"A terrific contribution to the critical study of whiteness transnationally, this lively, broadly learned, and methodologically sophisticated work shows that the 'enlargement' of the European Union only expanded political rights and economic opportunities for central and eastern Europeans within stark and contested limits. Assumptions regarding what made a united Europe cohere and of what nations and institutions should lead it continued to aggrandize Europe's north and west even as the lesser whiteness of those to the east was nominally acknowledged."

David Roediger, *University of Kansas, USA*

"In this much needed account, Dagmar Myslinska explores the interconnectedness between the legal environment, migration and evolving ideas about whiteness in the European Union. Drawing on detailed research, it provides an important insight into the changing dynamics of mobility, migration and bordering in the world around us."

John Solomos, *University of Warwick, UK*

"A valuable and original intervention that opens up the causes and consequences of hostility to Central and Eastern European migrants in Western Europe. Dagmar Myslinska unpacks and complicates existing debates on whiteness and, along the way, demonstrates that the racial politics of 'Brexit' were not exceptional but indicative of wider patterns found across Europe."

Alastair Bonnett, *Newcastle University, UK*

"Dagmar Myslinska's book levels a forceful, yet measured, critique of the entrenched inequality that has driven the European Union's treatment of Central and Eastern Europeans. It articulates the historical processes through which peripheralization has occurred, and evidences the contemporary manifestations of this inequality, with intricate clarity. Myslinska's impressive command of the historical, legal and sociological dimensions of her work render it all the more compelling."

Samantha Currie, *Monash University, Australia*

"This book powerfully demonstrates how East-West divides of old have been given a new lease on life via East-West mobility from the EU's newest member states. The author's postcolonial approach shows how the racialising logic of the EU legal framework for intra-European mobility call-upon, validate, and refresh East Europe's – and East Europeans' – continued marginality in Europe."

Jon Fox, *University of Bristol, UK*

Law, Migration, and the Construction of Whiteness

This book addresses the hidden dynamics of race within the European Union.

Brexit supporters' frequent targeting of European Union (EU) movers, especially those from Central and Eastern Europe (CEE), has been popularly assumed as at odds with the EU project's foundations based on the ideals of equality and inclusion. This book dispels that notion. By interrogating the history, wording, omissions, assumptions, and applications of laws, as well as policies, and discourses pertinent to mobility and equality, the argument developed throughout the book is that the parameters of CEE nationals' status within the EU have been closely circumscribed, in line with the entrenched historical positioning of the west as superior to the east. Engaging current legal, economic, political, and moral issues—against the backdrop of Brexit and contestations over EU integration and globalisation—this work opens avenues of thought to better understand the law's role in producing and sustaining social stratifications. Europe is a postcolonial space, as this book demonstrates. By addressing fractures within the construct of whiteness that are based on ethnicity, class, and migrant status, the book also provides a theoretically nuanced and politically useful understanding of contemporary European racisms.

This book will appeal to scholars, students, and others interested in migration, EU integration and EU citizenship, equality law, race and ethnicity, social policy, and postcolonialism.

Dagmar Rita Myslinska, PhD, is Associate Professor at Creighton University School of Law, USA.

Law, Migration, and the Construction of Whiteness

Mobility Within the European Union

Dagmar Rita Myslinska

LONDON AND NEW YORK

First published 2024
by Routledge
4 Park Square, Milton Park, Abingdon, Oxon OX14 4RN

and by Routledge
605 Third Avenue, New York, NY 10158

Routledge is an imprint of the Taylor & Francis Group, an informa business

© 2024 Dagmar Rita Myslinska

The right of Dagmar Rita Myslinska to be identified as author of this work has been asserted in accordance with sections 77 and 78 of the Copyright, Designs and Patents Act 1988.

All rights reserved. No part of this book may be reprinted or reproduced or utilised in any form or by any electronic, mechanical, or other means, now known or hereafter invented, including photocopying and recording, or in any information storage or retrieval system, without permission in writing from the publishers.

Trademark notice: Product or corporate names may be trademarks or registered trademarks, and are used only for identification and explanation without intent to infringe.

A GlassHouse book

British Library Cataloguing-in-Publication Data
A catalogue record for this book is available from the British Library

Library of Congress Cataloging-in-Publication Data
Names: Myslinska, Dagmar Rita, author.
Title: Law, migration, and the construction of whiteness : mobility within the European Union / Dagmar Rita Myslinska.
Description: Abingdon, Oxon [UK] ; New York, NY : Routledge, 2024. | Includes bibliographical references and index.
Identifiers: LCCN 2023042687 (print) | LCCN 2023042688 (ebook) | ISBN 9781032007373 (hardback) | ISBN 9781032007380 (paperback) | ISBN 9781003175377 (ebook)
Subjects: LCSH: European Union countries--Emigration and immigration. | Freedom of movement--European Union countries. | Migration, Internal--European Union countries. | European Union--Great Britain.
Classification: LCC KJE5170 .M97 2024 (print) | LCC KJE5170 (ebook) | DDC 342.2408/2--dc23/eng/20231005
LC record available at https://lccn.loc.gov/2023042687
LC ebook record available at https://lccn.loc.gov/2023042688

ISBN: 978-1-032-00737-3 (hbk)
ISBN: 978-1-032-00738-0 (pbk)
ISBN: 978-1-003-17537-7 (ebk)

DOI: 10.4324/9781003175377

Typeset in Sabon
by Taylor & Francis Books

For Alexander, who prompted me to grow and to love in ways I could not have imagined.

Contents

Acknowledgements		viii
Foreword		ix
1	Introduction: On the Peripheries of the EU and Whiteness	1
2	Margins of the EU Project: The East in Rhetoric and Accession Policies	15
3	Inequalities in the Experience of East-to-West Mobility: The Rights to Free Movement and Equality	69
4	Case Study: CEE Movers in Pre-Brexit Britain	160
5	Conclusions: Fractures and Peripheries, Past and Future	229
	Index	238

Acknowledgements

I am forever indebted to Nicola Lacey and Coretta Phillips, for their unwavering support, patience, and encouragement during the doctoral project that formed the starting point of this book. The thoughtful and sympathetic feedback from my doctoral examiners, the late Peter Fitzpatrick and Samantha Currie, provided further intellectual inspiration. Thanks also go to Floris de Witte, Damian Chalmers, Linda Mulcahy, and Lena Holzer for their generous and invaluable comments on various aspects of this project. Timothy Roesch provided superb editing assistance. I am grateful to Alex Dymock and Fatima Ahdash, who have been the most supportive, honest, and generous colleagues an academic could wish for. Finally, this work is a testament to the choices, hard work, and sacrifices of my parents, Iwonna and Jan. Their own refugee experience and ability to overcome challenges have not only served as an inspiration to me as a person, but are also the reason why I study migration and race, hoping to give a voice to those who otherwise may have none.

Foreword

Law, Migration, and the Construction of Whiteness: Mobility within the European Union represents a major shift in the study of whiteness and migration in Europe. Employing a methodology that draws upon qualitative and quantitative data, Dagmar Myslinska provides a compelling and rigorous analysis that intervenes in debates on intra-European racism and critical whiteness studies. This book makes several major contributions to the literature on human rights, migration studies, postcolonial studies, critical race studies, and critical whiteness studies. First, Myslinska shifts the frame by placing the human rights and economic rights of Central and Eastern Europeans at the center of her analysis of ethnic and racial discrimination in European Union legislation and policies. By providing a close reading of EU legislation and policies that discriminate Central and Eastern Europeans, this book offers a vocabulary and a set of cases that further develop the intersectional and interdisciplinary literature on racism and anti-racism in Europe. A second contribution is the introduction of a new methodology that is intersectional. Myslinska's close reading of legislation and policies represents a new template that illuminates the ways that ethnic inequality and racism shape the experiences of Eastern Europeans in postcolonial Europe. A third contribution is that Myslinska demonstrates the theoretical value of critical whiteness studies to analyses of human rights, civil rights, and economic equality in the EU. Her trenchant analysis of discrimination against Central and Eastern Europeans illuminates how ethnic inequality is reinforced and operates within European Union policies. This book opens up a new empirical arena for scholars devoted to studies of racism and anti-racism among white Europeans.

Myslinska employs a critical legal analytical lens to illuminate how Eastern Europeans are produced as 'not quite white' or not eligible for whiteness in the ways that distinguish them from Western Europeans. Shifting the frame to Europeans who are eligible for whiteness *outside* of the European Union, Myslinska's focus on migration policies revisits themes in an earlier wave of studies on European immigrants to the United States who were not perceived as Americans, unlike those of Northern and Western European origin, who were deemed to be 'white upon arrival'. American scholars of whiteness have demonstrated that for Irish, Italian, and Jewish immigrants, whiteness was an "achievement". A series of books including *Are Italians White: How Race is Made in America* (2003) edited by Jennifer Guglielmo and Salvatore Salaerno, *How Jews Became White Folks* by Karen Brodkin (1998), and *Not Quite White* by Matt Wray (2006), provided forceful analyses of the boundaries of whiteness and the centrality of national origin, class inequality, and stereotypes that shaped the meanings of whiteness.

By presenting a new vocabulary and a close analysis of the language of EU policies and practices, Myslinska's analytical approach offers a template for future research on racism and anti-racism. Employing close readings of the law, Myslinska introduces a new methodology that will be valuable to scholars devoted to critical analyses of race, racism, and whiteness. Central and Eastern Europeans have been neglected in contemporary sociological, historical, and cultural studies of race and racism in the European Union. Myslinska's innovative case study of ethnic discrimination in the EU expands a body of literature that originated in the United States—known as 'whiteness studies'. By shifting the analytical frame to Central and Eastern Europeans who are 'eligible for whiteness', but continue to face ethnic discrimination, Myslinska revisits and further develops themes found in earlier studies of working-class and poor immigrants from Southern and Eastern Europe in 19th century America whose status as 'white' was ambivalent and contested.

During the past three decades, the field of whiteness studies has grown dramatically. In 1997, a conference titled "The Making and Unmaking of Whiteness" was held at the University of California at Berkeley. Organized by Eric Klinenberg, Irene J. Nexica, and Matt Wray, all graduate students at the University of California, this conference represented a growing sub-field that came to be known as Whiteness Studies. In 2001, outputs of "The Making and Unmaking of Whiteness" conference were published by Duke University Press as an edited collection under the same title. A wave of studies published in the 1990s by scholars working in history, geography, law, labour studies, literature, film and media studies, and sociology reframed the study of race and racism in the United States to members of the dominant racial groups – that is, people socially and legally classified as white. New research in critical race studies began to examine the experiences of poor or working-class whites (Hartigan, 1999; Wray and Newitz, 1997), and of whites who emmigrated from Eastern and Southern Europe in the late 19th century and were considered "not quite white" (Brodkin, 1998; Frye Jacobson, 1998). Scholars of whiteness have noted that a core feature of whiteness is to become middle-class, to benefit from mobility across national borders, and to be free from cultural and racialized discrimination. Thus, whiteness is a form of privilege globally (Twine and Gardener, 2013; Leonard, 2010; 2013). More recently, whiteness studies have expanded from its birthplace in the United States to volumes about race and whiteness in other regions, including Sweden (Hübinette, Lundström and Wikström, 2023).

The role of migration policies in the ability of citizens to 'assert' or accomplish whiteness is not new. Scholars studying the border between the US and Mexico and the internal borders in the US where discrimination has restricted where Indigenous Americans and Blacks can live have been central in analyses of white supremacy. What is new is Myslinska's focus on the contemporary racialization of Central and Eastern Europeans as they struggle to have equal opportunities across a range of spheres including employment, civil rights, and access to upward mobility like their Western European counterparts.

In *Law, Migration, and the Construction of Whiteness*, Myslinska revisits theoretical questions that were introduced three decades ago by European American scholars in the United States including Ruth Frankenberg (1993), John Hartigan (1999), Matthew Frye Jacobson (1998), and others whose research innovated the then nascent field of whiteness studies. Myslinska expands the analysis of racism and discrimination in important ways. If the ability to move across borders is a central feature of being socially recognized as white, then scholars working in the fields of postcolonial studies, critical race studies, migration studies, and European studies will benefit greatly from Myslinska's analysis. This book should be required reading for scholars, policymakers, academics, and thought leaders who want to understand intersecting forms of discrimination in contemporary Europe. Most importantly, *Law, Migration, and the Construction of Whiteness* will inspire emerging scholars to rethink and revise the objects of analysis in this field. The equality rights of Central and Eastern Europeans deserve the same attention as the rights of Europeans who are not qualified physically for 'whiteness' by calling attention to the fractures within whiteness.

Professor France Winddance Twine
University of California, Santa Barbara

Bibliography

Brodkin, Karen (1998) *How Jews Became White Folks & What That Says About Race in America* (New Brunswick, New Jersey: Rutgers University Press)

Frankenberg, Ruth (1993) *White Women, Race Matters: the social construction of whiteness* (Minneapolis, MN: University of Minnesota Press)

Frye Jacobson, Matthew (1998) *Whiteness of a Different Color: European Immigrants and the Alchemy of Race* (Cambridge, MA and London: Harvard University Press)

Guglielmo, Jennifer and Salvatore Salerno (2003) *Are Italians White?: How Race is Made in America* (New York and London: Routledge)

Hartigan, John (1999) *Racial Situations: Class Predicaments of Whiteness in Detroit* (Princeton, New Jersey: Princeton University Press)

Hübinettte, Tobias, Catrin Lundström, and Peter Wikström (eds) (2023) *Race in Sweden: Racism and Antiracism in the World's First 'Colourblind' Nation* (London and New York: Routledge)

Levine-Rasky, Cynthia (ed) (2002) *Working through Whiteness: International Perspectives* (Albany, New York: State University of New York Press)

Leonard, Pauline (2010) *Expatriate Identities in Postcolonial Organizations: Working Whiteness* (New York and London: Routledge)

Leonard, Pauline (2013) Landscaping privilege: Being British in South Africa, in France Winddance Twine and Bradley Gardener (eds) *Geographies of Privilege* (New York and London: Routledge)

Rasmussen, Brander, Eric Klinenberg, Irene J. Nexica and Matt Wray (eds) (2001) *The Making and Unmaking of Whiteness* (Durham and London: Duke University Press)

Twine, France Winddance and Bradley Gardener (eds) (2013) *Geographies of Privilege* (New York and London: Routledge)

Van Houtum, Henk (2013) Human blacklisting: The global apartheid of the EU's external border regime, in France Winddance Twine and Bradley Gardener (eds) *Geographies of Privilege* (New York and London: Routledge)

Wray, Matt and Annalee Newitz (1997) *White Trash: Race and Class in America* (New York and London: Routledge)

Chapter 1

Introduction
On the Peripheries of the EU and Whiteness

The EU was explicitly founded on the premise of equality, inclusion, and unity. According to the European Commission, it 'arose from the ashes of World War Two',[1] to promote 'humanitarian and progressive values'.[2] Notably, 'human dignity, freedom, [and] equality' form the EU's 'spiritual and moral heritage'.[3] In 2012, the EU was awarded the Nobel Peace Prize for advancing the causes of peace, democracy, and human rights across Europe. The gradual geographical expansion of the EU has been linked to helping effectuate this benevolent vision. The accession of eight Central and Eastern European ('CEE') states[4] in 2004 was situated within the EU's 'historic task … to further the integration of the continent by peaceful means',[5] 'transcend … former divisions and … forge a common destiny'.[6]

But how effectively have those promises been met? EU institutions have been increasingly limiting the right of free movement and movers' access to social benefits, and have been tolerating western Member State policies targeting CEE movers.[7] Once the Eastern Enlargement began to materialise, popular and political attacks were levelled against potential movers from the eastern peripheries of Europe, leading to the imposition of transitional post-accession mobility derogations in all EU-15[8] states other than Sweden. Whereas the mobility of French au pairs, Spanish waiters, or British pensioners never raised public or political concerns, CEE movers have been targeted by anti-immigrant rhetoric across EU-15 states—portrayed as 'economic migrants' suitable only for menial jobs, criminals, and welfare scroungers (despite evidence to the

---

1 European Commission (1996).
2 European Commission (2014).
3 Charter of Fundamental Rights of the European Union, 26.10.2012.
4 Czechia, Estonia, Hungary, Latvia, Lithuania, Poland, Slovenia, and Slovakia.
5 European Commission (2001).
6 Treaty establishing a Constitution for Europe, 16.12.2004 (unratified).
7 As well as movers from Bulgaria and Romania, which acceded during the second wave of the Eastern Enlargement, in 2007.
8 Austria, Belgium, Denmark, Finland, France, Germany, Greece, Ireland, Italy, Luxembourg, the Netherlands, Portugal, Spain, Sweden, and the United Kingdom. After Brexit, EU-15 became EU-14.

DOI: 10.4324/9781003175377-1

contrary). Moreover, hostility against CEE movers has been accompanied by empirical evidence of their inequalities—such as de-skilling and exploitation in the employment context, and experiences of racism, hate crimes, and discrimination. Most poignantly perhaps, the origins of the Brexit referendum and its outcome were linked to Britons' popular opposition to the mobility of CEE workers. Even mainstream British politicians had racialised CEE movers as uncivilised, criminality-prone, cheap labourers, and welfare abusers. Meanwhile, CEE movers have been overlooked by equality discourse. Moreover, their experiences are not adequately captured in practice by anti-discrimination laws, which tend to focus on addressing racism only as it impedes free market competition, and to approach whiteness as homogeneously privileged. These realities have been given little attention by critical legal scholars.[9] The Eastern Enlargement process has been generally seen as benevolent and inclusive. When it comes to Brexit, academic and policy commentators have tended to approach anti-CEE sentiment as un-European and at odds with the EU project's emphasis on integration and fundamental rights, and have largely attributed it to the exceptional British Euroscepticism.

This book, however, presents a new perspective for thinking about these topics. By weaving together a doctrinal analysis of EU policies crucial to CEE mobility—notably the Eastern Enlargement process, the right of free movement, and movers' protections from racial discrimination—with a qualitative analysis of pertinent legal discourses, and by situating this legal analysis within available quantitative data evidencing CEE movers' inequalities, I argue that anti-CEE sentiment forms an integral part of the western-centric EU project. One of my contentions is that factors that culminated in Brexit are not exemplary. Instead, CEE movers' experience of racialisation and inequalities in the UK can serve as a case study of the lived experience of second-class EU citizenship on the Member State level, in line with the enduring EU-wide reproductions of historical power differentials and ideological otherings of the eastern peripheries of Europe. Omissions and inequalities in EU policies and discourses pertaining to mobility, social rights, and racial equality have helped to support the creation of a social reality filled with ethnic stratifications that have been enabling CEE movers' racialisation in the west, a position further reinforced in the UK by ineffective equality policies, CEE movers' absence from equality discourse, and the broader anti-CEE policy climate. Brexit not only exemplified the lack of a sense of a 'European' identity among EU nationals and the fragility of the EU as a construct, but it also exposed glaring failures concerning EU promises of equality and 'free' movement.

The book's innovative look at inequalities of east-to-west mobility and at peripheralisation of the east is bolstered by being situated within critical approaches to the study of race, including critical whiteness studies, which have

---

9 For critiques from other disciplines, see, e.g., Böröcz and Kovacs (2001); Engel-Di Mauro (2006).

not been adequately explored in the context of contemporary intra-EU dynamics, power relations, and racial contestations. Although 'race' is a construct, it produces and is reinforced by material aspects of lived experience which are steeped in historical, social, economic, and political power relations. As such, before racial constructs can be abolished and the possibility of change can be conceptualised, pre-existing racial categories must be employed to address the position of groups at each race's centre and at the margins. As US Justice Blackmun had noted in a key affirmative action case, '[i]n order to go beyond racism, we must first take account of race'.[10] As a construct, race 'has not only to do with colour, but with tying culture to bodies in a hierarchical way'.[11]

Racism has always constituted a part of European heritage, both historically and in the present, having been levelled not only against visible non-white ethnic minority groups, but also against whites. As a form of exclusion, racism can extend to 'any group that has been socially constructed as having a different "origin", whether cultural, biological and historical', that has been located in 'ethnic terms', through labels such as 'foreign', 'migrant', or 'minority'.[12] Whiteness has been deeply embedded within European history, and has been most contested at its boundaries. The significance of whiteness has been traced to the construction of the Roman Empire and of the Holy Roman Empire; hostility towards Saracens, Jews, and Gypsies; and antagonism towards non-white colonial subjects.[13] Slavs, the Irish, Southern Europeans, and lower socio-economic classes also have a long history of being racialised. Contemporary debates about whiteness can be observed in the concept of Fortress Europe, to keep (mostly non-white) third-country nationals—including refugees—out of the EU, and in widespread opposition to the potential accession of Turkey. Implicitly, the notion of a 'European' has been constructed based on (homogeneous, privileged) whiteness[14], which intersects with not only Christianity, but also certain socio-economic standing.

As the most significant post-war migration of people within Europe, CEE movers represent a remarkable group for a study of contemporary whiteness. In line with their historical inferiorisation and othering, white skin has not shielded them from the process of racialisation and the effects of racism. CEE nationals have been positioned as lesser than the imagined 'European' community that has been created by western thinkers. Since the Enlightenment, the CEE region has been subjected to the western gaze of presumed superiority, and the term 'Eastern' came to suggest lack of civilisation or modernity, and an inability to be fully 'European'.[15] The economically driven, imperialist concept of 'Mitteleuropa' was applied in the early 1900s to support German plans to

10 *Regents of the University of California v Bakke*, 438 U.S. 265 (1978).
11 See generally Garner (2007).
12 Anthias and Yuval-Davis (1983).
13 McVeigh (2010).
14 See generally Möschel (2014); Solanke (2009).
15 See generally, e.g., Boatcă (2007); Bakić-Hayden (1995).

impose economic and cultural hegemony over Poland, Czechia, and Hungary. In western discourses, CEE states continue to be perceived as a buffer zone between west and the dreaded east, and as a repository of otherness, not quite part of 'Europe' culturally or politically,[16] and fit only to serve as a subaltern source of cheap labour and exploitable markets to facilitate 'racial capitalism'.[17] Of course, it is true that CEE nationals have at times benefited from their (partial) whiteness—both historically, and in contemporary times. For example, post-war guest and volunteer worker schemes in many EU-15 countries welcomed displaced persons from the CEE region. The Eastern Enlargement was in part driven by western preference for Caucasian, Christian workers.[18] Their whiteness has made CEE movers preferred by employers for customer-facing positions. Moreover, CEE movers can more easily escape incidents of micro-aggression than those who differ phenotypically from white western majorities.

Nevertheless, CEE nationals' whiteness is degenerate, and in some contexts, has been disadvantageous. Anti-CEE outlook can be found in select EU policies and in EU discourses. Moreover, CEE nationals have been targeted by EU-15 policies limiting social rights, by western media, and by political and popular discourses. They have been racialised through the white majority's application of deprecatory features, which focus on their 'alien values', primitive character, and basic criminal nature. Poignantly, some white Britons questioned CEE movers' phenotypical whiteness, describing them as 'not quite white' or simply 'pale' in comparison to phenotypically black people.[19] Notably, their (partial) whiteness and consequent (partial) invisibility have complicated their access to anti-discrimination protections. Not forming a part of EU-15 societies or their colonial heritage, CEE movers are not considered an oppressed minority, and their status as immigrant outsiders is ambiguous. Despite documented incidents of discrimination and racism against them, they routinely get overlooked by western equality and integration policies and by advocacy groups. Moreover, policymakers, perpetrators of racism, and even CEE victims have difficulty conceptualising race-based subjugations they experience as 'racism', which in some ways makes this type of racism especially threatening. Such views, of course, reflect how naturalised white privilege is, rendering whiteness homogeneous and invisible.

One of the book's novel contributions is to expose this understudied fracture within whiteness. Revealing cracks within whiteness and its fabrication facilitates breaking down of white privilege. While doing so, I acknowledge that whites and blacks are racialised differently, with vastly different social and political ramifications, and I do not devalue racisms and discrimination suffered by other groups. Different forms of racism are not mutually exclusive, and I am

16 See generally, e.g., Todorova (2003).
17 Kalmar (2023).
18 A recent illustration of this preference can be seen in how Ukrainians fleeing Russia's invasion have been received with much more tolerance than any refugees from war-torn countries in the Middle East, Asia, or Africa.
19 Halej (2014).

mindful of the need to avoid creating hierarchies of disadvantage, which only detracts from non-majoritarian groups' need to come together to oppose oppression in all its forms.

By developing a critical legal methodology for studying fractures within whiteness—as an interrelated social, cultural, political, economic, and historical phenomenon rooted in ideas of postcoloniality, transnationality, and intersectionality—this book makes significant interdisciplinary contributions to European, migration, anti-discrimination, human geography, postcolonial, and critical whiteness scholarship. Notably, critical analyses of EU law have been fragmented, and largely focused on specific historical moments and on isolated areas of law.[20] Similarly, despite a plethora of economic, cultural, political, anthropological, and sociological studies of east-to-west mobility, explorations of how laws and legal discourse approach CEE nationals' mobility have been rare, discrete in scope,[21] or developed through shorter works only.[22] Finally, applications of legal analysis to whiteness studies have been infrequent, and typically limited to the US context, both contemporary[23] and historical.[24] While firmly situated within such critical works, this book offers a holistic critique of pre-accession policies and the Eastern Enlargement process, and of CEE nationals' positioning within the EU mobility and equality frameworks, before tracing it to the domestic case study of their experience of mobility to the UK.

Scholars have called for greater attentiveness to the role of inequalities, discrimination, and racialisation in migration studies, and for the need to contextualise migration within global political and social transformations.[25] Since racisms reflect a contemporary 'global hierarchy of human superiority and inferiority' that is re-produced politically, culturally and economically[26], modern axes of disadvantage and inequality have been splintering and increasing in complexity. This calls into question traditional approaches of race scholars, which have been based on the binary of privileged whites versus disadvantaged non-whites. This book begins to address such gaps. By engaging with contemporary economic, political, and moral issues, against the backdrop of Brexit and increasing contestations over EU integration, my research opens up avenues of thought to better understand law's role in social stratifications and power hierarchies. More generally, by exploring the continuing salience of the role of class and ethnicity transnationally, my research expands studies of policies, discourse, and lived experience at the intersection of race and migration, which is crucial given the accelerating rate of present-day migrations.

20 E.g., Adams et al. (2017); Williams (2004); Howard (2009); Solanke (2009). For a review of critical approaches to EU law, see Neuvonen (2022).
21 E.g., Currie (2008).
22 E.g., Barnard et al. (2018); Lewicki (2023).
23 E.g., Lopez (1996); Tehranian (2008).
24 E.g., Roediger (2005).
25 E.g., Erel et al. (2016); Romero (2008); García (2017); Grosfoguel (2004).
26 Grosfoguel et al. (2015).

In the process, the book poses questions about, and invites readers to engage in, a more nuanced analysis of the concept of EU citizenship and of how free the right to free movement really is. Although hindrances to mobility have typically been attributed to the limited scope of EU competence, I suggest that they can also be explained, in the context of CEE movers, by the ongoing unequal power dynamics between east and west, which is steeped in long-standing inferiorisation of the former. A better understanding of the evolving relationship between EU governance, rights, and citizenship is vital given that CEE mobility to the remaining western Member States has continued, if not accelerated, after Brexit. Furthermore, such scrutiny is necessary in order to make equality and social rights policies more responsive to contemporary mobilities, at both EU and Member State levels. More generally, my conceptual approach provides a platform for discussions about the role of east-to-west mobility within the continuing EU project. The arguments developed in this book have implications for studies of power dynamics between CEE and EU-14 states, and are needed more than ever in light of recent dis-integration pressures—posed not only by Brexit, but also by populist parties' resurgence across western Europe, and as illustrated by the disjoined responses to the 2015–16 'refugee crisis', the Covid-19 pandemic, and Russia's invasion of Ukraine.

Although much of the analysis presented in this book pertains to the whole CEE region and its nationals collectively, each CEE state's unique history, politics, migration patterns, and identity affect how its nationals[27] have experienced mobility. There are some significant similarities across the CEE region, however, that justify my collective approach. CEE nationals have had a long history of emigration to the west, oftentimes to face anti-Slavic sentiment. All CEE states experienced similar power imbalances with the west during their accession processes, and all have been treated alike under EU policies. Western political, media, and public discourses have tended to approach the CEE region as inferior, subsumed within the pejorative label 'Eastern Europe', which connotes a geopolitical as much as a geographical concept, and which conjures up western stereotypes of Polish plumbers, Ukrainian agricultural workers, and Romanian cleaners. And, against the broad EU backdrop, all CEE nationals have been poor in comparison to EU-15 nationals, as indicated, for example, by their GDPs per capita and by average minimum wages. Thus, while I am cognisant of the need to avoid essentialising the CEE region and its nationals as homogeneous, approaching them collectively facilitates my analysis.

Analytical Framework

The book's innovative look at east-to-west mobility is bolstered by being situated within the critical whiteness studies framework, which has not been adequately explored in the context of contemporary intra-EU dynamics, power relations, and racial contestations. The origins of whiteness studies stem from

---

27 Notably, Roma groups originating in the CEE region demand separate scrutiny.

approaching whiteness as a monolithic, abstract concept that endows all whites with privilege[28], which accrues through racism against and racialisation of inferiorised groups.[29] Whiteness has been normalised as the position of power, by being traditionally rendered invisible and unmarked.[30] Critical whiteness scholars have disrupted that image, by revealing and problematising the construction of white privilege through laws, discourse, economics, politics, and culture.[31] Degrees of whiteness differentiate between dominant and non-dominant white groups. Not only do people of colour get excluded from the concept of whiteness. Instead, it is a relational concept, constructed by positioning others at its borders or by dismissing them altogether as inferior.[32] Moreover, whiteness has permeable and shifting boundaries,[33] constructed through local, national, and global relations, in the past and presently.

Accordingly, contemporary scholars have sought to dismantle the idea that whiteness is a monolithic identity[34], by exposing its fractures and how closely circumscribed the locally privileged white norm is[35], with some phenotypically white people marginalised due to factors such as class[36], nationality, gender, or sexuality. The theory of intersectionality recognises that we are simultaneously members of many groups—such as those based on gender, religion, and sexual orientation—and these complex social categories shape the specific ways in which we access privilege, experience discrimination, and suffer inequalities.[37] Notably, access to white privilege is impacted by migration status and by class.[38] Historically, immigrants from Eastern Europe have been seen as 'degenerate whites', in both Europe and the United States.[39] Similarly, contemporary Caucasian migrants have had only partial access to white privilege—for example, Middle-Eastern[40] and Eastern European[41] migrants in the United States, and the Irish in the UK and the United States.[42] More specifically, CEE nationals' whiteness and racialisation in the west have been affected through their (lower) class—both historically, and today. According to Garner,[43] the increasing presence of CEE migrants in EU-15 states after the fall of communism in 1989 brought to the

---

28 E.g., McIntosh (1988).
29 See generally Frankenberg (1993).
30 See generally Bonnett (2000).
31 See generally Lopez (2005).
32 Said (1978).
33 See generally Linke (1999).
34 See generally Twine and Gallagher (2008).
35 E.g., Levine-Rasky (2013); Garner (2007).
36 See generally Pruitt (2015); Jones (2011); Mondon and Winter (2018).
37 See generally Delgado and Stefancic (2017).
38 See generally Levine-Rasky (2013); Wray (2006); Kindinger and Schmitt (2020).
39 Roediger (1991).
40 Tehranian (2008).
41 Sadowski-Smith (2018); Myslinska (2014).
42 Bronwen (2011).
43 Garner (2007).

foreground ethnic fractures within whiteness, further deepened by the Eastern Enlargement. This book's contribution lies in exploring in detail these fractures, which fall at the intersection of mobility, ethnicity, and class, and which are embedded within the intra-EU juridical, economic, and political apparatuses that maintain the edges of whiteness.

Studying whiteness is also rooted in ideas of postcoloniality. The relationship between critical whiteness studies and postcolonial analysis is symbiotic, and both intersect with an anti-capitalist stance[44] and with critical race theory. There are some obvious overlaps between postcolonial theory and critical studies of race. Both emerged out of and represent an intellectual challenge to racial oppression. Borrowing heavily from one another, both expose how race and racism constitute intricate parts of social histories and social systems. Both seek to create more racially-just societies. As W.E.B. Du Bois presciently noted a century ago, racial domination and economic exploitation within nation states are connected to imperial and international domination, accomplished not only through violent conflict, but also through economic policies.[45] Fitzpatrick has argued that today's globalism, fuelled by neoliberal economics, can be approached as a continuance of western imperialism, albeit without actual colonies.[46] Notably, western European states created the EU integration project as their empires were collapsing. In addition to exploring the effects of colonial exploitation,[47] postcolonial theory has engaged with modern colonisation processes, such as those found in the Middle East,[48] and the global South.[49] In the context of contemporary east-west relations, the postcolonial framework has been underutilised and fragmented, with a few notable exceptions of (non-legal) studies of the Eastern Enlargement's export of governmentality and economic controls,[50] and of western exclusionary politics and practices targeting CEE movers.[51] Building upon such works, I expand postcolonial critique by looking closely at the long-term peripheralisation of the CEE region through policies and legal discourses—both historical (pre-accession and enlargement), and ongoing (free movement and equality).

'Law, in essence, is language',[52] which is never objective, and which creates lived reality. By weaving together critical whiteness and postcolonial analytical frameworks, I re-examine historical and legal records to focus on the underlying interests that they further, while questioning the foundations of the current legal order and of conventional approaches to legal reasoning. In the process, I seek to replace

44 See generally Cole (2021).
45 Du Bois (2016).
46 Fitzpatrick (2001).
47 E.g., Fanon (1988); Said (1978); Garland and Chakraborti (2006).
48 E.g., Gregory (2004).
49 E.g., Kerner (2018).
50 E.g., Böröcz and Kovacs (2001); Engel-Di Mauro (2006).
51 E.g., Kinnvall (2016); Samaluk (2016).
52 Kalimo et al. (2018).

majoritarian interpretations with those in line with the experience of CEE movers. Drawing on critical race methodologies,[53] I use qualitative research methods to expose various forms of subjugation, arrive at an in-depth understanding of complex social processes, and gain insights about how legal systems operate in practice. I rely on documentary qualitative analysis because law is a highly verbal field, propagated through not only hard laws, but also soft laws and legal discourse. I view the binary distinction between binding hard laws (such as statutes and court judgements) and soft laws (such as recommendations, guidelines, declarations, resolutions, and statute preambles) as illusory.[54] Close analysis of soft laws is especially important when researching the EU's legal framework, because the EU is 'primarily a textual enterprise, a "print community" detailing its own development and practices'.[55]

In light of my theoretical standpoint, the availability of large numbers of relevant documents, and the complexity of the phenomena that I research, content analysis proved to be the most suitable method. To appreciate how the CEE region and its nationals have been situated within the EU project and approached by free movement and equality policies, my content analysis focuses on foundational EU Treaties and discourse pertaining to the EU's foundations and purpose; policies, soft laws, and general EU discourse pertaining to the EU's relationship with CEE states after 1989—including during the Eastern Enlargement process; laws and discourse concerning the right of free movement, social rights, and post-accession mobility derogations; and EU anti-discrimination legislation and caselaw, as well as equality discourse. Similarly, in the chapter devoted to the UK case study, I look closely at UK laws and discourses pertaining to migration, racism, equality, and CEE nationals. These authoritative primary sources, all created by EU and UK institutions and official representatives, are contextualised within relevant studies, such as of economic outcomes, where applicable. Data limitations are acknowledged throughout the book, as relevant.

Structure of the Book

Chapter 2 opens with a historical overview of the EU project's foundations and aims, as expressed through its policies and discourse. The chapter reveals an absence of CEE heritage in discussions of 'European' culture and instances of explicit othering of the east, and exposes the economic core within fundamental-rights foundational rhetoric. It then traces the economic and political dynamics of the relationship between the EU and CEE states—from before, to the aftermath of the fall of communism, and under discrete pre-accession agreements. The chapter looks closely at early incursions of western lenders

---

53 See generally Delgado and Stefancic (2017); Williams (1992).
54 See generally Trubek et al. (2006).
55 Williams (2003).

into the CEE region while still under communism, and the unequal impact of pre-2004 policies on CEE and EU-15 states, further exacerbated by the one-sided approach imposed by the west during the accession process. I contend that, amid economic and political chaos in the CEE region after 1989, the west misused its bargaining power to shape Eastern Enlargement policies so as to economically benefit western financial institutions and EU-15 states, while ignoring CEE states' interests and reinforcing east/west economic inequalities. This politically, legally, and economically unequal process was complemented by EU rhetoric othering the CEE region as being in need of civilising through westernisation. Both accession policies and discourse paved the way towards normalising CEE states' status as second-class Member States that are not fully deserving of EU membership, and towards reinforcing CEE nationals' status as not fully belonging to proper (white) 'Europe' and as not fully deserving of EU rights.

Chapter 3 exposes shortcomings of the rights of free movement and equality in the context of CEE nationals. The overarching argument is that both mobility and equality policies and discourses have been further normalising CEE nationals' second-class citizenship within the EU. The chapter first explains the significance of intra-EU mobility, and looks closely at CEE nationals' experience of mobility—replete with incidents of exploitation and discrimination in EU-15 states—and at the unequal impact of CEE mobility on the CEE and EU-15 regions. It then offers close analysis of the right to mobility as developed—and diminished, in the case of CEE nationals—by various EU institutions and by EU-15 states, including through the Citizens' Rights Directive 2004/38, its transposition, and related policies. The complex web of laws on social benefits has intersected with freedom of movement laws to further privilege EU-15 states' economic and political concerns. Moreover, CEE movers' inequalities in EU-15 states have been entrenched through inadequate ethnicity-based equality protections, which get triggered once CEE nationals engage in mobility. The Race Equality Directive 2000/43 and its transposed western policies have prioritised western economic concerns, while overlooking CEE movers' peripheral position. Meanwhile, CEE movers have been absent from the broader equality discourse, and their inequalities have been further naturalised by EU institutions' inadequate attention to reports of their racialisation and discrimination. The chapter then traces inequalities built into the Enlargement process not only to the obvious example of post-accession mobility derogations, but also to how CEE nationals not impacted by transitional derogations were disadvantaged in the aftermath of the Enlargement, and how CEE movers' rights have been diminished through recent EU and EU-15 policies.

Chapter 4 relies on a detailed analysis of CEE nationals' experiences and positioning in the UK—while it was still a Member State—as an illustrative case study to bolster arguments developed in the preceding chapters. It situates CEE movers within racism and equality debates in the UK, and addresses their uniquely disadvantaged positioning in the labour market. It then centres on

CEE movers' reception in the UK and on a close analysis of the post-accession Worker Registration Scheme, the right-to-reside test, and related hostile policies, drawing out their long-term negative consequences for CEE workers. Next, the chapter explores how CEE movers' experiences of discrimination and racialisation, and their unique positioning within the UK's hierarchies of privilege and disadvantage, have been overlooked by the British equality discourse and inadequately addressed by the Equality Act 2010. Finally, drawing on close analysis of race discrimination cases within the employment context, the chapter suggests that 'low-skilled' CEE workers have faced some unique challenges in asserting their equality rights, reinforced through unsuitable statutory definitions, adjudicators' discretionary analytical approaches, and practical hurdles.

The final chapter brings to the foreground links that can be drawn between the colonial-like EU integration project and the ongoing disadvantage and racialisation experienced by CEE movers in western Europe. By contextualising CEE mobility within both historical and contemporary transnational economic, cultural, and political power dynamics, the chapter arrives at a more nuanced picture of today's micro-level ethnic power relations which are shaping the boundaries of whiteness. It then offers suggestions for how adjudicators, legislators, the media, educators, and the public should take account of contemporary demographic changes, transnational contexts, globalisation, and intersectionality, to better reflect the nature of contemporary discrimination and racism. The chapter also explores broader consequences of my findings for how legal rules and institutional discourses define equality and the reality of 'race' when it comes to other groups of marginalised whites, and addresses the significance of my conclusions for the continuation and legitimacy of the EU project. The book's contributions to critical whiteness studies and postcolonial theory are brought to the forefront, as is the utility of both frameworks to studies of intra-EU mobility and of the experience of racialised whites. The book closes by contributing to the central goal of critical whiteness studies, through problematising the construction of white privilege and disrupting the conventional proclivity to essentialise whiteness in laws and legal discourses.

Bibliography

Adams, Maurice et al. (eds) (2017) *Constitutionalism and the Rule of Law: Bridging Idealism and Realism* (Cambridge: Cambridge University Press)

Anthias, Floya and Nira Yuval-Davis (1983) Contextualising feminism: Ethnic, gender and class divisions, *Feminist Review* 15: 62–75

Bakić-Hayden, Milica (1995) Nesting orientalisms: The case of former Yugoslavia, *Slavic Review* 54(4): 917–931

Barnard, Catherine et al. (2018) Beyond employment tribunals: Enforcement of Employment rights by EU-8 migrant workers, *Industrial Law Journal* 47(2): 226–262

Boatcă, Manuela (2007) The eastern margins of empire: Coloniality in 19th century Romania, *Cultural Studies* 21(2-3): 368–384

Bonnett, Alastair (2000) *White Identities: Historical and International Perspectives* (London: Prentice Hall)
Böröcz, József and Melinda Kovacs (eds) (2001) *Empire's New Clothes: Unveiling EU Enlargement* (Shropshire: Central Europe Review)
Bronwen, Walter (2011) *Outsiders Inside: Whiteness, Place and Irish Women* (London: Routledge)
Charter of Fundamental Rights of the European Union, OJ C 326, 26.10.2012
Cole, Michael (2021) Understanding critical whiteness studies: Harmful or helpful in the struggle for racial equity in the academy?, in Dave Thomas and Jason Arday (eds) *Doing Equity and Diversity for Success in Higher Education: Redressing Structural Inequalities in the Academy* 277–298 (London: Palgrave Macmillan)
Currie, Samantha (2008) *Migration, Work and Citizenship in the Enlarged European Union* (London: Routledge)
Delgado, Richard and Jean Stefancic (2017) *Critical Race Theory* (New York: NYU Press)
Du Bois, W.E.B. (2016) *The Souls of Black Folk* (Mineola: Dover Publications)
Engel-Di Mauro, Salvatore (ed) (2006) *The European's Burden: Global Imperialism in EU Expansion* (New York: Peter Lang)
Erel, Umut et al. (2016) Understanding the contemporary race–migration nexus, *Ethnic and Racial Studies* 39 (8): 1339–1360
European Commission (1996) *Europe... Questions and Answers: How Does the European Union Work?* (Brussels), http://aei.pitt.edu/15091/1/MOVE-HOWDOESTHEEUROPEAN UNIONWORK-1996_1.pdf
European Commission (2001) *Enlargement of the European Union: An Historic Opportunity* (Brussels), http://aei.pitt.edu/41185/1/A5181.pdf
European Commission (2014) *The European Union Explained: Europe in 12 Lessons* (Brussels), https://op.europa.eu/en/publication-detail/-/publication/009305e8-2a43-11e7-ab65-01aa75ed71a1
Fanon, Frantz (1988) *Black Skin, White Masks* (London: Pluto Press)
Fitzpatrick, Peter (2001) *Modernism and the Grounds of Law* (Cambridge: Cambridge University Press)
Frankenberg, Ruth (1993) *White Women, Race Matters* (Minneapolis: University of Minnesota Press)
García, San Juanita (2017) Bridging critical race theory and migration: Moving beyond assimilation theories, *Sociology Compass* 11(6): 1–10
Garland, Jon and Neil Chakraborti (2006) 'Race', space and place: Examining identity and cultures of exclusion in rural England, *Ethnicities* 6(2): 159–177
Garner, Steve (2007) *Whiteness: An Introduction* (London: Routledge)
Gregory, Derek (2004) *The Colonial Present: Afghanistan, Palestine, Iraq* (Malden: Blackwell)
Grosfoguel, Ramon (2004) Race and ethnicity or racialized ethnicities?: Identities within global coloniality, *Ethnicities* 4(3): 315–336
Grosfoguel, Ramon et al. (2015) 'Racism', intersectionality and migration studies: Framing some theoretical reflections, *Identities: Global Studies in Culture and Power* 22 (6): 635–652
Halej, Julia Oktawia (2014) *Other Whites, White Others: East European Migrants and the Boundaries of Whiteness*, PhD Dissertation (UCL, School of Slavonic and East European Studies)

Howard, Erica (2009) *The EU Race Directive: Developing the Protection against Racial Discrimination within the EU* (London: Routledge)

Jones, Owen (2011) *Chavs: The Demonisation of the Working Class in Britain* (London: Verso)

Kalimo, Harri et al. (2018) Of values and legitimacy—discourse analytical insights on the copyright case law of the Court of Justice of the European Union, *Modern Law Review* 81(2): 282–307

Kalmar, Ivan (2023) Race, Racialisation, and the East of the European Union: An introduction, *Journal of Ethnic and Migration Studies* 49(6): 1465–1480

Kerner, Ina (2018) Postcolonial theories as global critical theories, *Constellations* 25: 614–628

Kindinger, Evangelia and Mark Schmitt (eds) (2020) *The Intersections of Whiteness* (London: Routledge)

Kinnvall, Catarina (2016) The postcolonial has moved into Europe: Bordering, security and ethno-cultural belonging, *Journal of Common Market Studies* 54(1): 152–168

Levine-Rasky, Cynthia (2013) *Whiteness Fractured* (Farnham: Ashgate)

Lewicki, Aleksandra (2023) East–West inequalities and the ambiguous racialisation of 'Eastern Europeans', *Journal of Ethnic and Migration Studies* 49(6): 1481–1499

Linke, Uli (1999) *Blood and Nation: The European Aesthetics of Race* (Philadelphia: University of Pennsylvania Press)

Lopez, Alfred J (ed) (2005) *Postcolonial Whiteness: Critical Reader on Race and Empire* (New York: State University of New York Press)

Lopez, Ian Haney (1996) *White by Law: The Legal Construction of Race* (New York: NYU Press)

McIntosh, Peggy (1988) *White Privilege and Male Privilege: A Personal Account of Coming to See Correspondences through Work in Women's Studies*, Working Paper 189 (Wellesley College Center for Women)

McVeigh, Robbie (2010) United in whiteness? Irishness, Europeanness, and the emergence of a white Europe policy, *European Studies* 28: 251–278

Mondon, Aurelien and Aaron Winter (2018) Whiteness, populism and the racialisation of the working class in the United Kingdom and the United States, *Identities: Global Studies in Culture and Power* 26(5): 510–528

Möschel, Mathias (2014) *Law, Lawyers and Race: Critical Race Theory from the US to Europe* (London: Routledge)

Myslinska, Dagmar (2014) Contemporary first-generation European Americans: The unbearable "whiteness" of being, *Tulane Law Review* 88: 559–625

Neuvonen, Päivi Johanna (2022) A way of critique: What can EU law scholars learn from critical theory?, *European Law Open* 1(1): 60–88

Pruitt, Lisa R (2015) The false choice between race and class and other affirmative action myths, *Buffalo Law Review* 63: 981–1027

Roediger, David (1991) *The Wages of Whiteness: Race and the Making of the American Working Class* (New York: Verso)

Roediger, David (2005) *Working Toward Whiteness: How America's Immigrants Became White* (New York: Basic Books)

Romero, Mary (2008) Crossing the immigration and race border: A critical race theory approach to immigration studies, *Contemporary Justice Review* 11(1): 23–37

Sadowski-Smith, Claudia (2018) *New Immigrant Whiteness: Race, Neoliberalism, and Post-Soviet Migration to the United States* (New York: NYU Press)

Said, Edward (1978) *Orientalism* (New York: Pantheon)
Samaluk, Barbara (2016) Migration, consumption and work: A postcolonial perspective on post-socialist migration to the UK, *Ephemera* 3: 95–118
Solanke, Iyiola (2009) *Making Anti-Racial Discrimination Law: A Comparative History of Social Action and Anti-Racial Discrimination Law* (London: Routledge)
Tehranian, John (2008) *Whitewashed: America's Invisible Middle Eastern Minority* (New York: NYU Press)
Todorova, Maria (2003) Isn't Central Europe Dead?, in Christopher Lord (ed) *Central Europe: Core or Periphery?* 219–231 (Copenhagen: Copenhagen Business School)
Treaty establishing a Constitution for Europe, OJ C 310, 16.12.2004 (unratified)
Trubek, David et al. (2006) 'Soft law,' 'hard law' and EU integration, in Gráinne de Búrca and Joanne Scott (eds) *Law and New Governance in the EU and the US* 65–96 (Portland: Hart)
Twine, France Winddance and Charles Gallagher (2008) The future of whiteness: a map of the 'third wave', *Ethnic and Racial Studies* 31(1): 4–24
Williams, Andrew (2003) Mapping human rights, reading the European Union, *European Law Journal* 9(5): 659–676
Williams, Andrew (2004) *EU Human Rights Policies: A Study in Irony* (Oxford: Oxford University Press)
Williams, Patricia J (1992) *The Alchemy of Race and Rights* (Cambridge: Harvard University Press)
Wray, Matt (2006) *Not Quite White: White Trash and the Boundaries of Whiteness* (Durham: Duke University Press)

Chapter 2

Margins of the EU Project
The East in Rhetoric and Accession Policies

Throughout the Middle Ages and the Enlightenment, western authors described the eastern peripheries of Europe as a 'curious' and backwards region, filled with 'sad', 'poor', 'dirty villages', and populated by enslaved persons and undisciplined armies, living in 'cottages little different from savage huts', as if having 'been moved back ten centuries'.[1] Western intellectuals have historically relied on such discursive practices to imagine eastern parts of the European continent as inherently inferior to the west—politically, socially, ideologically, scientifically, and artistically. The long-standing mainstream scholarly and popular constructions of 'European' history and of the concept of 'Europe' have been replete with anti-Slavic sentiment and portrayals of the west as a superior site of civilisation, wealth, peace, and modernity, and of the east as primitive peripheries.[2] This view produced political and economic repercussions. The Polish-Lithuanian Commonwealth was wiped out during the 1700s, through partitions by Austria and the German state of Prussia. By the 1800s, the east was seen as a reservoir of cheap seasonal labour—especially for the neighbouring German states—and serfdom was introduced in the CEE region in response to western demand for cereals. The Germanic imperial concept of Mitteleuropa and expansionist Lebensraum ideology and policies propagated in the 1800s and early 1900s included racialising the CEE region's nationals as subhumans—worthy of forced labour, expulsion, or extermination—and imagining eastern reaches of Europe as up for grabs,[3] ultimately feeding into Nazi ideology. During the Cold War, the region continued to be not only geographically separated, but also conceptually inferiorised. It was described in western discourses as belonging to the 'Second World', more backwards than the western 'First World'. Over time, various nationalities of the eastern reaches of Europe became folded within the pejorative and essentialising label 'Eastern European', imagined as underdeveloped, backwards, and barbarian.[4]

1 Wolff (1994) (citation omitted).
2 See generally Todorova (2003).
3 See generally Meyer (1955).
4 See generally Lewicki (2023).

DOI: 10.4324/9781003175377-2

This chapter traces such western-centric perspectives through the EU's more contemporary rhetoric—about its identity, foundations, and priorities—and through the actual Eastern Enlargement process and policies. Through a holistic and long-term look at the EU's western-centric relationship with CEE states, this chapter reveals that the EU's foundational rhetoric prioritises western economic interests, continues to exclude the CEE region from the construction of 'Europe', and explicitly others it as inherently lesser and in need of civilising through westernisation. This disparaging rhetoric is interwoven with its actual policies, and underlies the EU's post-war relationship with the CEE region. Notably, even before the collapse of communism, the EU began to misuse its economic and political power to intensify inequalities between the east and the west. This one-sided approach culminated in pre-accession policies and accession treaty provisions aimed at economically benefiting western financial institutions and EU-15 states, while ignoring CEE states' and their nationals' interests. Ultimately, the EU facilitated growing economic inequalities in the region, paving the way towards normalising CEE states' status as second-class Member States and CEE movers' position as second-class EU citizens, not fully belonging to proper 'Europe'.

Western Gaze and Lofty Myths in EU Rhetoric

Any legal framework's goals, true meaning, and potential impact cannot be fully understood without appreciating its relevant legal discourse. Predominantly contained in non-binding soft-law[5] instruments, legal rhetoric elaborates laws and how they are interpreted, affecting what becomes think-able and do-able, by producing a social reality that reflects and reinforces existing power relations.[6] EU soft laws—which influence and are influenced by Member States' discourses and policies—offer are an especially important source of knowledge because, unlike nation states, the EU lacks its own media to disseminate its legal and political rhetoric. Since the first forerunner entity[7] to the EU was created in 1951, EU rhetoric has been widely disseminated by key EU institutions and their representatives, as well as by civil society members, scholars, and Member States themselves. The EU, however, tends to be approached by scholars as a pragmatic construct that does not rely on discourse to sustain its identity and policies, unlike nation states. Hence, with the exception of some critical scholars, who tend to be from disciplines other than law,[8] EU rhetoric remains under-studied. I hope to begin remedying this oversight.

---

5 Quasi-legal, non-binding documents, such as guidelines, declarations, codes of conduct, recommendations, and preambles of enforceable instruments.
6 See generally Delgado and Stefancic (2017).
7 European Coal and Steel Community, joined in 1957 by the European Atomic Energy Community and the European Economic Community. Throughout the book, references to 'EU' include references to its predecessor entities.
8 E.g., Böröcz and Kovacs (2001); Engel-Di Mauro (2006).

Limiting Our Imagination Through Myths

As 'a success story that is unrivaled globally',[9] the EU project has been framed as a benevolent mission characterised by cooperation and linear progress. EU policy statements have endowed the project's raison d'être with lofty ideals, frequently shrouded in dreams, myths,[10] and magical attributes. While seeking to legitimate[11] EU institutions and policies as progressive, inevitable, and universal, such narratives have normalised a praise-worthy view, hindering critiques of the EU project and any efforts to reduce shortcomings of its discrete policies.[12] Furthermore, they have delineated EU polity as being comprised of pre-Eastern Enlargement Member States only.

For example, in a 2009 book by the Council of the European Union,[13] *Europe: Giving Shape to an Idea*, 'Europe' is portrayed as having 'existed down the centuries as a myth, ... an idea, a source of identity'.[14] This vision assumed concrete shape through 'a Union of Member States working together ... in pursuit of a common destiny'.[15] The book's cover—an image of the European continent, shrouded in mist and clouds—evokes united Europe's mythical origins and inevitable destiny. It brings to mind the reaction of one of the participants at the 1948 Hague Congress, considered the first federal moment of modern European history: 'Where am I? In what epoch? In a dream? ... I hear a voice saying ... "We must here and now resolve that a European Assembly be constituted." ... Yes, it is a dream'.[16] This mythology has continued to permeate more contemporary EU discourse. When accepting the Nobel Peace Prize on behalf of the EU in 2012, the then-President of the European Council noted that the EU is guided by 'the idea of Europa[17] itself... speaking to us from the centuries'.[18] Notably, in such mythical, nostalgic references, pre-Eastern Enlargement Member States have served as a synecdoche for all of Europe, thus implicitly othering the east as not fully European.

On the eve of significant events, such as the Eastern Enlargement, efforts to disseminate such narratives to general audiences—including children—have tended to increase, further enshrining what is popularly think-able.[19] To make

---

9 European Commission (2014).
10 For a general discussion of the role of myths in law, see Fitzpatrick (1992).
11 Securing the appearance of legitimacy has been of particular importance to the EU—widely acknowledged to suffer from a legitimacy deficit.
12 For a discussion of how laudatory discourse prevents critique and reform initiatives, see generally Crenshaw (2011).
13 Governing institution that defines the EU's general political direction and priorities.
14 Council of the European Union (2009).
15 Id.
16 Brugmans (1970).
17 In Greek mythology, Europa was a Phoenician princess abducted by Zeus. The continent was named after her. She has served as a symbol of the EU.
18 Van Rompuy (2012).
19 E.g., European Commission (2002); European Commission (2004).

the EU's mission more relatable, alleged real-life stories are often used. For example, the Commission has praised integration through illustrative anecdotes, with titles such as, 'From a small farm to an online business thanks to EU funds'; 'Studying abroad, a life-changing experience'; and 'Saving lives through medical cooperation'.[20] On the tenth anniversary of the Eastern Enlargement, poignant statements attributed to CEE nationals were used to cement such accolades:

> [S]omeone came and waved a 'magic wand' over us. ... it was the EU ... of course. ... When I look at Poland ten years after its accession ... I ... feel a sense of pride. ... [W]e have finally managed to join the European family after several decades of troubled history ....[21]

Notably, the above excerpt implies that Poland (and, by implication, other CEE countries) did not belong to proper 'Europe' until they joined the EU.

Prioritising Economic and Integration Imperatives

By the 1980s, EU initiatives became firmly situated within fundamental-rights foundational narratives[22], disseminated widely by EU institutions. Various symbols, binding laws, soft laws[23], and audio-visual productions portray the project as having been created in order to promote 'humanitarian and progressive values'[24] and fundamental rights, which get nestled within the imagined 'cultural, religious and humanist inheritance of Europe'[25] and its 'spiritual and moral heritage'.[26] The European Court of Justice ('ECJ') situates fundamental rights as 'enshrined in the general principles of Community law',[27] having been 'inspired by the constitutional traditions common to the Member States'.[28] The European Parliament has commended the 'active role played by the European Union in the world as a defender of human rights'.[29] More discrete derivative concepts, such as pluralism, justice, solidarity, freedom, and equality get situated within this vision. They tend to be heavily emphasised during periods filled

---

20 European Commission (2012).
21 European Economic and Social Committee (2014).
22 See generally Smismans (2010).
23 E.g., 1977 Joint Declaration on Fundamental Rights; 1993 Resolution on the Respect for Human Rights in the European Community; 1995 Resolution on Human Rights in the World in 1993 to 1994 and the Union's Human Rights Policy.
24 European Commission (2014).
25 Treaty of Lisbon amending the Treaty on European Union and the Treaty establishing the European Community, 17.12.2007.
26 Charter of Fundamental Rights of the European Union, 14.12.2007.
27 *Stauder v City of Ulm*, Case 29/69, ECLI:EU:C:1969:57.
28 *Internationale Handelsgesellschaft mbH v Einfuhr- und Vorratsstelle für Getreide und Futtermittel*, Case 11/70, ECLI:EU:C:1970:114.
29 European Parliament (2009).

with identity and political anxieties—such as at the time surrounding the Eastern Enlargement—to connect the EU's fundamental-rights mythology to its actual policies, such as freedom of movement and equality acquis.[30] In addition to shaping the EU legal order and what is think-able, such narratives have served to bolster the EU's identity and legitimate its social order, normalising benevolent appraisals of the EU project's political and philosophical underpinnings and its policies.

But how stable is this vision? My review of EU discourse about its foundations and goals revealed fractures that open space for a more critical reading of what the EU is and what it does which comports with the western-centric content and impact of policies instrumental to the Eastern Enlargement. For one, this benevolent vision is historically inaccurate as it ignores the Dark Ages and the long history of European intolerances, brutality, slave trade, and imperialism. Instead, this imagined 'European' identity gets linked only to (sanitised versions of) periods such as the Renaissance and the Enlightenment, which 'improved the lives of the people ... to an extent unprecedented in the history of mankind'.[31]

Moreover, fundamental-rights narratives have always contained (western-centric) economic and integration goals. This, of course, is in line with how EU builders had at first conceptualised the project.[32] EU discourse often lists economic goals alongside dominant fundamental-rights narratives, in both hard- and soft-law instruments. For example, on the eve of the Eastern Enlargement, Europe was envisioned not only as 'a continent of democracy, freedom, peace and progress', but also of 'prosperity'.[33] Moreover, the EU's protection of human rights gets linked to its economic initiatives. For example, 'the internal market ... is an expression of our values, of the European idea of freedom ... under the rule of law',[34] that even serves to advance racial and ethnic equality:

> The appalling excesses of racism and xenophobia which were often rooted in economic causes demonstrated a need to structure economic relationships for the future in a new way .... The best way to fulfil ... objectives of its founding fathers ... is through a strong multilateral trading system.[35]

Advancing both fundamental rights and economic imperatives gets intertwined with integration. 'As far as Europe is concerned, change points in one direction only: full political and economic integration'.[36] The EU's mission at the time of

---

30 'Acquis communautaire' refers to cumulative body of EU laws.
31 European Economic and Social Committee (2000).
32 See generally Williams (2004).
33 European Commission (2003).
34 European University Institute (2006). Monnet Lectures were given annually between 1977 and 2006, by high EU officials, pro-integration western politicians, and other pro-integration public figures.
35 European University Institute (1995).
36 European University Institute (1985).

its foundation in the 1950s is portrayed as centred on enlargement to 'foster peace, prosperity and European values on the continent'.[37] Of course, those 'European values' from the 1950s were set by only a handful of western states. EU myths look far back in history to justify the inevitability of this mission. 'Europe [which] has existed down the centuries as a myth, ... an idea, a source of identity', that 'first appears with Dante', gets effectuated through a 'Union of Member States working together ... in pursuit of a common destiny'.[38] Thus, enlargement, whatever its terms, is made to appear inevitable and obvious, not to be questioned.

As explored in greater detail below and in later chapters, in the context of the Eastern Enlargement, economic and integration goals—made to look benevolent by being nestled within fundamental-rights rhetoric—have been privileging western Member States' interests, facilitating a social reality of continuing inequalities between the CEE region and western parts of the EU, and contributing to the experience of mobility by CEE nationals that has been 'free' in name only. As if pre-emptively, soon after the fall of the Iron Curtain, EU institutions portrayed the anticipated Eastern Enlargement as exemplary within the history of territorial expansion projects, thereby foreclosing any opportunity for seeing it as a neo-colonial endeavour:

> The idea of unification ... has sometimes meant an imperial vision of domination ... What we are now attempting to build is a Europe based on consensus and on popular support. This experiment is ... unique in human history... different from the experience of the great empires of the past ... and also different from that of the United States.[39]

As my analysis throughout the book suggests, however, the colonial characterisation is apt.

Emphasising Shared (Western) Heritage

In addition to legitimating its political framework and specific initiatives, EU rhetoric has been creating a sense of common polity among members of the dominant, privileged group that has created it. Since the establishment of the EU's precursor institutions, its architects have been enveloping the project's mythical foundations within references to the 'spirit' and identity of 'Europe', based on an allegedly shared 'European' cultural heritage.[40] The construct of 'a European idea' allegedly 'penetrat[es] ... deeply into the consciousness of the public'.[41] Despite the EU's limited competence to act in cultural matters,[42] in 1973, the Commission

---

37 European Commission (2013).
38 Council of the European Union (2009).
39 European University Institute (1992).
40 See generally Sassatelli (2009).
41 European Economic Community Commission (1961).
42 And only since the 1993 Maastricht Treaty.

issued the Declaration on European Identity.[43] Actively promoting a sense of shared culture has been bolstered through what Hobsbawn and Ranger term 'invented traditions'[44]—including embodiments of the Greek myth of Europa (on euro currency, on various EU buildings, and used as the name of the official EU website), exaggerations of historical figures (such as Charlemagne), and newly invented collective symbols and rituals (such as common passport, driving license, and car number plate designs; the 'United in Diversity' motto; the EU anthem[45]; and the annual Europe Day). Such rhetorical and cultural initiatives have been creating, to borrow Anderson's concept, an 'imagined community'.[46]

Notably, throughout such initiatives, the notion of 'Europeanness' has tended to be closely circumscribed, positioning the east at its conceptual peripheries—by relying on western symbols, locations, moments, and thinkers, stretching back to antiquity, while conflating them with all of 'Europe'. For example, Italy gets lauded for having contributed, more than any other country, to the foundations of 'European' cultural identity—through the Roman Empire, Roman law, and the Renaissance.[47] Aristotle, Cicero, Tocqueville, Durkheim, Hegel, Marx[48], Erasmus, Kant, Rousseau, and Voltaire[49] get mentioned frequently as the founders of 'European' heritage.[50] The EU's shared 'European' culture and institutional heritage often get linked to its founding fathers, described as '[v]isionary leaders',[51] characterised by 'great-heart[s]', 'deep wisdom', and 'iron will'.[52] All the founding fathers were western and white (and male). Although one could argue that such references simply reflect the original composition of the EU's forerunner entity,[53] they nevertheless normalise a western-centric vision of what constitutes 'Europe'.

Ideas about the intrinsic basis for shared identity and belonging within the EU, as linked to the EU's foundations, intersect with notions of whiteness.[54] Not all whites are perceived the same way. As critical whiteness scholars postulate, not all groups of Caucasians are able to fully benefit from their phenotypical whiteness.[55] Instead, intra-white fractures, based on factors such as ethnicity, class, culture, and nationality, determine how various groups are

43 European Communities (1973).
44 Hobsbawm and Ranger (1983).
45 Beethoven's 'Ode to Joy'.
46 Anderson (2006).
47 E.g., European University Institute (1984).
48 E.g., European Economic and Social Committee (1999).
49 E.g., European University Institute (1990).
50 This vision also overlooks British cultural and scientific contributions, in line with British (pre-Brexit) Euroscepticism.
51 European Commission (2013).
52 European University Institute (1977).
53 European Coal and Steel Community was founded in 1951 by Belgium, France, Germany, Italy, Luxembourg, and the Netherlands.
54 See generally El-Enany (2020).
55 See e.g., Levine-Rasky (2013).

portrayed in institutional discourse and popular narratives—and how they are approached by policies, as discussed later on in this chapter. In the process of emphasising shared (western) Europeanness, those from Eastern regions of Europe have been racialised as backwards and threatening.[56]

Explicit Othering of the CEE Region

To create a sense of commonality among members of the dominant group, legal rhetoric tends to other and racialise non-dominant groups, by propagating implicit and explicit discourses which assume other groups' inferiority and affect their outcomes. The rhetorical construction of 'European' cultural identity has not only imagined the project as a western endeavour, but has also relied on explicit references to 'outsiders', such as those geographically from beyond the EU's external borders—notably, communists during the Cold War, and third-country nationals today (especially Muslims). Moreover, my analysis indicates that explicit othering by both EU and western politicians has posited the CEE region as inferior and innately un-European, even once it was on its way to becoming a political part of the EU. Unfortunately, '[o]ppressive language' not only limits knowledge, but it 'is violence'.[57]

Soon after the collapse of communism in 1989, the then Commission President Jacques Delors instinctively assumed that the EU would serve as a 'lodestar', an ideal to which the CEE region aspired as it embarked on its postcommunist path.[58] At the same time, the prospect of mobility of CEE nationals to the west caused a sense of disquiet among EU bureaucrats, western politicians, and western publics. As discussed in the next chapter, othering rhetoric was especially prevalent in the context of restricting CEE workers' mobility after accession. In its 'Agenda 2000' plan,[59] the Commission justified postaccession mobility restrictions as being helpful in preventing 'problems' that would result from CEE workers' unrestrained mobility to the west. Since economic predictions at the time indicated that CEE nationals' unrestricted mobility would benefit EU-15 states economically, one can only assume that the Commission was concerned about the social impact of an influx of these othered, new citizens of the EU.

Notably, the 2004/2007 enlargement was the only one to be called 'eastern'. Although the immediately preceding enlargement had involved a geographically eastward expansion (to incorporate Austria, Finland, and Sweden in 1995), it was described through references to its date. Moreover, despite fears of postcommunist otherness, the absorption of East Germany into West Germany in 1990 was portrayed as a 're-unification'. Presumably, East Germany was

---

56 See generally Boatcă (2013).
57 Morrison (1994).
58 Delors (1990).
59 Commission of the European Communities (1997).

deemed as having been sufficiently 'European' prior to the Cold War to deserve such inclusive terminology. On the other hand, CEE states represented reaches of the continent somehow different than, and inferior to, the proper 'European' polity.

During the accession process itself, CEE states were represented by EU bureaucrats as backwards. In the annual Accession Country Regular Reports (1998–2002), drafted by the Commission to evaluate candidates' progress in meeting membership benchmarks, the Eastern Enlargement was framed as a 'civilising' mission, akin to how western European empires had historically portrayed their colonisation efforts. Notably, by taking in CEE countries, EU-15 states were portrayed as 'opening up to new people'[60] and preparing to 'embrace widely different peoples … and cultures',[61] rather than as expanding a pan-European union of equals. As an impoverished other, the CEE region had to be 'rescued' by western Europe, which was to serve as a 'mentor' and 'beacon to guide the applicants'[62] in their efforts to partake of some of the achievements of (western) Europe. The Eastern Enlargement presented western states, 'the heirs of a civilisation deeply rooted in religious and civic values', with an opportunity to spread their standards throughout the continent.[63] According to western bureaucrats, CEE countries were seeking to join the EU in order to 'liquidate' their 'social and civilisation backwardness',[64] rather than to reclaim their European heritage. Notably, in the context of demographic shifts brought about by the Eastern Enlargement, western 'shared values' that had held EU-15 societies 'together' became 'more important than ever',[65] as the pre-2004 (western) EU encountered a region that presented a threat to its principles and identity.

My review of more recent statements by western and EU politicians indicates that, despite its accession, the CEE region's heritage has not been added to the construction of the imagined 'European' community. Notably, CEE states have been accused of 'exporting their crime'[66] to the west. An alleged growth in prostitution in Denmark has been depicted 'as a result of the EU's expansion eastwards'.[67] Moreover, the 'mass migratory flows' of CEE nationals have been blamed for 'encouraging the free movement of diseases, such as tuberculosis … allow[ing] this disease to take hold amongst younger age groups in the [western] population'.[68] When responding to such comments made by EU-15 Members of the European Parliament, EU officials have been failing to address their racist stereotypes. Instead, they have been reiterating the limits of EU competence in such matters, allowing this biting rhetoric to be normalised.

60 Commission of the European Communities (2004).
61 Kok (2003).
62 European Commission (2003a).
63 Prodi (2000).
64 Organisation for Economic Co-operation and Development (1998).
65 Commission of the European Communities (2004).
66 European Parliament (2013).
67 European Parliament (2013a).
68 European Parliament (2014a).

In fact, EU institutions themselves have continued to position the CEE region as not quite European. Seven years after the Eastern Enlargement, the Commission noted that 'advanced countries (the United States, Japan and *Europe*) [had] returned to modest growth', whereas 'emerging and transition economies in *eastern Europe* ... have proved more resilient' to the 2008 economic crisis.[69] The concept of 'Europe' in this statement excludes eastern Europe. Although such differentiation might be attributed, to some extent, to historical differences in institutional and economic infrastructures between EU-15 and CEE states, it nevertheless continues to normalise discourse of eastern otherness and inferiority. Steeped in historical origins, such narratives have continued to this day. For example, ECJ discourse tends to prioritise values of western Member States, while normalising negative stereotypes to create an image of CEE nationals as socially and economically inferior to westerners, as not belonging to the proper EU polity, and as not quite deserving of EU law's protections.[70]

Strategic Interludes of Rhetorical Inclusion

The CEE region has been sporadically included in the grand vision of 'Europe', but only during discrete historical moments or for pragmatic reasons, rather than as an unequivocal indication of inclusivity. One such unique context was the euphoric period soon after the fall of communism—before CEE states' accession had become a clear possibility. For example, at the 1989 European Council summit, EU bureaucrats declared that the EU's objective was 'overcoming the divisions of Europe'.[71] During the 1990 Monnet Lecture, titled 'The Crisis of the Societies in the East and the Return to a Common Europe', the concept of 'Europe' was portrayed as a 'unifying' and 'continent-wide' idea.[72] Similarly, the Parliament expressed its intention to 'end ... the division of Europe into two blocs'.[73] Such statements likely reflected nothing more than an ideological rebuff to communism and an attempt to strengthen the legitimacy and reinforce the benevolent vision of the western order and the EU project. Moreover, as Schimmelfennig argues,[74] the EU's occasionally inclusive statements—stretching as far back as the post-war period of strong anti-fascist and anti-Soviet sentiments—had rhetorically entrapped it. That is, the EU could not backtrack on the long-standing pan-European rhetoric without losing its credibility.

Othering of the CEE region also diminished once the Eastern Enlargement became certain. By 2003, the Commission was situating the Enlargement within the task of integrating 'the continent',[75] and internal policy reports portrayed CEE states as having shared 'since the Middle Ages in the interplay of cultural

69 European Commission (2011) (emphases added).
70 See Myslinska (2021).
71 European Council (1989).
72 European University Institute (1990).
73 European Parliament (1995).
74 Schimmelfennig (2001).
75 European Commission (2003).

influences in continental Europe', with their Cold War separation having been merely 'a temporary aberration'.[76] Notably, the Joint Declaration 'One Europe', annexed to the 2003 Act of Accession, emphasised the 'inclusive' nature of the Enlargement, with the aim of making 'Europe a *continent* of democracy, freedom, peace and progress'.[77] In addition to reflecting rhetorical entrapment, such inclusive rhetoric was also likely intended to serve a pragmatic purpose—to garner EU-15 states' support for the Enlargement[78] once the EU had determined that it was the only method of bolstering EU-15 economies. I contend that inclusive discourse at the time of the Eastern Enlargement also served to legitimate the integration process and to help obfuscate any inequalities in the actual accession policies, while conveniently aligning with the EU's fundamental rights narratives. The EU's propagation of such more inclusive narratives at both the time of the fall of communism and the time of the Enlargement can be attributed to what Bell had termed 'interest convergence',[79] where the rights of marginalised groups are only supported when they serve interests of the group in power.

Economic and Political Dynamics of CEE States' Accession

In line with western-centric narratives discussed above, the Eastern Enlargement was conceptualised as being grounded in pre-2004 'European' values, that is, extending principles created in the 1950s to the whole continent. Rather than a coming together of equals, CEE states were to be absorbed *into* the western framework. This was to entail the undertaking of major adjustments in the acceding states, as their 'institutional framework and the ground rules ha[d] to be re-constructed'[80]—due to not only economic, but also to 'social disparities' between the west and the CEE region.[81]

Such narratives prompted me to wonder whether the actual processes and policies leading towards and enabling the Eastern Enlargement also reflected silencing or disadvantaging of the CEE region while prioritising western interests. What scholarship exists about the actual economic and political dynamics leading up to the Eastern Enlargement has been largely uncritical, often nestled within myths of the neutrality and benevolence of EU policies, and embedded

76 Kok (2003).
77 Act concerning the conditions of accession of the Czech Republic, the Republic of Estonia, the Republic of Cyprus, the Republic of Latvia, the Republic of Lithuania, the Republic of Hungary, the Republic of Malta, the Republic of Poland, the Republic of Slovenia and the Slovak Republic and the adjustments to the Treaties on which the European Union is founded, 23.9.2003 ('2003 Accession Treaty') (emphasis added).
78 Any accession must be ratified by all Member States.
79 Bell (1980).
80 Commission of the European Communities (1993).
81 E.g., Europe Agreement establishing an association between the European Communities and their Member States and the Czech Republic, 31.12.1994, Preamble.

within fundamental-rights narratives. Below, my critical and holistic look situates the Eastern Enlargement's process, policies, and immediate aftermath within the relevant historical, economic, social, and political contexts—to reveal how the west misused its bargaining position to benefit itself while increasing economic inequalities between the east and the west and normalising the post-accession relationship of unequals. Kalmar[82] has summed up this relationship as an embodiment of 'racial capitalism',[83] pursuant to which the subaltern periphery provides new markets and cheap labourers, while being placed behind an imagined racial barrier and being deprived of full access to rights that are afforded to the dominant countries.

CEE Region Before the Fall of Communism

Germany and the Soviet Union invaded Poland in 1939, throwing the entire CEE region into chaos. Stalin occupied and subsequently annexed the Baltic states of Estonia, Latvia, and Lithuania. By the end of WWII, approximately 40 million CEE nationals had perished. At the 1945 Yalta Conference, the United States, United Kingdom, and the Soviet Union configured the post-war 'reorganisation' of Germany and of the CEE region. New governments under Soviet auspices were then formed in Czechoslovakia, Hungary, and Poland, as well as in Bulgaria and Romania. Meanwhile, Slovenia was incorporated into Yugoslavia, which was re-established under new communist rule.

Under Soviet pressure, CEE states rejected the opportunity to participate in the Marshall Plan, the post-war US support for industrial and economic recovery in Europe. Instead, Stalin provided the CEE region, now under his firm political and economic control, with the Molotov Plan, which was later expanded into COMECON,[84] an economic and trade alliance within the Eastern Bloc. As a result, the CEE region[85] reoriented its trade towards the Soviet Union while curtailing its economic, political, and cultural links to the west. Exacerbated by wartime human casualties and decimation of infrastructure—as well as by post-war deportations, repatriations, and forced resettlements—living standards across the region deteriorated rapidly.

Throughout the post-war period, CEE industries were nationalised and farmland was redistributed through collectivisations. Economic restructurings prioritised heavy industry to service communist military forces. Although by the 1960s the CEE region was highly industrialised, it was plagued by economic stagnation and escalating consumer prices. By the mid-1970s, three decades of

---

82 Kalmar (2023).
83 See generally Robinson (2019).
84 The Council for Mutual Economic Assistance (1949 to 1991) included the Eastern Bloc (Czechoslovakia, Hungary, Poland, as well as Bulgaria and Romania) and socialist states outside Europe.
85 With the exception of Yugoslavia, which had a quasi-market economy and was more open to the west.

central planning had left most of the CEE region with an inability to innovate technologically, low production efficiency and slumping industrial output, shortages of food and basic consumer goods, low public health standards, and rampant corruption. The 1973 oil crisis further exacerbated these trends. As food rationing was introduced across the region, most CEE states became recipients of international food aid. Economic challenges contributed to social ills, such as high rates of alcoholism, prostitution, and drug addiction. Not surprisingly, this period saw public revolts in Czechoslovakia, Hungary, and Poland which were violently suppressed by communist leaderships.

To reduce public discontent, wide-ranging 'reforms' were introduced across the CEE region[86] in the 1970s and 1980s opening the door to western interference in the region's economic future. This included increased Soviet trade subsidies which made the region even more economically dependent on the Soviet Union. Simultaneously, CEE states' economic and political self-determination became further undermined by borrowing heavily from western governments,[87] the European Economic Community, and western banks and international financial institutions (i.e., the International Monetary Fund ('IMF'), and the World Bank). These loans were largely used to purchase obsolete western technologies and to increase access to consumer goods, neither of which benefited the region's long-term economic development. The Eastern Bloc's combined borrowing amounted to $80 billion in 1982,[88] resulting in staggering interest payments. For example, by 1980, Poland had become the third largest debtor in the world, with interest alone on its $24.1 billion foreign debt exceeding the value of all Polish exports.[89] Repayment efforts and structural adjustments imposed by western creditors significantly strained national budgets, further increased consumer prices, decreased welfare and infrastructure spending, and reduced wages. Foreign debt was rescheduled and debt tenures were extended—in Poland in 1981 (accompanied by the imposition of martial law[90]), in Romania in 1982, and in Yugoslavia in 1983. Furthermore, where allowed by communist leadership, the west began to increase its investment in CEE states, especially in Hungary and Czechoslovakia. By the late 1980s, these economic initiatives had left CEE states economically entwined with the west, while still being politically dominated by the Soviet Union, with no ability to determine their own long-term political or economic paths.

---

86 Having been annexed by the Soviet Union, Baltic states were not as affected by such initiatives. Instead, they experienced severe economic difficulties, as Soviet industrial production was even more heavily oriented towards militarisation, and the economy was even more tightly controlled by the party.
87 Especially from West Germany, France, and the UK. Incidentally, they became some of the largest host states for CEE movers.
88 See Nove et al. (1982).
89 See Tittenbrun (1993).
90 After martial law was imposed, Poland stopped making interest payments, yet western regimes continued to extend it credit.

Aftermath of the Fall of the Iron Curtain

As part of 'glasnost' (openness) and 'perestroika' (restructuring) policies introduced in the mid-1980s, Gorbachev slowly allowed greater self-governance in the Eastern Bloc. The resultant public pressure led to a cascade of events in 1989: the legalisation of the Solidarity trade union and free elections in Poland; crossings of thousands of East Germans into West Germany; the dismantling of barbed-wire barriers between Hungary and Austria; and the tearing down of the Berlin Wall. In December 1989, Gorbachev and George Bush released a joint statement that the Cold War between the two superpowers had ended. This was quickly followed by democratic elections that ended communist rule in the Baltic States, and by Slovenia's declaration of independence from Yugoslavia.[91]

The CEE region soon became marred by chaos as its ideological, political, economic, and social systems collapsed. More than four decades of central planning had left CEE economies with deeply distorted structures which were further destabilised after COMECON disintegrated in 1991. Each CEE state—especially the newly independent Baltic nations and Slovenia—was faced with the urgent tasks of overhauling state institutions or creating new ones, and implementing macroeconomic stabilisation efforts to address escalating inflation and fiscal deficits, amid infighting among multiple new political parties which lacked any experience of long-term economic or political planning.

The Visegrád Group

The three largest CEE states (Czechoslovakia, Hungary, and Poland) faced staggering post-1989 political and economic challenges. Poland's economic crisis was the most severe within the CEE region, with 250%[92] inflation and GDP contraction exceeding 7% by 1990.[93] One-third of Poles were living in poverty, and 15% were unemployed by 1991,[94] while prices increased by 600% between 1989 and 1991.[95] In Hungary, as inflation reached 35% in 1991, stern austerity measures were implemented accompanied by currency devaluations and the selling of key economic sectors to foreign investors.[96] Similarly, at the time of its dissolution in 1993, Czechoslovakia was suffering from high levels of unemployment (in excess of 13% in the Slovak Republic), rapid inflation, and substantial currency devaluation.[97] Overall, the post-1989 period was characterised

---

91 By 1989, communism was also toppled in Bulgaria and Romania. With a history of political repression more severe than in CEE states, both countries were plagued by political and economic crises, which caused widespread doubt about their abilities for independent recoveries without EU accession.
92 Belka (2013).
93 Flamm (2012).
94 Ekiert and Kubik (2004).
95 Myant and Cox (2008).
96 Bod (2019).
97 Vienna Institute for International Economic Studies (2019).

by economic declines, hyperinflations, and drastic decreases in real wages which produced high social costs, exacerbated by increasing unemployment and deep cuts in social spending.

As key creditors, western financial institutions swiftly began to play a more prominent role in the region. After COMECON's dissolution in 1991, the IMF pressured Poland and Hungary to end their trade relations with other CEE states. Unable to service their foreign debts, and hence not able to borrow abroad anymore, they were then compelled by the IMF and the World Bank to quickly transform into market-oriented economies, in a first such attempt in European history. Post-1989 economic transformation measures were the most severe in Poland, with the IMF's conditioning its continued financial support on economic 'shock therapy'—which no western state had ever imposed on itself for fear of detrimental effects on livelihoods,[98] and which has been subsequently heavily criticised and later modified by western financial institutions themselves.[99] A term borrowed from electroconvulsive therapy of inducing generalised seizure to manage some treatment-resistant mental illnesses, economic 'shock therapy' entailed a rapid overhaul of macro- and micro-economic practices to liberalise the economy. This 'reform' package included swiftly increasing interest rates, liberalising prices, and expanding privatisations, with the most viable Polish enterprises getting acquired by western Fortune-500 companies. Furthermore, IMF-prompted legal 'reforms' allowed foreign-owned companies in Poland to repatriate all their after-tax profits and exempted them from Polish licensing laws. Although Hungary already exhibited some free market elements before 1989, it was similarly pressured to overhaul its economy and to quickly privatise, selling some of its most profitable companies to foreign investors. In Czechoslovakia, although at first, large enterprises were privatised via the voucher system and sold to Czech nationals, by the mid-1990s, the most successful companies (including Škoda) and banks were acquired by foreign investors.

With no experience of independent or multi-party governance, this period was also politically tumultuous across the CEE region. Initial democratic elections were marred by conflicts among multiple political parties (with some holdovers from the communist era) and were plagued by the communist tradition of short-term political thinking with no consensus about how to chart independent national paths. For example, more than 100 parties participated in the first free parliamentary elections in Poland in 1991, and 13 candidates ran for office in the 1995 presidential elections. Between 1989 and 1993, Poland had two presidents and seven prime ministers (two of whom did not even form cabinets) and frequent votes of no-confidence. Hungary was similarly crippled by divisive elections and political infighting, particularly between groups wanting to eliminate all vestiges of communism and those that had absorbed the former communist elite. Emerging from an

---

98 See generally Glasman (1996).
99 Balázs et al. (2014).

especially rigid communist rule, Czechoslovakia also faced political instability. This was further fuelled by nationalistic pressures which culminated in the Slovaks' decision to form a separate country in 1992.

As a response to such instabilities, political elites in the Visegrád countries supported free-market capitalist models. Many preferred capitalism for pragmatic reasons: perceiving it as a quick fix, associating it with democracy, stability, and security from the Soviet Union, or valuing it as a symbolic break from the communist past and a method to increase their legitimacy in western eyes.[100] Although blue-collar workers, conservative scholars, post-communist political factions, and the Catholic Church had envisioned either a planned or a mixed economy for post-communist CEE states—at least in part to avoid high social and political costs of a drastic economic transformation—non-market options soon became impossible due to the rapid privatisations of the early 1990s and the increasing western ownership of CEE businesses and banking systems. Some experts also perceived the free-market model as less risky than developing new economic models particularly as non-governing politicians—splintered into many small parties—failed to present persuasive alternatives.

Moreover, CEE political elites tended to perceive EU accession[101] as an indispensable element of free-market economics. They saw no feasible economic alternatives to joining the EU, especially after COMECON was dissolved in 1991. Capital infusions from non-EU countries, such as the United States, were uncertain and would have carried similar risks as those from EU institutions. Finally, the Swiss and Norwegian models of relations with the EU were not feasible due to the comparatively low levels of CEE states' economic development. With no suitable alternatives, the Visegrád states were placed on an unequal footing in their relationships with the EU, as they hoped to ingratiate themselves with the west so that accession would indeed materialise.

The Baltic States

Having been occupied since WWII by the Soviet Union, the Baltic states inherited especially inefficient economies. This was particularly notable in Lithuania, which had the largest agricultural sector in the Baltic region. Furthermore, the collapse of the Soviet Union in 1991 severely disrupted their trade and financial channels resulting in sharply falling outputs and real incomes, rapid price increases, and escalating budget deficits. They emerged as independent states with lower GDPs and higher inflation than their CEE counterparts. For example, between 1990 and 1994, real GDP in Lithuania declined by approximately 70% while inflation reached 1,180% in 1992.[102] As unemployment increased due to industrial restructurings, the Baltics were faced with sharp declines in living standards.

---

100 See generally Ash (1990).
101 For Slovakia, joining the EU also represented a symbol of its new independence.
102 See generally Vilpišauskas (2014).

Due to these economic struggles, Baltic governments sought IMF assistance in 1991. In exchange for promises of financial support, the IMF set up 'advice' missions in each Baltic country which shaped their economic, legal, and financial policies while training their government officials. According to the IMF, there was 'no choice—or even debate'—in following its guidance regarding swift transition to market economies.[103] The IMF engaged the World Bank in shaping Baltic 'reforms', with financial disbursements made conditional on adhering to their financial and structural policies. Quick privatisations and economic restructurings were adopted with significant social costs. Repeated banking crises resulted in more stringent regulatory and supervisory oversight by the IMF, the World Bank, and the European Bank for Reconstruction and Development. The IMF placed long-term experts in the Baltic states' central banks and ministries of finance. Although IMF financial policies were not necessarily successful, the IMF did not provide any domestic leeway to shape their implementation. For example, in the mid-1990s, a rising budget deficit in Latvia fuelled domestic pressure to reverse some recently implemented trade liberalisation policies. The IMF, however, resisted this and instead suggested a re-tightening of fiscal policy. Similarly, the IMF opposed calls in Lithuania for trade protection particularly in the agricultural sector. In both Latvia and Lithuania, IMF's continued financial support was conditioned on strictly following its demands.

Outputs across the Baltic region continued to plummet through the mid-1990s, much more than in Visegrád countries, due to the more severe systemic and trade shocks. To reduce inflations, current account deficits were increased across the Baltic states. IMF then suggested remedying this through foreign direct investment ('FDI'). FDI was largely directed towards companies operating in financial, commercial, and construction service areas and hence did not contribute to the modernisation of manufacturing, to the improvement of trade balances, or to the enhancement of longer-term economic performance. By the early 2000s, all three Baltic states experienced large and rising deficits in their balance of payments, while their productivity and income growth stagnated and consumption became increasingly financed through foreign loans.

Furthermore, the newly independent Baltic states' political landscapes were tumultuous. In addition to having to create new constitutions and institutions, much political energy was diverted towards political scuffles which were particularly turbulent given ethnic and linguistic divides with in Baltic societies.[104] Compared to the Visegrád states, the Baltics had even fewer economic or political alternatives to chart their independent paths due to their smaller sizes, less developed economies, and post-war Soviet isolation. Further incentivised by the ongoing geopolitical risk of having Russia as a neighbour, very few in the region questioned their aspirations to transform into free-market economies and to join the EU.

103 Knöbl and Haas (2003).
104 Under Soviet occupation, Baltic states were subjected to an influx of Russian workers, to Russify their cultures.

Slovenia

Slovenia entered its post-communist period on a stronger economic footing than other CEE states. Economic freedoms had been broader in Yugoslavia than in the rest of the CEE region. Post-war collectivisation attempts were unsuccessful, and industry was not subjected to central planning after 1965. Despite its communist one-party political system, Yugoslavia never joined the COMECON, and its trade remained heavily oriented towards western Europe. Slovenia was the wealthiest of the Yugoslav republics and the richest CEE state. For example, in 1990, its income per capita exceeded $6,000[105] which was similar to that of Greece and Portugal. Although in some respects, its economy resembled other CEE states' systems—with significant industrialisation and a small service sector—Slovenia was more open and market-oriented, with prices and imports relatively free and with significant experience of entrepreneurship and self-employment under communism. After 1989, it did not experience industrial or consumer goods shortages. Moreover, having been prohibited under the Yugoslav regime from borrowing externally, the Slovenian budget was typically balanced. As a result, after Slovenia declared its independence from Yugoslavia in 1991, its economic reforms were the least drastic in the region. With a low share of FDI and little need for foreign loans, Slovenia was able to resist IMF's pressure for rapid economic transition. Adopting a gradual path towards privatisations and opening to foreign capital, it quickly achieved currency convertibility which spared it from hyperinflation common in the region. Nevertheless, Slovenia did initially suffer from a sharp decrease in real GDP (of more than 9% in 1991) and an increase in unemployment (of more than 8% in 1991), in part due to a reduction in exports to the former communist countries (especially to the former Yugoslav markets).

Moreover, its post-communist political environment was challenging and this contributed to its decision to seek EU accession. Civil unrest accompanying Yugoslavia's breakup negatively affected its production and exports. Moreover, intense political infighting plagued Slovenia during its first decade of independence, resulting in the ousting of the first Minister-President, parliamentary paralysis, and the formation of a new government. Similarly to the new Baltic states, Slovenia also faced the challenge of creating the legal and administrative institutions of a new state. Moreover, Slovenia was not in a position to chart its own course due to its small size and the growing instability in the Yugoslav region. Its situation became especially precarious after other CEE states made it clear that they were seeking to accede. Due to a history of trade openness with the west and the relatively low costs of post-communist economic transition, Slovenians exhibited little opposition to market reforms or EU accession.

---

105 See generally Pleskovic and Sachs (1994).

Role of the EU Before 2004

Before the fall of communism in 1989, political relations between CEE states and the EU as a collective[106] were largely non-existent, and only a few formal economic links existed between them. Under Soviet pressure, CEE countries refused to recognise the European Economic Community ('EEC') —the EU's precursor—under public international law. Except for Slovenia's sectoral trade arrangements with select EU-15 Member States, economic relations were also limited. Starting with the 1980 (non-preferential) trade agreement with Romania,[107] the EEC entered into a few sectoral agreements with Czechoslovakia, Hungary, and Poland, but they were limited to certain industrial products, textiles, steel, and specific meats. These first-generation trade agreements did not contain a commitment to eliminate discriminatory quantitative restrictions. In the case of Czechoslovakia and Poland (which were already members of the GATT[108]), these agreements largely reflected the already-existing (limited) commitments under the GATT which permitted quantitative restrictions on eastern exports. Furthermore, EEC's anti-dumping rules significantly impeded eastern exports to western Europe thereby eliminating any economic advantage the east might have derived from lower production costs.

Gorbachev's increasing openness towards the west, further incentivised by his efforts to bolster the declining Soviet economy and his political clout within the Eastern Bloc, resulted in the signing of the one-page 1988 Joint EEC-CMEA Declaration[109] which envisaged establishing 'official relations' and developing cooperation in areas and through methods to be determined later. Although the Declaration resulted in the establishment of diplomatic relations, its practical implications were limited. Any 'cooperation' would not include commercial policy measures because they were outside the competence of the CMEA as a collective entity. Moreover, although the Declaration was binding on EU Member States, it did not bind CMEA states individually. It did, however, facilitate the conclusion of EEC trade and cooperation agreements with CEE states.

---

106 Political relations between *individual* EU Member States and CEE states did exist, albeit largely formal and superficial.
107 Council Regulation No 3338/80 of 16 December 1980 on the conclusion of the Agreement on the establishment of the Joint Committee and the Agreement on trade in industrial products between the European Economic Community and the Socialist Republic of Romania, 29.12.1980.
108 General Agreement on Tariffs and Trade, replaced by the World Trade Organisation in 1995.
109 Council Decision of 22 June 1988 on the conclusion of the Joint Declaration on the establishment of official relations between the European Economic Community and the Council for Mutual Economic Assistance, 24.6.1988. Council for Mutual Economic Assistance was synonymous with COMECON.

Trade and Cooperation Agreements

When the Iron Curtain started to crumble, the EU began to pay greater attention to CEE states' economic and political paths. EU bureaucrats strongly encouraged CEE electorates to support pro-western and pro-capitalist domestic political parties. Between 1988 and 1993, all CEE states[110] and the EU signed second-generation Agreements on Trade and Commercial and Economic Cooperation ('T&C Agreements') to provide timetables for the gradual elimination of quantitative trade restrictions against CEE exports to the EU. Because the EU negotiated trade matters separately with each CEE country, these agreements' provisions were not uniform. All except Slovenia's,[111] however, shared the same central features—discussed below—including numerous policies disadvantageous towards CEE states.

Although these agreements accorded contracting parties the most-favoured-nation treatment, their protectionist provisions benefited the west. In the case of CEE states that were members of the GATT, this merely largely reaffirmed pre-existing commitments under the GATT. Notably, exports of goods in which CEE countries tended to be competitive—including coal, steel, textiles, and agricultural products—were excluded from trade preferences. In the agricultural sector, of great economic significance to most CEE states, most T&C Agreements contained a non-binding stipulation for joint committees between the EU and the pertinent CEE state to consider 'the possibility of granting each other reciprocal concessions on a product-by-product basis'.[112] Furthermore, all goods were to be traded between the contracting parties at market-related prices, thus eliminating any advantage that the more affordably produced CEE goods might have had when sold in the west.

In addition to being protectionist towards the existing (western) Member States in areas in which CEE states were especially competitive, the T&C Agreements contained other provisions that were likely to disadvantage CEE states and to benefit the west. For one, the most-favoured-nation clauses were reciprocal, so that CEE states were required to provide non-discriminatory market access to western exports—for example, by streamlining their import license systems, abolishing import quotas, and treating EU companies similarly to domestic ones. Western consumer goods were anticipated to be more appealing to CEE consumers than domestic goods, especially if provided at market-related prices, crowding out CEE producers. The T&C Agreements also facilitated foreign investment opportunities. Given economic and labour cost differences, investment was expected to largely flow from west to east.

---

110 Similar T&C Agreements were also signed with Bulgaria (1990) and Romania (1991).
111 Slovenia's T&C Agreement reflected pre-existing EU trade relations with Yugoslavia.
112 E.g., Agreement between the EEC and the Polish People's Republic on trade and commercial and economic cooperation, 22.11.1989 ('T&C Agreement Poland'), Article 12.

It is true that the T&C Agreements contained safeguard clauses that enabled CEE states to reinstate quantitative restrictions if they experienced, or were at risk of, injury from imports of any EU product for which restrictions had been abolished. However, these safeguards' practical benefits to CEE states were insignificant. For one, these rights were reciprocal, so that, if a CEE state were to apply safeguards, the EU could deviate from its obligations in respect of 'substantially equivalent trade'[113] or even do so in a retaliatory way. Moreover, safeguard clauses were to be implemented only upon the contracting parties' consultation and agreement. More generally, joint committees composed of the contracting parties' representatives monitored the T&C Agreements' implementation. Given the EU's clout and CEE states' aspirations to increase their links with the EU, such oversight largely functioned to keep CEE states on their best behaviour.

Notably, T&C Agreements did not guarantee accession. Instead, they merely 'recogniz[ed]' that the EU and CEE states 'desire[d] to establish' wider-ranging 'contractual links' which would 'permit further development at a later stage'[114] or would 'extend the relations already existing between them'.[115] By the time T&C Agreements were signed with the Baltic states in 1992, any possibility of accession was made explicitly conditional. The contracting parties were 'desirous of creating favourable conditions' to promote economic cooperation by developing economic links to contribute to 'progress towards the objective of an association agreement in due course, when [such] conditions [were] met'.[116] Furthermore, in order to make any increasing economic links possible, the Baltic states were explicitly obligated to meet a new benchmark—having to prove to the EU's satisfaction that they were respecting human rights principles in all their domestic and external policies.

The sense of conditionality was even more apparent in the financial instruments that accompanied all of the T&C Agreements, which prioritised expansion of the EU's internal market to benefit western states while overlooking long-term economic development and aspirations for self-sufficiency within the CEE region. Any EU financial aid to CEE states was conditioned on their successful ongoing 'cooperation' and on satisfactory outcomes of 'exchanges' with EU representatives 'of commercial and economic information on all matters

---

113 E.g., Agreement between the EEC and the Hungarian People's Republic on trade and commercial and economic cooperation, 30.11.88 ('T&C Agreement Hungary'), Article 7.
114 E.g., T&C Agreement Poland, Preamble.
115 E.g., T&C Agreement Hungary, Preamble.
116 E.g., Agreement between the EEC and the Republic of Latvia on trade and commercial and economic cooperation, 31.12.92 ('T&C Agreement Latvia'), Preamble. It was not until 1994 that the EU expressed an intention to develop closer relations with the three Baltic countries—due to perceiving them as a gateway to the expanding Russian economy, and a buffer against potential illegal migration, smuggling, and drug trade from farther east. See Press Release (1994).

which would assist the development of commercial and economic cooperation'.[117] The most significant pre-accession financial instrument, PHARE[118], was financed by international financial institutions with close links to the EU—the World Bank, the European Bank for Reconstruction and Development, and the European Investment Bank. PHARE's stated goals included providing CEE states with western technical expertise to aid their economic transformation into market economies. CEE states were afforded a mix of aid, investment, and trade concessions which continued to maintain restrictions against CEE exports of 'sensitive' products[119] and which were subject to the recipient states' continued economic and political 'reforms' in line with IMF requirements. The programme emphasised large infrastructure projects and hence was likely to encourage CEE states to concentrate on exports and on developing large-scale western-type institutions like stock exchanges, rather than on enabling internal competitive conditions that would facilitate economic self-sufficiency or long-term prosperity. In addition, under PHARE, CEE states were expected to purchase EU agricultural surpluses at (western) market prices even though many CEE states were self-sufficient in that area.

Despite not guaranteeing accession, the T&C Agreements—supplemented through PHARE provisions and ongoing IMF pressure—prompted wide-ranging economic and institutional reforms across CEE states. Instituted in the hopes that links with the west would expand, many of these 'reforms' brought immediate benefits to western markets and investors by promoting foreign investment and cross-border transactions. For example, Poland's 1989 Act on Foreign Currencies[120] introduced internal currency convertibility, led to its devaluation to boost cross-border capital transactions, and abolished state monopoly in international trade. Poland also liberalised foreign trade, lifted price controls, and legalised private enterprises. Similarly, Hungary further liberalised foreign trade by limiting the need for import and export licenses.[121] Foreign investments in up to 50% of company equity no longer required the Hungarian government's approval. To facilitate their repatriation, dividends paid to foreign investors in Hungarian currency were converted by the National Bank of Hungary into the hard currency of the foreign investment.[122]

---

117 E.g., T&C Agreement Latvia, Article 13.
118 Poland and Hungary Assistance for the Restructuring of the Economy. See Council Regulation (EEC) No 3906/89 of 18 December 1989 on economic aid to the Republic of Hungary and the Polish People's Republic, 23.12.1989. PHARE was later extended to all CEE states, as well as Bulgaria and Romania. During 2000–2006, PHARE was supplemented by ISPA (Instrument for Structural Policies for Pre-Accession) support for environmental and transport infrastructure, and SAPARD (Special Accession Programme for Agriculture and Rural Development) support for the agricultural sector.
119 I.e., coal, steel, textile, and agricultural products.
120 Prawo dewizowe [The Act on Foreign Currencies], Dziennik Ustaw [Polish Journal of Laws] 1989, No 6, Item 33.
121 See generally Pogany (1991).
122 Economic Associations Act, Act VI of 1988 (Hungary).

Moreover, foreign entities became allowed to own equity in Hungarian joint ventures, buy shares of existing corporations or own Hungarian enterprises outright, and could carry out any economic activity lawful under Hungarian law.[123] Hungary also implemented ad hoc methods of reducing potential risks to foreign investors. For example, the sale of shares of Tungsram, a major light bulb producer, to a consortium of Austrian banks in 1990 was accompanied by the Hungarian government's guaranty that the consortium would be reimbursed for any loss incurred in connection with its subsequent resale.

Through this first wave of pre-accession initiatives, rather than reversing Cold War divisions between the east and west (as it had promised to do soon after the fall of the Iron Curtain), the EU began to shape the course of the CEE region's post-communist developments, prioritising short- and long-term economic benefits accruing to western Member States and financial institutions. At the same time, it prompted the CEE region to restructure its political and economic frameworks in line with IMF requirements, thereby binding the region's future to western financial institutions and markets and turning CEE states into dependent economies.[124]

Europe Agreements

By the early 1990s, the EU began to expand trade associations with CEE states which were deemed to have evidenced satisfactory commitment to economic and political reforms expected by the EU. After the first 'Europe Agreements' with CEE states were entered into in 1993—with Poland, Hungary, and the CSFR[125]—they were extended to all CEE countries by 1999. Although the EU has historically used association agreements with various non-European countries, it had done so only twice before in the context of countries desiring to accede—with the UK in 1954, and Greece in 1961, when the EU was much smaller and its economic and political structures were less developed and thus arguably in greater need of protecting. In line with provisions of the T&C Agreements, the Europe Agreements with CEE states reinforced the EU's one-sided approach. CEE states had no voice in Brussels at the time, and they were marred by political and economic challenges which only deepened power imbalances between the east and the west. This unequal approach might have also reflected the fact that (western) Member States were not supportive of CEE states' accession, having even opposed calling these documents 'Europe' agreements.

All Europe Agreements with the CEE states pertained to the same topics: political reforms and high-level dialogue; (limited) application of free movement

123 Foreign Investment Act, Act XXIV of 1988 (Hungary); Transformation of Economic and Business Organizations and Companies Act, Act XIII of 1989 (Hungary).
124 See generally Kennedy and Webb (1990).
125 Czechoslovakia was renamed the Czech and Slovak Federative Republic in 1990. The Europe Agreement with CSFR was never ratified due to its dissolution into the Czech and Slovak Republics in 1992.

rules pertaining to capital and goods; legislative 'harmonisation' (i.e., approximation of CEE laws to EU acquis); and economic and financial relations. All these provisions prioritised legislative re-writing in CEE states to support the EU's internal market. Without committing itself to CEE states' accession or to providing any pre-accession aid, the EU required CEE states' adoption of the acquis in specified key areas of political and economic activity—including banking, customs, competition, financial services, taxation, and environmental protection. Moreover, CEE states became obligated to 'facilitate the setting up of operations ... by Community companies and nationals', affording them 'treatment no less favourable' than that accorded to their own nationals and companies.[126] This right of establishment was further supported by '[f]reedom of financial transfers arising from commercial transactions, the provision of services, investment operations', and by permitting unlimited 'repatriation of capital invested and the gains from this capital'.[127] National treatment also applied to public procurement. Although the rights of establishment and of bidding for public contracts were reciprocal, this carried little practical significance because CEE firms were not competitive in the west.

In addition, Europe Agreements imposed protectionist trade measures in favour of pre-existing EU states, continuing the EU's approach under the T&C Agreements. Although duties and quotas on some products were to discontinue within ten[128] years of signing the Europe Agreements, the EU welcomed imports of CEE goods which were not competitive on western markets (such as computers), while being protectionist of 'sensitive' western sectors (such as textiles, coal, steel, and agriculture). Concessions for CEE exports were the least generous for agricultural products despite the great economic significance of this sector to the CEE region. In addition, CEE states continued to be subject to GATT's anti-dumping measures, which limited their ability to benefit from selling their more affordably manufactured goods in the west. The EU did make use of these various protective measures[129]—for example, by imposing anti-dumping duties on Hungarian and Polish exports of seamless pipes and tubes of iron and non-alloy steel[130] and by invoking safeguards to reimpose quotas on steel exports from the Czech and Slovak Republics.[131]

126 E.g., Europe Agreement establishing an association between the European Communities and their Member States and the Republic of Hungary, 31.12.1993 ('Europe Agreement with Hungary'), Article 44.
127 E.g., id., Articles 60 and 63.
128 Or five years, in Poland's case.
129 For a general critique of Europe Agreements' protectionist and disadvantageous measures towards the CEE region, see Hartnell (1993).
130 Council Regulation 1189/93 of 14 May 1993, 15.5.1993.
131 Decision No 1/93 of the EC-Czech Republic and Slovak Republic Joint Committee of 28 May 1993, 29.6.1993; Commission Decision No 1970/93/ECSC of 19 July 1993 opening and providing for the administration of tariff quotas in respect of certain ECSC products originating in the Czech Republic and the Slovak Republic imported into the Community (1 June 1993 to 31 December 1995), 23.7.1993.

Notably, all Europe Agreements with CEE states employed multiple forms of conditionality dictated unilaterally by the EU. For starters, even the conclusion of agreement negotiations was conditioned on the EU's satisfaction that sufficient political and economic 'reforms' were being carried out in respective CEE states. All implementation criteria under the agreements were set unilaterally and monitored by the EU. To ensure compliance, the Europe Agreements established Association Councils, composed largely of representatives of the existing Member States, to 'supervise the implementation' of their provisions in CEE states.[132] Moreover, all contained unilateral suspension clauses pursuant to which either party could 'denounce' the agreement for any reason. Either party could also take any 'appropriate measures' if it determined, in its discretion, that the other had failed to fulfil any obligation under the agreement.[133] Although these safeguards were reciprocal, their practical implications were unequal. Given CEE states' accession aspirations, the east-west political and economic power imbalances, and the Europe Agreements' indefinite nature, CEE states felt compelled to continue being on their best behaviour.

Further conditionality was added with each subsequent set of Europe Agreements with CEE states. Some of these later terms also painted an image of the CEE region as defective and differentiated from the west's imagination of itself. Whereas Europe Agreements with the Visegrád countries did include references to their commitment to human rights in (non-binding) preambles, all later Europe Agreements made human rights an 'essential element' and a binding obligation to inform all CEE policies and a condition of trade terms or any development aid to be provided by the EU.[134] The EU's authority to judge CEE states' human rights obligations provided it with yet another discretionary ground to apply unilateral suspension clauses. Arguably motivated by ethnic struggles that developed by the mid-90s in the former Yugoslavia and the former USSR Republics, inclusion of binding human rights provisions also signalled that the region was more crude than the west. Furthermore, the 1998 Europe Agreements with the Baltic states also contained an obligation to 'cooperate' closely on crime prevention—including combating 'illegal' immigration, drugs trafficking, and organised crime.[135] Having lost their independence through Soviet annexation, the Baltics were seen as especially crime-ridden, embodying the far reaches of proper 'Europe' in the western

---

132 E.g., Europe Agreement establishing an association between the European Communities and their Member States and the Republic of Poland, 31.12.1993 ('Europe Agreement with Poland'), Article 102.
133 E.g., Europe Agreement establishing an association between the European Communities and their Member States, acting within the framework of the European Union and the Republic of Slovenia, 26.2.1999 ('Europe Agreement with Slovenia'), Article 123.
134 E.g., Europe Agreement establishing an association between the European Communities and their Member States and the Republic of Lithuania, 20.2.1998, Article 2.
135 E.g., id., Article 102.

imagination. The EU was particularly concerned with controlling Baltic emigration to EU states which was anticipated to 'pose serious ... problems'.[136] This anxiety is consistent with the west's historical approach towards the region as not belonging to 'Europe'.

The Europe Agreements' one-sided conditionality provisions were reinforced through accompanying financial programmes, which paved the path for further western economic incursions into the CEE region. Any aid or support the EU considered providing (without guaranteeing it) depended on CEE states' 'work towards fulfilling the necessary conditions' of pre-accession including adopting free-market economic policies.[137] Despite benevolent-sounding section headings within the Europe Agreements, such as 'Financial cooperation', all relevant benchmarks were to be unilaterally decided and applied by the EU. CEE states would become eligible for PHARE grants and European Investment Bank loans only if they restructured their economies in accordance with details determined after 'consultation' with the EU.[138] Decisions to provide any such funding, and its amounts, were to be closely coordinated with the IMF, the International Bank for Reconstruction and Development (part of the World Bank), and the European Bank for Reconstruction and Development. Continuing the long-standing east-west power dynamic, any assistance under Europe Agreements was also subject to CEE states' satisfying all of the IMF's requirements including implementing economic and political changes to support macroeconomic restructurings. IMF's surveillance, carried out mainly through 'consultations' pursuant to the IMF's Articles of Agreement,[139] entailed intensified IMF team visits to candidate states to review and shape their economic policies. Any EU aid was to be concentrated in technical assistance rather than in investment or economic support which would have improved long-term economic prospects in the CEE region. For example, PHARE, the largest of the microeconomic funding measures foreseen, focused on providing financial and technical support to the CEE region for implementing pro-EU market economic reforms. The programme also subsidised traineeships for CEE civil servants, facilitating western influence on the development of civil societies and political institutions in the CEE region.

Although the Europe Agreements with CEE states asserted that they were built upon a (non-binding) 'recognition' that the parties wished to 'establish close and lasting relations which would allow' CEE states to 'take part in the process of European integration',[140] they did not provide a timetable for the start of accession negotiations. All of the agreements were entered into for an

---

136 European Economic and Social Committee (1992).
137 E.g., Europe Agreement with Poland, Article 1.
138 E.g., Europe Agreement with Hungary, Article 99.
139 Articles of Agreement of the International Monetary Fund, adopted at the UN Monetary and Financial Conference on 22.07.1944, Article IV.
140 E.g., Europe Agreement with Poland, Preamble; Europe Agreement with Hungary, Preamble.

unlimited duration placing CEE states in a 'holding pattern'[141] until such time as the EU decided they were ready to progress towards greater integration. This prompted the Visegrád countries to submit a request that the EU set a timetable for their accession.[142] The subsequent 1993 Copenhagen Summit Conclusions, however, simply reiterated that accession might take place once CEE states were deemed 'able to assume the obligations of membership by satisfying the economic and political conditions required'.[143]

Accession Partnership Agreements

The 1998 Accession Partnership Agreements between the EU and CEE states imposed a timetable for further short- and long-term reforms in the CEE region to 'help the candidate countries in their preparations for membership'.[144] The misleadingly named 'partnerships' prioritised (1) further privatisations and restructurings of steel, agricultural, and coal sectors in the CEE region, and (2) abolishing barriers to the free movement of goods, capital, and foreign direct investment all largely flowing from west to east. The agreements were updated in 1999 and in 2001 in accordance with the EU's evolving priorities.

Despite such extensive adjustments, the Accession Partnership Agreements limited potential pre-accession aid to CEE states. For one, all investment projects envisioned under assistance provisions had to be co-financed by CEE states—not an easy feat given their fiscal challenges at the time. Moreover, any assistance was conditioned on CEE states' 'respecting' all conditions under the Europe and Partnership Agreements and on having taken further steps towards satisfying the EU-set Copenhagen accession criteria.[145] All relevant benchmarks were to be determined at the EU's discretion. Regular Commission reports and Association Committee reviews of CEE states' implementation of the agreements' requirements demanded not only evidence that CEE states had incorporated the acquis into domestic legislations but also proof of its 'effective implementation and enforcement'.[146] As with the T&C Agreements and Europe Agreements, any inequitable impact of these policies on CEE states and their nationals was overlooked.

---

141 See Böröcz (2001).
142 Commission (1992).
143 European Council (1993).
144 E.g., Council Decision of 30 March 1998 on the principles, priorities, intermediate objectives and conditions contained in the accession partnership with the Czech Republic, 23.4.1998 ('Accession Partnership with Czech Republic'), Article 1.
145 E.g., Council Decision of 6 December 1999 on the principles, priorities, intermediate objectives and conditions contained in the Accession Partnership with the Republic of Estonia, 28/12/1999, Article 5.
146 E.g., Accession Partnership with Czech Republic, Article 3.

Unequal Impact of pre-04 Policies on CEE and EU-15 States

Through these post-1989 EU policies, CEE economic and political futures were inequitably moulded to support western economic growth. In fact, on one rare occasion, the EU even expressly acknowledged this reality—outright admitting that the entire post-1989 process of CEE integration was driven by the EU's desire to increase its exports and create new investment opportunities.[147]

i. Trade

The overall trade impact of pre-accession policies reflected new export opportunities for western suppliers. EU exports to the CEE region intensified throughout the 1990s, consisting mainly of machinery equipment, agricultural products, chemical products, transport equipment, and textiles, some of which would later get re-imported into the EU after (much more affordable) processing in the CEE region. CEE countries had well-developed industries in these products and did not need western imports. On the other hand, western markets were difficult for CEE exporters to penetrate at least in part due to western nationals' lack of preference for CEE products and the imposition of barriers to such exports. Moreover, the infusion of foreign capital under PHARE increased the value of CEE currencies which further lowered demand for CEE products in the west.

Despite the Europe Agreements' liberalisation of trade, by 1993 they had actually produced an increase in the EU's trade surplus with the CEE region prompting the then-Prime Minister of Poland to complain to the EU that the existing Member States had been the main beneficiaries of these agreements.[148] CEE states, as well as Bulgaria and Romania, tended to suffer significant trade deficits with the EU throughout the late 1990s and even after accession. For example, by 2000 Poland suffered a $13 billion deficit in its trade with the EU[149] and did not achieve a trade surplus with the EU until 2013.[150] This was particularly problematic given the collapse of trade with the former communist countries which made eliminating CEE inventories very challenging.

ii. Foreign Investment

At the same time, western investment in the CEE region accelerated. Legislative changes implemented in the CEE region pursuant to the Europe Agreements paved the way for an influx of foreign investment which was noted with approval in various contemporaneous EU and (western) Member States' reports. For example, the Polish legislature changed 130 statutes by 1994 to effectuate its Europe Agreement. Similar changes were quickly implemented in

---

147 European Commission (2001).
148 Suchocka (1993).
149 Hofbauer (2006).
150 MSZ (2014).

Hungary and the Czech Republic. New domestic laws committed CEE states to the free movement of western services (particularly financial services) and western capital through both increased direct investments by western companies already established in the CEE region and the establishment of new western companies.[151]

The most intrusive form of foreign investment, foreign direct investment ('FDI'), soon came to dominate capital flow from west to east. It entails foreign control of recipient business operations—including voting shares, technology, crucial skills, and management—by either establishing operations outright or by acquiring tangible, income-generating assets. By 2004, the average inward FDI stock was 38.5% of GDP across the CEE region with that figure amounting to more than 54% in Hungary and more than 75% in Estonia.[152] Notably, nearly half of FDI was directed towards sectors such as public utilities and financial institutions[153] which would not bring about any immediate economic benefits to CEE states. In the tradeable sector, most FDI was prompted by EU-15 states' desire to increase their market shares in CEE states, exploit wage differentials, and export human-capital-intensive products and technologies.[154] Although some of the larger CEE enterprises dominated by foreign firms experienced improved productivity and wage increases, FDI resulted in significant overall costs for CEE states. By its very nature, FDI produced tax-income losses for CEE states already struggling with budget deficits. This effect was reinforced by CEE states' tax-reduction packages which were adopted to effectuate the acquis. Notably, increased FDI pushed some CEE businesses out of the market, especially those in sensitive sectors such as agriculture, textiles, clothing, coal, steel, and chemicals—which had historically constituted some of the largest CEE producers and employers. More generally, increased FDI reinforced CEE dependency on western investors and on western technologies further limiting the CEE region's ability to chart its own economic and political paths.

iii. Banking

Driven by banking policy reforms in line with the acquis, foreign control of CEE banks also accelerated. For example, in Hungary, shares of foreign ownership in registered banking capital amounted to 60% by the end of 1997.[155] By 2000, foreign equity constituted the majority of assets in most banks operating in Poland—approaching 70% of the sector's total assets.[156] Banks in Estonia also became dominated by foreign owners by 2001.[157] By 2004, foreign banks

---

151 Commission (1997).
152 See Éltető (2014). A decade later, inward FDI stock to GDP exceeded 80% in Estonia and Hungary. Id.
153 European Commission (2001).
154 Id.
155 Commission of the European Communities (1998).
156 Commission of the European Communities (2001).
157 Commission of the European Communities (2002).

held majority shares throughout the banking sectors in all CEE states as banking became the sector with the highest private and foreign participation. Although foreign bank ownership might expand some companies' access to credit, it also increases credit risk and the potential for capital flow volatility by connecting such companies to global economic shocks. Moreover, foreign bank ownership limits small- and medium-sized enterprises' access to capital and pushes many domestic banks out of business. In the long run, foreign bank ownership bound the CEE region's financial futures even more closely to western economies while benefitting western stockholders and investors.

iv. Foreign Debt

According to the Europe Agreements' provisions, CEE states were encouraged to seek additional financial assistance from western international financial institutions and commercial banks. As a result, foreign debt across the CEE region continued to increase, hampering its long-term economic independence and growth. For example, in Hungary by 1993, gross foreign debt amounted to more than 65% of the GDP[158], and throughout the decade, public proceeds from privatisations were mostly used to reduce foreign debt.[159] In Poland, foreign debt service payments accounted for more than 17% of its budget expenditures by 1995[160] and more than 30% of company debts were in foreign currencies by 1998.[161] In Slovenia, foreign debt increased from 1.9 billion ECU in 1994 to 4.1 billion ECU (£360 million) in 1998.[162]

High levels of foreign debt exposed CEE states to the uncertainty of exchange-rate fluctuations while channelling a substantial proportion of domestic revenues into debt service payments and away from investing in economic growth. As markets and capital became concentrated in the hands of foreign investors and governments, CEE states' dependency on the west deepened, further worsened by the sizeable east/west trade imbalances. At the same time, IMF/EU loan packages had limited CEE states' abilities to conduct loser budgetary policies. Hofbauer aptly likens the overall pre-accession economic relationship between the EU and the CEE region to the latter's becoming 'an economic colony of … the IMF and the World Bank'.[163]

---

158 Id.
159 Foreign-currency denominated debt continued to be high after accession. For example, in 2013, it amounted to 80% of all public indebtedness in Lithuania, and 40% in Hungary.
160 Senior Nello and Smith (1997).
161 Lommatzsch et al. (2004).
162 Commission of the European Communities (1998a).
163 Hofbauer (2006).

v. Social Impact on CEE States

As the Eastern Enlargement approached, most CEE states were faced with declining economic activity, GDP contraction, increasing budget deficits, and periods of inflation and recession, in no small part due to staggering foreign debt repayments and implementing IMF- and EU-driven economic and structural 'reforms'. Overall, the collective debt ratio[164]—which serves as a key indicator for the sustainability of government finance—of CEE states, Bulgaria, and Romania increased from 35.9% of their collective GDPs in 2000 to 36.5% in 2001[165] and was predicted to continue growing.[166] Their average government deficit (comparing net borrowing to net lending) was also increasing. It constituted 3% of GDP in 1999, 3.1% in 2000, and 3.8% in 2001 and was also anticipated to keep expanding.[167] Budget deficits lessened CEE states' ability to benefit from pre-accession EU funding sources all of which required matching CEE state funding. In response, each CEE government adopted various domestic economic and austerity measures, such as increasing excise taxes,[168] freezing or decreasing social benefits and pensions, and increasing the retirement age, all of which produced high social costs.

Social inequalities increased across the CEE region during the pre-accession period. Employment declined annually across CEE states, as well as in Bulgaria and Romania, by an average of 1.5% between 1995 and 1999.[169] By 2000, average unemployment in the CEE region was 13% and approached 25% among workers younger than 25.[170] Increased flexibilisation and deregulation of the labour markets, adopted across the CEE region to attract FDI, further increased unemployment, with particularly high rates for young people and low-skilled workers, and in rural areas. Due to state budget difficulties, unemployment benefits were slashed. Meanwhile, currency devaluations increased import prices and demand for exports contributing to inflationary pressures and increased consumer prices. With Soviet-era social security systems dismantled and the IMF's and EU's insistence on diverting social spending towards servicing foreign debt, educational and health systems also suffered. Rates of crime, suicide, and alcoholism increased. It is thus not surprising that many CEE nationals felt that they had no choice but to move to EU-15 states after accession.

Overall, the substance of pre-accession policies and their impact were anything but equal or fair despite the benevolent-sounding names of all key pre-accession agreements (Trade & Cooperation Agreements, Europe Agreements,

---

164 Comparing public debt to GDP.
165 With country variations, of course—for example, it was less than 5% in Estonia.
166 Commission of the European Communities (2002a).
167 Id.
168 Imposed on manufacturers, retailers, or consumers of various goods or services.
169 Commission (2001).
170 Balázs et al. (2014).

and Accession Partnership Agreements). The EU shaped almost every area of domestic policy-making in the CEE states through the combination of passive leverage (attractiveness of EU membership and lack of feasible alternatives) and active influence (requiring extensive pre-accession economic, political, and legal 'reforms'). In collaboration with western financial institutions, the EU opportunistically took advantage of the east-west power differentials while reinforcing CEE states' economic difficulties. The uneven playing field was further entrenched through the 2001 Treaty of Nice[171] which protected EU-15 states' blocking influence over new policies in the soon-to-be-enlarged EU and through the Council's introduction in 2002 of new limits on EU expenditures until 2006.[172] Overall, leading up to the Eastern Enlargement, the west's approach towards CEE states had posited them as second-class future Members while fortifying pre-existing east-west inequalities.

The Accession Process

The relationship of unequals continued during the accession 'negotiation' process and in the EU's use of conditionality through Accession Treaty provisions. The EU's apparent motivations for allowing the CEE region to accede help to explain this one-sided approach especially when contextualised within the value system expressed through its previously-discussed long-standing rhetoric. The Eastern Enlargement would serve several obvious strategic goals, including controlling a potential influx of undocumented CEE migrants, strengthening the EU's security and political structures, and expanding its political clout on the world stage. Economic motivations—increasing trade,[173] and gaining access to cheaper labour—appear to have been particularly significant. Notably, the Eastern Enlargement served the EU's 2000 Lisbon Strategy goals of achieving global economic competitiveness and freedom of capital.[174] At the 1997 Luxembourg Summit, EU-15 leaders had already determined that CEE states' accession would constitute a better alternative for reinvigorating their economies than what could be accomplished through domestic policy reforms.[175] This enlargement's overall economic benefits to the old Member States were predicted to vastly exceed any anticipated costs.[176] The EU's calculated tactic should be further contextualised, as previously discussed, within both the long-standing western ideology of approaching the east as an inferior region and the core economic priorities embedded within the EU's foundational narratives. At

---

171 Treaty of Nice amending the Treaty on European Union, the Treaties establishing the European Communities and certain related acts, 10.3.2001.
172 Council of the European Union (2002).
173 Commission of the European Communities (1993).
174 Supported by deregulation of the labour markets, and the growth and decreased regulation of the finance sector.
175 See generally Likic-Brboric (2011).
176 See generally Trzeciak (2012).

the same time, CEE nationals' whiteness likely facilitated the Enlargement as western publics found them more palatable than non-white workers.[177]

The EU's One-Sided Approach Towards Negotiations

At its meeting in Copenhagen in 1993, the European Council concluded that, to join the EU, CEE states would have to demonstrate to the EU's 'satisfaction' that they possessed 'stability of institutions guaranteeing democracy, the rule of law ... a functioning market economy, as well as the capacity to cope with competitive pressure and market forces within the Union'.[178] The EU deemed CEE states' adoption of the internal-market acquis particularly critical.[179] There was 'no question of modifying' these Copenhagen criteria.[180] Moreover, these benchmarks were never defined precisely and thus provided the EU with leeway in dictating pre-accession policies.

After CEE states submitted their applications for EU membership between 1994 and 1996, formal discussions commenced in 1998. This was followed by several years of further re-writing of CEE laws in line with the acquis and additional economic policy changes as required by western financial institutions and the EU. Although the EU would often refer to the entire accession process as 'negotiations' based on 'cooperation',[181] it was predicated on non-negotiable, one-way adjustments prompting some scholars to liken the process to a discretionary 'extension of club membership'[182] or even 'a takeover'.[183] Unlike during prior enlargements, CEE governments were not even ensured a clear understanding of the acquis which was not fully translated by EU institutions—despite their legal obligation to do so—into CEE languages before accession.[184] Not being fully informed of what accession entailed further disadvantaged CEE legislators who already lacked appropriate expertise and experience to form well-educated opinions on the wide range of EU legislation. CEE voices were silenced while new laws were being imposed by the west.

The EU's imposition of its norms and rules, through a take-it-or-leave-it approach, was more extensive, inflexible, and intrusive than in prior enlargements. Unlike in all earlier enlargements,[185] CEE states were not given an option to

---

177 See generally McVeigh (2010). Degrees of whiteness also help to explain, at least in part, the EU's greater openness to Ukrainian refugees than to those from the Middle East or south-central Asia.
178 European Council (1993).
179 Commission (1997).
180 Commission (2001).
181 E.g., Commission of the European Communities (1993).
182 Jileva (2004).
183 Hofbauer (2006).
184 Less than 30% of it had been translated into CEE languages by 2000. The entire acquis was translated and published only in March 2006, 22 months after accession.
185 For example, the UK and Denmark obtained derogations from the Justice and Home Affairs acquis; and several EU-15 states opted out of Schengen and the economic and monetary union.

permanently derogate or opt out from any parts of the acquis. Furthermore, the EU employed conditionality widely—first in trade relations and regulatory alignment supporting operations of the single market and then in shaping domestic policies more generally. The EU's conditionality package was highly ambiguous, which afforded the EU further flexibility in defining accession conditions. The overall outcome of the 'negotiation' process was very distant from CEE states' initial demands and heavily in the EU's favour. Any CEE successes in obtaining concessions were largely illusory and did not involve actual practical compromise or sacrifice by the west. For example, Poland's receipt of higher Common Agricultural Policy[186] ('CAP') subsidies than the EU had initially offered merely involved the EU's moving already-secured structural funds to direct payments.[187] Notably, any concessions made by the EU were not driven by benevolence or by approaching the CEE region as an equal. Rather, they constituted a tactical move—to prevent CEE states from seeking more meaningful concessions and to reduce post-Enlargement political repercussions of a resentful CEE voting bloc.[188] The discrepancy of power between the EU and the candidate states—more significant than during prior enlargements—facilitated this aggressive export of EU rules.

This one-sided approach was accompanied by intensified pre-accession monitoring reminiscent of imperial preoccupation with recording, standardising, and classifying. This comprised verbal and written instructions, regular written reviews, EU representatives' visits to CEE capitals, and the posting of EU experts at specific CEE government ministries to oversee 'reforms'. Frequent expert reports were used to pressure CEE states to swiftly and diligently follow the EU's demands and to compete with one another in doing so. The Commission's final Comprehensive Monitoring Report, published half a year before the Enlargement, raised 39 areas of 'serious concern' that had to be resolved before accession, such as inspections and control of Lithuanian and Polish fishing fleets and computerisation of Latvian tariff and transit systems.[189] In hindsight, the Commission noted that the '2004 enlargement was the best prepared in the history of the EU' as 'the EU [had] defined precise accession criteria[190] ... [and had] closely monitored the efforts of the candidate countries against the conditions'.[191] Through the publication of official reviews, EU

---

186 Created in 1962, to reflect the needs of western states (especially France), CAP provides funding to Member States to support rural economics and the farming sector.
187 Notably, this was disadvantageous for Poland's economy—increasing Poland's budgetary deficit (since co-financing would have to be covered from the national budget), and turning funds normally used to modernise regional economies into subsidies for land ownership.
188 See generally Trzeciak (2012).
189 European Commission (2003b).
190 As noted earlier, the Copenhagen criteria were anything but precise.
191 European Commission (2006).

experts were also constructing and controlling the dominant, idealised narratives about the accession process being benevolent and exemplary of western civilisation.

Accession Treaty Safeguard Clauses

Furthermore, the EU employed extensive conditionality after the conclusion of accession 'negotiations' and after signing of the Accession Treaty[192] in April 2003. Accession Treaty safeguard clauses were broader during the Eastern Enlargement than in any previous enlargement through the expansion of previously used safeguard provisions and the adoption of new ones. Any old Member State could ask the Commission to invoke these safeguard clauses against any new Member State for up to three years after accession in 2004 if it unilaterally determined that 'difficulties' existed which it deemed to be 'serious and liable to persist in any sector of the economy'.[193] Moreover, upon the request of any EU-15 state or on its own initiative, the Commission could invoke two new safeguards in cases of 'a serious breach' (or an imminent risk thereof)[194] in the functioning of the internal market[195] or 'serious shortcomings' (or an imminent risk thereof) in the transposition of justice and home affairs acquis[196] (i.e., recognition in the area of criminal law or civil matters). Only the economic safeguard clause was reciprocal, whereas the remaining two were available to EU-15 states only. All safeguard provisions were broadly defined and left much discretion to the EU to prevent CEE states' ability to benefit from accession. Notably, although the economic and internal-market safeguards could only be invoked within three years of accession, any responsive measures—temporarily suspending any rights under the acquis deemed directly related to the triggering conditions—could be adopted indefinitely until the invoking state or the Commission deemed the situation to have been satisfactorily remedied by the relevant CEE state.

In its final monitoring report before the Enlargement, the Commission noted 39 areas across the CEE region of serious concern to the single market[197] against which it was considering applying the internal-market safeguard clause. Given that any responsive EU measures could be indefinite and applied at the EU's discretion, this sent a strong signal to the CEE region to continue to be on its best behaviour, not only at the time of accession, but also afterwards. Moreover, several EU representatives did announce that they intended to use this safeguard provision, thereby exerting additional pressure on CEE states to

192 2003 Accession Treaty.
193 Id., Article 37.
194 Id., Article 38.
195 E.g., energy, transport, telecommunications, agriculture, and consumer and health protection sectors.
196 2003 Accession Treaty, Article 39.
197 Commission (2003c).

fulfil all the accession requirements to the EU's satisfaction. For example, the then-Commissioner for Health and Consumer Protection pointed out, less than a year before accession, that '[m]any problems need to be resolved and significant improvements need to be made between now and accession .... If deficiencies remain, safeguard measures can be triggered to ensure that standards are maintained'.[198] Pressure was intensified as accession approached. The then-Enlargement Commissioner emphasised the Commission's zero-tolerance policy regarding new Members' correct implementation of the acquis and noted that the EU would not hesitate to use safeguard clauses. In particular, he predicted that safeguard measures were 'likely to be invoked concerning food safety. Slaughterhouses and dairy producers could thus be barred from exporting'.[199] Similarly, the then-Director General for Enlargement warned that if CEE states did not correctly implement all the acquis by November 2003—when the Commission was to present its final monitoring report on accession readiness—the 'introduction of the so-called protective clauses would be inevitable'.[200] Although none of the safeguard clauses were ultimately applied to CEE states[201], they nevertheless reinforced the unequal power dynamic between the west and the east and naturalised the reality of second-class membership afforded to CEE states.[202]

Accession Referenda in CEE States

In early 2003, all CEE states held public referenda on joining the EU. Although the majority of those who voted in all CEE states approved accession, this should not be seen as tantamount to unequivocally embracing it. Some media outlets did voice opposition to accession—for exploiting CEE states economically,[203] for turning them into sources of cheap labour for EU-15 economies, and for likely leading to significant job losses and the collapse of some economic sectors.[204] Groups that expected to be disadvantaged economically by accession opposed

198 Byrne (2003).
199 Week in Europe (2004).
200 EU Observer (2003).
201 Safeguard clause was applied to Romania, however. In 2011–12, Spain suspended Romanians' right of free movement to enter Spain.
202 Bulgaria and Romania were subjected to additional conditionalities and monitoring. Under a new postponement clause, the Council could postpone their accession by one year if the Commission determined that implementation of the acquis was insufficient. To trigger this clause in the case of Romania, only a majority vote by the Council was required. In addition, under the new 'cooperation and verification' mechanism, both states were subjected to bi-annual monitoring by the Commission, focused on fighting corruption and organised crime, and on instituting judicial reforms. Failure to make sufficient progress could have triggered the internal-market or justice-and-home-affairs safeguard clauses. The Commission did not lift this monitoring mechanism for Bulgaria until 2019 and for Romania until 2022.
203 E.g., Motas (2011); Urbanowicz (2002).
204 E.g., Thorpe (2003).

it—those who were older, less educated, living in rural areas, or involved in manual labour. Devout Catholics and social conservatives perceived the west as a threat to traditional values. After decades of Soviet occupation, some Baltic state nationals feared any foreign influence and Russian-speaking minorities therein opposed it for ideological reasons. Such sentiments appear reflected in public opinion polls. For example, in 1998, 65% of poll respondents across the CEE states, Bulgaria, and Romania supported accession (largely due to economic reasons), 8% opposed it, and the remaining 27% had no opinion and/or anticipated abstaining from accession referenda.[205] In 2002, 42% of poll respondents anticipated that EU membership would bring as many advantages as disadvantages, 12% that it would cause mostly disadvantages, and 12% had no opinion.[206] Notably, although only 33% perceived accession as advantageous for their countries, almost half expressed willingness to vote for accession.[207] Apparently, some CEE nationals felt that accession was a foregone conclusion[208] or that their countries did not have any viable alternatives-especially as Eurosceptic groups across the CEE region were not well-organised and did not present well-formulated alternatives to accession.

Turnout at accession referenda across the region was low (e.g., 46% in Hungary) even threatening to invalidate referenda results in some countries.[209] Compared to pre-referenda polls, a slightly higher percentage of participants supported accession. This is likely due to the fact that Eurosceptic factions across the region had encouraged voter abstention rather than a 'no' vote. The perception that a positive outcome was a foregone conclusion might have also fostered voter apathy likely skewing outcomes in support of EU membership. As a result, mandate strength was fairly low across the region—with bottommost in Hungary at 37%.[210] Only Slovenia and Lithuania achieved mandate strengths of 50–60% with the remaining five countries at 40–50%.[211]

Notably, CEE nationals were not well-informed about the ramifications of accession. For example, in a 2001 poll,[212] 67% of Hungarian respondents considered themselves not very well or not at all informed about accession. On the eve of the referendum, 40% of Poles reported that they were not very well informed, and 4% not informed at all, about accession.[213] This reflected, at

---

205 Eurobarometer (1998).
206 Eurobarometer (2003).
207 Id.
208 For example, in a May 2003 poll, most Poles did in fact assume that Poland would join the EU regardless of the result of the referendum. See The Economist (2003).
209 To increase participation, Lithuania, Slovakia, Poland, and the Czech Republic held referenda over two days.
210 At 46% turnout, with 84% voting in support.
211 Congressional Research Service (2003).
212 Eurobarometer (2001).
213 Eurobarometer (2003).

least in part, the fact that the accession 'negotiation' process had lacked transparency or involvement of the third sector. Furthermore, some CEE nationals supported accession simply because they were disenchanted with their domestic political elites and political cleavages. For example, Poles had higher esteem for EU institutions than for Polish ones.[214] Lacking information and mistrusting their domestic politicians also made the publics vulnerable to rhetorical manipulation by pro-EU political elites across the region. While Eurosceptic factions were fragmented and lacked media access, CEE political elites—supported with EU funding[215]—often appealed emotively to their citizenries' western consumer aspirations. The widely used 'return to Europe' slogan also likely tapped into some voters' desire to assert their 'Europeanness' in a rebuke to the western-centric view of 'Europe', reminiscent of how colonised subjects attempted to elevate themselves through assimilating and reproducing their oppressor's language and ideology.[216]

Post-Accession Landscape

The Enlargement entailed CEE states' transposition of the acquis—composed of more than 10,000 documents arranged into 31 accession chapters[217]—which became effective immediately. Upon accession, all EU financial commitments under PHARE, ISPA, and SAPARD ceased. These policy changes necessitated significant spending in the CEE region and substantial contributions to the EU budget. Meanwhile, post-accession EU support to some key CEE sectors—notably, agriculture—was to be smaller than to EU-15 states. Such inequalities were further entrenched through EU-15 states' adoption of new policies in anticipation of the Enlargement such as making it easier to reach decisions through qualified majority voting. Given that EU-15 states had much more experience in coalition-building, this was intended to benefit them—in line with how Behr had described the entire accession process as 'an epitome of structural violence'.[218]

---

214 Roguska (2003).
215 €10 million per year for campaigns across candidate states.
216 See generally Fanon (1988).
217 Free Movement of Goods; Free Movement of People; Freedom to Provide Services; Free Movement of Capital; Company Law; Competition Policy; Agriculture; Fisheries; Transport Policy; Taxation; EMU; Statistics; Social; Energy; Industrial Policy; Small and Medium Enterprises; Science and Research; Education and Training; Telecommunications and Information; Culture and Audio-visual Policy; Regional Policy and Co-ordination; Environment; Consumers and Health Protection; Justice and Home Affairs; Customs Union; External Relations; Common Foreign and Security Policy; Financial Control; Finance and Budgetary Provisions; Institutions; and Miscellaneous.
218 Behr (2012).

Accession's Immediate Aftermath

Some experts had anticipated the accession to negatively impact vital sectors of CEE economies—especially agriculture, heavy industry, and banking.[219] Moreover, increasing free markets and competition could have been predicted to work to the detriment of CEE companies which were structurally disadvantaged compared to western companies. These concerns materialised in part due to mandatory spending that was imposed on CEE states. Pursuant to the EU's Agenda 2000[220] framework for 2000–06, adopted by EU-15 states in anticipation of the Enlargement, CEE states were required to incur high facilities spending in numerous sectors including education, technical research, transport, and environmental protection. Notably, they were expected to invest in renewable energy and higher ecological standards while reducing big mining and industrial plants. The EU's carbon-dioxide emission limits increased production costs in the coal, construction, chemical, and steel industries[221] across the CEE region. This increased consumer prices, made some businesses not profitable, and forced many to shut down and cut jobs. Looking at the example of Poland, which, before accession, used to be Europe's biggest coal producer, these policies turned it into an importer of coal.[222] Emission limits became even more stringent pursuant to the EU's 2013–20 and 2021–30 Emissions Trading System policies.

Any EU aid or funding CEE states could receive after accession were significantly offset by their contributions to the EU budget. CEE states were generally unable to take advantage of EU aid programmes as those required matching CEE funding—a challenge given CEE states' budgetary struggles. Moreover, the EU had capped regional aid (aimed at supporting economic development in disadvantaged regions across the EU) to the new Member States at 4% of their respective GDPs. Within two years of the Enlargement, the top seven recipients of EU funds were EU-15 states.[223] At the same time, CEE states were required to make considerable contributions to the EU budget immediately after accession, offsetting any EU structural aid to the CEE region, especially in the first few years after accession. This was particularly the case with Hungary, Poland, the Czech Republic, Slovakia, and Slovenia.[224] For example, in 2004, the EU provided Poland with €2.42 billion in structural aid while Poland contributed €1.31 billion to the EU budget. In 2005, those amounts were, respectively, €4.01 billion and €2.38 billion and, in 2006, €5.05 billion and €2.55 billion.[225]

---

219 E.g., Szczerbiak (2002).
220 Commission of the European Communities (1997).
221 European Parliament (2013b).
222 European Parliament (2014).
223 European Commission (2007).
224 Clemens and Lemmer (2006).
225 Kundera (2014).

The agricultural sector offers a poignant example of the inequitable and damaging impact of EU policies on the CEE region. By 1999, 14% of all workers across the CEE region, Bulgaria, and Romania were employed in agriculture, and the sector produced 12% of the region's exports.[226] Due to this economic significance and the territorial dominance of rural areas in the CEE region, agricultural policies represented a particularly sensitive issue to the acceding states during accession 'negotiations'. Whereas in all prior enlargements, free trade in agricultural products and full CAP subsidies became implemented for acceding states immediately after their accession on the same terms as for pre-existing Member States, the west opposed following this approach towards CEE states. A ten-year transitional period was applied to CEE agriculture, supplemented by protectionist trade measures, to benefit EU-15 farmers.

Starting with the preparatory deliberations in the 1990s, EU experts and western politicians opposed extending CAP payments to the new entrants because they feared that the more affordable and plentiful agricultural labour and land in the CEE region would pose a competitive advantage. Reflecting western interests, the Commission came to prioritise providing resources to EU-15 farmers while also reducing direct aid to CEE farmers. In anticipation of the Enlargement, the EU implemented the most far-reaching CAP reforms since its inception in 1962. Overall, CAP funding was reduced, and it was redirected away from agricultural production and towards environmental protection.[227] Direct payments to CEE farmers began in 2004, at 25% of what EU-15 farmers were receiving, to be slowly increased over the ten-year transitional period. Two support systems were created—one for EU-15 states, with room to differentiate support based on farm sizes, headage, regional specialisation, and needs. The only CEE state included in this preferential support system was Slovenia which had the smallest agricultural sector among the acceding states. Another support framework became applicable to the remaining seven CEE states, with annual lump sum grants conditioned on farmer compliance with the new, more demanding environmental protection, food safety, and animal welfare standards all of which increased CEE farmers' expenditures and decreased their profits. Moreover, any payment amounts were determined based on production levels at the time of the Enlargement which, for many CEE states (most notably, Hungary), were even lower than in the 1980s, having been negatively impacted by post-communist economic transformations.

As a result of all these initiatives, significant inequalities in direct CAP payments could still be observed at the end of the ten-year transitional period. For example, in 2013, payments per hectare were €527 in Greece but only €89 in Latvia. Disparity in payments between EU-15 and CEE farmers continued

---

226 Commission (2001).
227 Council Regulation (EC) No 1257/1999 of 17 May 1999 on support for rural development from the European Agricultural Guidance and Guarantee Fund, 26.06.99.

under the 2014–2020 programming period.[228] Persisting inequalities in policies proposed to take effect under the 2023–2027 CAP reforms prompted CEE states' agriculture ministers to complain to the EU in 2018.[229] This resulted in extensive negotiations and an agreement on new CAP, reached in June 2021, promising to provide more flexibility for Member States to adapt measures to local conditions. It remains to be seen how this will be effectuated.

In addition, the new, post-accession CAP programme permitted the Commission to regulate its price interventions[230] in various CEE agricultural products. The Commission has used this power to protect western agricultural production while disregarding high costs incurred by CEE farmers. For example, fearing that CAP payments would incentivise rye production in the CEE region (especially in Poland), the Commission abolished rye price intervention thus removing rye farmers' protections of an artificial price floor. Similarly, after stock of maize within the EU increased by 40% soon after the Enlargement (mostly due to significant production in Hungary), the Commission ended its intervention for maize with no notice period that would have allowed corn producers to adapt to the new environment.

Furthermore, the ten-year transitional period also pertained to protectionist trade measures to benefit western farmers which sidestepped normal competition rules. Whereas CEE states were not permitted to freely export their agricultural products to EU-15 states, they were required to immediately open their markets to EU-15 exports which put competitive pressure on the CEE region's agricultural sector.[231] This further increased pre-accession trade imbalances. Notably, the EU imposed transitional quotas on the region's production of EU-sensitive commodities such as cereals, sugar, pork, poultry, and dairy which had constituted CEE states' key agricultural outputs. Moreover, the EU required that any shortages of these products in CEE states be offset by imports from other Member States, such as Germany, which resulted in increased prices for CEE consumers.[232]

Before their implementation, all these agricultural policies were predicted to produce an increasingly uneven distribution of income and profits among CEE and EU-15 farmers.[233] Their impact indeed proved detrimental to the CEE region in both economic and social terms. CEE farmers were forced to incur high labour and capital costs associated with changing their operations in line

---

228 European Council, Reform of the Common Agricultural Policy post 2013, www.consilium.europa.eu/en/policies/cap-reform/.
229 Teffer (2018).
230 If a commodity's market price falls to an appointed 'intervention price' (usually 10–20% below its target price), national intervention agencies purchase all items that cannot be sold at that price, thereby reducing supply and preventing further price drop.
231 Similar transitional protectionist trade measures and unequal support systems were applied to Bulgaria and Romania in 2007, and to Croatia in 2013.
232 European Parliament (2013c).
233 E.g., Inotai (2000).

with EU regulations, for example, by shifting from growing quota to non-quota products, increasing the use of biotechnology and organic farming, and engaging in afforestation. Adopting the required quality, production, processing, and hygiene regulations resulted in increased production costs across the CEE region which was further exacerbated by EU-imposed VAT increases on agricultural machinery and supplies. EU funding was not sufficient to reimburse most CEE farmers for these costs. Notably, farming lots smaller than 1 hectare—which had been particularly common in Poland and the Baltic states—were not eligible for CAP funding. Moreover, preconditions for some EU requirements could not be met easily—such as the required buffer zones around organic farming. Many CEE farms did not survive these post-accession transformations. For example, within two years of accession, 1.5 million Polish farms were liquidated[234] while many Hungarian agribusinesses went bankrupt within the first few years of accession.[235] At the same time, expanded production mechanisation and reduction in labour-intensive farming further displaced farm workers. Increased unemployment and social tensions left many rural workers with little choice but to seek work in EU-15 states and resulted in further demographic erosion in many CEE rural areas.

Unequal Long-Term Impact

Whereas CEE states have benefited from the increased geo-political stability and security of joining the EU,[236] economic consequences of the Eastern Enlargement on the CEE region have been more difficult to evaluate. Generally, studies of European integration's enduring economic effects remain inconclusive, largely due to methodological difficulties and country heterogeneities. Some research suggests that GDP and productivity increases, as well as unemployment decreases, across the CEE region within a decade after enlargement might be attributable to accession.[237] However, it is very difficult to directly link such developments to the effects of accession as opposed to purely domestic factors or geopolitical forces beyond the EU. Notably, if such benefits could indeed be attributed to accession, they are linked not to the receipt of (limited) EU aid but rather to greater trade integration with EU-15 states and to the departure of CEE workers for the west as discussed in greater detail in the following chapter. Moreover, economic improvements have not been observed equally in all CEE states. Accession can be more clearly linked to GDP and labour productivity increases in Hungary (which had already adopted components of the free market before EU interference) and in smaller (Slovenia) and less economically developed states (the Baltics) whereas it has had the least positive

---

234 Zielonka (2007).
235 Burger (2009).
236 Accompanied by NATO's post-1989 expansion.
237 E.g., MSZ (2014).

economic impact on the Czech and Slovak Republics.[238] Notably, although economic gaps between the pre- and post-04 Member States have been decreasing over time, CEE states collectively continue to significantly lag behind EU-15 states in terms of their GDPs per capita[239] and minimum wages.[240]

Importantly, long-term economic improvements according to financial benchmarks do not necessarily impact people's lives. Indeed, the CEE region has experienced high social costs of western-driven policy changes as inequalities within the region have increased. Large urban areas have expanded and flourished in many ways since 2004, whereas many former industrial areas and rural regions have been left with poor public services, collapsing infrastructures, population declines, and a sense of decay. The accession's impact on individual CEE nationals has also been uneven depending on their age, education, and socio-economic class. In some economic sectors, CEE workers have experienced halving of real wages while capital owners saw doubling of their capital returns.[241] And all CEE nationals have had to contend with increasing prices and higher costs of living—further intensified by EU VAT regulations.[242] Many have also been trapped by a proliferation of precarious and illegal work, especially in Latvia and Poland.

It is thus not surprising that post-accession public opinion about EU membership across the CEE region has not been entirely enthusiastic—with increasing support for Eurosceptic parties. For example, ten years after accession, due to increasing economic inequalities, Poles, Hungarians, and Lithuanians expressed disappointment about the functioning of free-market economies in their countries.[243] Only 40% of those polled in 2019 in the Czech Republic agreed that EU membership had generally benefited their country.[244] By 2021, 39% of Poles (who used to be one of the most pro-accession publics) agreed with the statement that Poland would face a better future outside the EU.[245] Slovenians, Czechs, Hungarians, and Romanians have also tended to agree with such statements significantly more than EU-15 nationals.[246]

Unhappy with where their countries have headed since the Enlargement, many CEE nationals have felt compelled to try to better their lives by relying on the right of free movement. Although data collection pertaining to mobility is imperfect, approximately 5 million CEE nationals appear to have moved to EU-15 states

---

238 Campos et al. (2019).
239 E.g., World Bank (2021).
240 E.g., Eurostat (2023).
241 See Levchenko and Zhang (2012).
242 Council Implementing Regulation (EU) No 282/2011 of 15 March 2011 laying down implementing measures for Directive 2006/112/EC on the common system of value added tax, 23.3.2011.
243 CBOS (2014).
244 Pew Research Center (2019).
245 Eurobarometer (2021).
246 See, e.g., Eurobarometer (2016).

between 2004 and 2014, including significant numbers of highly-skilled workers, leading to concerns about brain drain. Some studies have linked this exodus, composed mostly of young workers, to depressing GDPs in CEE states in the first decade after accession despite considerable remittances being sent back to the region.[247] Moreover, mobility has not been unproblematic for CEE workers who have often experienced exploitation and racialisation in EU-15 states, as discussed in the following chapters.

On the other hand, research has consistently shown significant economic benefits of the Eastern Enlargement to EU-15 states—in line with pre-accession predictions that it was going to be a 'phenomenally good bargain'.[248] Within five years of the Enlargement, benefits of expanded trade[249] and increased demand for EU-15 exports—which also created more jobs in the west—had greatly outweighed the EU's financial assistance to CEE states.[250] Moreover, financial assistance to the CEE region had directly benefited EU-15 states, by having been largely used to create business and investment opportunities for western companies in the CEE region. Western companies' investment in the CEE region has been linked to long-term increased corporate profits and a suppression of wages in the CEE region.[251] Of course, these benefits have not been uniformly distributed among EU-15 states, with the largest beneficiaries being Austria and Germany and the smallest being Portugal.[252] As a German Eastern Business Association's board member remarked in 2022, '[o]ur close economic ties with the region make a decisive contribution to Germany's global competitiveness. Without Central and Eastern Europe, we would not be in such a good position today'.[253] Critically, the west gained sources of affordable materials, and—even more significantly—of cheap flexible labour, comprised largely of young, educated workers, to revitalise their aging populations. Finally, by shifting the EU's eastern borders, the EU-15 region reduced the risk of an influx of undocumented migrants and alleged crime from even farther east. The CEE region also proved to serve as a buffer zone between western Europe and the political instabilities in the east including the post-2020 Russian proxy state in Belarus and the chaos unleashed by Russia's invasion of Ukraine in 2022.

Conclusions

The Eastern Enlargement and CEE nationals' mobility have been embedded within a western-centric set of values and ideologies. Foundational EU rhetoric

---

247 For example, during 2004–11, Poland received more than €26 billion in remittances. See Kundera (2014).
248 Neueder (2003).
249 Trade between the old and new Member States grew from €175 billion in 1999 to approximately €500 billion in 2007. See European Commission (2009).
250 CEE aid represented approximately 0.2 % of the aggregate EU-15 GDP in 2009. See id.
251 E.g., Dullien (2017).
252 Levchenko and Zhang (2012).
253 Emerging Europe (2022).

posits the EU project as benevolent and inevitable, while tending to conceal its pro-western economic core. Moreover, in EU discourse, only the west constitutes the imagined community of 'Europe'. Given its political foundations and the fact that EU-15 representatives had controlled EU institutions until 2004, it is not surprising that the EU was at first conceptualised as a western project. Since the Eastern Enlargement, however, EU rhetoric should have become more inclusive, especially in light of its emphasis on fundamental rights and equality. Why has it not?

I contend that remnants of the long-standing inferiorisation of the east remain—in the continuation of othering or exclusionary discourses and in policies privileging western interests. Europe's idea of itself still depends on (western) imperialist attitudes[254] fuelled by globalisation and increased migration. Intra-EU east-to-west mobility, accompanied by ongoing instances of othering, continue to play a role in this process. For example, in a 2013 letter to the European Council for Justice and Home Affairs, representatives of Austria, Germany, the Netherlands, and the UK complained about the alleged financial abuse of western 'benefit magnet' Member States by CEE 'immigrants'.[255] Leading up to the 2017 Rome Summit, France, Germany, Italy, and Spain endorsed a 'multiple-speed' Europe, with a smaller subset of 'core' Member States cooperating more closely to shape EU policies, prompting concerns in the CEE region that it might be (further) relegated to the periphery in EU decision-making while more powerful states, such as Germany, would amplify their dominance. Perhaps it comes as no surprise that, after Brexit, the two London-based EU agencies were relocated to Paris and Amsterdam despite the fact that several CEE states had requested to host them. Notably, western-centric discourse has been normalised and rendered almost invisible, attesting to the strength of western conceptual dominance. It is difficult to imagine references to a 'European' culture and heritage discussed in this chapter to have been solely based on cultural accomplishments and practices of the CEE region.[256] Such discourse would be noticeable to most readers, whereas reliance on exclusively western references tends to be unreflexively accepted as 'normal'.

East/west inequalities also are reflected in and intensified through EU policies.[257] Western-driven pre-accession policies, the Enlargement process, and select aspects of the acquis have taken advantage of and reinforced CEE states' unequal position to the west. Rather than a 're-unification' of Europe, the actual Eastern Enlargement process and policies were in line with the rhetorical positioning of the CEE region as an eastern other and with the western-centric economic core of the EU project. As if attempting to pre-empt potential criticism, on the 25th anniversary of

254 See generally Ponzanesi and Blaagaard (2011).
255 Mikl-Leitner et al. (2013).
256 Or of non-white thinkers.
257 For a general discussion of how EU laws have ignored concerns of 'peripheral' states, companies, and their workers (including all CEE states, as well as Bulgaria and Romania), see Kukovec (2015).

the fall of the Iron Curtain, the Commission noted that, in evaluating the Eastern Enlargement, it is important 'to avoid pitfalls of an "imperialist" categorization'.[258] My research, however, reveals that such characterisation is apt. The legal, political, and economic frameworks behind CEE states' accession and membership reflect imperial attributes and have served the interests of western financial institutions and EU-15 states—before the Enlargement and since. Any benefits accrued by CEE states at the time of their accession appear only ancillary and are more aptly attributable to interest convergence rather than to benevolent intentions on the part of the pre-04 EU. It is true that historically, more powerful countries have often approached weaker ones in an opportunistic fashion. However, the EU's self-interested actions towards the CEE region and misuse of bargaining power have taken place in the context of the EU project's promises of equality between all Member States and between all Europeans. The reality has been a far cry from promises of the Eastern Enlargement as an undertaking to 'transcend ... former divisions and ... forge a common destiny'[259] of a united Europe.

Bibliography

Act concerning the conditions of accession of the Czech Republic, the Republic of Estonia, the Republic of Cyprus, the Republic of Latvia, the Republic of Lithuania, the Republic of Hungary, the Republic of Malta, the Republic of Poland, the Republic of Slovenia and the Slovak Republic and the adjustments to the Treaties on which the European Union is founded, OJ L 236, 23.9.2003 ('2003 Accession Treaty')

Agreement between the EEC and the Hungarian People's Republic on trade and commercial and economic cooperation, OJ L 327, 30.11.88

Agreement between the EEC and the Polish People's Republic on trade and commercial and economic cooperation, OJ L 339, 22.11.1989

Agreement between the EEC and the Republic of Latvia on trade and commercial and economic cooperation, OJ L 403, 31.12.92

Anderson, Benedict (2006) *Imagined Communities: Reflections on the Origin and Spread of Nationalism* (New York: Verso)

Articles of Agreement of the International Monetary Fund, adopted at the UN Monetary and Financial Conference on 22.07.1944

Ash, Timothy Garton (1990) *The Magic Lantern: The Revolutions of '89 Witnessed in Warsaw, Budapest, Berlin, and Prague* (New York: Random House)

Balázs, Péter et al. (2014) *25 Years After the Fall of the Iron Curtain: The State of Integration of East and West in the European Union* (Brussels: European Commission)

Behr, Hartmut (2012) EUrope—history, violence and 'peripheries', *Review of European Studies* 4(3): 7–17

Belka, Marek (2013) *How Poland's Membership Helped Transform its Economy* (Washington: Group of Thirty)

---

258 Balázs et al. (2014).
259 Treaty Establishing a Constitution for Europe, signed on 29 October 2004, OJ 2004/C 310, 16.12.2004 (unratified), Preamble.

Bell, Derrick (1980) Brown v. Board of Education and the interest-convergence dilemma, *Harvard Law Review* 93: 518–533

Boatcă, Manuela (2013) Coloniality of labor in the global periphery: Latin America and Eastern Europe in the world-system, *Review (Fernand Braudel Center)* 36(3-4): 287–314

Bod, Peter (2019) Hungarian economic policy between 1989 and 2019, *Economy & Finance* 6(1): 17–42

Böröcz, József (2001) The Fox and the Raven: The European Union and Hungary Renegotiate the Margins of Europe, in Jozsef Böröcz and Melinda Kovacs (eds) *Empire's New Clothes: Unveiling EU Enlargement* 51–110 (Shropshire: Central Europe Review)

Böröcz, József and Melinda Kovacs (eds) (2001) *Empire's New Clothes: Unveiling EU Enlargement* (Shropshire: Central Europe Review)

Brugmans, Hendrik (1970) *L'idée européenne 1920–1970* (Bruges: De Tempel)

Burger, Anna (2009) *The Situation of Hungarian Agriculture*, Paper Presented at International Scientific Conference, 27–29 May (Vilnius), https://ageconsearch.umn.edu/record/90651/files/THE%20SITUATION%20OF%20HUNGARIAN%20AGRICULTURE.pdf

Byrne, David (2003) Speech: Food safety—Completion of farm to fork approach, 27 June (Brussels), http://europa.eu/rapid/press-release_SPEECH-03-329_en.htm

Campos, Nauro et al. (2019) Institutional integration and economic growth in Europe, *Journal of Monetary Economics* 103: 88–104

CBOS (2014) *Polish Public Opinion: Opinions about Market Economy*, March (Warsaw), www.cbos.pl/PL/publikacje/public_opinion/2014/03_2014.pdf

Charter of Fundamental Rights of the European Union, OK C 3030, 14.12.2007

Clemens, Johannes and Astrid Lemmer (2006) *Financing the EU Budget—Present Situation and Perspectives*, CESifo DICE Report 1/2006, https://core.ac.uk/download/pdf/6631155.pdf

Commission (1992) Joint Statement by the Foreign Ministers of the European Community and the Visegrád countries, *Bulletin of the European Communities*, October, No 10, pp 127–128

Commission (1997) Agenda 2000: For a stronger and wider Union, COM (97) 2000, 15.07.1997

Commission (2001) *Making a success of enlargement—Strategy Paper and Report of the European Commission on the progress towards accession by each of the candidate countries*, COM/2001/0700 final, 13.11.2001

Commission Decision No 1970/93/ECSC of 19 July 1993 opening and providing for the administration of tariff quotas in respect of certain ECSC products originating in the Czech Republic and the Slovak Republic imported into the Community (1 June 1993 to 31 December 1995), OJ L 180, 23.7.1993

Commission of the European Communities (1993) Green Paper: European Social Policy—Options for the Union, COM/93/551 final, 17.11.93

Commission of the European Communities (1997) Agenda 2000—Commission Opinion on Poland's Application for Membership of the European Union, DOC/97/16, 15.07.97

Commission of the European Communities (1998) Regular report on Hungary's progress towards accession, COM (98) 700 final, 17.12.98

Commission of the European Communities (1998a) Regular report on Slovenia's progress towards accession, COM (98) 709 final, 17.12.98

Commission of the European Communities (2001) Regular Report on Poland's Progress Towards Accession, 13.11.2001, SEC (2001) 1752

Commission of the European Communities (2002) Regular Report on Estonia's progress towards accession, SEC (2002) 1402 final, 9.10.02

Commission of the European Communities (2002a) Enlargement Papers: Main Results of the April 2002 Fiscal Notifications Presented by the Candidate Countries, No 13, November (Brussels)

Commission of the European Communities (2004) Green Paper—Equality and non-discrimination for all in an enlarged EU, COM (2004) 379 final, 28.05.2004

Congressional Research Service (2003) European Union Candidate Countries: 2003 Referenda Results, 26 September, www.everycrsreport.com/files/20030926_RS21624_7b4adfe763b7a99e6d0a9dbc048d8916b20affc2.pdf

Council Decision of 22 June 1988 on the conclusion of the Joint Declaration on the establishment of official relations between the European Economic Community and the Council for Mutual Economic Assistance, OJ L 157, 24.6.1988

Council Decision of 30 March 1998 on the principles, priorities, intermediate objectives and conditions contained in the accession partnership with the Czech Republic, OJ L 121, 23.4.1998

Council Decision of 6 December 1999 on the principles, priorities, intermediate objectives and conditions contained in the Accession Partnership with the Republic of Estonia, OJ L 335, 28/12/1999

Council Implementing Regulation (EU) No 282/2011 of 15 March 2011 laying down implementing measures for Directive 2006/112/EC on the common system of value added tax, OJ L 77, 23.3.2011

Council of the European Union (2002) Presidency Conclusions, Brussels, 14702/02, 26.11.2002, www.consilium.europa.eu/media/20917/72968.pdf

Council of the European Union (2009) *Europe: Giving Shape to an Idea* (London: Anthem Press)

Council Regulation No 3338/80 of 16 December 1980 on the conclusion of the Agreement on the establishment of the Joint Committee and the Agreement on trade in industrial products between the European Economic Community and the Socialist Republic of Romania, OJ L 352, 29.12.1980

Council Regulation (EEC) No 3906/89 of 18 December 1989 on economic aid to the Republic of Hungary and the Polish People's Republic, OJ L 375, 23.12.1989

Council Regulation 1189/93 of 14 May 1993, OJ L 120/34, 15.5.1993

Council Regulation (EC) No 1257/1999 of 17 May 1999 on support for rural development from the European Agricultural Guidance and Guarantee Fund, OJ L 160/80, 26.06.99

Crenshaw, Kimberlé (2011) Race, reform, and retrenchment, *German Law Journal* 12(1): 247–284

Decision No 1/93 of the EC-Czech Republic and Slovak Republic Joint Committee of 28 May 1993, OJ L 157, 29.6.1993

Delgado, Richard and Jean Stefancic (2017) *Critical Race Theory* (New York: NYU Press)

Delors, Jacques (1990) Speech to the European Parliament: 'Presenting the Commission's Programme for 1990', 17 January (Strasbourg)

Dullien, Sebastian (2017) Eastern resentment of Germany spells trouble for Berlin and Brussels, 5 October (European Council on Foreign Relations), https://ecfr.eu/article/commentary_eastern_resentment_of_germany_spells_trouble_for_berlin_and_brus/

Economic Associations Act, Act VI of 1988 (Hungary)

Ekiert, Grzegorz and Jan Kubik (2004) *Rebellious Civil Society, Popular Protest and Democratic Consolidation in Poland, 1989–1993* (Ann Arbor: University of Michigan Press)

El-Enany, Nadine (2020) *(B)ordering Britain: Law, Race and Empire* (Manchester: Manchester University Press)
Éltető, Andrea (2014) *Mind the Gap – Integration Experiences of the Ten Central and Eastern European Countries* (Budapest: Institute for World Economics)
Emerging Europe (2022) FDI strengthens Central and Eastern Europe's economies, 30 November, https://emerging-europe.com/news/fdi-strengthens-central-and-eastern-europes-economies/
Engel-Di Mauro, Salvatore (ed) (2006) *The European's Burden: Global Imperialism in EU Expansion* (New York: Peter Lang)
EU Observer (2003) Acceding states warned over slow take-up of rules, 1 May, https://euobserver.com/enlargement/11070
Eurobarometer (1998) Central and Eastern Eurobarometer 8: Public Opinion about the European Union—Ten Countries' Survey, March, www.gesis.org/eurobarometer-data-service/survey-series/central-eastern-eb/study-profiles/ce-eb-8/
Eurobarometer (2001) Candidate Countries Eurobarometer 2001.1: Life in the Candidate Countries, Attachment to Nationality and Identification with Europe, Contact with Other Countries and Cultures, and European Union Enlargement
Eurobarometer (2003) Candidate Countries Eurobarometer 2003.2, www.icpsr.umich.edu/web/ICPSR/studies/04107/summary
Eurobarometer (2016) Standard Eurobarometer 85, europa.eu/eurobarometer/surveys/detail/2130
Eurobarometer (2021) Standard Eurobarometer 94, Public Opinion in the European Union, europa.eu/eurobarometer/surveys/detail/2355
Europe Agreement establishing an association between the European Communities and their Member States and the Czech Republic, OJ L 360, 31.12.1994
Europe Agreement establishing an association between the European Communities and their Member States and the Republic of Hungary, OJ L 347, 31.12.1993
Europe Agreement establishing an association between the European Communities and their Member States and the Republic of Lithuania, OJ L 51, 20.2.1998
Europe Agreement establishing an association between the European Communities and their Member States and the Republic of Poland, OJ L 348, 31.12.1993
Europe Agreement establishing an association between the European Communities and their Member States and the Republic of Slovenia, OJ L 51, 26.2.1999
European Commission (2001) Enlargement Papers: The economic impact of enlargement, No 4, June (Brussels)
European Commission (2002) Media Pack: The Enlargement of the European Union (Luxembourg), https://op.europa.eu/en/publication-detail/-/publication/7d68e06e-1dc3-4ec1-9f7b-d124a2fefbb0
European Commission (2003) Enlargement of the European Union: An Historic Opportunity (Brussels), https://op.europa.eu/en/publication-detail//publication/5d510696-c6c5-401f-b605-244b365b1054
European Commission (2003a) More unity and more diversity: The European Union's Biggest Enlargement (Brussels), https://eurlex.europa.eu/resource.html?uri=cellar:57b37ead-e06a-4aac-a079-c62a5e06fbbe.0012.02/DOC_1&format=PDF
European Commission (2003b) Comprehensive monitoring report of the European Commission on the state of preparedness for EU membership of the Czech Republic, Estonia, Cyprus, Latvia, Lithuania, Hungary, Malta, Poland, Slovenia and Slovakia, COM (2003) 0675 final

European Commission (2004) Europlus: Come and Visit the Countries Wishing to Join the European Union! (Luxembourg), https://op.europa.eu/en/publication-detail/-/publication/ab0ae68a-1efe-42ad-8ccf-28ffde568aa0

European Commission (2006) EU Enlargement—20 Myths and Facts about Enlargement (Brussels), https://op.europa.eu/en/publication-detail/-/publication/0c9d9c2a-7e25-4e79-bd82-8dd1a14407d5

European Commission (2007) EU budget 2006 Financial Report (Luxembourg), https://www.europarl.europa.eu/meetdocs/2004_2009/documents/dv/tran20071120accountscom2006_/tran20071120accountscom2006_en.pdf

European Commission (2009) Good To Know About EU Enlargement (Brussels), https://op.europa.eu/s/xuah

European Commission (2011) Annual Report 2011 on the European Union's development and external assistance policies and their implementation in 2010, SEC (2011) 0880 final, 6.07.2011

European Commission (2012) The EU: What would it mean for me? Four Stories, Four People (Brussels), https://op.europa.eu/en/publication-detail/-/publication/ef43562c-0764-4a5e-8454-a0513b556e66

European Commission (2013) Enlargement—Extending European Values and Standards to More Countries (Luxembourg), https://op.europa.eu/en/publication-detail/-/publication/6b289b12-ad64-462d-9b35-645f211db8d6

European Commission (2014) The European Union Explained: Europe in 12 Lessons (Brussels), https://publications.europa.eu/en/publication-detail/-/publication/009305e8-2a43-11e7-ab65-01aa75ed71a1/language-en/format-PDF/source-88244208

European Communities (1973) Bulletin of the European Communities No 12, 14.12.1973, pp 118–122

European Council, Reform of the Common Agricultural Policy post 2013, www.consilium.europa.eu/en/policies/cap-reform/ (last accessed 29 June 2023)

European Council (1989) Conclusions of the Presidency, Strasbourg, 8–9 December, www.consilium.europa.eu/media/20580/1989_december_-_strasbourg__eng_.pdf

European Council (1993) European Council in Copenhagen, 21–22 June 1993, Conclusions of the Presidency, SN 180/1/93 Rev 1, Bulletin of the European Communities, No 6/1993, http://aei.pitt.edu/1443/1/Copenhagen_june_1993.pdf

European Economic and Social Committee (1992) Opinion on Immigration Policy, 92/C 40/104, 17.02.92

European Economic and Social Committee (1999) Opinion on the role and contribution of civil society organisations in the building of Europe, OJ C 329

European Economic and Social Committee (2000) Opinion on the Communication from the Commission to the Council, the European Parliament, the Economic and Social Committee and the Committee of the Regions—Towards a European Research Area, 2000/C 204/16

European Economic and Social Committee (2014) 10th Anniversary of the EU Enlargement (Brussels), www.eesc.europa.eu/sites/default/files/resources/docs/qe-02-14-519-en-n.pdf

European Economic Community Commission (1961) Fourth General Report on the Activities of the Community, http://aei.pitt.edu/30807/1/67557_EEC_4th.pdf

European Parliament (1995) Minutes of the Sitting of Friday, 22 September, OJ C 269, 16.10.1995

European Parliament (2009) Resolution of 14 January 2009 on the situation of fundamental rights in the European Union 2004–2008 (2007/2145(INI)), OJEU C 46 E/48

European Parliament (2013) Written Questions by Members of the European Parliament and their answers given by a European Union institution, OJ C 111E, 18.4.2013
European Parliament (2013a) Written Questions by Members of the European Parliament and their answers given by a European Union institution, OJ C 75E, 14.3.2013
European Parliament (2013b) Written Questions by Members of the European Parliament and their answers given by a European Union institution, OJ C 228E, 7.8.2013
European Parliament (2013c) Written Questions by Members of the European Parliament and their answers given by a European Union institution, 2013/C 203 E/01, 17.07.2013
European Parliament (2014) Written Questions by Members of the European Parliament and their answers given by a European Union institution, OJ C 229, 17.7.2014
European Parliament (2014a) Written Questions by Members of the European Parliament and their answers given by a European Union institution, OJ C 377, 23.10.2014
European University Institute (1977) 1st Jean Monnet Lecture: Europe's Present Challenge and Future Opportunity, 27 October
European University Institute (1984) 7th Jean Monnet Lecture: European Union or Decline: To be or not to be, 24 May
European University Institute (1985) 8th Jean Monnet Lecture: European Union: One Character in Search of an Author, 23 November
European University Institute (1990) 13th Monnet Lecture: The Crisis of the Societies in the East and the Return to a Common Europe, 23 November
European University Institute (1992) 15th Jean Monnet Lecture: The Future of Europe, 5 November
European University Institute (1995) 17th Jean Monnet Lecture: The European Union—A Stage of Transition, 10 February
European University Institute (2006) 25th Jean Monnet Lecture: Uniting in Peace: The Role of Law in the European Union, 31 March
Eurostat (2023) Minimum wage statistics, https://ec.europa.eu/eurostat/statistics-explained/index.php?title=Minimum_wage_statistics
Fanon, Frantz (1988) *Black Skin, White Masks* (London: Pluto Press)
Fitzpatrick, Peter (1992) *The Mythology of Modern Law* (New York: Routledge)
Flamm, László (2012) The Crisis and Euroscepticism in Central and Eastern Europe, *L'Europe en Formation* 2 (365): 305–421
Foreign Investment Act, Act XXIV of 1988 (Hungary)
Glasman, Maurice (1996) *Unnecessary Suffering: Managing Market Utopia* (London: Verso)
Hartnell, Helen (1993) Association agreements between the EC and Central and Eastern European states, *Acta Juridica Hungarica* 35(1-2): 225–236
Hobsbawm, Eric and Terence Ranger (eds) (1983) *The Invention of Tradition* (Cambridge: Cambridge University Press)
Hofbauer, Hannes (2006) EU Enlargement: Political recognition of an economic process, in Salvatore Engel-Di Mauro (ed) *The European's Burden: Global Imperialism in EU Expansion* 53–70 (New York: Peter Lang)
Inotai, Andras (2000) *Reflections on the timing of EU Enlargement*, Working Papers 107 (Budapest: Institute for World Economics)
Internationale Handelsgesellschaft mbH v Einfuhr- und Vorratsstelle für Getreide und Futtermittel, Case 11/70, ECLI:EU:C:1970:114, 17 December 1970
Jileva, Elena (2004) Do norms matter? The principle of solidarity and the EU's eastern enlargement, *Journal of International Relations and Development* 7(1): 3–23

Kalmar, Ivan (2023) Race, racialization and the East of the European Union: An introduction, *Journal of Ethnic and Migration Studies* 49(6): 1465–1480

Kennedy, David and David Webb (1990) Integration: Eastern Europe and the European Economic Communities, *Columbia Journal of Transnational Law* 28: 633–675

Knöbl, Adalbert and Richard Haas (2003) *IMF and the Baltics – A Decade of Cooperation*, Working Paper 03/241 (Brussels: IMF) www.elibrary.imf.org/view/journals/001/2003/241/article-A001-en.xml

Kok, Wim (2003) Report to the European Commission: Enlarging the European Union: Achievements and challenges, 26 March (Florence: European University Institute), https://hdl.handle.net/1814/2515

Kukovec, Damjan (2015) Law and the periphery, *European Law Journal* 21(3): 406–428

Kundera, Jaroslaw (2014) The economic effects of 10 years of membership of Poland in the EU, *Research in Social Change* 6(1): 61–98

Levchenko Andrei and Jing Zhang (2012) Comparative advantage and the welfare impact of European integration, *Economic Policy* 27(72): 567–602

Levine-Rasky, Cynthia (2013) *Whiteness Fractured* (Farnham: Ashgate)

Lewicki, Aleksandra (2023) East–West inequalities and the ambiguous racialisation of 'Eastern Europeans', *Journal of Ethnic and Migration Studies* 49(6): 1481–1499

Likic-Brboric, Branka (2011) EU enlargement, migration, and asymmetric citizenship: Political economy of inequality and the demise of the European social model, *Globalizations* 8(3): 277–294

Lommatzsch, Kirsten et al. (2004) Poland's economy prior to EU accession, *Economic Bulletin* 41(4): 113–118

McVeigh, Robbie (2010) United in whiteness? Irishness, Europeanness, and the emergence of a white Europe policy, *European Studies* 28: 251–278

Meyer, Henry (1955) *Mitteleuropa: In German Thought and Action 1815–1945* (The Hague: Springer)

Mikl-Leitner, Johanna et al. (2013) Letter to Alan Shatter, President of the European Council for Justice and Home Affairs, www.statewatch.org/news/2013/apr/eu-4-ms-welfare-letter-to-irish-presidency.pdf

Morrison, Toni (1994) *The Nobel Lecture in Literature 1993* (New York: Knopf)

Motas, Maciej (2011) Gdyby nie Unia, to byśmy krówki pasali? [If not for the Union, we would have been raising cows?], *Konserwatyzm*, 5 July, www.konserwatyzm.pl/gdyby-nie-unia-to-bysmy-krowki-pasali

MSZ (Ministerstwo Spraw Zagranicznych [Ministry of Foreign Affairs] (2014) Polskie 10 Lat w Unii—Raport [Report on Poland's Ten Years in the European Union] (Warsaw), https://dziennikurzedowy.msz.gov.pl/resource/10lat_PLwUE.pdf

Myant, Martin and Terry Cox (eds) (2008) *Reinventing Poland: Economic and Political Transformation and Evolving National Identity* (London: Routledge)

Myslinska, Dagmar (2021) Not quite right: Representations of Eastern Europeans in ECJ discourse, *International Journal of Politics, Culture, and Society* 34: 271–307

Neueder, Franz (2003) Costs and benefits of EU enlargement, *Intereconomics* July/August: 190–195

Nove, Alec et al. (eds) (1982) *The East European Economies in the 1970s* (London: Butterworths)

Organisation for Economic Co-operation and Development (OECD) (1998) Preparing civil servants for EU: The case of Poland, Meeting of Heads of Civil Service in the

Ten Candidate Countries to the European Union, 10–12 November, www.sigmaweb. org/1850843.htm

Pew Research Center (2019) European public opinion three decades after the fall of communism, www.pewresearch.org/global/wpcontent/uploads/sites/2/2019/10/Pew-Research-Center-Value-of-Europe-report-FINAL-UPDATED.pdf

Pleskovic, Boris and Jeffrey Sachs (1994) Political independence and economic reform in Slovenia, in Olivier Jean Blanchard et al. (eds) *The Transition in Eastern Europe* 191–220 (Chicago: University of Chicago Press)

Pogany, Istvan (1991) Recent developments in the law relating to foreign investment in Hungary, *ICSID Review—Foreign Investment Law Journal* 6(1): 114–118

Ponzanesi, Sandra and Bolette B Blaagaard (2011) Introduction: In the name of Europe, *Social Identities* 17(1): 1–10

Prawo dewizowe [The Act on Foreign Currencies], Dziennik Ustaw [Polish Journal of Laws] 1989, *No* 6, Item 33

Press Release (1994) Commission launches global policy for the Baltics, 27 October

Prodi, Romano (2000) Speech: Catching the tide of history: Enlargement and the future of the Union, 11 October (Brussels: Paul-Henri Spaak Foundation), http://europa.eu/rapid/press-release_SPEECH-00-374_en.htm

Robinson, Cedric J (2019) *On Racial Capitalism, Black Internationalism, and Cultures of Resistance* (London: Pluto Press)

Roguska, Beata (2003) Polska Droga do Unii Europejskiej [Polish Road to the European Union], in Krzysztof Zagorski (ed) *Polska Europa—Swiat: Opinia Publiczna w okresie integracji [Polish Europe—The World: Public Opinion During the Integration Period]* (Warsaw: CBOS)

Sassatelli, Monica (2009) *Becoming Europeans: Cultural Identity and Cultural Policies* (London: Palgrave Macmillan)

Schimmelfennig, Frank (2001) The community trap: Liberal norms, rhetorical action, and the Eastern enlargement of the European Union, *International Organization* 55(1): 47–80

Senior Nello, Susan and Karen E Smith (1997) The consequences of Eastern enlargement of the European Union in stages, RSC Working Paper No 97/51 (Florence: European University Institute), http://cadmus.eui.eu/handle/1814/1529

Smismans, Stijn (2010) The European Union's fundamental rights myth, *Journal of Common Market Studies* 48(1): 45–66

Stauder v City of Ulm, Case 29/69, ECLI:EU:C:1969:57, 12 November 1969

Suchocka, Hanna (1993) Letter to Jacques Delors et al, Agence Europe, Nr 5995, 4 June

Szczerbiak, Aleks (2002) *The Political Context of EU Accession in Poland*, Briefing Paper (London: Royal Institute of International Affairs)

Teffer, Peter (2018) Five east European states prevent new CAP consensus, *EU Observer*, 20 March, https://euobserver.com/economic/141381

The Economist (2003) Come on try getting excited: The Poles sound diffident about what should be a historic moment, 5 June

Thorpe, Nick (2003) Hungarians lukewarm about EU, *The Guardian*, 14 April

Tittenbrun, Jacek (1993) *The Collapse of 'Real Socialism' in Poland* (London: Janus Publishing)

Todorova, Maria (2003) Isn't Central Europe dead?, in Cristopher Lord (ed) *Central Europe: Core or Periphery* (Copenhagen: Copenhagen Business School)

Transformation of Economic and Business Organizations and Companies Act, Act XIII of 1989 (Hungary)

Treaty Establishing a Constitution for Europe, signed on 29 October 2004, OJ 2004/C 310, 16.12.2004 (unratified)

Treaty of Lisbon amending the Treaty on European Union and the Treaty establishing the European Community, OJ C 306, 17.12.2007

Treaty of Nice amending the Treaty on European Union, the Treaties establishing the European Communities, OJ C 80, 10.3.2001

Trzeciak, Sergiusz (2012) *Poland's EU Accession* (London: Routledge)

Urbanowicz, Juliusz (2002) Kopenhaskie rozwiązanie [Copenhagen Solution], *Wprost* Nr 1047, 22 December, www.wprost.pl/tygodnik/37218/Kopenhaskie-rozwiazanie.html

Van Rompuy, Herman (2012) European Union Nobel Lecture: From war to peace: A European tale, 10 December, www.nobelprize.org/prizes/peace/2012/eu/lecture/

Vienna Institute for International Economic Studies (2019) Czechoslovakia was one of the most rigid and conservative countries in the former Eastern Bloc, 10 December, https://wiiw.ac.at/czechoslovakia-was-one-of-the-most-rigid-and-conservative-countries-in-the-former-eastern-bloc-n-414.html

Vilpišauskas, Ramūnas (2014) Lithuania's double transition after the re-establishment of independence in 1990: Coping with uncertainty domestically and externally, *Oxford Review of Economic Policy* 30(2): 223–236

Week in Europe (2004) Week in Europe 12–18/4/04 (Prague: ICEU), www.agris.cz/Content/files/main_files/52/130341/Week_040419_EN.doc

Williams, Andrew (2004) *EU Human Rights Policies: A Study in Irony* (Oxford: Oxford University Press)

Wolff, Larry (1994) *Inventing Eastern Europe: The Map of Civilization on the Mind of the Enlightenment* (Palo Alto: Stanford University Press)

World Bank (2021) GDP per capita (current US$) – European Union, https://data.worldbank.org/indicator/NY.GDP.PCAP.CD?locations=EU&most_recent_value_desc=false

Zielonka, Jan (2007) *Europe as Empire: The Nature of the Enlarged European Union* (Oxford: Oxford University Press)

Chapter 3

Inequalities in the Experience of East-to-West Mobility

The Rights to Free Movement and Equality

According to EU institutions, the free movement of persons is 'a fundamental freedom, and a core element of European citizenship'.[1] Enshrined as a fundamental principle in EU Treaties, and developed through the Citizens' Rights Directive 2004/38, other secondary legislation, and ECJ case law, the right to free movement entitles each EU citizen[2] to work and reside in other Member States while enjoying equal treatment with host state nationals in the employment context and in access to social and tax advantages. As a prerequisite for the exercise of most other EU rights—including the right to equality—and a tangible symbol of integration, the free movement right carries great social, economic, and political importance. It has become widely regarded—by politicians and scholars alike—as a central aspect of the European integration project. As consistently indicated through Eurobarometer surveys,[3] the EU public prizes the right of free movement as a key EU achievement.[4] Intra-EU mobility has been increasing over time. Close to 14 million EU citizens lived in another Member State in 2021. Driven by employment opportunities, post 04 mobility has been largely directed from the CEE region towards EU-15 states. CEE nationals, however, have not been afforded access to mobility on equal terms due to unequal EU and western state policies, disparaging discourses, and experiences of exploitation and discrimination in host states.

Whereas western EU nationals' mobility has generally been a welcomed and celebrated phenomenon, CEE movers have been portrayed in EU-15 popular and political discourse as not only 'labour migrants', 'benefit scroungers', and 'benefit tourists' but also as 'criminals' and 'drunks'.[5] Coming from countries denigrated as backwards and parasitic, CEE movers get stamped in western parlance with the collective pejorative label 'Eastern Europeans'. Such descriptors are indicative of the underlying contestation over east-to-west mobility in

1 European Parliament (2009).
2 As well as citizens of Iceland, Lichtenstein, Norway, and Switzerland.
3 E.g., Eurobarometer (1986); Eurobarometer (2013).
4 It is true that the value of the free movement right has not been accepted by all EU nationals—especially not by stayers.
5 E.g., Financial Times (2011). See generally Drzewiecka (2014); Sobis (2016).

DOI: 10.4324/9781003175377-3

laws, political rhetoric, media portrayals, and public discourses. Whereas, before the Eastern Enlargement, intra-EU labour mobility did not pose a threat—either real or imagined—to host states' welfare regimes, labour markets, or social cohesion, the right to free movement became highly politicised once CEE nationals' mobility was on the horizon, and it became one of the most contested topics during the Eastern Enlargement process. Various surveys conducted between 2000 and 2003 indicated that about 40% of EU-15 nationals opposed granting civil rights to lawful CEE migrants and 20% favoured their repatriation.[6] Responding to public anxieties, transitional derogations included in the 2003 Accession Treaty enabled EU-15 states to limit CEE workers' mobility for up to seven years. They diminished the concept of equality and degraded the scope of CEE states' EU membership while reinforcing the long-standing western approach towards CEE nationals as not fully belonging to the 'European' community.

Since the Enlargement, public opposition to CEE nationals' mobility, embraced by both far-right populist and mainstream political parties, has been widespread across EU-15 states. For example, in 2007, when CEE mobility to the UK was at its highest, 34% of British survey respondents felt that EU-14 nationals should be given priority to immigrate to the UK, whereas none supported that approach for CEE nationals.[7] Renewed popular and political debates about 'benefit tourism' and 'poverty immigration' spread across EU-15 states when the transitional mobility limitations were coming to an end. In a 2011 survey, the majority of nationals in every EU-15 state other than Sweden and Luxembourg agreed with the statement that the internal market had 'flooded' their country with too much 'cheap labour'.[8] In a 2013 letter to the President of the European Council for Justice and Home Affairs, Ministers representing Austria, Germany, the Netherlands, and the UK called for limitations on the mobility of intra-EU 'immigrants' due to CEE movers' alleged abuses of social systems in 'benefit magnet' states.[9] Popular hostility towards CEE movers also contributed to the outcome of the 2016 Brexit referendum, as discussed in the next chapter.

Embedded within this broader context, and in line with the social, economic, and political inequalities discussed in the previous chapter within which the CEE region was situated when it entered the EU, CEE nationals' access to the free movement right has been free in name only. The west's unequal pre-accession approach towards the CEE region, reinforced through othering discourse, has also been reflected in CEE nationals' unequal access to mobility. Their experiences in EU-15 states have been marred by exploitation and racism, in line with the

6   See Erel (2007).
7   Ipsos MORI (2007). Bulgarians and Romanians fared particularly poorly—with 8% of those polled stating that they should not be allowed to enter the UK at all, which is higher than for any other white group measured.
8   Eurobarometer (2011).
9   Mikl-Leitner et al. (2013).

long-standing western peripheralisation of the east, while underscoring a hierarchy of Europeanness and of whiteness. Throughout this chapter, I demonstrate how both the conceptualisation and application of the free movement right[10]—as well as of social and equality rights which are necessary to facilitate mobility—have been perpetuating and exacerbating power differentials between east and west while not only disregarding CEE movers' interests but also othering and turning them into second-class EU citizens.

Experience and Impact of CEE Nationals' Mobility

Given the restrictions they had experienced behind the Iron Curtain, CEE nationals have greatly valued the free movement right due to not only its practical but also symbolic implications. CEE mobility peaked soon after 2004. By 2007, approximately 2 million[11] CEE nationals resided in EU-15 states. This number increased to approximately 4.5 million by 2011. As the most populous state in the CEE region, Poland has produced the largest group of CEE movers. Before the Eastern Enlargement, most CEE migrants resided or worked in Germany. The biggest destination countries since the Enlargement have been Germany and the UK, with significant numbers of CEE movers also in Austria, Spain, Italy, Ireland, and France. In 2020, approximately 3 million CEE nationals lived in Germany and 2 million in the (post-Brexit) UK. Oftentimes de-skilled, exploited, and victimised through discrimination and racism in western states, CEE movers' experiences have been a far cry from EU rhetoric about the benevolence of the EU project, its unflinching respect for fundamental rights, and the occasional portrayals of the Enlargement as a 'reunification' of Europe and the east's 'return' to Europe. Furthermore, the significant outflow of CEE nationals has drained populations across the CEE region and has been linked to some negative long-term effects. Meanwhile, EU-15 host states have been shown to steadily benefit from CEE workers' labours. EU institutions have largely tolerated this unequal reality.

CEE Movers' Exploitation and Discrimination in EU-15 States

A deep schism can be observed between the EU's promises of 'a strong social Europe that is fair, inclusive and full of opportunity'[12] and the reality of CEE movers' experiences in EU-15 host states. CEE movers have faced significant barriers to political and social integration. They have been documented to suffer discrimination in the social sphere[13] ranging from micro-aggressions to

---

10 See also Myslinska (2019).
11 Numbers are approximate (and likely larger), as host and sending states do not keep detailed statistics, and Europeans cross borders unregistered.
12 European Commission (2021).
13 E.g., Gilmartin and Migge (2015).

incidents of blatant racism and physical attacks. Moreover, they have often been relegated to substandard housing including through temporary and hot-bedding arrangements. Some have also experienced homelessness. Even CEE children have been exposed to bullying and discrimination at schools not only by students but also by teachers.[14]

CEE movers' unequal outcomes have been particularly prominent and well-documented in the employment context.[15] Across EU-15 states, CEE nationals have been overrepresented in '3D' jobs (i.e., dirty, dangerous, and demeaning) and in 'low skill', temporary, and poorly-paid employment oftentimes in the secondary labour market and in sectors that suffer from high rates of precarity[16] including cleaning, agriculture, food processing, construction, manufacturing, wholesale, retail, accommodation, food service, care, and transport. Such sectors are associated with higher risks of exploitation and discrimination with very limited opportunities for upward mobility. CEE movers have often been disproportionately recruited via employment agencies, especially as factory operatives and care workers, which further reinforces their precariousness. De-skilling and brain squandering have been prevalent among CEE movers. For example, during the first decade after accession, approximately 30% of all Polish movers (including 50% of those with tertiary-level education) had jobs for which they were formally overqualified. Although CEE movers have increasingly also included those employed in high-skilled roles and persons electing to settle long-term in host states, they have continued to predominantly fill low-paid, temporary positions. Their de-skilling and wage penalties have been shown to be more permanent than of other foreign workers.[17] This effect has been exacerbated by western employers' reluctance to train and promote them.[18]

CEE movers have been consistently shown to experience poor working conditions, sometimes rising to the level of abuse and forced labour. While those who are foreign-born often experience difficulties in the workplace—further fuelled by increasing labour flexibilisation and decreasing labour regulation enforcement across EU-15 states over the last few decades—CEE workers have been documented as especially prone to suffering unfair treatment, harassment, bullying, and discrimination.[19] CEE nationals employed in low-paid sectors have been particularly at risk of being underpaid, forced to live in sub-standard tied accommodations, pressured to work more hours than permitted under labour regulations, and denied statutory breaks and annual leave, on top of often having unlawful deductions made from wages and not being provided

14 E.g., Sime et al. (2022).
15 This is especially significant as CEE movers' mobility has been motivated by employment, and they have had higher rates of employment in host states than host state nationals or non-EU migrants.
16 See e.g., Engbersen et al. (2017); Verwiebe et al. (2014).
17 E.g., Sirkeci et al. (2018).
18 E.g., French (2012).
19 E.g., Kofman et al. (2009).

required paperwork. Within a decade of the Enlargement, the majority of employment discrimination complaints across EU-15 states were brought by CEE workers.[20] More generally, national occupational health and safety authorities have been reporting greater numbers of discrimination incidents against CEE than EU-15 movers.[21] As my illustrative review of discrimination cases in the UK employment context in the next chapter demonstrates, CEE movers have faced bullying, abuse, harassment, and racial discrimination at work. In an extreme example of exploitation, in 2006, 119 Polish seasonal farm workers were freed from a modern-slavery camp in Italy replete with incidents of rape, torture, debt bondage, and suicide.[22]

I am not discounting the fact that CEE workers have also benefited economically and socially from mobility and have not been completely devoid of agency. Notably, some benefits which CEE nationals have been able to garner from their mobility stem from their skin colour. In addition to being shielded, at times, from expressions of racism that target non-whites, CEE movers' whiteness has made them more employable in front-end jobs and in the home-care sector both of which require interacting with customers.[23] Nevertheless, western employers often target CEE workers specifically through their hiring strategies due to them being seen as expendable, exploitable guest workers, more willing to work for lower wages, in poorer employment conditions, and at higher productivity rates, all while being more compliant than other workers.[24]

The Covid-19 pandemic exacerbated these trends and provided them greater conspicuousness. Starting in the spring of 2020, at the peak of border closures, Austria and other western states increased their efforts to recruit temporary healthcare workers from the CEE region to provide care for vulnerable persons and for those infected with Covid. Moreover, Austria, Germany, the Netherlands, and the (post Brexit) UK implemented special initiatives, including through the creation of 'travel corridors', to target seasonal CEE farm workers. Their exploitation became well documented. When transporting workers via special charter flights and train journeys, western recruiters frequently violated local quarantine rules. In addition to experiencing normal risks associated with precarious work, these CEE workers' health was at risk especially because EU-15 states had higher Covid rates than in the CEE region and CEE movers were employed in sectors with higher rates of Covid transmission.[25]

In the agricultural sector in Italy, Germany, Sweden, and the Netherlands, seasonal CEE workers found themselves in overcrowded and unhygienic

20 European Parliament (2014).
21 Groenendijk et al. (2013).
22 BBC News (2006).
23 E.g., Drinkwater et al. (2006).
24 E.g., MacKenzie and Forde (2009).
25 They also risked bringing Covid back to CEE states, which were less able to shoulder its high public health costs. In fact, the first cases of Covid in the CEE region were linked to movers' return visits from EU-15 states during Christmas break.

working and living conditions, lacking protective equipment or onsite medical assistance, and unable to self-quarantine.[26] Many agricultural employers implemented 'de-facto quarantine with simultaneous work opportunity' so that workers who became ill with Covid continued to work and share accommodations albeit with half as many people as customarily.[27] In June 2020, one of the largest Covid outbreaks in Europe was reported in Germany at Europe's biggest slaughterhouse and meatpacking plant. It affected more than 1,500 workers—mostly Poles as well as many Bulgarians and Romanians. Company officials blamed the workers themselves for bringing Covid from the CEE region. The regional government erected a fence around the plant, protected by police and security officers, to force workers to remain in company dormitories. This was intended to protect the local German population outside the plant while increasing Covid infection rates among the workers inside.

CEE movers who were already in EU-15 states at the time of the pandemic's outbreak and who remained in their host states also experienced particularly difficult conditions exacerbated by their pre-existing inequalities. Due to being often employed in precarious arrangements, and in industries principally affected by the pandemic (such as hospitality, food service, and retail), CEE workers were at a higher risk of losing their jobs. For those in tied accommodations, job loss also led to the loss of housing. Their resultant challenges were often intensified by limited financial resources and inadequate or no access to host states' safety nets. Notably, if let go, many had no access to government rescue packages which tended to prioritise companies and their direct employees. Some reports also suggest that CEE movers faced increased discrimination in accessing social benefits during this period. Destitute, some became trapped in their host countries oftentimes living in overcrowded accommodations or even becoming homeless. Those who remained employed were overrepresented in sectors with higher rates of Covid (e.g., care) and in industries where it is difficult to physically distance (e.g., manufacturing, and food processing). Lab-confirmed Covid tests in the UK, for example, indicate that non-British whites were more likely to suffer from Covid and experienced higher rates of Covid-related fatalities than white UK populations.

The prevalence of CEE movers' experiences of exploitation and discrimination in EU-15 states must be contextualised within east/west economic inequalities as well as within both historical and contemporary western policies that have inferiorised the east and extracted its nationals' labour. EU impediments to CEE nationals' access to western labour markets before the Eastern Enlargement resulted in a significant proportion of CEE migrants engaging in irregular, temporary, and circular migration—associated with risks of undocumented, poorly-paid, and de-skilled employment.[28] Although those who were residing in the EU

---

26 See generally Andriescu (2020).
27 See generally Weisskircher et al. (2020).
28 In addition to lawful post-war migration from east to west (including CEE soldiers, workers from displaced-persons camps, and ethnic Germans returning to Germany)

unlawfully before 2004 became regularised at the time of the Enlargement, pre-04 experiences have had repercussions for how both CEE workers and western employers approach their labour market positionality. Furthermore, post-accession mobility derogations (discussed below) have been directly linked to their labour exploitation.[29]

The European Parliament has acknowledged that transitional mobility restrictions had resulted in 'more illegal work, the promotion of the black economy and worker exploitation', as well as in discrimination against CEE workers.[30] Similarly, the European Commission has recognised that post-accession restrictions on their labour market access had produced increased incidence of undeclared work and false sham employment, had caused CEE movers to experience negative social consequences and inequalities in EU-15 states,[31] and had pushed some to remain in their host countries after losing their jobs rather than risking not being allowed back in under transitional restrictions.[32]

More generally, CEE movers' experiences of exploitation and discrimination can be connected to the EU's conceptualisation of CEE mobility as responsive to western employers' needs within a neoliberal economic climate of increasing labour flexibilisation, promulgating austerity measures, and expanding fortification of the EU's external borders.[33] I contend that the long-standing western approach racialising the CEE region as inferior and uncivilised has also had repercussions for not only shaping the Eastern Enlargement process but for moulding and normalising the unequal experience of mobility by CEE nationals as well. Notably, their racialisation intensified during the pandemic as westerners blamed CEE workers for bringing Covid to the west and for spreading it. For example, German employers attributed the aforementioned slaughterhouse outbreak to seasonal CEE workers. German newspapers and politicians blamed 'Eastern Europeans' for the spread of Covid.[34] Similarly, Britons accused 'scumbag' 'Eastern Europeans' for high rates of Covid transmission in the UK.[35]

EU Institutions' Perspectives on CEE Movers' Experiences

Despite becoming aware soon after the Eastern Enlargement that CEE movers were experiencing exploitation and inequalities in the west, the EU has tended to overlook or minimise these experiences thereby normalising CEE movers'

   and waves of refugees (oftentimes clandestinely fleeing following discrete political crises, such as the Hungarian Revolution of 1956).
29 See generally Carrera and Atger (2009).
30 E.g., European Parliament (2006).
31 E.g., Guild et al. (2007); Commission of the European Communities (2008); European Commission (2008).
32 European Commission (2011).
33 See generally Lewicki (2023).
34 See ibid.
35 Anthony (2020).

poor treatment. Notably, EU institutions have avoided attributing such incidents to any policy shortcomings within EU-15 states or to flaws of the free movement right or related EU policies. Moreover, EU institutions have failed to situate CEE movers' exploitation and discrimination within the wider dynamics of east-west political and economic inequalities. This approach persisted even in the aftermath of widespread reports of exploitation exacerbated by the Covid pandemic. Furthermore, in reports specifically examining labour or migrant exploitation or discrimination more generally, EU institutions have tended to exclude CEE movers from such discussions, thereby suggesting that only non-white (and non-Christian) ethnic groups can be vulnerable or disadvantaged. In effect, they have been normalising CEE movers' experiences of second-class EU citizenship while prioritising western economic interests.

As mentioned earlier, EU institutions did acknowledge, within the first two years after the Enlargement that CEE movers were overrepresented in unlawful and precarious employment and that they often faced exploitation and inequalities in EU-15 labour markets. Notably, the Commission's observations in 2006 that transitional arrangements had resulted in many CEE movers' engagement in unlawful employment appeared motivated not by a concern for their wellbeing but by institutional preference for lawful migration and documented employment as those are 'easier to control' by the receiving states.[36] By 2008, EU reports also noted that CEE movers' experiences in EU-15 states were often marred by de-skilled employment, poor living conditions, poverty, poor educational outcomes, and hindrances in access to healthcare and other social services.[37] Yet the Commission did not recommend any policy initiatives to address these findings. Moreover, in its report on transitional arrangements, the Commission had simultaneously noted that CEE movers tended to be highly qualified and that they were relieving labour shortages in low-skill sectors such as construction, domestic services, hospitality, and catering.[38] Thus, the Commission tacitly approved of CEE movers' de-skilling. Additionally, in a 2013 general report on mobile workers' rights, the Commission recognised that CEE movers have been particularly prone to experiencing discrimination in access to housing and social benefits as well as in employment—including receiving lower wages than other workers for comparable jobs, and being more pressured to work unofficially.[39] However, the Commission did not tie this observation to the need for more detailed studies or for initiatives to protect CEE movers. Similarly, drawing on labour statistics accumulated over the first decade of CEE mobility, the European Parliament concluded that CEE movers had been experiencing lesser rates of lawful full-time employment and greater concentration in low-skill sectors than all other foreign-born workers.[40] It did not,

---

36 Commission of the European Communities (2006).
37 E.g., European Commission (2008).
38 Commission of the European Communities (2006a).
39 European Commission (2013).
40 European Parliament (2014).

however, condemn such inequalities, call for further research, or recommend that policy measures be implemented to alleviate such occurrences.

Furthermore, whenever Members of the European Parliament ('MEPs')[41] have brought examples of exploitation and discrimination faced by CEE movers to EU institutions' attention, EU representatives have expressed little concern for the movers' wellbeing. For example, MEPs had asked the European Parliament to address the institutionalised, 'blatant witch-hunt' by western politicians,[42] working conditions resembling 'modern-day slavery',[43] and EU-15 proposals to (further) curb CEE nationals' mobility and access to social benefits.[44] In responding, the Parliament has routinely failed to condemn CEE movers' poor treatment in EU-15 states as violations of fundamental rights. Instead, it has critiqued such discriminatory treatment only for reducing the potential economic benefits of mobility to the receiving (western) states. Thereby, the Parliament has helped to entrench CEE nationals' positioning as fungible, exploitable labour in the service of EU-15 economies, while further naturalising east/west inequalities and the economic core of the freedom of the right to movement.

Even in the context of discussing movers' increasingly visible exploitation during the Covid pandemic, EU institutions showed little concern for the wellbeing of CEE movers. Instead, they continued to prioritise (low-paid, precarious) CEE workers' economic importance to EU-15 states. Notably, within weeks of the imposition of national lockdowns and measures to limit free movement—illustrating how limited the reach of EU citizenship and how fragile the right of free movement can be in practice—the EU emphasised that mobility restrictions should be loosened to safeguard economic interests and the functioning of the internal market. In particular, mobility of workers in 'critical occupations' or 'essential services' (e.g., healthcare, and food sectors) was to be secured to preserve supply chains and the single market.[45] Since movers in these sectors tend to come from the CEE region—a fact which was not mentioned—the EU's priority was to maintain mobility's benefits to western states, with no concern about how movers themselves might be impacted by Covid. Notably, the Commission encouraged the creation of air corridors to facilitate temporary, ad hoc mobility of workers in essential services,[46] with no foresight about the consequent exacerbation of exploitative working conditions or about increased exposure of such workers to Covid. Throughout 2020[47] and 2021,[48] EU institutions continued to urge Member

---

41 As of 2023, there are 705 MEPs. They are elected by direct universal suffrage in each Member State, for a five-year period. The number of MEPs to which each Member State is entitled roughly corresponds to its population size.
42 European Parliament (2014a).
43 European Parliament (2014b).
44 E.g., European Parliament (2014c).
45 E.g., European Commission (2020).
46 European Commission (2020a).
47 E.g., Council Recommendation 2020/1475, 14.10.2020.
48 E.g., European Parliament (2021).

States to facilitate mobility, and to even lessen domestic quarantine requirements for movers who worked in essential occupations, in order to safeguard workings of the internal market. Since most mobility has been from east to west, this worry was directed at protecting western economies.

Notably, EU institutions overlooked CEE workers in reports devoted to protecting groups especially exposed to the pandemic's effects. Subscribing to a view of whiteness as homogeneous and uniformly privileged, the EU does not consider CEE movers to be vulnerable or racialised despite scholarly arguments and lived experience evidence to the contrary. For example, in one of its first guidelines urging Member States to better protect 'vulnerable groups' from heightened Covid risks and from pre-existing inequalities that had been exacerbated by Covid, the Commission mentioned 'racialised minorities' (that is, asylum seekers, undocumented migrants, Roma, non-whites, and non-Christians), the homeless, disabled persons, domestic violence victims, and LGBTQI groups.[49]

Although by the summer 2020, EU institutions began to acknowledge that many seasonal essential workers faced precarious working conditions and increased Covid risks, they did not draw attention to the plight of CEE seasonal workers. For example, in its June 2020 resolution on safeguarding essential workers, the European Parliament[50] acknowledged that the pandemic had exacerbated social dumping and precariousness for many cross-border (i.e., frontier) and seasonal workers—especially those working in agriculture, construction, and healthcare sectors in EU-15 states.[51] But it failed to mention how those sectors and employment arrangements are predominantly populated by CEE workers and how the pandemic had worsened their exploitation. Furthermore, by noting that cross-border and seasonal workers tend to come 'from impoverished and vulnerable regions', the Parliament implied that there are select sending regions across the EU that produce movers' vulnerabilities rather than acknowledging that their exploitation occurs at western employment sites, in western societies, and within western antagonistic political milieus. The Parliament also observed that vulnerable workers tend to originate from 'minority' groups, which, in the EU's understanding, refers to non-Caucasians and non-Christians. As always, the Parliament did not link precarious working conditions to any potential failings of the internal market or to intra-EU inequalities but instead portrayed them as aberrations by connecting them to localised subcontracting practices and inadequate domestic labour law enforcement.

Similarly, the Commission's guidelines to better protect seasonal workers during the pandemic were particularly inadequate in the context of CEE movers. The guidelines merely reminded Member States of their pre-existing obligations under EU policies and were limited to ensuring the protection of seasonal workers 'in the context of the coronavirus pandemic'.[52] Again, there

---

49 European Commission (2020b).
50 European Parliament (2020).
51 European Parliament (2020a).
52 European Commission (2020c).

was no attention drawn to CEE workers despite listing sectors which are heavily staffed by CEE movers and plagued by precarious conditions (e.g., tourism and agriculture). Notably, the guidelines failed to recognise such workers' exploitation beyond the context of the Covid pandemic, did not recommend any specific actions to improve their conditions, and did not propose any new EU initiatives.[53] Fundamentally, the need to issue such guidelines at all demonstrates the long-standing institutional failures to make mobile and migrant workers' vulnerabilities—which have been known to both national and EU institutions for years—a key issue when designing policies in support of the internal market.

It is only in response to a public outcry, after significant media and NGO attention, that the Commission acknowledged—albeit only in passing—how CEE movers had suffered in EU-15 states during the pandemic. In its annual report on labour mobility in 2021, the Commission referred to poor living, safety, and working conditions experienced during the pandemic by seasonal workers from Poland as well as from Bulgaria and Romania.[54] These observations, however, were limited in scope to only seasonal workers and to the context of the pandemic, thus portraying any such exploitation as a temporary, discrete aberration. Without placing any blame on western employers, western regulatory frameworks, or failures of the internal market, and without proposing any remedial action, the Commission normalised experiences of exploitation during non-pandemic times and of workers who are not seasonal. Furthermore, instead of problematising exploitation, the Commission reiterated the need to further facilitate mobility to continue benefiting western economies.

Negative Long-term Impact of Mobility on the CEE Region

Although CEE nationals' mobility has been linked to some positive short-term effects[55] on sending states, it has produced considerable negative long-term effects on the CEE region which EU institutions have tended to minimise. By 2009, outflow of CEE nationals resulted in 1.1% GDP loss across CEE states—especially high in Poland (1.9%), Slovakia (1.5%), and Lithuania (1.15%). By 2012, mobility decreased cumulative real GDP growth across the CEE region by

---

53 In 2020, however, the Parliament added social conditionality clause to the Common Agricultural Policy, making the payment of subsidies to agrobusiness operators conditional on providing adequate work conditions, starting in 2025. The policy is limited in scope, as it applies to agricultural workers only, and it did not create any new rights or enforcement mechanisms.
54 European Commission (2022). Notably, the Commission attributed Poles' increased return mobility between 2016 and 2019 to improving economic conditions in Poland, with no mention of their racialisation and exploitation in the west.
55 Such as reduced excess supply of labour; contributions of returnees' new skills and intangible human capital to domestic development; and receipt of remittances (although remittances have also been linked to reduced labour force participation and decreased GDPs).

an average of 7%—particularly high in the Baltic region.[56] Although during the 2010s, GDP growth across CEE states was generally positive, long-term economic concerns arose due to outflows of workers. Both independent[57] and EU-sponsored[58] studies have linked CEE mobility to negative long-term effects across the CEE region including labour shortages, significant skills mismatches, decreases in productivity and incomes per capita, long-term unemployment, breakups of family units, and erosion of public funding (particularly for pensions and medical services). Notably, CEE nationals engaging in mobility have tended to be younger, better skilled, and more educated than stayers. Brain drain of highly-skilled CEE nationals has inhibited innovation as well as social and political improvements in the region. Between 2004 and 2016, the share of high-skilled movers tripled across the EU, largely driven by movers from Poland, Slovakia, and the Baltic states, as well as from Bulgaria and Romania. The Baltic states and Slovakia have experienced an especially significant exodus of medical professionals to EU-15 states leading to severe medical care deficits particularly in smaller towns and villages.[59]

Mobility-driven population drain, exaggerated by low reproduction rates, has been significant across the CEE region. For example, within a year of the Eastern Enlargement, the working-age population had shrunk by 3.3% in Lithuania. By 2008, labour force across the whole CEE region had contracted by 1.16%, with Poland and Slovakia especially affected. Between 2000 and 2010, CEE states had lost on average 3.7% of their populations. In Lithuania, population declined by 10.4%. Predictions indicate further significant population decreases across the CEE region largely driven by intra-EU mobility. Latvia, Lithuania, and Poland, as well as Romania, are expected to experience some of the biggest relative population declines in the world by 2050—of approximately 40% on average—including many workers engaged in healthcare and care sectors.[60] In addition to aforementioned economic and social concerns, population drain has been linked to the rise of radical-right and authoritarian politicians.[61] Since the 2008 global financial crisis, labour mobility has increased exclusively among certain CEE sending countries—Hungary, Slovakia, and Poland, as well as Bulgaria and Romania. Radical-right parties have flourished in these states typically advocating xenophobia, conservative social values, authoritarian government institutions, and media censorship, consequently giving rise to concerns over democratic backsliding.

56 Similarly, the long-term impact of mobility has been negative on Bulgaria and Romania. Despite substantial remittances, by 2011, mobility was linked to 9.2% decrease in their collective GDP and 2.5% decrease in output per capita.
57 E.g., Horridge and Rokicki (2018). See generally Patuzzi and Benton (2020).
58 E.g., Holland et al. (2011).
59 Similar outflow has occurred from Bulgaria and Romania. For example, in 2020, 25% of doctors trained in Romania worked abroad, prompting the Romanian government to propose restricting its nationals' mobility.
60 Organisation for Economic Cooperation and Development (2020).
61 Finnsdottir (2019).

Notably, some of this exodus of CEE workers has been further fuelled by EU fiscal policies, especially those adopted in response to the 2008 economic crisis, which have made living in the CEE region more difficult for many. For example, the EU imposed fiscal control and austerity measures on Latvia which produced especially detrimental effects on its health care provision. Hungary received bailout packages from the IMF which entailed implementing strict spending cuts including freezing public sector wages, raising the retirement age, and reducing welfare provision.[62] Slovenia and Slovakia, as parts of the Eurozone, were forced to implement austerity measures in accordance with the European Monetary Union's guidelines. More generally, since the European Monetary Union coordinates economic and fiscal policies of all Member States, its post-crisis emphasis on austerity has had negative repercussions for all CEE states, exacerbating pre-existing east/west economic inequalities.

EU institutions have tended to avoid associating CEE nationals' mobility with such negative developments in the CEE region. For example, four years after the Enlargement, the Commission attributed brain drain and labour shortages in CEE states to their domestic economic and demographic factors, without referring to any research in support of such a conclusion.[63] The Commission also sought to minimise the significance of any negative developments that might be linked to mobility emphasising, for example, that labour shortages have been mostly sector-specific, that some workers were likely to return, and that increasing enrolment rates in tertiary education across CEE states would eventually compensate for the outflow of skilled labour. More recently, EU institutions have attributed population drain across the CEE region to aging[64] and to the Covid pandemic and have emphasised that it has been confined to rural areas.[65]

It was only after the Committee of the Regions[66] lobbied the EU in 2020 to provide compensation to CEE states for brain drain[67] that the EU finally acknowledged that mobility has been 'imbalanced' and 'uneven'.[68] But again, the EU emphasised mobility's positive effects on CEE states and placed the responsibility on the sending states to make their de-populated regions more appealing to potential stayers. Moreover, the Commission admitted in 2023 that 'acute' population declines in some CEE states can be linked to 'high levels of emigration', noting that this 'can exacerbate existing economic, social and territorial inequalities, and provoke political divides'.[69] But the EU has continued

---

62 Similarly, Romania was forced by the IMF to institute some of the most severe austerity measures in Europe.
63 European Commission (2008a).
64 E.g., European Commission (2020d).
65 E.g., European Commission (2021a).
66 The EU's assembly of local and regional Member State representatives.
67 Committee of the Regions (2020).
68 Council of the EU (2020).
69 European Commission (2023).

to fail to acknowledge large-scale structural causes behind such processes. As I argue throughout this book, CEE population drain is attributable to economic and social inequalities between eastern and western parts of the EU reinforced through long-standing and contemporary western policies and discourse peripheralising the east.

Economic Benefits of CEE Mobility to EU-15 States

On the other hand, EU-15 states have greatly profited from CEE mobility. In addition to enriching host state cultures, intra-EU mobility has economically benefited receiving EU-15 states by increasing their outputs and public finances, promoting economic growth, and allowing for better matching of labour demand and supply.[70] On average, CEE movers have been contributing more to EU-15 fiscal purses than native or non-EU workers have[71] especially after post-accession transitional mobility derogations ended in 2011. Despite contrary public and political rhetoric, CEE movers have been shown to rely less on public welfare than host states' native populations do and have not disproportionately crowded out native workers or lowered their wages. As shown by independent studies[72] and noted by EU institutions,[73] the combined GDP of EU-15 states between 2004 and 2009 increased by up to 1% due to post-2004 mobility. More recent studies have confirmed CEE movers' positive impact on EU-15 collective GDP, GDPs per capita, and employment rates.[74] Furthermore, CEE mobility has been associated with overall improvements in labour market integration of *all* foreign workers as measured by increased probability of labour market entry within one year after arrival in host countries.[75] The greatest positive economic effects of CEE mobility have been observed in states with the largest numbers of CEE workers—that is, the UK, Ireland, and Germany.[76] For example, by 2011, 3% of Ireland's GDP could be attributed to CEE mobility.[77]

CEE workers' benefits to EU-15 economies have derived from their high degree of responsiveness to changing labour opportunities in the west.[78] Transitional mobility restrictions likely facilitated this demand-driven CEE mobility as EU-15 states were given discretion to choose the numbers and types of CEE workers they would admit, while national restrictions on residence rights and access to social benefits incentivised CEE movers to take up any jobs available—including through precarious and flexible arrangements—and disincentivised them from

---

70 See, e.g., Barslund and Busse (2014); European Commission (2020e).
71 See, e.g., Nyman and Ahlskog (2018); Dustmann and Frattini (2014).
72 E.g., Holland et al. (2011).
73 E.g., European Commission (2013a).
74 E.g., Kahanec and Pytliková (2017).
75 Kosyakova and Brücker (2021).
76 Organisation for Economic Co-operation and Development (2012).
77 Holland et al. (2011).
78 Kahanec et al. (2016).

relying on benefits in host states. Moreover, CEE movers have had high employment rates—hovering at close to 80%, with Poles' rate as high as 90%. These rates have been higher by at least 10% than those of host state nationals.

EU institutions have long praised CEE workers' responsiveness to the needs of the increasingly flexible western labour markets as an effective adjustment mechanism.[79] Despite acknowledging that labour market flexibilisation relies heavily on precarious jobs[80] and has resulted in poor working conditions and inadequate social protections for workers, the Commission has supported it[81]— a far cry from its fundamental-rights rhetoric discussed in the preceding chapter. Similarly, according to the European Parliament, to address unemployment and labour shortages across the EU, 'it is essential to take steps to provide greater flexibility ... increase mobility, and make the markets more adaptable'.[82] The EU's support of flexibilisation, praise of CEE workers' willingness to participate in flexible western labour markets and under precarious conditions, and an acknowledgement of EU-15 economies' need for such workers became especially poignant during the Covid pandemic, as previously discussed. This neo-liberal economic approach poses little, if any, burden on EU-15 state welfare systems as precarious workers often do not qualify for social benefits or have difficulty proving their eligibility. Notably, as I will further address below, while reaping the benefits of CEE labour, both EU institutions and EU-15 states have been erecting more stringent impediments to precarious movers' access to social rights.

The Right to Free Movement

How can CEE nationals' actual experience of mobility be situated within EU and western state policies and discourses on the freedom of movement right and ancillary rights that support mobility? As my discussion below indicates, the right of free movement continues to be inextricably linked to economic goals. Despite grandiose narratives about fundamental rights and the creation of EU citizenship in 1993, the adoption of the Citizens' Rights Directive 2004/38 did not reshape its economic core. Furthermore, EU-15 states have expended ongoing efforts to curtail movers' rights—targeting CEE nationals. EU institutions have tolerated, and at times directly facilitated, this approach. Meanwhile, protections from ethnic discrimination under the Race Equality Directive 2000/43 have been particularly inadequate in the context of racialised whites, and the broader equality discourse has overlooked CEE movers' racialisation. Moreover, both equality policies and discourse have been connected to facilitating

---

79 E.g., European Commission (2012).
80 Including fixed-term, part-time, on-call, zero-hour, and freelance contracts, and temporary employment agency arrangements.
81 E.g., Commission of the European Communities (2006).
82 European Parliament (2006).

the workings of the internal market, rather than to protecting human rights. Although CEE states were not involved during the adoption of either of these two directives, as both preceded the Eastern Enlargement, the continued marginalisation of CEE nationals' interests through policies and discourses pertaining to free movement, social rights, and equality attests to the dominance of western priorities including western host states' economic interests.

Background

Since the beginnings of the EU project, mobility and social prerogatives have been inextricably linked with economic goals. The EU's foundational documents refer to a 'social market economy' which seeks to imbue the single internal market with social protection attributes. That is, the EU strives for a 'highly competitive social market economy', in order to promote the 'well-being of its people', through rights such as free movement.[83] The types of persons who were initially afforded access to mobility indicate its economic core and the inherent preference for temporary movement of workers that responds to specific labour needs. Pursuant to the 1951 Treaty of Paris,[84] blue-collar workers in the steel and coal sectors were encouraged to cross borders for temporary employment to aid post-war recovery across western Europe. The 1957 Treaty of Rome[85] established a common market based on the free movement of goods, people, services, and capital, mandating that free movement rights become extended to all workers (except those in the public sector). This aim was then realised through successive binding legislations including Regulation 15/61[86] which provided Member State nationals with the right to take up employment in other Member States as long as there were no host state workers available for the job. However, it was not until 1968[87] that mobile workers' rights were fully implemented within the six founding Member States on the same conditions as those afforded to host-state nationals.

Building upon Treaty equality rights,[88] Regulation 1612/68 granted workers protections from nationality discrimination in host states in employment,

---

83 Consolidated version of the Treaty on the Functioning of the European Union, Article 3.
84 Treaty Establishing the European Coal and Steel Community.
85 Treaty Establishing the European Economic Community.
86 Council Regulation 15/61 of 16 August 1961 on initial measures to bring about free movement of workers within the Community. See also Directive of 16 August 1961 on administrative procedures and practices governing the entry into and employment and residence in a Member State of workers and their families from other Member States of the Community.
87 Regulation 1612/68 of the Council of 15 October 1968 on freedom of movement for workers within the Community.
88 Specifically, Treaty Article 12 prohibits 'any discrimination on grounds of nationality' that falls '[w]ithin the scope of application of this Treaty', and Article 39 prohibits nationality discrimination in 'employment, remuneration and other conditions of work and employment'. See Treaty Establishing the European

remuneration, and other conditions of work. EU institutions' prohibition of discrimination against mobile workers was guided by broad economic goals rather than by concerns with improving workers' wellbeing. For example, the Commission has acknowledged that the goal of nationality anti-discrimination protections is to reduce employers' use of worker exploitation as 'an instrument of competition'[89] which would inhibit the EU's economic success. This is in line with Derrick Bell's observation that steps to promote equality tend to be taken when they benefit the dominant group.[90]

Looking back to the 'aspirational view' ascribed to Jean Monnet,[91] that the purpose of EU integration is to 'unite[] men, not to build a coalition of governments',[92] western politicians have linked the EU project and the common market to the idea of a collective citizenship. Experts tend to approach free movement as the embodiment of EU citizenship.[93] A closer look at the legislative history of the construct of EU citizenship reveals that, in addition to its political and symbolic values, it has been largely limited to its economic importance, in line with the long-standing western approach towards the free movement right. The 1957 Treaty of Rome conferred some elements of a collective citizenship—including the right of free movement of workers, with the affiliated rights of residence and coordinated social security benefits. Notably, as noted in its Preamble, these rights were created in order to develop a common market and 'establish the foundations of an ever closer union among the European peoples'.[94] Thus, citizenship, free movement (of workers), and economic priorities were acknowledged as inherently linked.

In 1990, Spain proposed that EU citizenship be recognised as a Treaty right[95] in order to strengthen territorial cohesion across the EU, inspire public loyalty to the integration project, and improve its democratic legitimacy. The resultant 1993 Maastricht Treaty created the construct of EU citizenship, automatically available to all persons who are citizens of EU Member States, and mandated that '[e]very citizen of the Union shall have the right to move and reside freely within the territory of the Member States'.[96] In practice, the impact of this Treaty addition has been more limited than the grandiose language might

Community (Nice Consolidated Version) ('EC Treaty'). The ECJ defines movers' equality rights broadly—to include 'all rights or benefits which in any way impact on the ability ... to exercise the right to move and reside' in other Member States. See *Elsen v Bundesversicherungsandstalt fur Angestellte*, Case C-135/99, ECLI:EU: C:2000:647.
89 Commission of the European Communities (1993).
90 Bell (1980).
91 French politician often called 'The Father of Europe' due to his efforts in establishing the European Coal and Steel Community.
92 Committee of the Regions (2000).
93 E.g., Everson (1995).
94 Treaty Establishing the European Economic Community, Preamble.
95 Spanish Delegation, Intergovernmental Conference on Political Union (1990).
96 Treaty on European Union, Article 8a(1).

suggest as the right of citizenship is 'subject to the limitations and conditions laid down in the Treaties and by the measures adopted to give them effect'.[97] Notably, pursuant to Article 49, the Council was instructed to issue legislation to bring about 'freedom of movement for workers' only. Both the Treaty's implementing EU policies—such as the Citizens' Rights Directive 2000/43 (discussed below)—and the margin of discretion left to the Member States when effectuating mobility and related policies have been shaping the scope and practice of citizenship and free movement rights since then, prioritising their economic core. Notably, while strengthening connections between EU citizenship and movers' rights, the ECJ has often referred to arguments about labour concerns in EU-15 states[98]—favouring western economic needs while making citizenship conditional on making sufficient employment contributions.

The freedom of movement right is also inherently linked to having equal access to welfare and other host-state support. Pursuant to Treaty rights, all mobile EU citizens are entitled to equal treatment with respect to all benefits (which includes social and tax advantages) falling within the scope of EU law. Movers' access to social rights on par with host sate nationals has been reaffirmed through several market-enabling legislations. Notably, Regulation 883/2004 mandates the coordination of social security benefits systems, without harmonising them, so that Member States determine the types and amounts of benefits to be granted to movers. It pertains to social security (contributory) benefits and special non-contributory cash benefits ('SNCB') (e.g., sickness, maternity/paternity, old-age, survivor, unemployment, family, pre-retirement, work accident, and occupational disease benefits).[99] Moreover, Regulation 492/2011[100] mandates equality of mobile workers and jobseekers in access to training, housing, social and tax advantages, and jobseekers' assistance.

EU competence in the sphere of social policies is limited, however, and Member States control the configuration and distribution of social rights. Notably, under Directive 2004/38, Member States have been afforded wide discretion in conferring social assistance to movers and having the ability to expel movers who become an 'unreasonable burden' on their social assistance systems, as discussed below. In addition to imposing direct transitional post-accession mobility derogations, the main leeway that Member States have had in trying to affect the free movement right has been through their social benefits frameworks which turned welfare provisions into an especially sensitive issue in the context of the accession of states with greater economic asymmetries and which helps to explain EU-15 states' ongoing efforts to curtail CEE movers' social rights.

97 Ibid., Article 21.
98 E.g., *Martínez Sala v Freistaat Bayern*, Case C-85/96, ECLI:EU:C:1998:217.
99 Regulation 883/2004 of the European Parliament and Council of 29 April 2004 on the coordination of social security systems.
100 Regulation 492/2011 of 5 April 2011 on freedom of movement for workers within the Union.

Finally, the right to free movement is also intrinsically connected to broader protections from discrimination in host states beyond just those prohibiting nationality discrimination. Unfortunately, the Race Equality Directive 2000/38 has been particularly unfit for protecting CEE movers' rights. It reflects EU-15 states' economic and political interests. CEE movers' concerns have also been overlooked or silenced in the broader EU equality discourse and soft law instruments. Overall, the right to equality—like the right to free movement to which it has been intimately linked—has been limited in practice and indicates a schism between EU ideals and actual policies. In the process, CEE movers' status as second-class EU citizens has been naturalised, thereby entrenching inequalities and fractures within whiteness.

Movers' Rights under the Citizens' Rights Directive 2004/38

By the late 1990s, the Commission had been placed on alert due to frequent reports pertaining to various domestic administrative procedures hindering mobility. To address this, the Commission assembled the High Level Panel on the Free Movement of Persons. Its 1997 report[101] prompted the Commission to recommend adopting a directive to strengthen the freedom of movement right. Despite the Maastricht Treaty's provision of the free movement right to all EU citizens in 1993, the Commission proposed extending mobility to all citizens, without formalities, for up to six months only. To strengthen the right of free movement, however, it also recommended creating a new right of permanent residence after four years of residence in host states.[102] With the impending Eastern Enlargement, however, EU-15 states sought to water down the Commission's proposals, especially after their fears of 'welfare tourism' became increasingly politicised in response to the ECJ's expansive rulings in *Martinez Sala*[103] in 1998 (that even economically inactive movers may appeal to Treaty non-discrimination principles to access social assistance benefits in host states) and *Grzelczyk*[104] in 2001 (that Member States may not limit access to subsistence allowance to lawfully residing movers including those economically inactive).

Because EU-15 states desired to have the new instrument agreed upon before the Eastern Enlargement, so that CEE states could not voice any opposition to it, the Citizens' Rights Directive 2004/38[105] was adopted fairly swiftly. Signed two days before the Enlargement took place, the Directive consolidated dispersed pre-existing legislative instruments (two regulations and nine directives) and ECJ rulings

101 Report of the High Level Panel on the Free Movement of Persons, COM 7035/97.
102 European Commission (2001).
103 *Martínez Sala*, Case C-86/96, ECLI:EU:C:1998:217.
104 *Grzelczyk v Centre public d'aide sociale d'Ottignies-Louvain-la-Neuve*, Case C-184/99, ECLI:EU:C:2001:458.
105 Directive 2004/38/EC of 29 April 2004 on the right of citizens of the Union and their family members to move and reside freely within the territory of the Member States.

pertaining to mobility, residence, and social rights—shaping the current scope of the right of free movement. The Directive strengthened substantive and procedural safeguards available to EU citizens who elect to engage in free movement. Notably, it expanded the right to reside in other Member States to all EU citizens for up to three months without any formalities or conditions (Article 6), extended movers' right to be joined by family members (Article 3), and granted a new right of permanent residence after five years of lawful residence in a host state (Articles 16–17). On the other hand, at western states' urging, the Directive endowed Member States with greater discretion than had been available previously to limit movers' access to residence and social rights. Importantly, the right to reside for longer than three months is provided only to (1) 'workers' and self-employed persons (or those able to retain such status upon becoming involuntarily unemployed), and (2) those who are economically inactive but possess 'comprehensive sickness insurance' and 'sufficient resources' so as not to become a burden on the social assistance system of the receiving state (Article 7).

Key Provisions of the Citizens' Rights Directive

In line with pre-existing EU law, workers' rights are privileged under Directive 2004/38. According to Article 7(1), workers (including self-employed individuals) have an automatic right to reside in other Member States for longer than three months without any conditions. The ECJ has defined the concept of a 'worker' broadly[106]—as applying to anyone engaging in any 'effective' and 'genuine' employment activity which is more than purely marginal and ancillary.[107] The ECJ does not require minimum working hours or wages.[108] 'Worker' status also cannot be denied simply due to a short period of employment but only on the basis of an individual assessment of the overall employment relationship.[109] Thus, those employed under fixed-term or training contracts or in part-time work can qualify as workers. Relying on the host state's social security system to supplement insufficient income does not automatically prevent such individuals from qualifying as workers—even if their main aim of securing work in a host state was to obtain access to its public assistance.[110] From day one of qualifying as a worker, equal access to the host state's social security benefits[111] (Regulation 883/2004, Article 3),

---

106 *Trojani v Centre public d'aide sociale de Bruxelles*, Case C-456/02, ECLI:EU:C: 2004:488.
107 *Ninni-Orasche v Bundesminister für Wissenschaft, Verkehr und Kunst*, Case C-413/01, ECLI:EU:C:2003:600.
108 Even working fewer than 5.5 hours per week has been found sufficient.
109 *Vatsouras and Koupatantze v Arbeitsgemeinschaft Nürnberg*, Case C-22/08, ECLI:EU:C:2009:344.
110 *Ninni-Orasche*, Case C-413/01, ECLI:EU:C:2003:600.
111 That is, (1) contributory benefits (including old-age pensions, survivor's pensions, disability benefits, sickness benefits, birth grants, unemployment benefits, family allowances, and healthcare benefits), and (2) special non-contributory cash benefits

social and tax advantages[112] (Regulation 1612/68, Article 7(2)), and social assistance (Directive 2004/38, Article 24(2)) follows. The ECJ has supported workers' receipt of all these benefits.

The Directive's legislative history and the politicisation of CEE movers' anticipated abuse of rights in EU-15 states help to explain the vagueness of some of the Directive's provisions and the resultant discretion afforded to host states to limit movers' access to residence rights. This has been particularly significant in the context of movers who do not qualify as 'workers'. Notably, under Article 7(1)(b), to reside in host states for longer than three months, economically inactive movers—such as students, pensioners, or those who are long-term unemployed—must demonstrate having 'sufficient resources' (so that they do not become an 'unreasonable burden' on the social assistance system of receiving states) and 'comprehensive sickness insurance', neither of which is defined in the Directive. Determining 'sufficient resources' is a fact-intensive, individualised process to be made at the host state's discretion and based on the host state's cost of living, although the Directive forbids host states from laying down specific fixed amounts (Article 8(4)).

Member States are endowed with discretion to deny economically inactive movers' access to social assistance (means-tested and non-contributory benefits) during the first three months of residence (Article 24(2)). After that period, however, economically inactive movers' access is to be the same as that of host state nationals albeit movers must also demonstrate self-sufficiency so that they do not lose their right to reside. Before its more restrictive post-2010 jurisprudence (discussed later on in this chapter), the ECJ used to afford economically inactive movers access to social benefits as long as they could demonstrate a 'real link' to host-state society based on a holistic determination of factors such as the duration of stay in the host country, intentions, and family situation.[113] Pursuant to the ECJ, the test was to be broad and flexible and would not be satisfied only when it was inconceivable that a real link exists.[114] The test could even be met by recently unemployed movers since they do not lose worker status for at least six months following involuntary unemployment (Article 7(3)).[115] However, as discussed below, several EU-15 states used the Directive's vagueness to adopt policies to limit economically inactive (CEE) movers' access to social security and to SNCBs.

Like all economically inactive movers, those who enter another Member State to seek employment must demonstrate being self-sufficient and having sickness

---

(such as income support or jobseeker's allowance). Non-contributory benefits fall outside the scope of EU law.
112 Such as benefits associated with improving professional qualifications (e.g., study maintenance grants).
113 *Swaddling v Adjudication Officer*, Case C-90/97, ECLI:EU:C:1999:96.
114 *Office national de l'emploi v Ioannidis*, Case C-258/04, ECLI:EU:C:2005:559.
115 Expiration of a fixed-term contract can amount to involuntary unemployment. *Ninni-Orasche*, Case C-413/01, ECLI:EU:C:2003:600.

insurance (Article 7(1)). Article 14(4)(b) prohibits first-time jobseekers' expulsion, however, as long as they are 'continuing to seek employment' and are deemed to have a 'genuine chance' of finding employment—that is, if they can demonstrate some prospects of finding employment, even after having been searching for more than six months.[116] This protection from expulsion has been interpreted by the ECJ as providing first-time jobseekers with the right to reside in other Member States without having to prove self-sufficiency.[117] The ECJ has supported the mobility of first-time jobseekers, perceiving it to be necessary to encouraging labour mobility. Furthermore, even though under Article 24(2) host states may deny access to social assistance for as long as jobseekers remain in that status, the ECJ has limited the scope of that provision by ruling that it does not apply to social benefits 'intended to facilitate access to the labour market'—such as jobseeker's allowance which must be granted whenever a jobseeker can demonstrate a 'real link' with the host country's labour market. To demonstrate this, a jobseeker may present evidence of having been invited to job interviews, registering as a jobseeker with employment agencies, and participating in events organised by such agencies over the course of a 'reasonable' period of time even without ever having worked.[118] By facilitating the movement of jobseekers, EU law better responds to (western) employers' needs and has promoted (CEE) movers' undertaking any labour arrangements including precarious and flexible ones.

The Directive endows receiving states with the ability to terminate residence rights of (1) economically inactive movers who lack 'sufficient resources' or 'comprehensive sickness insurance' (if they have not yet become permanent residents), and (2) first-time jobseekers who are not deemed to be continuing to seek employment or to have a genuine chance of finding it (Article 14). As discussed below, during the 2010s, the ECJ became more restrictive by interpreting 'sufficient resources' and 'unreasonable burden' tests stringently so as to endow host states with great discretion to impede mobility of movers who do not qualify as 'workers'. As intra-EU mobility has been mostly from east to west, all these discretionary clauses have served primarily to protect EU-15 states. Moreover, provisions tied to 'sufficient resources' have functioned as a greater impediment to the rights of CEE as opposed to EU-15 movers due to CEE states' lower average GDPs. For example, in 2003, Latvia's GDP (in terms of purchasing power) represented 42% of the EU-25 average GDP, and both Poland's and Lithuania's represented 46% of the EU-25 average. On the other hand, Austria's stood at 121%, the UK's at 119%, France's at 113%, and Germany's at 108% of the EU-25 average.[119] Despite the fact that wages and GDPs have been increasing across the CEE region, significant wage differentials

---

116 *The Queen v Immigration Appeal Tribunal, ex parte Antonissen*, Case C-292/89, ECLI:EU:C:1991:80.
117 *Collins v Secretary of State for Work and Pensions*, Case C-138/02, ECLI:EU:C:2004:172.
118 *Prete v Office national de l'emploi*, Case C-367/11, ECLI:EU:C:2012:668.
119 Eurostat (2004).

between east and west persist. For example, in 2016, average hourly labour costs amounted to just under €31 in EU-15 states and to approximately €11 in CEE states. Today, monthly gross minimum wages continue to vary considerably between CEE and EU-14 states. For example, they are €2,080 in Germany and €1,709 in France but only €743 in Poland and €620 in Latvia.

EU-15 States' Restraints on CEE Movers' Rights

Directive 2004/38 was to be transposed into domestic legislations in EU-15 states by 2006. Transposition approaches varied from amending pre-existing laws to adopting entirely new measures. Many states, however, failed to timely, effectively, and precisely transpose the Directive into domestic laws. Between the end of the transposition period and early 2007, the Commission initiated infringement proceedings against Belgium, Germany, Luxembourg, Finland, Sweden, and the UK for improper or inadequate transposition. At the end of 2008, the Commission reported that the overall transposition efforts had been 'rather disappointing'.[120] By that time, not a single Member State had transposed the Directive correctly in its entirety. Moreover, not a single Article of the Directive had been transposed accurately by all the Member States. It is true that directive transpositions are always marred by problems and delays—largely dependent on how unpopular a new measure is with voters, domestic leadership priorities, administrative capacity, legal complexity and ambiguity of a specific directive,[121] as well as the chosen method of transposition.[122] However, several features of Directive 2004/38 should have facilitated its swift transposition. Notably, many of its parts reflect pre-existing EU law which EU-15 states should have been already following, and the vagueness of several of its provisions should have appealed to Member States as it preserved their significant discretion in key areas.

Resistance among EU-15 states to transposing the Directive was motivated, at least in part, by opposition to the looming mobility of CEE nationals. Notably, EU-15 states narrowly interpreted the Directive's key provisions, took advantage of the vagueness of some of its terms (e.g., 'sufficient resources') and of the inherent domestic flexibility in interpreting them, and failed to transpose some of its safeguards. Discretion in the Directive's domestic applications opened space for subjective decision-making and inconsistent access to mobility rights even within Member States. The widespread anti-CEE sentiment and populist discontent across EU-15 states at the time of the Eastern Enlargement and since has further disadvantaged CEE movers.

In addition, many EU-15 states adopted additional statutory and discretionary administrative measures—some in contravention of the Directive—to limit

---

120 Commission of the European Communities (2008a).
121 See generally Koning and Luetger (2008).
122 Doing so through primary legislation takes longer than through secondary regulations.

movers' rights of entry, residence for more than three months, permanent residence, and access to social assistance.[123] Restrictive approaches across EU-15 states were motivated by concerns over CEE movers' alleged welfare tourism. Some EU-15 policies—or their discretionary applications—directly targeted CEE movers. Moreover, even if restrictive domestic regulations applied to all movers, they have had a disproportionately negative effect on CEE nationals due to east/west economic differentials and the propensity of CEE movers to be employed in precarious and low-paid positions in EU-15 states. Transposed Directive provisions, and supplementary restrictive EU-15 measures and practices, became applicable before 2011 to CEE movers to whom transitional post-accession mobility derogations did not apply and to all EU movers after 2011.

Complaints lodged by movers help to illustrate some of the EU-15 policies and practices that were adopted contemporaneously with the Directive's transposition and with the Eastern Enlargement to target CEE nationals' mobility. For example, individual complaints that EU institutions received during 2006–08 revealed various national administrative measures to limit mobility rights beyond what is sanctioned by the Directive.[124] Movers have often been required to present additional documentary evidence when applying for entry or for permanent residence, which are not required under the Directive, such as work permits, proof of not having a criminal record, evidence of satisfactory living conditions, and documentation of the legality of income sources.

A study commissioned by the European Parliament in 2009[125] exposed various EU-15 efforts to limit the scope of the Directive's rights—often via secondary domestic legislations and the use of administrative discretion—which disproportionately affected the rights of CEE nationals. For example, when accessing administrative services in some EU-15 states such as Belgium, CEE nationals have had to use different service counters than EU-15 nationals. A disproportionate number of complaints made to the Commission's Citizens Signpost Service[126] have pertained to CEE nationals' rights of entry and residence in EU-15 states. Notably, CEE nationals have reported being questioned upon arrival in EU-15 states regarding the purpose of their entry, contrary to the Directive. CEE nationals have also disproportionately complained about receiving notices of termination of their right to remain in EU-15 states due to recourse to social assistance in breach of Article 14(3) of the Directive. Disappointingly, despite having initially instituted several infringement procedures

---

123 See generally Blauberger and Schmidt (2017).
124 Commission of the European Communities (2008a).
125 European Parliament (2009). As of February 2023 there have been no newer comprehensive EU reports issued on the right of free movement, except in the contexts of (1) transitional arrangements imposed against Bulgarian, Romanian, and Croatian nationals, and (2) Covid.
126 Citizens Signpost Service assists EU citizens in asserting their EU rights. Free of charge and available in all EU languages, it provides advise, and makes referrals to the Solvit network for problem-solving.

in the context of transposition defects, EU institutions have voiced little opposition to such additional domestic measures or discretionary practices developed across EU-15 states to target CEE movers' rights. Indicative exemplars of restrictive, and at times discriminatory, EU-15 approaches are discussed below.

i. Right of Residence For Up To Three Months

Under Article 6(1) of the Directive, for residence of up to three months, movers must simply present a valid ID card or passport. There are no other requirements or conditions that must be satisfied. In Belgium, however, EU citizens were required to report their presence to the authorities within ten days of arrival unless they were staying in a hotel or were imprisoned or hospitalised. A €200 fine was imposed against those failing to comply.

ii. Right of Residence For More Than Three Months

Under Article 7(1)(b), economically inactive movers who desire to reside in host states for more than three months must have 'sufficient resources' (as not to become 'a burden' on host social assistance systems) and 'comprehensive sickness insurance' though neither of these terms is defined by the Directive. Article 8(4) mandates that 'sufficient resources' cannot be set at a fixed amount through Member State policies but must instead 'take into account the personal situation' of each mover. Article 8(4) is somewhat ambiguous, however, which reflects the intensive debates regarding 'sufficient resources' among EU-15 Member States and the Commission leading up to the Directive's adoption immediately before the Eastern Enlargement. Although it requires host states to consider the personal situation of each mover, it permits domestic thresholds to be set at the level at which host-state nationals become eligible for social assistance benefits. Many EU-15 states implemented strict rules and administrative practices when transposing and applying 'sufficient resources' and 'comprehensive sickness insurance' requirements, leading to restrictions on economically inactive movers' residence and social rights.[127]

For starters, many EU-15 states did not adopt a clear legislative definition of 'sufficient resources'. Some automatically linked it to national minimum income levels or levels at which host-state nationals became eligible for social assistance (e.g., in Belgium, France, the Netherlands, Austria, and Ireland). Connecting the 'sufficient resources' requirement to social assistance eligibility thresholds deviated from holistic personal evaluations and disadvantaged movers from poorer regions of the EU and those who were in low-paid employment. Notably, many EU-15 states (including Belgium, Germany, Finland, Ireland, Italy, Luxembourg, the Netherlands, and Sweden) imposed specific stringent evidentiary requirements, obligating movers to present work permits or to prove

---

127 See generally Mantu and Minderhoud (2019).

satisfactory housing conditions, without taking into account personal circumstances holistically. Some EU-15 states implemented the 'sufficient resources' clause in an overly vague and discretionary manner. For example, in Ireland, determination of resources was to be based on a 'detailed examination' of the personal circumstances of the mover, with no clarity as to what such a potentially intrusive and subjective examination entailed.

EU-15 states also interpreted the 'comprehensive sickness insurance' requirement in restrictive ways, to impose impediments on movers from poorer Member States and those in low-paid employment. The Commission had made it clear that this requirement could be satisfied through having any type of sickness insurance, obtained in any state, as long as it provided comprehensive coverage and did not create a burden on the host state's public finances.[128] EU-15 states, however, came up with methods to make this requirement difficult to satisfy. For example, in France, economically inactive movers were automatically excluded from the national health service. Similarly, in Sweden, registering with the Swedish tax authority was a prerequisite for accessing public health insurance thereby making it impossible to access for economically inactive movers. Moreover, none of the Swedish private health insurance plans were judged by Swedish authorities to satisfy the Directive's requirements. In the UK, the Home Office opined that having access to the public national health service was insufficient, so movers would need to obtain additional coverage. Similarly, Ireland required movers to present documentation from private insurance providers of having a comprehensive private insurance plan.

More generally, various administrative formalities that are more demanding than those dictated under the Directive were imposed across EU-15 states to impede movers' right of residence for more than three months. For example, Article 14(2) allows host states to verify that movers satisfy conditions of eligibility for residence of more than three months but mandates that such verification must 'not be carried out systematically' and may only be imposed if there is 'reasonable doubt' pertaining to eligibility. Denmark, Ireland, France, Italy, and Austria, however, did not prohibit systematic verification of the conditions attached to the right of residence. Moreover, under Article 8(1), host states are permitted to require movers residing therein for more than three months to have to register with relevant authorities. According to Article 8(2), however, any such registration obligation may not be imposed until after three months from the date of arrival. Moreover, if imposed, any such requirement must result in the issuance of registration certificates immediately upon registration and any sanctions imposed for failure to comply must be 'proportionate and non-discriminatory'. France, however, required movers to register with local authorities *within* three months of entry and imposed fines of between €450 and €750 for failure to do so. Belgium adopted an inconsistent approach—although movers were *not* required to obtain registration certificates for stays

---

128 Commission of the European Communities (2009).

exceeding three months, they could be detained if unable to present a registration certificate when asked to do so by government officials. Moreover, movers who could not produce documents deemed necessary by Belgian authorities to obtain a registration certificate in the first place could be automatically expelled—action which is not permitted under the Directive.

EU-15 states also attempted to reduce the Directive's general protections against expulsion. Although under Article 14(3) host states are not permitted to expel movers as 'an automatic consequence' of their recourse to social assistance therein, Austria, Belgium, Germany, Denmark, France, Ireland, and Italy did not prohibit detention and expulsion as an automatic consequence of such recourse. Moreover, in Belgium, before obtaining permanent residence, the right to reside could be terminated automatically upon reliance on social assistance for more than three months at any point during residing therein. EU-15 states were also threatening movers whose applications for social assistance were unsuccessful with the loss of their residence rights thus likely deterring some movers from applying for support in the first place. In some host states, including Finland and Italy, automatic expulsions due to lacking sufficient resources were disproportionately exercised against CEE nationals as well as those from Romania.

iii. Retention of Worker Status

Across EU-15 states, various approaches were also adopted to limit rights afforded to former workers. Under Article 7(3) of the Directive, former workers (including those who were self-employed) retain their worker status if they become (i) involuntarily unemployed (as long as they register as jobseekers with the host state employment office) or (ii) temporarily unable to work as a result of an illness or accident. In the case of those involuntarily unemployed, worker status is retained indefinitely if they had worked for more than a year in the host state, and it is retained for at least six months if they had worked for less than a year. Austria, Belgium, Germany, France, Ireland, Italy, the Netherlands, Sweden, and the UK did not provide for the retention of worker status under Article 7(3). Instead, they created more narrow provisions for the retention of the right of residence only which does not confer the same extent of rights as afforded to those categorised as workers. This enabled EU-15 states to expel former workers and to deny them access to social rights which is particularly problematic for low-paid workers. It also impeded such former workers' ability to accrue the time necessary to be eligible for permanent residence.

iv. Right of Permanent Residence

EU-15 states also attempted to directly limit the right of permanent residence which the Directive had created. Under Article 16(1), movers who had resided lawfully for a continuous period of five years in the host state have the right of permanent residence therein. Even though no such limitation exists in the Directive, Belgium and the UK failed to take into account periods of residence acquired by EU citizens prior to their countries' accessions to the EU in order to target CEE nationals who might have been residing in EU-15 states before 2004. Despite the fact that such CEE nationals' status became regularised in host states at the time of the Enlargement, they could not become eligible for permanent residence until 2009—unlike EU-15 nationals. The ECJ ultimately found this approach to be unlawful in some circumstances, ruling that the time residing in a host state before the Eastern Enlargement counts towards the five-year period but only if pre-accession residence had satisfied conditions specified under the Directive[129] (for example, qualifying as a 'worker' or being financially self-sufficient). Furthermore, Austria, Belgium, Germany, Denmark, Ireland, and Sweden failed to implement Article 17 which had created exceptions to the five-year residence requirement for movers no longer working due to reaching pension age, taking up early retirement, or becoming permanently incapacitated.

In addition, EU-15 states adopted strict evidentiary requirements to make the right of permanent residence very difficult to access in practice. Under the Directive, proving eligibility for permanent residence is not onerous. Upon verifying the duration of an applicant's residence, the host state is obliged to issue, as soon as possible, a document certifying permanent residence (Article 19). Continuity of residence 'may be attested by any means of proof in use in the host' state, and can be broken only by expulsion decisions duly enforced against the mover (Article 21). Many EU-15 states, however, required movers to present detailed proof of their continuous residence and excluded those who had relied on (or even ever applied for) social assistance during the five-year period. Austria, Finland, Denmark, and the UK imposed inconsistent, discretionary, and burdensome requirements on the types and numbers of documents that movers had to produce to prove that their residence had been lawful and continuous. French authorities sometimes demanded that applicants present registration certificates even though France did not require that movers register with the authorities at any time after arrival (and some local authorities would even refuse to issue residence certificates to movers). Notably, providing documentation such as employment contracts, tax documentation, tenancy agreements, or utility bills attesting to the five-year continuous presence would have been particularly onerous for CEE movers since they have been overrepresented in precarious and temporary work, circular mobility, semi-lawful employment (often without written contracts), and temporary living arrangements. Moreover, in Belgium, authorities routinely rejected permanent residence applications of self-employed movers, also disproportionately common among CEE nationals, especially during the post-accession transitional period.

129 *Ziolkowski and Szeja v Land Berlin*, Joined Cases C-424/10 and 425/10, ECLI:EU:C:2011:866.

v. Equal Treatment and Access to Social Assistance

Under Article 24(2), host states are not obliged to confer social assistance only to economically inactive movers during their first three months of residence or to first-time jobseekers (for as long as they remain in that status). Several EU-15 states, however, applied this provision far too broadly. For example, Germany adopted Social Security Act 2006 to automatically exclude all jobseekers and economically inactive movers who were not yet permanent residents from access to social assistance benefits—including unemployment insurance under Social Code Book II. Additionally, pursuant to a new German law adopted in 2007, movers were not eligible for child benefits or jobseeker's allowance until they had worked in Germany for a continuous period of at least five years.

Moreover, under the Directive, permanent residency leads to equal treatment in access to all EU rights, including social assistance and maintenance for studies. In practice, however, some EU-15 states tried to limit rights that follow from permanent residence. For example, when movers who had already obtained permanent residence applied for social benefits in Austria or Germany, they were required to provide documentation supporting their residency eligibility – for a new, independent examination.

vi. Entry and Residence Restrictions on Public Policy Grounds

Under Article 27(1), host states are permitted to restrict freedom of movement on grounds of public policy, public security, or public health as long as such restrictions are not invoked 'to serve economic ends'. The Directive provides detailed material and procedural safeguards for applying these restrictions. For example, according to Article 27(2), measures taken on grounds of public policy or security must comply with the proportionality principle,[130] and must be 'based exclusively on the personal conduct of the individual concerned'. Previous criminal convictions alone do not justify restrictions. Instead, the person's conduct 'must present a genuine, present and sufficiently serious threat affecting one of the fundamental interests of society'. Furthermore, before making an expulsion decision due to public policy or security reasons, host states must take into account individual circumstances such as length of residence, age, family and economic circumstances, integration within the host state, and continuing links with the country of origin (Article 28). Once a mover obtains permanent residence, expulsion decisions may only be taken on 'serious' grounds of public policy or security. Movers who have resided in a host state for the previous ten years or more may be expelled only on 'imperative grounds of public security'.

All EU-15 states other than Greece and Portugal transposed these material safeguards too narrowly and applied broad administrative discretion to limit

---

130 That is, they must be necessary and appropriate to attain the objective pursued.

the rights of entry and residence under policy grounds. Several EU-15 states did not prohibit residence restrictions from being invoked for economic reasons. Irish regulations provided that EU nationals could be refused entry where their personal conduct was found contrary to public policy or security, with no requirement that it presents a genuine and serious threat. Italy and Finland automatically expelled movers who had committed crimes of certain gravity, without respecting the principle of proportionality, and used this ground disproportionately against CEE movers as well as Romanians.

Procedural protections against limitations on entry and residence rights were also more limited in EU-15 states than under the Directive. Article 30 requires that EU citizens must be provided adequate notification if they are refused entry or residence on grounds of public policy and that such notice must include information about how to lodge an appeal. Furthermore, Article 31 demands that such persons have access to redress procedures while remaining in the host state, including the right to ask for an interim order to suspend removal until after the redress decision has been taken. All EU-15 states other than Spain and Portugal failed to provide sufficient procedural safeguards under these Articles. For example, France denied any procedural safeguards in cases which it deemed to be of absolute urgency, so that movers could be expelled without written notice and without the right of redress. In the UK, movers denied entry or residence rights were not informed about their right of redress. Moreover, regulations adopted in the UK in 2006 allowed appeals of entry refusals and of deportation orders only after departing the UK, which made such appeals much more challenging for movers to advance.

vii. Prohibition of Levelling Down

According to Article 37, Member States are not permitted to diminish movers' rights which were more favourable under pre-existing domestic policies than the rights afforded by the Directive. However, French regulations adopted in 2007 lowered pre-existing social support standards available to movers. Presented as a response to alleged benefit forum shopping by movers, they prevented jobseekers from accessing minimum income support, health coverage, and non-contributory family benefits. Given their timing and the populist rhetoric in France at the time, one can only assume that they were adopted to target CEE movers.

viii. Additional, Long-term Limitations on CEE Movers' Rights

In addition to narrowing rights afforded by the Directive during its transposition, as well as through additional related policies and procedures, EU-15 states also targeted CEE movers by adopting new measures to limit rights that fall beyond the scope of the Directive. For example, in Ireland, citizenship laws were changed in 2004 so that individuals born in Ireland to non-Irish parents would no longer automatically become Irish citizens unless one of the parents had been lawfully resident in Ireland for at least three out of the four immediately preceding years. Moreover, an act proposed in 2008 (though ultimately scrapped) would have allowed deportation without notice of any individuals present in Ireland without a lawful residence right. Ireland and the UK also limited economically inactive movers' access to social security and to SNCBs by adopting new right-to-reside tests in 2004 which had to be satisfied in addition to the 'habitual residence' test under EU Regulation 883/2004. The new tests were especially difficult for CEE movers to satisfy due to their overrepresentation in part-time jobs and in the gig economy.

Movers' Protections from Ethnicity-Based Discrimination

The right of mobility and the experience thereof are inextricably linked to the right of equality. As mentioned earlier, EU institutions have long recognised that, to facilitate mobility and reap its benefit to the aggregate EU economy, the freedom of movement right must be supported by Treaty and secondary measures against nationality discrimination. Nationality anti-discrimination protections, however, are insufficient to account for discrimination due to race as the two concepts do not always overlap. Notably, nationality non-discrimination protections do not have a horizontal effect[131] which formalistically implies that nationality discrimination committed by individuals does not exist—or is unworthy of EU law's protection. Moreover, as discussed throughout the book, CEE nationals have been racialised in the west and their exclusion, exploitation, and discrimination often stem not simply from having non-host state nationalities, but rather from being essentialised as 'Eastern European' and inherently less white than EU-15 state nationals.

Drafted once the Eastern Enlargement was on the horizon and adopted only four years before it—and hence, with no input from CEE states—the Race Equality Directive 2000/38 expanded the principle of equal treatment to prohibit direct discrimination, indirect discrimination, harassment, and victimisation due to racial and ethnic origin in various contexts, including employment, education, social protections, social advantages, and access to goods and services (including housing). EU institutions have repeatedly praised the Race Equality Directive as a stellar achievement[132]—one of 'the most advanced legal [equality] frameworks'[133] and 'the most comprehensive and far-reaching anti-discrimination legislation to be found anywhere in the world'.[134]

Despite such grandiose rhetoric, racial discrimination has historically been perceived by EU bodies as problematic mostly to the extent that it distorts the

---

131 That is, they cannot be invoked against individuals before national courts.
132 For a general critique of the Race Equality Directive, see e.g., Howard (2009).
133 Commission of the European Communities (2004).
134 Commission of the European Communities (2005).

functioning of the common economic market. Meanwhile, social justice issues have been largely relegated to national agendas. Hence, the EU's early equality initiatives addressed nationality and gender discrimination to facilitate (western European) workers' mobility and participation in the labour market. They had focused on socio-economic equality only, while failing to address other roots of social disadvantage. According to Somek,[135] the core of all EU equality policies continues to stem from a desire to facilitate the functioning of the neoliberal economic market. My analysis below reveals that both the Race Equality Directive and contemporary equality discourse indeed continue to exemplify the economic core of equality rights. This, once again, brings to mind Derrick Bell's interest convergence theory. Moreover, both discourse and racial equality policies overlook the needs of racialised whites such as CEE movers, and some of the Directive's provisions are especially poorly suited for protecting them.

Legislative History of the Race Equality Directive 2000/43

Anti-foreigner, anti-migrant, and racist attitudes have been prevalent for decades across Europe. For example, in 1997, 33% of EU-15 nationals polled considered themselves to be 'very' or 'quite' racist against immigrants,[136] which at the time included CEE nationals. EU citizens see racial discrimination as an ordinary part of life and the most widespread form of discrimination in the EU. Discrimination appears particularly common in the context of employment,[137] as further confirmed by outcome studies.[138] Surveys of ethnic minorities indicate that Caucasians, including intra-EU movers, who do not belong to the dominant (white) ethnic group in a given host country can experience increased risk of discrimination.[139] Almost a decade after the Eastern Enlargement, the Commission observed that movers were 'still perceived in most of the EU as holding a status closer to that of third-country nationals than to that of national workers'.[140] CEE movers have been particularly affected by racism, especially frequently noted in the employment and housing contexts.[141]

In addition to the fact that racism and discrimination tend to be underreported, such survey data likely fails to fully capture their extent, particularly as race-based discrimination across the EU has become more furtive during the past few decades and more concealed within appeals to patriotism, culture, and

---

135 Somek (2011).
136 Eurobarometer (1997).
137 E.g., Eurobarometer (2007); Eurobarometer (2015).
138 E.g., Jefferys (2015).
139 E.g., European Commission (2022a). In its discussion of findings and recommendations, however, the Commission excluded anti-white discrimination, implicitly signalling that anti-white racism is not an issue worthy of its attention.
140 European Commission (2013).
141 E.g., European Union Agency for Fundamental Rights (2009).

class. While drawing overt distinctions between whites and non-whites has become publicly unacceptable, salient boundaries have become more prominent between white EU movers and white host-state populations. Notably, public prejudices and discrimination faced by CEE movers—termed by scholars 'racialisation'[142]—have been exhibited across EU-15 states not only through impediments to mobility but also through exclusions from full participation in the economic, political, and social spheres of their host states.

EU institutions' motivations for addressing racial and ethnic discrimination, however, have been not only contextualised within aims to prevent distortions of the internal market but also steeped in concerns for non-white, non-Christian victims only. By the 1980s, EU institutions began to note the apparent rise in racist and xenophobic attitudes across the EU—attributed to increasing immigration from outside the EU, escalating racial tensions in Member States with colonial legacies, and the growing appeal of populist, right-wing politicians. After extreme right-wing parties recorded considerable electoral successes in France and other Member States in 1984, the European Parliament established a committee to analyse racism and fascism in Europe, which recommended EU-level action. In response, the Commission, Council, and Parliament issued the first official acknowledgement that racism was an issue of concern to the EU, through the (non-enforceable) Joint Declaration Against Racism and Xenophobia.[143] Concurrently, activists were pressuring EU institutions to implement measures to combat racial discrimination[144] against non-European, non-Christian minorities (such as Turkish and Moroccan guest workers). Attacks perpetrated in several western states in the early 1990s against migrants of Jewish, Muslim, African, and South Asian backgrounds added further impetus.

My analysis of contemporaneous EU debates and the broader equality discourse revealed a similar focus on the need to better protect non-European (largely, non-white) immigrants. The increasing presence of post-1989 CEE migrants in western states and the prospect of CEE nationals' post-accession mobility were overlooked in EU discourse. It is possible that (predominantly white) EU officials could not foresee widespread prejudices against Caucasian intra-EU movers or could not conceptualise such incidents as 'racism'. Such is the naturalised, homogenising power of white privilege. This silence might also have been due to a more pernicious motive—an unwillingness to deem any potential unfair treatment of CEE nationals as deserving of anti-discrimination protections. After all, EU institutions were clearly aware of east/west power differentials in the context of the Eastern Enlargement and of inequalities built into the accession process. EU institutions also knew that EU-15 states had consistently opposed CEE nationals' mobility and acknowledged on several

---

142 E.g., Rzepnikowska (2019).
143 OJ 1986 C 158.
144 See generally Solanke (2009).

occasions that CEE mobility would likely lead to experiences of prejudice and inequalities, as mentioned earlier. Nevertheless, any such awareness did not become part of the racial equality agenda.

The Parliament's efforts were facilitated by the increasingly well-organised NGO network across the EU which led to the creation of the Starting Line Group ('SLG') in 1991. Composed of more than 300 (western) state and EU-level NGOs and legal experts, the SLG was dominated by Dutch and British activists. Migrant rights organisations encompassed under its umbrella were concerned with protecting the rights of refugees and immigrants from outside Europe, including guest workers as well as Jews and Roma. Most of the SLG's constituent groups were well-established and engaged in addressing historical domestic equality causes. Concerns with the treatment of white European movers were not on domestic agendas at the time. Moreover, migrant-advocacy groups comprising the SLG had failed to create EU-wide momentum to increase migrant inclusion[145] and had settled on supporting measures focused on attaining formal, as opposed to substantive, equality.

Disappointingly, although the SLG did propose some of the most innovative provisions of the new directive which moved beyond the EU's pre-existing anti-discrimination regime—such as increasing victims' access to courts and providing institutional support for litigants—it tended to situate its proposals only within economic concerns. Echoing how EU institutions have tended to support equality measures, the SLG often drew on market-integration arguments noting that the lack of racial equality protections presented a barrier to workers' mobility, their economic integration, and the success of the single market. Even if this was merely a strategic move to increase the political persuasiveness of its arguments, the SLG's recommendations and drafts were steeped in market discourse—further reinforcing the economic core of the EU's equality and fundamental-rights rhetoric discussed in the preceding chapter.

The Commission only came to embrace the SLG's efforts after the release of the 1995 Kahn Report[146] which concluded that racism permeated the daily lives of 'foreigners' and 'national citizens from minority groups' across EU-15 states. Even with the support of both the Parliament and the Commission, however, the SLG's proposals faced opposition from EU-15 politicians. Notably, although Member States had many prior opportunities to amend EU foundational Treaties to endow the EU with competence in this field—including through the 1993 Maastricht Treaty which had created EU citizenship—they had expressed no interest in doing so. Due to EU-15 politicians' pressure, some of the most significant SLG proposals were scrapped—including those providing NGOs with standing to sue independently, permitting class actions, and

---

145 More generally, migrants have tended to lack political power in the EU—due to their relatively small numbers, diverse origins and interests, temporariness, and low political engagement of some groups.
146 Kahn (1995).

endowing the new directive with direct effect. EU-15 states also objected to SLG proposals to extend the scope of protections beyond the employment field. The EU, however, successfully resisted EU-15 opposition on that point, believing protections in access to goods, services, and education necessary to further facilitate workers' mobility.

With the Commission's support now secured, EU institutions began discussing how to amend foundational Treaties to provide EU competence in the anti-discrimination field. This was driven inexclusively, if at all, by human rights concerns. Although both the Parliament and the Commission increasingly relied on fundamental rights rhetoric, this was likely a tactical move to help justify expanding the EU's competence. As mentioned in the preceding chapter, by that time, fundamental rights rhetoric had become well-propagated as the key EU foundational myth. Notably, the Council only succumbed to extending the EU's competence due to racism's negative effects on the internal market and due to contemporaneously increasing EU efforts to coordinate external immigration policies.[147] The Commission also acknowledged another benefit of a new equality legislation. It was expected to provide 'excellent publicity' for the EU—especially useful before the upcoming Parliamentary elections.[148]

The 1997 Treaty of Amsterdam endowed the Council, 'acting unanimously on a proposal from the Commission', with discretionary power to 'take appropriate action to combat discrimination' based on racial or ethnic origin, as well as sex, religion or belief, disability, age, or sexual orientation.[149] The ground of 'racial or ethnic origin' under the Treaty is more narrowly phrased than the typical race-based grounds under international human rights instruments which oftentimes explicitly encompass race, colour, language, national origin, social origin, and birth or other status.[150] A single Member State could prevent the Council from reaching the unanimity required to adopt any anti-discrimination measures. Overall, the limited scope of this new Treaty provision reflected the EU's having to accommodate reluctance among EU-15 states, all of which must have agreed to ratify a Treaty amendment. Notably, even after this Treaty modification, some EU-15 states continued to oppose EU legislation in this field for various reasons, including its being domestically unpopular.

The Commission proposed the Race Equality Directive in December 1999. It was adopted by the Council in June 2000—at record speed, likely as a symbolic

---

147 As illustrated in the next chapter, increasing immigration controls are often accompanied by expanded formal anti-discrimination laws, and both are prompted by anti-migrant antagonism.
148 Commission of the European Communities (1996).
149 Treaty of Amsterdam amending the Treaty on European Union, the Treaties establishing the European Communities and certain related acts, Article 13.
150 E.g., UN International Covenant on Civil and Political Rights; UN International Convention on the Protection of the Rights of All Migrant Workers and Members of Their Families; European Convention for the Protection of Human Rights and Fundamental Freedoms.

rebuff to the contemporaneous electoral successes of extreme right-wing parties across EU-15 states such as of the Freedom Party in Austria. Although motives for the Directive's adoption were not always consistent or straightforward, one thing is certain: none of the key EU institutions, pan-European advocacy groups, or western politicians considered the treatment of white movers or of racialised whites when drafting or adopting the Directive.

Key Provisions of the Race Equality Directive

The Race Equality Directive 2000/43 converges labour market and fundamental rights justifications for prohibiting discrimination. Its 28 (non-enforceable) preamble recitals frame racial and ethnic equality within the EU's respect for fundamental rights, as well as within economic objectives such as achieving a high level of employment. Composed of nineteen articles that span three pages, the Directive provides 'a framework for combating discrimination' on the grounds of 'racial or ethnic origin' in EU states (Article 1). Although states may implement broader anti-discrimination provisions than those specified in the Directive, any pre-existing domestic protections could not be reduced during its transposition. The Directive aims to attain formal—as opposed to substantive—equality. This is evident in its title ('implementing the principle of equal treatment'), and its stated purpose ('putting into effect in the Member States the principle of equal treatment') (Article 1). Moreover, although the Directive recognises that positive action might be necessary to bring about substantive equality, it does not mandate it.[151] National discrimination sanctions for violating anti-discrimination law must be 'effective, proportionate and dissuasive' (Article 15). The ECJ has determined a rather low threshold for this, requiring sanctions to simply fulfil the principles of (1) equivalence (not being less favourable than those governing similar domestic actions); (2) effectiveness (not rendering the exercise of EU rights 'practically impossible or excessively difficult'); and (3) non-regression (not lessening pre-existing national measures).[152] That being said, for the first time under EU law, Member States became required to designate bodies tasked with promoting equal treatment, providing independent aid to victims, and conducting research on discrimination (Article 13). Finally, drawing on EU fundamental rights rhetoric, the ECJ has ruled that the Directive does have horizontal direct effect.[153] Thus, individuals can rely on it in disputes with other individuals or private entities before national courts.

The Directive prohibits both direct and indirect discrimination. Aiming to attain formal equality, direct discrimination is defined as being 'treated less

---

151 '[W]ith a view to ensuring full equality in practice, the principle of equal treatment shall not prevent any Member State from maintaining or adopting specific measures to prevent or compensate for disadvantages linked to racial or ethnic origin' (Article 5).
152 *Bulicke v Deutsche Büro Service GmbH*, Case C-246/09, ECLI:EU:C:2010:418.
153 *CHEZ Razpredelenie Bulgaria AD v Komisia za zashtita ot diskriminatsia*, Case C-83/14, ECLI:EU:C:2015:480.

favourably than another [person] is, has been or would be treated in a comparable situation' (Article 2(2)(a)). Indirect discrimination occurs when 'an apparently neutral provision, criterion or practice would put persons of a racial or ethnic origin at a particular disadvantage compared with other persons' (unless such a provision meets the proportionality test) (Article 2(2)(b)). Because some Member States and employers do not collect data broken down by racial and ethnic origins, this definition does not rely on the test of disproportion (i.e., statistical evidence that a provision or practice disadvantages a substantially higher proportion of the ethnic/racial group to which a claimant belongs). According to the ECJ, 'particular disadvantage' includes not only 'serious, obvious or particularly significant cases of inequality' but also practices where 'it is particularly persons of a given racial or ethnic origin who are at a disadvantage'.[154] Thus, indirect discrimination might be found when a measure, albeit formulated in neutral terms, 'works to the disadvantage of far more persons possessing the protected characteristic than persons not possessing it'.[155] However, according to *Jyske Finans*, it is necessary to perform not merely a general abstract comparison but 'a specific concrete comparison, in the light of the ... treatment in question'.[156] A genuine and determining occupational requirement might justify either direct or indirect discrimination (if it satisfies the proportionality test) (Article 4), which further diminishes the Directive's ability to attain substantive equality.

Once a claimant presents sufficient evidence to establish a presumption of direct or indirect discrimination, the Directive shifts the burden of proof to the respondent (Article 8). The ECJ has interpreted this not to constitute a particularly onerous burden for claimants. For example, in *Firma Feryn*[157], the ECJ deemed an employer's public statement that it would not recruit 'immigrants' sufficient to create a presumption of direct discrimination. In *Meister*,[158] the Court even drew an inference unfavourable to the respondent, which is not mandated by the Directive's text. Despite satisfactory qualifications, Ms Meister was not invited for a job interview and the employer refused to provide her the file of the person who was appointed to that position. Although the Court ruled that claimants were not entitled to such information, it also held that adverse inferences may be made against respondents who refuse to make such disclosures.

Furthermore, Article 2(3) prohibits harassment, that is, 'unwanted conduct related to racial or ethnic origin' which is undertaken 'with the purpose or effect of violating the dignity of a person and of creating an intimidating, hostile, degrading, humiliating or offensive environment'. Notably, this broad

154 Ibid.
155 Ibid.
156 *Jyske Finans A/S v Ligebehandlingsnævnet*, Case C-668/15, ECLI:EU:C:2017:278.
157 *Centrum voor gelijkheid van kansen en voor racismebestrijding v Firma Feryn NV*, Case C-54/07, ECLI:EU:C:2008:397.
158 *Meister v Speech Design Carrier Systems GmbH*, Case C-415/10, ECLI:EU: C:2012:217.

definition does go beyond just formal equality as it allows claims based simply on the effects of a perpetrator's conduct. Instructing others to discriminate (Article 2(4)) is also proscribed. Finally, states are required to introduce measures to protect individuals from victimisation, i.e., 'any adverse treatment or adverse consequence as a reaction to a complaint or to proceedings aimed at enforcing compliance with the principle of equal treatment' (Article 9).

All these prohibitions apply to both private and public sectors—including public bodies—in the contexts of (1) employment (access to employment, promotion, vocational training, working conditions, dismissal, pay, and involvement in trade organisations) and (2) social protections (social security, healthcare, social advantages, education, and access to and supply of goods and services that are publicly available, such as housing) (Article 3(1)). Thus, the Directive reinforces EU provisions facilitating the free movement right, including access to social rights.

Key Weaknesses of the Directive

The Directive's uncertain stance and limitations stem not only from the practical constraints involved in its adoption, but also from the complicated western approach towards curbing racism. According to Fitzpatrick,[159] racism has been fundamental to the creation of a 'European' identity and to western liberal notions of equality. In order to operate and gain legitimacy, modern anti-discrimination law always requires some groups to be excluded by the polity. Notably, several of the Directive's provisions seem especially ill-suited for protecting the rights of small, poorly-organised groups which lack political power, such as CEE movers. As explained below, racialised whites often fall outside the Directive's grasp. Superficially, this can be attributed to the fact that the roots of western anti-discrimination law stem from inequalities experienced by non-white colonial subjects who are perceived as inherently lesser than white (western) Europeans. I argue that not adequately addressing CEE movers' ethnic discrimination is also in line with the long-standing peripheralisation of the east and its nationals. Furthermore, overlooking CEE movers' needs facilitates EU-15 states' ability to derive economic benefits from their labour. Meanwhile, their whiteness—albeit degenerate—complicates whether their racialisation is perceived as racism.

i. Individual Enforcement

Arguably, the Directive's greatest inherent limitation is that it can only be enforced through individual litigation. Private litigation based on past individual incidents of discrimination, with no possibility of class action, is inefficient and insufficient to address widespread, structural, or institutional discrimination. Notably, it does not create space for coalition-building that class actions facilitate and does little for

---

159 Fitzpatrick (1987).

disadvantaged groups' inclusion or political empowerment. Moreover, this approach overlooks pre-existing disadvantages faced by some groups and such disadvantages' contributory underlying socio-economic conditions, and it ignores the complex power relations between different ethnic groups. It encourages adjudicators to rely more on their own (typically majoritarian) values and forms of understanding, while devaluing evidence going beyond just the individual dispute before them such as of conditions of exclusion and racialisation that some groups tend to face in EU-15 states. In the context of my study group, individual litigation does little to address circumstances when, for example, all CEE nationals (or all workers of a specific CEE nationality) tend to be treated poorly by an employer and are disadvantaged collectively in the labour market—as illustrated in the next chapter through my discussion of discrimination cases in the UK employment context. It also does not take into account negative public and media discourses or the broader western rhetoric of othering the CEE region that racialises and embeds CEE nationals' experiences of mobility within a specific ideology of inequality.

Moreover, individual claims place the entire burden (of initiating claims, obtaining advice, collecting evidence, and paying filing fees) on individual claimants. This disadvantages CEE movers since they tend to be low-paid, overworked, engaged in precarious employment, and lacking in access to well-organised advocacy groups. Although the Directive instructed Member States to ensure that domestic equality-rights organisations have legal standing to support claimants or to sue on their behalf (Article 7(2)), my review of UK employment tribunal cases (discussed in the next chapter) revealed that this might not have often been put into practice in the context of CEE movers. Finally, a remedial framework based on individual cases fails to serve as a meaningful deterrent to perpetrators or to provide a remedy to the whole group affected by discrimination—for example, to CEE claimants' co-workers of the same or other CEE nationalities who often tend to be exploited collectively in their places of employment. Conceptually, reliance on individual claims to address discrimination implies that racist attitudes and actions are merely aberrations and this therefore naturalises the status quo as fundamentally fair.[160]

ii. Lack of Definitional Specificity

The Directive leaves many key terms,[161] legal tests,[162] and Member State obligations[163] vague or undefined, placing much discretion in the hands of national lawmakers. Some of this vagueness stems from the function of EU directives to merely specify results to be attained without dictating particular means to be employed. Moreover, the Directive's vagueness likely served a

---

160 See generally Williams (1992).
161 E.g., 'racial origin', 'ethnic origin', 'proportionate aims'.
162 E.g., how to evaluate evidence offered in support of discrimination claims.
163 E.g., enforcement procedures; designation of equality bodies.

pragmatic purpose. Had the Directive's terms been more exacting, EU-15 states might not have adopted it due to concerns over sovereignty, transposition burdens, and the need to accommodate diverse domestic political, economic, and social priorities. Regardless of the reasons, leaving much discretion to EU-15 lawmakers is problematic in the context of publicly and politically unpopular groups such as CEE movers.

As very few cases under the Directive have been referred to the ECJ so far,[164] the interpretation of many crucial provisions (including those pertaining to harassment, positive action, and victimisation) has been left largely within the ambit of national lawmakers. This necessitates that my analysis rely more heavily on the Directive's legislative history and on the broader EU equality discourse—as well as on the Directive's application at the Member State level (in the next chapter)[165]—to speculate about how some of its provisions might be implemented. Given that the Directive's legislative history and the EU's equality discourse (further discussed below) have focused on the protection of long-standing national minorities and non-European migrants, it seems unlikely that the ECJ will interpret the Directive to robustly protect the rights of (non-Roma) CEE movers. This is particularly doubtful since the Court has traditionally favoured economic freedoms over equality or human rights concerns, as illustrated also in its approach towards the freedom of movement right, analysed throughout this chapter. Notably, ECJ interpretations of the Race Equality Directive—and its companion legislation, the Employment Equality Directive 2000/78—have drawn heavily on gender equality law which has had strong roots in promoting economic competition.

In addition, the Directive's frequent lack of specificity makes it more difficult for EU institutions to monitor its effectiveness. Unfortunately, with little direction or oversight, national legislators are even less likely than EU institutions to protect or monitor the rights of politically powerless groups which are unpopular with domestic voters. Being subject to more political and social pressure than EU officials might be, national policymakers are even more likely to be swayed by negative public opinion of CEE movers which has been prevalent in western discourses. National lawmakers have little to gain, yet much to lose, by seeking to protect outsider groups—especially those which are not widely recognised by domestic policy regimes as victims of racism, a tendency reinforced through the traditional view of whiteness as homogenously privileged. This inclination to overlook movers' rights is further reinforced by the fact that domestic lawmakers tend to be native-born and to belong to domestic ethnic majorities, with personal experiences that are far removed from the day-to-day

---

164 By February 2023, only eight ECJ judgments had substantively engaged with the Race Equality Directive. More generally, the ECJ has not heard as many equality cases as proceedings in other fields.
165 Moreover, Member State level analysis is necessary because EU equality laws cannot provide market corrections, which remain within Member States' scope of responsibility.

lives of CEE movers. Although vague definitions also present an opportunity for better national protections than what the Directive mandates, my analysis in the next chapter of how the transposed Directive has been applied in the UK indicates that this potential might be rarely utilised to protect CEE nationals.

iii. 'Racial or Ethnic Origin' Ground

The protected ground of 'racial or ethnic origin', left undefined by the Directive, is too limited in practice in the context of migrants and movers. The Directive does not apply to 'difference of treatment based on nationality' (Article 3(2)). The law is not settled on whether it covers language or accent discrimination. Thus, in some cases, nationality (or language) discrimination might serve as a proxy for ethnic discrimination yet escape the reach of EU law. Furthermore, the Directive does not reflect the reality of today's racisms, which have increasingly relied on markers such as different cultural practices. Notably, the Directive does not address inequalities that stem from simply being a 'migrant' or being 'foreign' (as opposed to having a specific foreign nationality), factors that have been found to lead to disadvantage, discrimination, and prejudice.[166] Listing such additional grounds as has been done in numerous international anti-discrimination instruments—and, arguably, as implied by ECJ jurisprudence[167]—would have made the Directive more reflective of movers' equality needs. Although in theory victims could argue that factors such as 'foreignness' can be brought under the 'ethnic origin' category, my illustrative review in the next chapter of cases brought by CEE claimants in the UK employment context indicates that such arguments have not been advanced by claimants or by judges, even where there was an opportunity to do so.

Finally, the Directive does not acknowledge that the experience of inequality often stems not from a victim's race or ethnicity alone, but rather, from an intersection with other factors—such as class, gender, religion, and sexual orientation. This is problematic for CEE movers whose exploitation often appears facilitated by the intersection of their ethnicity and low socio-economic status in EU-15 states. Notably, recent EU reports on fundamental rights and racial justice prompted by the BLM movement and the Covid pandemic (discussed below) have increasingly recognised the importance of intersectionality and structural racism, yet this is not captured by the Directive or by other binding EU instruments.

---

166 See generally Equality and Diversity Forum (2011).
167 In *Firma Feryn*, the ECJ interpreted an employer's public statement that it would not recruit 'immigrants' as within the Directive's scope. Moreover, in *CHEZ Razpredelenie Bulgaria*, the Court noted that 'ethnicity' refers to 'societal groups marked in particular by common nationality, religious faith, language, cultural and traditional origins and backgrounds'. *Jyske Finans*, however, made clear that country of birth is not synonymous with 'ethnic origin', although it can constitute a relevant factor. That being said, *Firma Feryn* and *Jyske Finans* concerned non-EU immigrants, and *CZEZ* dealt with Roma claimants, so it is uncertain if the Court would extend this line of reasoning to (non-Roma) CEE movers.

iv. Use of Comparators

The use of comparators supports a formal notion of equality. It ignores any existing inequalities or social disadvantages and allows for levelling down since the law is complied with as long as two like persons are treated alike—even if equally badly. In addition, using imprecise or incorrect comparators presents an inherent danger of reaching flawed decisions. There are particular risks of relying on both over and under-inclusive comparators in the context of CEE movers, especially in the employment setting. Staffing agencies' involvement, labour market segregation, and some (low-paying) employers' preference for CEE workers have resulted in 'low-skill' CEE movers' tendency to congregate at specific employer sites, constituting a substantial proportion or even the vast majority of some workforces. This makes it difficult to find an actual comparator in some cases. It is true that adjudicators have the flexibility to use hypothetical comparators. However, that approach presents risks, especially given that rigorous methodologies for creating hypothetical comparators require a long line of cases, which is not yet existent for post-04 CEE movers.

If judges look at all migrant groups, all white migrants, or all EU movers as the standard, their comparison will not reflect the specific prejudices that CEE workers have faced in western labour markets. For example, white immigrants from English-speaking countries (oftentimes laudatorily termed 'expats') and western EU movers (especially from the more affluent north-western states) are privileged economically and culturally over CEE movers. Moreover, even using all CEE movers as the standard presents challenges. Among CEE movers, Poles have faced especially high rates of de-skilling in the labour market, stereotyping by employers about their good work ethic (which supports their exploitation), and widespread negative media, political and public portrayals, including associations with criminality. On the other hand, if comparator characteristics are too limited, facts pertaining to CEE movers' widespread racialisation might get overlooked. Moreover, narrowly defining comparator traits risks obscuring intersectionality. For example, a Lithuanian female worker might suffer discrimination due to her ethnicity, national origin, migration status, language skills, gender, and socio-economic status. Focusing solely on her specific ethnic origin is likely to overlook all the other intersecting grounds of disadvantage.

As my illustrative discussion in the next chapter reveals, employment tribunals in the UK—which has had one of the most advanced non-discrimination frameworks among EU-15 states—have indeed struggled with finding correct comparators, especially hypothetical ones, when it comes to CEE claimants. UK adjudicators often appear not well versed in the unique experiences of CEE movers and unfamiliar with (or not inclined to acknowledge) the broader socio-cultural context that affects them. This is likely facilitated by how naturalised CEE movers' racialisation and experiences of disadvantage have become, by the lack of advocacy initiatives on their behalf, and by the scarcity of ECJ case law addressing their experiences.

v. Indirect Discrimination

The definition of indirect discrimination, despite being broader than under previous EU (gender) equality legislation, is also inadequate in the context of my study group. For starters, an indirectly discriminatory provision or practice may be 'objectively justified by a legitimate aim' if 'the means of achieving that aim are appropriate and necessary' (Article 2(2)(b)). This proportionality justification not only generally weakens protections from indirect discrimination but also appears especially problematic in practice, given EU-15 policymakers' accountability to domestic majorities which have tended to express strong antipathy towards CEE movers. Moreover, transposed domestic laws need not require the use of statistical evidence to establish indirect discrimination, and there is nothing stopping national lawmakers from discouraging the use of such evidence or discounting its value. Although obtaining statistical data is often cumbersome and expensive for claimants, in some cases, it constitutes key evidence. Notably, institutional discrimination—for example, higher refusal rates of CEE movers trying to access public services in EU-15 states—is more difficult to prove without statistical evidence. Since today's expressions of racism have become less overt and, in the case of CEE movers, are often cloaked in calls to nationalism or preferences for cultural similarities, they are more likely to escape the Directive's grasp without the use of statistical evidence.

vi. Harassment

Demonstrating harassment, which requires evidence of both conduct and environment elements,[168] is also problematic for CEE movers, notably in the employment context. Widespread incidents of microaggression directed against CEE workers might not be overt enough to be unlawful. Since sporadic, isolated, or less overt incidents of racism are not prohibited, employers might avoid liability if they perpetrate only one incident per worker, against multiple CEE employees, as long as such individual incidents would not be deemed by adjudicators to create a generally degrading environment for all such workers. Although the ECJ has not yet explained the 'hostile environment' element, an Advocate General opinion indicates that it refers to ongoing, long-term, collective measures from which all members of an ethnic group suffer[169]—in line with how the 'hostile environment' element has been interpreted in the context of gender equality. Since low-paid CEE workers often work alongside many other CEE workers, an employer's harassment of many workers individually can be a widespread practice, yet not necessarily actionable, particularly if at least a few

---

168 '[U]nwanted conduct ... with the purpose or effect of violating the dignity of a person and of creating an intimidating, hostile, degrading, humiliating or offensive environment' (Article 2(3)).
169 See *CHEZ Razpredelenie Bulgaria*, Case C-83/14, Opinion of AG Kokott, ECLI:EU: C:2015:170.

of such workers are not targeted or if workers of various CEE ethnicities (instead of just the claimant's specific ethnicity) are targeted. Also, the Directive does not impose vicarious liability on employers for harassment initiated by their employees or by third parties (e.g., vendors, contractors, or customers). Given how strong anti-CEE sentiment has been in EU-15 states, it is not unlikely that non-CEE employees or third parties harass CEE workers with impunity.

The Directive's Ineffectiveness in Practice

Delays and errors in the Directive's transposition, which was to be finalised in EU-15 states by July 2003, reduced all movers' access to protections from racial discrimination. Twelve of the EU-15 states failed to transpose the Directive on time. In addition to the typical transposition challenges, issues were caused by the pre-existence of divergent national equality legislations that reflected domestic race relations.[170] In 2004, after the Commission initiated infringement procedures, the ECJ found Austria, Finland, Germany, Greece, and Luxembourg in breach of their Treaty obligations for not having transposed the Directive fully. Continuing errors in defining the Directive's key terms and in narrowing its scope[171] prompted the Commission to launch infringement proceedings during 2005–07 against all EU-15 states except Luxembourg. In 2007— when all EU-15 states had finally transposed the Directive—the Commission sent reasoned opinions to eight EU-15 states, asking them to revise flawed national laws such as those limiting the scope of protections to the employment field only.

Despite instituting multiple infringement actions, the Commission had praised the overall transposition process and had even applauded Member States for their 'unprecedented commitment' to prioritising anti-discrimination measures.[172] In addition to being inaccurate, this reinforces the long-standing conceptualisation of the EU as a benevolent project that champions fundamental rights. On the rare occasion when the Commission acknowledged that the Directive has failed to prompt more domestic court proceedings, it has continued to minimise finding any fault with the EU equality framework or with national equality laws. Instead, it has blamed any shortcomings on victims' underreporting of discrimination and on generic issues with access to justice.[173] The European Parliament has been more critical, noting 'with

---

170 To this day, there is no consensus among politicians or scholars from various Member States as to what racial equality means in principle or in practice.
171 Most frequent errors included: incorrect definitions of direct or indirect discrimination, or harassment; excessively wide exceptions; cumbersome enforcement mechanisms; limiting equality associations' power to help victims; making the burden of proof overly demanding on claimants; and narrowing the Directive's scope of applicability (often to the employment field only).
172 European Commission (2009).
173 E.g., European Commission (2014).

concern, the unsatisfactory state of implementation' of the Directive.[174] Of course, the Commission's being more accommodating than the Parliament of Member States' priorities is in line with the institutional approach that was displayed during the Directive's drafting process. Unfortunately, lack of consistent institutional pressure has further weakened any potential the Directive might have had to improve domestic equality laws.

The Directive has had little impact on the actual incidence of discrimination, which remains prevalent across the EU. According to the Fundamental Rights Agency, the EU body specifically tasked with collecting and analysing data on fundamental rights, the Directive had brought about little improvement in tackling racial discrimination a decade after its transposition, as 'discrimination remains part of the daily experience of too many Europeans', especially in the employment context.[175] Moreover, forms of discrimination that are made unlawful might give false comfort that discrimination is being tackled. Thus, it becomes more difficult to recognise forms of disadvantage or inequality that do not fit the closely delineated causes of action[176], and this is further complicated by the fact that racist attitudes and behaviours are often covert and difficult to identify or get misattributed to factors such as cultural antipathy.

In the context of CEE movers, this becomes especially problematic. In addition to the fact that some of the Directive's provisions are unfit for protecting CEE movers, as discussed earlier, their whiteness might amplify the Directive's ineffectiveness. Some western civil society members assume that racial anti-discrimination laws apply to non-whites and non-Christians only and that whites cannot be victims of racism.[177] This erroneous view has even been subscribed to by some white victims of racism, likely decreasing their reliance on anti-discrimination law. The oversight of CEE movers in the Directive's legislative history and in the broader EU equality discourse (discussed below) have only served to reinforce this outlook. The traditional white/black binary contributes to the limiting view that whiteness is homogeneous and that white privilege is equally accessible to all Caucasians, which makes anti-white discrimination more difficult to perceive, acknowledge, and address.[178] Although contemporary critical scholars have drawn attention to fractures within whiteness[179] and have acknowledged how whites not belonging to the group in power—for example, those of lower socio-economic status[180]—are vulnerable to discrimination, CEE movers and racialised whites more generally have tended to be overlooked by western equality protections.

---

174 European Parliament (2005).
175 European Union Agency for Fundamental Rights (2013). This has been attributed to transposition errors, victims' lack of awareness, costliness of bringing claims, insufficient remedies, and fear of victimisation.
176 See generally Crenshaw et al. (1995).
177 E.g., Kelner (2016); Krishnan (2016).
178 See generally Frankenberg (1997).
179 See generally Levine-Rasky (2013).
180 E.g., Pruitt (2015).

Broader EU Equality Discourse

More generally, racialised whites have been disregarded by EU equality discourse. EU reports issued in the context of tackling racial and ethnic discrimination have consistently overlooked the unequal experiences of CEE movers and of white outsider groups more generally except for Roma and long-standing minorities within CEE states. This stance has further naturalised (non-Roma) CEE movers' inequalities and racialisation. Although recent reports have acknowledged that discrimination remains prevalent in general, despite the adoption of the Race Equality Directive, EU institutions have continued to focus on the rights of non-EU migrants and non-Caucasians only. They have also tended to minimise how commonplace CEE movers' discrimination has been and have been silent regarding how peripheralising EU policies and discourses have been implicated in that process. Instead, they have attributed racism to local-level economic and political structures.

For example, the Commission's 2014 report on the application of the Race Equality Directive[181] acknowledged that discrimination is widespread, especially in the employment context and particularly on grounds of ethnic origin. However, when referring to discrimination faced by 'ethnic or immigrant minority groups', the report did not mention movers. The report referred to only women, Roma, persons with disabilities, and LGBTQI groups as vulnerable to discrimination. Similarly, in a staff working document about national equality bodies, only Roma, gay, and disabled persons were listed.[182] When addressing fundamental rights more broadly, EU institutions have similarly focused on protecting non-EU migrants and long-standing national minorities (especially Jews, Muslims, and Roma).[183] This approach was even adopted in reports released after the Brexit referendum, despite evidence of a concomitant spike in violence against CEE movers in the UK. For example, in a 2017 report on EU citizens' rights, the Parliament did not mention CEE movers when discussing a recent 'rise in xenophobia and racism in the EU'.[184] Other recent reports have similarly focused on the need to protect refugees, Roma, Jews, Muslims, Africans, and groups deemed to be vulnerable (children, the disabled, and women), with no mention of intra-EU movers.[185]

Spurred only by the Covid pandemic and the BLM movement, the EU has made some recent strides in its thinking about racism and has begun to recognise structural racism and intersectionality in its discourse. Racialised whites, such as CEE movers, have continued to be overlooked in such discussions, however. For example, the Commission's EU Anti-Racism Action Plan 2020–25[186] recognises

---

181 European Commission (2014).
182 European Commission (2021b).
183 E.g., European Parliament (2005).
184 European Parliament (2017).
185 E.g., European Commission (2018); European Commission (2019).
186 European Commission (2020f).

the existence of structural racism, that is, organisational and institutional policies created over time that perpetuate racial inequity. However, the Action Plan overlooks CEE movers from its discussion of 'racialised' groups and mentions 'ethnic origin' only in the context of Roma and persons of non-Christian or non-Caucasian descent. Notably, it links such groups' subjugation to the historical roots of racism—colonialism, slavery, and the Holocaust—implicitly minimising the role of contemporary processes in propagating racisms. The Commission's subgroup on national implementations of the Action Plan has also acknowledged intersectionality (i.e., each person's multiple, intersecting social categorisation factors of disadvantage such as race and class) and unconscious racial bias (i.e., learned stereotypes about certain groups of people that are formed outside of conscious awareness).[187] Its report, however, also limits the EU's focus to protecting non-EU migrants and non-Caucasians[188] and reiterates the historical roots of racisms against such groups. The first ever EU Anti-Racism Summit, held in 2021, reiterated this approach,[189] which was restated again at the 2022 summit.[190] Although recent institutional acknowledgements of structural racism and intersectionality are to be commended, EU institutions have continued to overlook how both concepts play a role in CEE movers' racialisation.

In line with such reports that have consistently undermined racism experienced by CEE movers, EU support for integration measures has targeted non-EU migrants, Roma, Muslims, and non-white groups.[191] Moreover, whereas all EU-15 states have had mandatory nationwide integration measures for non-EU migrants, they have tended to lack such initiatives for EU movers. Some national integration measures have even explicitly excluded EU citizens, including in Austria, Germany, the Netherlands, and the UK.

Reports by EU agencies and EU-sponsored groups devoted to tackling racism have similarly disregarded CEE movers. Even when noting that those who are foreign-born are particularly susceptible to discrimination, the Fundamental Rights Agency (and its predecessor, the European Monitoring Centre on Racism and Xenophobia), the European Network Against Racism (ENAR), and Equinet have focused on the need to protect only Roma, Muslims, Travellers, Jews, refugees, non-whites, and non-EU migrants.[192] Moreover, even when acknowledging that all movers experience discrimination in accessing employment, housing, banking services, and education these entities entities have not called for greater equality protections for CEE movers.[193] In line with EU

---

187 European Commission (2022b).
188 See also Council of the EU (2022).
189 See European Anti-Racism Summit (2021).
190 See European Anti-Racism Summit (2022).
191 E.g., European Commission (2020g).
192 E.g., European Monitoring Centre on Racism and Xenophobia (2006); European Network Against Racism (2009); European Union Agency for Fundamental Rights (2012); Crowley (2020).
193 E.g., European Union Agency for Fundamental Rights (2018).

institutions' discourse, when explaining the new Anti-Racism Action Plan, the ENAR emphasised that the current equality legislation is not sufficient to protect 'marginalised' groups, but defined them to include only non-EU migrants, Roma, women, non-Caucasians, non-Christians, persons with disabilities, and LGBTQI groups.[194] Notably, although ENAR recommended adding nationality as a protected ground under race equality legislation, its discussion was limited to non-EU migrants and non-Caucasians. Similarly, ENAR's 2021 report on violence faced by 'racialised' groups[195] overlooked white movers. Furthermore, although it brought to the foreground the construction of whiteness as a race, it approaches whiteness as homogeneous, with privilege bestowed on all whites equally. Finally, the latest European Equality Law Review, the bi-annual publication produced by a Commission-sponsored network of legal experts in non-discrimination policies, made no mention of movers. It referred to Roma, persons with disability, and LGBTQI groups.[196] It overlooked the significance of foreignness to the experience of inequalities. Migrant status was mentioned only once and only in the context of intersectionality with LGBTQI status. Similarly, the network's 2022 report on structural racial discrimination, which spanned 114 pages, made no single mention of movers, despite frequent references to 'migrants' (that is, non-EU migrants) and 'ethnic minorities' (that is, non-Caucasians).[197]

Context Leading to the Imposition of Transitional Mobility Derogations

Before the Eastern Enlargement, CEE nationals' rights to work or reside in the EU were very limited. Under communist rule, lawful emigration was severely restricted except for some ethnic and religious minority groups under bilateral agreements. A small number of CEE nationals would defect each year from behind the Iron Curtain. Although the ability to emigrate from the CEE region was slightly liberalised in the 1980s, CEE nationals were required until 2001 to obtain visas to enter EU countries. Pre-accession agreements between the EU and each CEE state, discussed in the preceding chapter, did not provide CEE nationals with many routes to enter the EU lawfully. The Agreements on Trade and Commercial and Economic Cooperation focused on just that, with no mention of mobility. The Europe Agreements liberalised free movement of capital, goods, and services only. EU states could continue applying their domestic immigration rules to CEE nationals, although they were not permitted to make them more demanding than they had been at the time of signing their respective Europe Agreements. Although CEE nationals lawfully employed (or self-employed, if they could demonstrate sufficient resources) in EU states in accordance with domestic immigration laws

---

194 European Network Against Racism (2022).
195 European Network Against Racism (2021).
196 European Commission (2022c).
197 European Commission (2022d).

were entitled to protection from nationality-based discrimination in the employment context,[198] this was of little practical impact as so few CEE nationals were able to access lawful employment in the first place. Furthermore, as non-EU immigrants, CEE migrants could not access social benefits in EU states unless they were refugees or family members of EU citizens.

Estimates indicate that, on the eve of the Eastern Enlargement in 2004, approximately 1.5 million CEE nationals lawfully resided in EU-15 states, predominantly in Germany, Italy, and Austria. Most were there as refugees, as family members of EU nationals, or pursuant to a few ad hoc bilateral agreements that focused on temporary-worker schemes responsive to specific western-employer needs. Except for refugees and EU family members, CEE migrants tended to be mostly male, heavily engaged in temporary migration, and employed in low-paid jobs. Migration statistics, of course, suffer from data limitations and also overlook undocumented migrants, which was not uncommon among CEE nationals due to the restricted exit and entry regimes before the Enlargement.

As soon as the prospect of CEE nationals' mobility to the west began to materialise, western citizenries began to sternly oppose it. Despite labour shortages across EU states at the time, western politicians embraced post-accession mobility restrictions. Although EU institutions adopted a more pragmatic approach at first, they soon followed suit, without giving much thought about how withholding this fundamental right from CEE nationals was at odds with its grand rhetoric and with the post-Maastricht Treaty construct of EU citizenship. Seven-year post-transitional mobility derogations were imposed through the 2003 Accession Treaty, further reinforced through a variety of indirect EU-15 measures targeting CEE movers' rights, which were broader in scope and more difficult to justify pragmatically than the transitional measures that had been used in one prior enlargement.

EU Institutions' Approach Towards CEE Nationals' Mobility

Although EU institutions did not give the possibility of CEE nationals' mobility much thought when first formalising relations with the CEE region soon after the fall of communism, there is no indication that they contemplated imposing transitional mobility derogations if, or when, CEE states were to accede. Notably, this stance was motivated by pragmatic, rather than human rights, considerations. By the late 1990s, the Commission deemed restrictions on CEE mobility to be unnecessary for protecting EU-15 economies due to predictions of the arrival of only small numbers of CEE workers[199] who were expected to be largely well-educated

---

198 *Land Nordrhein-Westfalen v Pokrzeptowicz-Meyer*, Case C-162/00, ECLI:EU:C:2002:57.
199 Of between 41,000 and 335,000 movers per year in the first few years following the Enlargement, and long-term movement of no more than 2–4 million. This was lower than the expected post-04 inflows of non-EU and EU-15 movers.

and mostly engaged in temporary mobility. Moreover, various pre-Enlargement studies concluded that EU-15 states would benefit economically from unrestricted CEE workers' mobility, which was anticipated to alleviate bottlenecks in western labour markets, boost demand for goods, and address labour needs in light of ageing populations. Western labour organisations—including the European Trade Union Confederation and the Union of Industrial and Employers' Confederations of Europe—supported unrestrained CEE mobility. In fact, Member States with the greatest inflow of CEE movers were forecast to reap the greatest economic benefits. Some experts even argued that an influx of CEE workers was *necessary* for continued western economic growth.[200]

Nevertheless, in response to public fears about an impending arrival of CEE nationals, the Commission slowly began to acknowledge the possibility of mobility restrictions.[201] Disappointingly, although the Commission opposed extensive post-accession mobility derogations, it never acknowledged any conceptual difficulties with withholding this fundamental EU right from CEE nationals. Instead, it focused on pragmatic reasons only—expecting transitional arrangements to be ineffective and difficult to negotiate with CEE states and reiterating that CEE mobility would benefit EU-15 economies.[202] In line with long-standing narratives about the benevolence of the EU project and its policies, the Commission eventually came to justify post-accession derogations as beneficial to the CEE region itself by reducing labour shortages and brain drain therein.[203] Similarly, despite having supported the inclusion of the free movement right in the Europe Agreements with CEE states, the European Economic and Social Committee[204] embraced transitional derogations as advantageous to prospective CEE movers themselves, claiming the derogations would alleviate potential xenophobic reactions against them in EU-15 states.[205]

Notably, although there was some level of institutional awareness that CEE movers would be facing prejudices in the west and that their mobility would produce some negative effects on the CEE region, no efforts were contemplated to directly address such projections. More generally, no attention was devoted to CEE nationals' human rights during the Enlargement process. EU reports dedicated to equality issues specifically in the context of the Enlargement overlooked these new EU citizens' rights and instead emphasised that anti-discrimination

---

200 See generally Stalford (2003).
201 E.g., Commission of the European Communities (1997).
202 After the Enlargement, the Commission continued to question the utility of transitional derogations, but again, its critique was dominated by interest convergence between greater CEE workers' mobility and stronger western economic growth. E.g., Commission of the European Communities (2006b).
203 See generally Dougan (2004).
204 An advisory assembly composed of employers, employees, and representatives of various other economic interests.
205 European Economic and Social Committee (2001).

measures in an enlarged EU should focus on long-standing national minorities, non-Christians, non-EU nationals, and stateless persons.

For example, in the 2005 'Resolution on the Protection of Minorities and Anti-Discrimination Policies in an Enlarged Europe',[206] the Parliament mentioned CEE movers in only three of 63 paragraphs, noting that, like all 'foreign' groups, they should be integrated into host communities. Revealingly, when addressing discrimination against 'recent immigrants', the Parliament referred to non-EU immigrants only,[207] despite the fact that in the first year after the Enlargement more than one million CEE nationals had already moved to EU-15 states. Overall, CEE movers were portrayed as inherently foreign from EU-15 citizenries yet not foreign enough to deserve anti-discrimination protections. Similarly, in the Commission's 2004 'Green Paper: Equality and Non-Discrimination in an Enlarged European Union', the section titled 'Dealing with issues linked to the enlargement of the EU' only addressed protecting long-standing national minorities within CEE states such as Roma, Jews, and Muslims.[208] Furthermore, in the aforementioned Green Paper, the Commission focused on the significance of anti-discrimination policies to the EU's long-term economic growth and to labour market integration. As with the Race Equality Directive's legislative history, it is not clear if such absences reflect a mere oversight, an inability to recognise 'xenophobia' against Caucasians as racism, or an unwillingness to deem CEE victims of racism as deserving of the EU's protections. Regardless of the actual reasons, embedding equality and enlargement policies within discourse focused on market imperatives, while overlooking CEE movers, has helped to naturalise CEE nationals' unequal experience of mobility.

EU-15 States' Approach Towards CEE Nationals' Mobility

Western citizenries have steadily opposed CEE nationals' mobility to the west. Anxieties were voiced as soon as the Berlin Wall fell in 1989 crumbling the physical and ideological barriers between east and west. In 1991, 63% of EU citizens polled wished to restrict CEE immigration and 20% desired to ban it altogether.[209] Leading up to the Enlargement, western publics—particularly in Germany and Austria, due to their geographical proximity to the CEE region—began to express increasing concerns about an 'invasion' of undesirables. For example, the then-chief of the German police union proclaimed that the lifting of border controls with Poland would be 'an invitation to criminals'.[210] Across EU-15 states, various trade unions, the press, and the publics focused on unsubstantiated fears of benefit tourism and social dumping. Two years before

206 OJ 2005 C 124 E/405.
207 Although movers are not migrants in the legal sense, EU discourse has at times subsumed CEE movers under the 'migrant' label.
208 COM (2004) 379 final.
209 Eurobarometer (1991).
210 Johnstone (2007) (citation omitted).

the Enlargement, almost half of EU-15 nationals surveyed expected a 'considerable' post-accession influx of CEE nationals and, among those, 76% characterised it as a 'negative' development.[211] The instinctive assumption that many CEE nationals would move to western states was reinforced by a sense of western superiority and also reflected east/west economic inequalities. Meanwhile, opposition to CEE mobility was fuelled by the anticipated negative impact of CEE nationals on western cultures—an anxiety compounded by increasing globalisation and domestic fiscal concerns.

In 2000, then-German Chancellor Schröeder proposed seven-year transitional mobility derogations. This is despite the fact that approximately 45,000 CEE workers were forecast to arrive annually in Germany during the first few years after the Enlargement, while an annual inflow of more than 300,000 workers was needed to keep a stable working-age population. More generally, western politicians' opposition to CEE mobility, despite aging western populations and significant labour shortages at the time in many EU-15 states, is also in line with their use of migration as a scapegoat for any shortcomings of neoliberal political and economic policies which, in turn, has been driving the rise of right-wing, anti-immigrant populism across Europe in recent decades. Notably, some western politicians even argued that mobility derogations would benefit CEE nationals themselves by protecting them from labour exploitation in EU-15 states. Thus, similarly to the EU, they foresaw—without condemning—unequal treatment of CEE movers in the west, bringing to the foreground fractures and hierarchies within whiteness and within access to EU citizenship rights.

Transitional Mobility Derogations

Whereas workers' access to the free movement right has traditionally been privileged, that hierarchy was temporarily reversed in the context of CEE nationals. The 2003 Accession Treaty expressly blocked[212] the application of EC Treaty Article 39(2) which had abolished discrimination against movers in the context of employment. Specifically, Member States could derogate for up to seven years from Articles 1 through 6 of Regulation 1612/68 (pertaining to workers' mobility) and from provisions of Directive 68/360 (pertaining to mobile workers' residence rights).[213] As Currie notes, transitional derogations 'by their very nature [were] designed to protect the interests of the older Member States'.[214] This is in line with how the whole accession process was orchestrated, as I have argued in the preceding chapter. Moreover, transitional

---

211 Eurobarometer (2002).
212 E.g., 2003 Accession Treaty, Annex XII, s 2 (pertaining to Polish nationals); 2003 Accession Treaty, Annex X, s 1 (pertaining to Hungarian nationals).
213 Later repealed by the Citizens' Rights Directive 2004/38.
214 Currie (2008).

derogations reinforced a sense of commonality among EU-15 nationals while differentiating, stigmatising, and essentialising those from the CEE region.

Pursuant to the Accession Treaty, EU-15 states were provided wide discretion in restricting CEE workers' mobility during the transitional period.[215] For the first two years after accession, EU-15 states could apply their pre-accession domestic immigration measures as long as employers prioritised EU workers (including CEE workers) over non-EU workers. Of course, EU-15 states were free to make their national measures more restrictive *up to that date*—and many in fact did. Moreover, the requirement that employers prefer EU over non-EU workers had limited practical implications, because it could be satisfied by favouring only EU-14 applicants over non-EU immigrants. Before the end of the initial two-year phase, the Council was to 'review' the functioning of domestic transitional arrangements—although this process had no binding effect. Thus, in practice, Member States could decide unilaterally to continue imposing their national measures during the second (three-year) phase after simply notifying the Commission. Thereafter, states that had been applying restrictive measures had the discretion to continue doing so for two additional years 'in case of serious disturbances' of their labour markets or merely in response to 'a threat thereof'. No EU authorisation was required, and the concept of 'serious disturbances' was never clarified.

In addition, special safeguard measures were put in place. Any Member State that had not initially applied transitional restrictions could request, at any point before the end of the seven-year period, that the Commission authorise its use of mobility restrictions. This safeguard provision could be applied if a state had experienced—or merely foresaw—labour market disturbances that 'could seriously threaten the standard of living or the level of employment in a given region or occupation'.[216] Any restrictions authorised under this provision would be in place until conditions were deemed to have returned to 'normal'. Again, none of these terms were defined. Moreover, in 'urgent and exceptional' cases, Member States could unilaterally suspend the application of the free movement acquis at any point before the end of the seven-year period. Although neither of these safeguards was applied in the aftermath of the 2004 Enlargement, they indicate how much leeway EU institutions were willing to provide to EU-15 states in undermining CEE nationals' right of free movement.

---

215 Transitional derogations were reciprocal, so that each CEE state was permitted to limit labour market access to nationals of any state that had imposed mobility derogations against it. The practical effect of this measure was negligible, however, as EU-15 nationals had little interest in seeking employment in the CEE region. Providing reciprocity was merely a strategic move by the EU, to enhance the fabricated impression that CEE states were equal partners during the accession process—which was anything but equal, as my discussion in the preceding chapter has shown.

216 E.g., 2003 Accession Treaty, Annex XII, s 7.

Transitional derogations were not challengeable under EU law. Article 18 of the EC Treaty allows the adoption of EU measures to limit the free movement right.[217] The ECJ did not have jurisdiction to challenge the legality of derogations because they were an integral part of the Accession Treaty which constitutes primary law. That being said, since any limitations on the free movement right must be interpreted strictly,[218] the Commission could have brought infringement proceedings against any Member State for imposing overly broad direct mobility restrictions. No such procedures were initiated, however.

Moreover, although post-accession mobility derogations applied only to CEE workers[219] and jobseekers, access to mobility of other types of CEE nationals was significantly impeded under other Accession Treaty provisions, through secondary legislation, and due to practical constraints. For example, economically inactive individuals, retirees, and students had to demonstrate financial self-sufficiency and possession of comprehensive sickness insurance to access mobility. Since the concept of self-sufficiency is tied to the living standard in a host state, it would have been inherently difficult for CEE nationals to satisfy this test given the economic and wage differentials between CEE and EU-15 states. Mobility derogations also did not apply to self-employed persons. Although legally not a very onerous standard to meet, becoming self-employed requires financial resources and familiarity with local markets and practices. These hurdles would have been difficult for CEE nationals to overcome, due to economic reasons and because of their restricted access to EU-15 states before 2004. Transitional measures also did not apply to CEE nationals who had been working lawfully in any EU-15 state for an uninterrupted period of at least 12 months prior to Enlargement, as long as they remained in that state for the first 12 months after accession. The rights of such workers, however, could be limited at the discretion of host states. Notably, this provision carried little practical significance given how few CEE nationals had access to lawful employment opportunities in EU-15 states before the Enlargement. Furthermore, their propensity to engage in short-term migration and in informal employment caused many of them to lack an uninterrupted 12-month period of work. Overall, compared to workers, the categories of CEE nationals to whom transitional derogations did not apply constituted small potential numbers of movers who were less likely to be eligible for public benefits in host states. Thus, they did not pose much of an economic or psychological threat to the west.

---

217 'Every citizen of the Union shall have the right to move and reside freely within the territory of the Member States, subject to the limitations and conditions laid down in this Treaty and by the measures adopted to give it effect'.
218 Any limits on fundamental freedoms (such as free movement) must be narrowly interpreted, applied in a non-discriminatory manner, justified by imperative requirements in the general interest, suitable for securing the attainment of their objective, and may not go beyond what is necessary to attain those objectives.
219 Except posted workers, who rely on the right to freedom of movement of services.

Although access to the free movement right has always been differentiated, post-accession transitional policies created a patchwork of partial access to post-Maastricht EU citizenship rights and thus contradicted the foundational Treaty right to equal treatment regardless of nationality that underlies the EU integration project. The Accession Treaty and its legislative history were silent about CEE nationals' EU citizenship rights and did not offer any justification for mobility derogations. More generally, EU institutions and western politicians did not invoke the concept of citizenship during the accession process, indicating the substantial gap between the right of EU citizenship on the books and the actual experience of mobility, which reinforced CEE movers' racialisation and marginalisation.

Comparison to Mobility Restrictions During Earlier Enlargements

The right to mobility was less controversial during prior EU enlargements. The first enlargement incorporated Denmark, Ireland, and the United Kingdom in 1973, expanding the EU's population by 31% (from 209 to 273 million). Although Dutch and French politicians did express concerns about potential disruptions to their labour markets, further stoked by economic anxieties caused by the oil crisis that occurred later that year, no mobility restrictions were contemplated. During the 1995 accession of Austria, Sweden, and Finland—which added 29 million new EU citizens—free-movement rules were made fully applicable to the new Member States a year before accession. Transitional mobility restrictions were imposed, however, during the Southern Enlargement—for six years against Greek nationals (in 1981) and for seven years against those from Spain and Portugal (in 1986). The Southern Enlargement restrictions were justified at the time by the expansion of the EU population by 21% (58 million) and the fact that the pre-existing Member States were not experiencing any labour shortages at the time.

Mobility derogations imposed during the Eastern Enlargement were more difficult to warrant than during the Southern Enlargement. Although CEE states acceding in 2004 increased the EU's population by 19% (74 million), EU-15 states were experiencing significant labour shortages at the time. Predictions about EU-15 states' economic benefits from unrestricted mobility of the new Member States' nationals were well substantiated during this Enlargement, unlike during the Southern accession. Moreover, the 2004 mobility restrictions were inconsistent with two new Treaty provisions—the Maastricht Treaty's expansion of the free movement right to all Member State nationals and the creation of the borderless Schengen Area through the 1999 Amsterdam Treaty.

Despite being less defensible, post-04 mobility derogations were more restrictive than in the aftermath of the Southern Enlargement. Notably, all EU-15 states were given the flexibility to apply their own domestic restrictions rather than having to follow uniform restraints imposed by the EU.

During the Southern Enlargement, only Luxembourg had been permitted to adopt its own transitional rules—likely due to its small size and an already high proportion of foreign workers. This is indicative of just how much anxiety CEE mobility had provoked among western publics and politicians and of how problematic it was to the western psyche.

CEE Nationals' Rights During the Transitional Period

CEE Workers' Rights

Austria, Belgium, Finland, France, Germany, and Luxembourg had declared from early on in the accession process that they planned to apply tight restrictions on CEE workers' and jobseekers' mobility. Likely due to their geographical proximity to CEE states, Austria and Germany spearheaded these efforts. Once they had voiced their plans, other EU-15 states designed a variety of direct restrictions, in a 'race to the bottom'[220]—including annual quotas, bilateral agreements, seasonal permits, sector-specific permits, and general work permits (typically tied to domestic workers' unavailability). Some of these measures approached CEE nationals in a manner identical to non-EU migrants. Despite healthy economies in most EU-15 states, and 'low-skill' labour shortages in many (including the UK, Germany, and France), all EU-15 states except Sweden applied direct or indirect barriers to CEE nationals' mobility. The UK and Ireland did not apply direct derogations but adopted registration requirements (discussed in the next chapter). Although most EU-15 states—with the notable exceptions of Germany, Austria, Belgium, and Denmark—began to ease their direct restrictions after 2006, they did not do so immediately after it had become evident that CEE mobility was not threatening their labour markets and was indeed benefiting them economically. During the final transitional phase (2009–11), Austria and Germany continued to apply their direct mobility derogations, while Ireland and the UK persisted in maintaining their indirect measures.[221] Since such restrictions were difficult to justify by practical concerns, they were clearly motivated at least in part by anti-CEE animus and served as a symbolic rebuff to 'Eastern Europeans'.

Moreover, all EU-15 states other than Sweden adopted restrictions on post-2004 CEE workers' access to social assistance or social security benefits, for example, by defining 'worker' status more narrowly than under EU law, imposing additional entry or residence requirements, or expanding host state powers to expel movers who were reliant on (or had merely applied for) benefits. As discussed earlier in this chapter, some of these measures were implemented in

220 Boeri and Brücker (2005).
221 Similarly, most EU-15 states imposed even more stringent transitional derogations against Bulgarian and Romanian workers in the aftermath of the 2007 accession. Moreover, Spain invoked the accession safeguard clause to re-introduce mobility restrictions against Romanian workers during 2011–12, allegedly justified due to Spain's high unemployment rate.

the context of transposing the Citizens' Rights Directive 2004/38, and some via ancillary measures adopted near the time of the Enlargement or shortly thereafter. Such measures were applied notwithstanding the lack of empirical evidence to suggest that Member States with liberal welfare policies were at risk of disproportionately attracting CEE movers or that CEE movers intended to rely on host state welfare systems.

Notably, nothing in the Accession Treaty had endowed Member States with the right to impose restrictions falling outside of direct labour market access limitations. Anything not expressly excluded by the Accession Treaty was subject to the general EU equality principles—specifically EC Treaty Article 12 (prohibiting discrimination on grounds of nationality) and Article 39 (prohibiting nationality discrimination in employment). Thus, although Member States were permitted to limit CEE workers' access to their labour markets pursuant to the Accession Treaty, once that access was granted, host states were technically not allowed to restrict access to any benefits that accrue from 'worker' status. Indeed, pursuant to provisions of Regulation 1612/68 that were not explicitly excluded through the Accession Treaty, mobile EU workers and jobseekers were entitled to equal treatment in the context of employment conditions, access to social[222] and tax advantages, and access to housing. Furthermore, CEE movers were also automatically entitled to the protections of Regulation 1408/71, explicitly mentioned in the Accession Treaty,[223] which guaranteed equality of treatment in respect to both non-contributory and contributory social security benefits. Although indirect mobility impediments were in contravention of EU law, EU institutions largely remained silent and presented very little, if any, opposition to them.

CEE Self-Employed Movers' Rights

Transitional mobility derogations did not apply to self-employed CEE nationals, so, from the day of accession, they had the same rights as workers from EU-15 states. The ECJ has defined self-employment status broadly as working for oneself and being solely responsible for one's own business failures or successes.[224] Self-employed movers merely needed to abide by applicable national laws, such as those pertaining to registering keeping records, and paying income taxes. Although legally not an onerous standard to satisfy, becoming self-employed would have been difficult for CEE nationals to accomplish financially and due to historical restrictions on their travel, as already mentioned. Furthermore, self-employed CEE movers were subjected to a variety of restrictive measures adopted

---

222 'Social advantages' have been interpreted broadly by the ECJ—to include discretionary benefits, benefits granted after employment is terminated, and at least some benefits not directly linked to employment (such as the right to be accompanied by a mover's partner).
223 2003 Accession Treaty, Annex II.
224 *Centros Ltd v Erhvervs- og Selskabsstyrelsen*, Case C-212/97, ECLI:EU:C:1999:126.

across EU-15 states in the context of transposing Directive 2004/38 and via ancillary policies and practices discussed earlier in this chapter.

Although reliable data is not available as Member States did not consistently record self-employed movers, perhaps as many as 10% or 20% of all CEE movers during the transitional period accessed EU-15 states through self-employment. Given that CEE workers' access to EU-15 states was restricted during the transitional period, it is unclear how many CEE nationals felt pushed into self-employment in order to be able to gain such access and how many might have engaged in sham self-employment, which carries even greater economic and social risks than those normally associated with self-employment. Moreover, although self-employed CEE movers were entitled to benefit from social rights akin to western workers, they often encountered administrative difficulties in accessing social benefits. For example, host state officials used a wide margin of discretion when determining whether to accept CEE movers' evidence of valid self-employment.

CEE Economically Inactive Movers' Rights

Mobility derogations also did not apply to economically inactive CEE nationals—such as students, pensioners, and the unemployed—so that, from the day of accession, they could fully rely on the free movement right. Even before the Citizens' Rights Directive 2004/38 was transposed in 2006, economically inactive EU citizens could reside in other Member States pursuant to Directive 90/364 as long as they possessed sickness insurance and sufficient resources as not to become an unreasonable burden on host-state public finances. According to the ECJ's interpretation of Directive 90/364, determination of sufficiency had to be individualised and holistic, based on all the resources that might be available to a mover including from third parties.[225] However, since sufficiency depends on the cost of living in a host state, the sufficiency standard was difficult for many CEE nationals to satisfy as, on average, they were less wealthy than EU-15 nationals. For example, in 2003, CEE countries' GDPs (in terms of purchasing power) ranged from 42% (Latvia) to 77% (Slovenia) of the EU-25 average.

Economically inactive CEE movers gained access to ancillary rights, such as social and tax advantages, on par with comparable EU-15 movers. Until becoming more restrictive in the mid 2010s, the ECJ was instrumental in protecting access to social benefits of economically inactive movers, requiring only that they demonstrate a 'real link' to the host state society based on a holistic determination of factors such as length of presence in the host country, intention to remain there, and family links to the host state.[226] This test was broad and flexible and would only fail to be met when it was

---

225 *Baumbast and R v Secretary of State for the Home Department*, C-413/99, ECLI:EU:C:2002:493.
226 *Swaddling*, Case C-90/97.

inconceivable that a real link existed.[227] However, being heavily fact-specific, this assessment provided host states with much discretion to deny access to CEE nationals—as indeed illustrated by cases referred from EU-15 courts to the ECJ after 2010 (discussed below). In addition, when transposing Directive 2004/38, EU-15 states narrowed many of its provisions and adopted additional restrictive policies to diminish economically inactive CEE movers' rights in EU-15 states, as discussed earlier.

It is difficult to determine the precise extent to which this post-accession transitional framework affected the actual numbers of CEE movers, which is further complicated because not all Member States kept detailed statistics. Overall, between 2 and 3 million CEE nationals appear to have moved to EU-15 states by 2011—more than doubling their pre-accession presence. What is clear, however, is that mobility derogations had a negative effect on CEE workers' experiences in the west, leading to higher rates of exploitation and discrimination. When the first two-year phase of transitional restrictions was coming to an end, the European Parliament noted that they had constituted 'a major contributory factor' to CEE movers' frequently illicit employment and experiences of exploitation and discrimination in EU-15 states.[228] Despite this acknowledgement, however, there was no institutional response on the part of the EU to address CEE movers' poor treatment. More generally, post-accession mobility derogations, combined with various additional EU-15 approaches to limit CEE nationals' rights, not only transformed CEE states into 'restricted-exit homelands or reservations'[229] but also entrenched the long-standing view of CEE nationals as not belonging to the EU polity, with long-term negative repercussions for their experience of mobility.

CEE Movers' Rights Since the End of the Transitional Period

Directive 2004/38 continues to be in force today. Its transposed domestic policies—as well as oftentimes restrictive ancillary measures (discussed earlier)—became applicable to all CEE nationals accessing EU-15 states after any national transitional measures had come to an end by 2011. In the last decade, EU institutions have increasingly imposed their own limitations on the mobility of economically inactive movers and have tended to acquiesce to further EU-15 state efforts to limit the rights of even movers who are workers. Such measures have deliberately targeted CEE movers and have had a disproportionately negative impact on them.

Notably, with a more restrictive turn starting with its 2013 *Brey* judgment, the ECJ began to rely more heavily on a strict, technical interpretation of EU secondary laws while moving away from its prior 'constitutional' Treaty-based rhetoric about EU citizenship and free movement rights. Moreover, the ECJ has been painting a picture of CEE claimants, especially those deemed to be economically

---

227 *Ioannidis*, Case C-258/04.
228 European Parliament (2006).
229 Böröcz and Kovacs (2001).

inactive, as inherently socially, morally, and economically inferior, and not part of the 'European' polity. Arguably, ECJ judges[230] have been taking into account the increasing politicisation of CEE movers' rights across EU-15 states[231]—particularly when the transitional post-04 restrictions ended in 2011, as (even more stringent) transitional limitations against Bulgarians and Romanians were coming to an end in 2014, and as the UK began to openly question the right to free movement in the context of Brexit. Increasingly restrictive ECJ jurisprudence reflects what EU-15 states had aimed to achieve with some of the provisions of Directive 2004/38, adopted at their insistence, that afford Member States significant flexibility to curb (CEE) movers' residence and social rights. Moreover, in addition to acquiescing to directly discriminatory measures implemented against mobile CEE workers in the context of the UK's membership re-negotiation attempts, the EU had proposed amending secondary regulations to do so itself. Tellingly, EU rhetoric has continued to focus on the economic core of the free movement right—and its implicit economic benefits to the west—implying that only good 'market citizens' are deserving of the protections of EU law, while persisting to ignore CEE nationals' rights and the broader background of their exploitation and inequalities amid increasing flexibilisation of the labour market. This approach has continued in even the most recent discourse devoted to increasing social protections across the EU.

Recent restrictive measures have continued to perpetuate a 'xenosceptic' legal and administrative culture[232] by signalling that EU workers who come from poorer states, who are employed in low-paid or precarious jobs, or who might present a risk of not sufficiently contributing to EU-15 economies do not belong in the west. Once western labour shortages became sufficiently overcome and CEE mobility became highly politicised again after the transitional derogations expired, CEE nationals' access to mobility became gradually lessened through EU and various EU-15 policies. As with post-accession mobility derogations, western preferences have continued to be prioritised, reproducing the social, economic, and political power that EU-15 states wield over their second-class CEE neighbours.

Situating CEE Movers within the Current EU Mobility Framework

Workers

Recent EU statutory instruments have reinforced the traditional mobility hierarchy, privileging the rights of workers. For example, Regulation 492/2011

---

230 Although CEE experts joined the ECJ in 2004, as both Judges and Advocates General, the majority of its staff has continued to be from EU-15 states. Each Member State nominates a judge whose nomination is then ratified by all other Member States.
231 See generally Blauberger et al. (2018). Davies (2018) argues, however, that what has changed have been the types of cases brought before the ECJ, with increasingly more outlier cases dealing with movers who are less well integrated into host societies.
232 See generally O'Brien (2015).

defines workers' right to free movement broadly, as including 'all matters relating to the actual pursuit of activities as employed persons', and 'conditions for the integration of the worker's family'.[233] Directive 2014/54[234] denounces any 'unjustified restrictions and obstacles' to workers' mobility. Similarly, the ECJ has continued supporting workers' mobility, by defining the 'worker' category broadly, in line with its jurisprudence from before the adoption of Directive 2004/38. For example, the Court extended worker status to a full-time student who had entered a host state with the intention to study and was employed only part-time.[235] The Court has also persisted in defining the right to retain 'worker' status broadly. For example, in *Saint-Prix*, the Court extended worker status (and hence entitlement to income support) to a woman who had stopped working due to complications from pregnancy and childbirth as long as she were to return to work within a 'reasonable' time—to be determined based on individual factual circumstances.[236]

Moreover, in recent caselaw, the Court has been reiterating that self-employed persons are entitled to the same rights as employed workers, including to the retention of worker status under Article 7(3) of Directive 2004/38 after becoming involuntarily unemployed. For example, in *Gusa*[237] and *Tarola*,[238] the Court ruled that self-employed movers can retain 'worker' status after becoming involuntarily unemployed, as long as they register as jobseekers, which leads to retention of the right to reside and of eligibility for social benefits. Moreover, in *Dakneviciute*,[239] the Court ruled that self-employed women retain the right to reside under the Directive during pregnancy and following childbirth, thus enjoying access to child benefits and other social benefits. Notably, these three judgments were prompted in the context of low-paid, self-employed movers from Eastern Europe who had worked in EU-15 states[240] in precarious, part-time employment arrangements but became inadvertently unemployed and hence needed host state support during a period of vulnerability. Rather than characterising these judgments as inherently 'expansive' of workers' rights, one could argue that the Court has simply been responsive to

---

233 Regulation 492/2011, Recital (6).
234 Directive 2014/54/EU, Article 3. Despite its symbolic value, the Directive did not create substantive mobility or equality rights. Notably, six EU-15 states deemed their pre-existing legislations sufficient and did not implement any changes to their domestic policies.
235 *L N v Styrelsen for Videregående Uddannelser og Uddannelsesstøtte*, Case C-46/12, ECLI:EU:C:2013:97.
236 *Saint Prix v Secretary of State for Work and Pensions*, Case C-507/12, ECLI:EU:C:2014:2007.
237 *Gusa v Minister for Social Protection*, Case C-442/16, ECLI:EU:C:2017:1004.
238 *Tarola v Minister for Social Protection*, Case C-483/17, ECLI:EU:C:2019:309.
239 *Her Majesty's Revenue and Customs v Dakneviciute*, Case C-544/18, ECLI:EU:C:2019:761.
240 Gusa and Tarola were Romanian nationals living in Ireland, and Dakneviciute was a Lithuanian national living in the UK.

the effects of increasing labour market flexibilisation across the EU and the resultant dire social consequences—especially for those who are self-employed—which had intensified in the aftermath of the 2008 economic crisis.

Importantly, one should not assume that these recent rulings supporting workers' mobility are driven solely, or even predominantly, by human rights concerns. By facilitating workers' mobility, the ECJ has been enabling CEE workers' continuing contributions to the western labour markets. Indeed, the economic core of the right to free movement has come to the foreground in this recent jurisprudence. Notably, in the *Gusa* decision, the Court engaged in a subjective discussion of how the claimant was deserving of access to social benefits due to having relied on his family (rather than the public purse) for financial support upon his arrival in the host state and due to thereafter having worked and paid taxes for four years. The Court implied that movers become deserving of access to EU rights if their economic activity is deemed to have been sufficient. This, of course, not only departs from EU statutory provisions but also introduces a subjective, qualitative approach to judicial interpretation. Moreover, unlike in its earlier jurisprudence, judicial analysis in these three recent decisions did not rely on EU citizenship or other Treaty rights. Instead, these decisions have focused on market citizenship.

Other EU institutions have recently become more explicitly responsive to EU-15 initiatives to limit mobile workers' access to social rights. This became especially evident during David Cameron's attempts to renegotiate the UK's membership in the EU. Following his 2013 campaign proclamation that '[f]ree movement within Europe needs to be less free',[241] Cameron was seeking to extend the application of post-2010 ECJ decisions (discussed below) that constrained economically inactive movers' access to benefits to also impose such restrictions on workers. Under the 2016 'New Settlement'[242] between the UK and the EU, EU workers were to be denied access to in-work benefits and social housing for the first four years of residing in the UK. This approach was allegedly justified due to the exceptional impact of CEE movers on the UK's welfare system. Moreover, workers' entitlement to child benefits was to be indexed based on the cost of living in the children's countries of residence. This targeted and disadvantaged CEE circular movers whose children remained with family members in their home states.

Although the New Settlement proposal challenged the principle of non-discrimination between EU and national workers, the European Council assented to it, noting that it was warranted by 'conditions of necessity' brought about by the large influx of (CEE) movers into the UK. The Commission was in support of these initiatives as well. It is not clear what evidence the UK had presented to warrant such measures, which are incompatible with both the free movement and anti-discrimination acquis. The Commission simply declared that 'the kind

---

241 Cameron (2013).
242 Ultimately voided by the Commission due to the 2016 Brexit referendum outcome.

of information provided' by the UK indicated that 'the type of exceptional situation that the proposed safeguard mechanism is intended to cover exists in the United Kingdom'.[243] This is despite the fact that a study requested by the Commission three years earlier had found no evidence of benefit tourism and had indicated mobility's economic benefits to receiving states.[244]

One could argue that the EU's acquiescence to the 'New Settlement' was prompted by its unique context—the first ever attempt to leave the EU by a Member State which had always been Eurosceptic and which had been a major player within the EU. However, EU institutions contemporaneously exhibited a more general and more far-reaching willingness to prioritise EU-15 states' efforts to limit (CEE) workers' rights. Noting that 'Member States have the right to define the fundamental principles of their social security systems and to enjoy a broad margin of discretion to define and implement their social and employment policy'[245]—including discretion to limit mobile workers' rights—the Council[246] declared its intention to propose amending: (1) Regulation 883/2004 (on the coordination of social security systems) to allow child benefits indexation across the EU, and (2) Regulation 492/2011 (on workers' and job-seekers' equality in access to training, housing, social, and tax advantages) to provide an 'alert and safeguard mechanism' to respond to inflows 'of workers from other Member States of an exceptional magnitude over an extended period of time, including as a result of past policies following previous EU enlargements'.[247] The child benefit indexation proposal—vociferously supported by Austria, Germany, Belgium, Luxembourg, and the Netherlands—caused deep divisions between CEE and EU-15 states. The 'alert and safeguard mechanism'—reminiscent of the Enlargement safeguard provisions and post-accession mobility derogations that targeted CEE workers—would have enabled host states to limit access to non-contributory benefits linked to employment for up to four years from the start of an employment relationship. Targeting CEE movers, these proposals would have legitimised direct discrimination of mobile workers, while eviscerating the concept of EU citizenship. Albeit both plans were ultimately abandoned after the Brexit referendum, they provide a clear indication of the extent to which EU institutions have been willing to undermine even workers' rights in order to prioritise EU-15 interests.

Economically Inactive Movers

Until the early 2000s, the ECJ had been affording economically inactive movers access to some social benefits not available to them under secondary EU

---

243 European Commission (2016).
244 ICF GHK (2013).
245 European Council (2016).
246 The Council is composed of Member State heads of state, and thus CEE representatives represent a numerical minority within it.
247 European Council (2016).

legislation by expansively interpreting Treaty provisions. The Court retracted on this approach during the last decade, however, by narrowly reading secondary legislation. In effect, the rights of mobile first-time jobseekers, former workers who no longer retain 'worker' status, and those who have never been economically active in host states have been curtailed. Furthermore, such movers became discouraged from even applying for social benefits as that might jeopardise their residence right. This has had a particularly detrimental effect on movers who arrive in host states with lesser resources and who are employed in low-paid positions—such as CEE movers.

The *Brey* decision suggested that an economically inactive mover's entitlement to a means-tested SNCB, such as compensatory supplement benefit, *could* be an indication of not having 'sufficient resources'.[248] Hence, such a mover's right to reside in a host state for longer than three months under Directive 2004/38 could be called into question. Pursuant to the subsequent ruling in *Dano*, an economically inactive mover's application for social assistance benefits automatically terminates the right to reside without the need for an individual assessment.[249] Member States are not required to provide access to SNCBs to economically inactive EU citizens—at least not to those who, like Ms Dano, had never been employed in the receiving state and were not searching for work. In effect, Member States may attach conditions of residence (from Directive 2004/38) to the provision of SNCBs with a social assistance component—limiting access to such benefits even if they are available under Regulation 883/2004. Thus, the *Dano* judgment disconnected the freedom of movement right from the non-discrimination principle, in response to EU-15 state concerns about hypothetical risks allegedly presented by economically inactive movers from the CEE region.

In *Alimanovic*,[250] the Court went a step further by directly narrowing the rights of economically inactive movers under Directive 2004/38. After having worked for eleven months in Germany, Ms Alimanovic became involuntarily unemployed and was provided social assistance for six months in accordance with Article 7(3)(c) of Directive 2004/38. Afterwards, she was re-classified as a first-time jobseeker and German authorities relied on Article 24(2) of the Directive (permitting states to withhold social assistance from first-time jobseekers) to discontinue her social assistance. Despite widely-available evidence to the contrary, the Court accepted EU-15 states' welfare-magnet arguments and concluded that, even if an individual social assistance claim did not place an unreasonable burden on a national social security system, a host state could retract a mover's residence right by arguing that such claims taken collectively would constitute a burden. Moreover, the Court opined that an expulsion decision based on host state arguments that a mover is presenting an

248 *Pensionsversicherungsanstalt v Brey*, Case C-140/12, ECLI:EU:C:2013:565.
249 *Dano v Jobcenter Leipzig*, Case C-333/13, ECLI:EU:C:2014:2358.
250 *Jobcenter Berlin Neukölln v Alimanovic*, Case C-67/14, ECLI:EU:C:2015:597.

unreasonable burden to the national social assistance system does not require an individual assessment. Thus, host states are entitled to automatically prevent mobile jobseekers' access to certain SNCBs which constitute social assistance under Directive 2004/38 (but are not intended to facilitate access to the labour market). Furthermore, once a former worker no longer retains worker status under the Directive, after becoming involuntarily unemployed, she might be eligible for social assistance only if she possesses a residence right independent of merely the non-expulsion provision of the Directive (which pertains to former workers who continue to seek employment).

The *Alimanovic* judgment also narrowly construed the 'intended to facilitate access to the labour market' test[251] so that only benefits that are *necessary* to jobseekers' ability to access host-state labour markets cannot be withheld from economically inactive movers during their first three months of residence or to first-time jobseekers under Article 24 of the Directive. Thus, for example, the Court found German legislation denying social assistance to newly arrived jobseekers to be compatible with EU law. This stance was reiterated in *Garcia-Nieto*, in which the ECJ held that jobseekers are never eligible for unemployment benefits because they inherently contain a social assistance element—that is, their primary aim is the preservation of dignity, rather than the facilitation of access to the labour market.[252] Consequently, jobseekers can be automatically excluded from access to social assistance even during their first three months of residence in a host state.

In *Commission v United Kingdom*, the ECJ extended its *Dano* ruling—that economically inactive movers are not eligible for SNCBs with a social assistance element—to all social security benefits (including family benefits).[253] The case pertained to the legality of the UK's new right-to-reside test, implemented to limit CEE movers' access to social security benefits, which does not appear in Regulation 83/2004. The Court imported *Dano*'s approach of not requiring an individual assessment and *Brey*'s principle of permitting Member States to impose conditions on economically inactive movers' access to SNCBs into Article 4 of Regulation 883/2004 (regarding social security benefits such as child benefits and child tax credits). Moreover, the Court reversed its prior approach towards the burden of proof so that Member States are now presumed to be acting in a lawful, non-discriminatory manner when denying access to social benefits as long as they attribute their actions to the need to protect their public finances from (hypothetical) benefits payable to movers.

---

251 According to the ECJ, in view of the establishment of EU citizenship, jobseekers have the right to equal treatment in claiming benefits of financial nature intended to facilitate access to the host labour market, although host states may grant them only to jobseekers who have a real link to the host labour market. E.g., *Vatsouras and Koupatantze*, Case C-22/08.
252 *Vestische Arbeit Jobcenter Kreis Recklinghausen v García-Nieto*, Case C-299/14, ECLI:EU:C:2016:114.
253 *Commission v United Kingdom*, Case C-308/14, ECLI:EU:C:2016:436.

Through such judgements, the ECJ has not only facilitated EU-15 states' restrictions on mobility when it comes to CEE nationals,[254] but has also propagated an image of 'Eastern Europeans' as socially and economically inferior, and not quite deserving of EU law's protection. For example, the Court in *Dano* engaged in a subjective discussion of the claimant's personal circumstances which were not relevant to the legal issues before it. By mentioning how Ms Dano, a Romanian national in Germany, had been receiving public support for her child, 'whose father's identity is not known', had lacked any educational certificates or professional training, could not write in German, had never worked, and had not provided evidence of having looked for work, the ECJ portrayed her as of no use to German society, and implicitly, as not deserving of protections of EU law. The Court thus suggested that mobility is not a right, but instead a privilege, not intended for the under-paid or under-educated socio-economic class within the EU.[255]

More generally, my analysis of ECJ discourse in select free movement[256] and criminal cases has revealed how the Court often refers to irrelevant facts and negative assumptions to create an inferiorising image of CEE movers—as socially, educationally, and economically inferior to westerners, and as lacking the ability to conform to (western) middle-class practices. Discursively associated by the Court with illegality, poverty, poor judgement, and defect, CEE movers tend to be portrayed as not belonging to the proper EU polity, and not quite deserving of EU law's protections.[257] By silencing CEE nationals' voices and interests, while disregarding the background of east/west socio-economic and political power differentials and the precariousness experienced by many CEE workers in the west, such racialising discourse normalises ethnicity- and class-based stereotypes. It also helps to further contextualise EU and western policies targeting CEE movers, as well as evidence of their unequal outcomes in the west.

In the recent *Jobcenter Krefeld* judgment,[258] however, the ECJ refused to extend its *Alimanovic* approach—that host states could rely on Article 24(2) of Directive 2004/38 to deny social assistance to EU movers with residence rights based solely on jobseeker status—to cases where the right of residence derives from a separate instrument. The Court ruled that the right of residence under Article 10 of Regulation 492/2011 (for a parent taking care of a child enrolled in general education in host state) would not be suspended even if the parent lost their 'worker' status (and the related residence right under the Directive). Such parent would continue being eligible for social assistance. The Court determined that German legislation which automatically excluded economically inactive movers from subsistence benefits even if they had a right of residence under secondary legislation, such as

254 Notably, all the cases discussed in this subsection pertained to movers from poorer regions of the EU, who were residing in Germany or the UK.
255 See also De Witte (2019).
256 *Dano*, Case C-333/13; *Ziolkowski and Szeja*, Joined Cases C-424/10 and 425/10.
257 Myslinska (2020).
258 *Jobcenter Krefeld Widerspruchsstelle v JD*, Case C-181/19, ECLI:EU:C:2020:794.

Regulation 492/2011, was contrary to equal treatment provisions under Regulation 492/2011 (on workers' access to social and tax advantages) and under Regulation 883/2004 (on the coordination of social security systems). Thus, national authorities cannot automatically exclude movers from social assistance benefits if they lack residence right under the Directive. Instead, states must first individually assess if they might have a right to reside that derives from another EU regulation.

It is too early to say whether *Jobcenter Krefeld* represents an expansive turn in the ECJ's jurisprudence or whether the German policy at issue simply embodied an attack on the non-discrimination principle that was too manifest for the Court to ignore. This judgment might be attributable to its specific factual circumstances—the German measure in effect targeted the welfare of children, who appeared integrated in Germany and whose (single) parent had been in paid full-time employment, which he had subsequently resumed after a period of having been deemed unfit to work. Notably, in reaching its conclusion, the Court engaged in close reading of secondary EU laws, rather than referring to fundamental Treaty rights as it used to do in its pre-*Brey* jurisprudence. Moreover, as critical scholars point out, judicial application of anti-discrimination law occasionally offers a sense of resolution to make law appear effective, thereby legitimating pre-existing unequal social conditions.[259]

EU Discourse on Free Movement and Social Rights

In line with both post-2010 ECJ caselaw and EU institutions' increasing tendency to acquiesce to western efforts to limit movers' rights, EU rhetoric in the last decade has focused on maximising economic benefits that EU-15 economies can reap from mobile CEE workers. The frequency of such proclamations visibly spiked in the last decade—likely due to increased public and political consternation across EU-15 states when transitional mobility derogations against Bulgarians and Romanians were coming to an end, and due to amplified politicisation of CEE mobility surrounding Brexit. In line with the economic core of foundational EU narratives discussed in the preceding chapter, free movement is valued largely in the context of those who make economic contributions to host states. Occasional statements about free movement being a fundamental right remain merely a vacuous rhetoric. Moreover, to reinforce economic benefits of workers' mobility to (western) employers, EU institutions have continued to support labour flexibilisation. Despite having access to reports documenting incidents of exploitation linked to increasing flexibilisation—especially in sectors where CEE workers are disproportionately represented—EU institutions have shied away from explicitly mentioning CEE workers as being particularly vulnerable. Although the EU's competence in the area of social rights remains limited, such discourse has further normalised CEE movers' experiences of inequality and exploitation in EU-15 states, where they have been approached as second-class, fungible workers.

259 E.g. Delgado and Stefancic (2017).

For example, the Parliament's 2014 'Resolution on respect for the fundamental right of free movement in the EU'[260] called on Member States to facilitate mobility as a key component of the internal market, pointing to studies indicating how movers contribute to host state budgets more than national workers do. The Parliament drew attention to mobile workers' particularly significant contributions to healthcare, agriculture, and construction sectors. Although all these sectors have tended to be disproportionately populated by movers from the CEE region, they were not mentioned explicitly. There was also no reference to the high levels of precariousness and exploitation in these sectors, despite such incidents having come to EU institutions' attention by then. Notably, the Parliament acknowledged—in one recital—that political scapegoating of movers *might* lead to 'a rise in racism and xenophobia'. Again, there was no mention that movers have indeed been victims of racism and discrimination, or that this has particularly affected CEE movers. More generally, the Parliament's unease about racism appears driven not by human rights concerns, but by how it might decrease movers' contributions to host state economies by distorting the internal market.

Moreover, on occasions when the Parliament has acknowledged that mobile workers have been facing increasingly precarious host labour markets, such remarks appear motivated by a concern about how this leads to unfair competition and compromises the efficiency of the internal market. For example, in its 2016 resolution on social dumping,[261] the Parliament contemned it due to its market distortion and negative budgetary consequences for host state finances. Notably, while observing that precarious work has become especially prevalent in construction, healthcare, catering, transport, and domestic services sectors, the Parliament did not draw attention to the fact that these sectors have been disproportionately populated by CEE workers. Similarly, CEE workers were not mentioned in its 2017 resolution on precarious work,[262] which noted that precarious and part-time work have been increasing, especially in sectors such as agriculture, construction, travel, and accommodation.

More generally, the Parliament supports increasing flexibilisation of the labour market, opining that it can benefit both employers and workers—a view of which I remain sceptical. In fact, in the aforementioned resolution on precarious work, the Parliament justified employers' reliance on short-term agricultural contracts, by attributing them to the sector's 'natural constraints'.[263] As well-documented, the seasonal agricultural sector has been particularly plagued by exploitation and labour law violations—as vividly demonstrated during the Covid pandemic (discussed earlier). In further defence of flexibilisation, the Parliament proclaimed that

---

260 European Parliament (2014d).
261 European Parliament (2016).
262 European Parliament (2017a).
263 Ibid.

'atypical' and 'new forms of' employment are not always precarious.[264] Although some 'atypical' work arrangements might not involve precariousness or exploitation, explicitly defending them normalises flexible employment relations, while minimising their well-documented association with greater risk of exploitation. Notably, the Parliament critiqued precarious work not only for the resultant individual harms, but also for the consequent tax income loss to host states. In addition, when noting that it is the most vulnerable workers who are at greatest risk of precarious conditions, the Parliament drew attention to persons with disabilities, women, and those of non-white ethnic or minority religious origins—failing to acknowledge how CEE movers have also been consistently prone to such risks.

Prioritising movers' benefits to host economies, defending labour flexibilisation for benefiting (western) employers, and overlooking CEE workers' exploitation also permeate EU rhetoric in the context of the new 'European Pillar of Social Rights', which promises to facilitate free movement and access to social and economic rights for all EU citizens. Proclaiming the Pillar in 2017, the Commission[265] emphasised 20 general principles essential to achieving 'fair' and 'well-functioning' labour markets across the EU—such as increasing opportunities, inclusivity, and social protections. These principles largely reiterate pre-existing EU discourse, and focus on the position of domestic workers, while paying little attention to the needs of mobile workers. Notably, economic and social concerns remain fused, and labour flexibility continues to be praised for benefitting (western) employers. There is no mention of social rights to which economically inactive movers might be entitled. Moreover, the Pillar lists some groups as vulnerable to exclusion, including Roma, women, homeless persons, young workers, persons with disabilities, and LGBTQI individuals. The express mention of one (or more) serves to exclude all others.[266] Thus, CEE movers' vulnerabilities are overlooked and their inequalities implicitly normalised. Prompted only by the Covid pandemic, the largely symbolic Pillar led to the Commission's 2020 European Pillar of Social Rights Action Plan,[267] a set of (non-enforceable) targets for the EU and all Member States to accomplish by 2030—such as increasing employment rates, expanding skills training, and reducing poverty—with no guidance on how such goals are to be reconciled with the EU's support for increasing labour flexibilisation and precarity. Again, exploitative conditions frequently faced by CEE workers in EU-15 states were not mentioned.

Similar patterns of rhetoric permeate other EU institutions' social protection initiatives that complement and reinforce the Pillar of Social Rights. Social rights are consistently justified by references to workers' economic benefits to

---

264 Ibid.
265 European Pillar of Social Rights (2017).
266 The rule of *expressio unis est exlusio alterius* holds as much truth when interpreting discourse as when applied to statutory construction.
267 European Commission (undated).

host economies, and CEE movers are overlooked as a group vulnerable to exploitation and to denial of social rights. For example, in its 2019 recommendation on ensuring workers' access to social protections,[268] the Council of the EU fused economic and welfare concerns, aiming to achieve a 'highly competitive social market economy' within the EU. Referring to the Pillar of Social Rights, the Council reiterated that both employers' and workers' rights should be protected, and that social protection initiatives must not disadvantage small and medium-sized business enterprises. Notably, the recommendation valued social protections not only as a means to reduce workers' poverty, but also to facilitate their participation in the labour market. Although the Council did recognise that many national benefit entitlement schemes disadvantage self-employed workers and those on non-standard contracts (e.g., seasonal, and agency workers), it did not condemn such employment arrangements or domestic measures limiting such workers' protections. Nor did it draw attention to the fact that CEE movers are overrepresented on non-standard contracts. Instead, it merely observed that 'there is scope to tailor the rules more'.

With impetus provided by the Covid pandemic, the European Council adopted the Porto Declaration[269] in 2021, to work towards a 'social Europe', as part of the EU's 'distinctive social model' which links social cohesion to prosperity. The Porto Declaration is intended to strengthen the implementation of the Social Rights Pillar, to achieve an 'inclusive, … just and jobs-rich' post-pandemic recovery that is based on a 'competitive economy'. Adequate working conditions, equal treatment, and 'fair mobility' are meant to facilitate fair competition within the internal market.[270] Notably, although the Declaration mentions goals such as reducing inequalities, poverty, and exclusion, the only groups labelled as vulnerable to such risks are the unemployed, the elderly, persons with disabilities, young people, and women. Furthermore, the European Council—which defines the overall political direction and priorities of the EU—has noted that its support for both the Social Rights Pillar Action Plan and the Porto Declaration must be situated specifically in the context of post-Covid economic recovery,[271] implicitly devaluing the need for protecting social rights during non-pandemic times.

Recent EU-15 State Limits on Access to Free Movement and Social Rights

Since it is at the host state level that EU nationals get to effectuate their free movement right, current EU policies and discourse about free movement and

---

268 Council Recommendation of 8 November 2019 on access to social protection for workers and the self-employed.
269 European Council (2021).
270 President of the European Commission et al. (2021).
271 European Council (2021a).

social rights must be placed within relevant EU-15 frameworks. Although studies have consistently indicated that movers—especially those from east to west—have been primarily motivated by labour needs in host states, and have been contributing more to their host states' fiscal purses than using up in services, western politicians have been exploiting them as scapegoats for failures of domestic economic policies. The economic crises during 2008–12, the end of transitional mobility derogations against Bulgarians and Romanians in 2014, increasing EU and national austerity measures, and Brexit debates have served to further politicise CEE movers' rights across EU-15 states in the past decade. To address public anxieties, EU-15 states have continued to come up with new domestic policies and discretionary practices—some arguably in contravention of EU law—to limit movers' access to entry, residence, and social rights, amplifying their restrictive efforts from the time of the Directive's transposition. Such measures have targeted CEE movers, and have disproportionately disadvantage them. Meanwhile, EU institutions have largely tolerated such increasing incursions on mobility, equality, and social rights.

For starters, EU-15 states adopted various measures to make it more difficult for movers to access the right of residence for more than three months, especially for EU nationals not recognised as 'workers'. For example, whereas pursuant to Article 14(4)(b) of Directive 2004/38, first-time jobseekers cannot be expelled as long as they can 'provide evidence that they are continuing to seek employment and that they have a genuine chance of being engaged', Belgian authorities have been demanding that jobseekers present 'detailed evidence' of 'actively looking' for work or risk losing residence right after only three months of presence. Similarly, German courts have been applying wide discretion when determining whether jobseekers have a 'genuine chance' of finding employment. In 2014, the UK adopted a requirement that jobseekers who had been in the UK for more than six months needed to provide 'compelling evidence' that they were likely to find employment or they would risk losing jobseekers' allowance and the right of residence. Moreover, even those considered to be legitimate jobseekers became no longer entitled to housing benefits or the newly introduced Universal Credit,[272] which is restricted to workers.

Moreover, EU-15 states have been implementing methods to interpret 'worker' status even more narrowly than at the time of the Directive's transposition, to deny residence (and social) rights to movers who are low-waged or engaged in precarious employment, and to those who become involuntarily unemployed. Although EU laws do not impose specific minimum hour, duration, or remuneration thresholds to be considered a 'worker', Belgian authorities frequently refuse to recognise residence rights of movers engaged through short-term or atypical contracts, such as zero-hour contracts through employment agencies. Germany imposes a minimum work requirements, of eight hours

---

272 Which merged various means-tested benefits for the unemployed and for persons on low income.

per week. Furthermore, German courts have been determining 'worker' status arbitrarily when it comes to non-standard forms of employment—sometimes requiring earning thresholds of €450 per month, or considering factors such as continuity and regularity of work, or having a contractual right to paid sick leave. In the UK, 2014 legislative changes increased both the general thresholds and the burden of proof imposed on movers to qualify as 'workers'. Movers became required to (1) demonstrate evidence of having been earning €150 a week for the previous three months (equivalent to working 24 hours a week at the UK's then minimum wage) and pass an individual assessment or (2) pass an individual assessment that their work was 'genuine and effective' despite falling below that threshold. The UK increased the minimum weekly income threshold in 2018, to €185.

Furthermore, EU-15 states have been adopting administrative approaches to limit movers' ability to retain worker status after becoming involuntarily unemployed. For example, interview-based data indicates that involuntarily unemployed movers in Belgium have been receiving expulsion orders after only five months of unemployment, even if they provide proof of registering as jobseekers, actively looking for a job, and learning the local language.[273] This is despite the fact that under Directive 2004/38, they are entitled to retain worker status for at least six months (as long as they register as jobseekers).

Since 2011, EU-15 states have also been implementing particularly burdensome initiatives to limit movers' access to social benefits, by often combining access restrictions with a high burden of proof, and by treating benefit claims as grounds for retracting residence rights. For example, in 2011, Austria adopted a new statutory provision to deter alleged 'welfare migration'. Eligibility for SNCBs, such as supplementary pensions, became limited to those who could prove that they have sufficient resources so as not to rely on social assistance benefits during their entire (anticipated) period of residence in Austria. Moreover, those who had applied for SNCBs at any point during their stay in Austria could be considered as lacking 'sufficient resources', and thus risk losing their residence right. Although in the 2013 *Brey* judgment, the ECJ found this general statutory exclusion to be incompatible with EU law because it lacks an individual assessment, Austria did not change its rules, but instead slightly adjusted their administrative implementation, so that movers become eligible for supplementary pension as long as they were deemed to be lawfully residing in Austria. However, receiving SNCBs can still lead to losing residence right due to not having 'sufficient resources'. Thus, movers are deterred from even applying for such benefits.

Arguably emboldened—and, in some cases, vindicated—by the ECJ's restrictive judgments during 2013–16 regarding the rights of economically inactive movers, EU-15 states have been further limiting their access to residence and social rights.[274] In Sweden and Denmark, *Brey* and *Dano* judgments led to intensified

---

273 Schiek et al. (2015).
274 See generally Mantu and Minderhoud (2019).

political debates about CEE nationals' 'benefit tourism' and to governmental guidelines to restrict access to benefits in line with *Dano*. Courts in the Netherlands, Austria, Finland, Ireland, and the UK began to automatically consider economically inactive movers who cannot prove having looked for work to be an 'unreasonable burden' if they had received social support for as little as one day. Moreover, when determining 'sufficient resources', Italy, Belgium, and the UK began to impose arbitrary thresholds and to refuse to accept non-EU spousal income as part of that calculation. Various efforts to limit movers' access to social benefits have also been adopted in Germany since 2014. Amid media and political attacks on 'welfare cheaters' and 'poverty migrants' from Eastern Europe, the 2014 Freedom of Movement Act/EU imposed more stringent eligibility tests for social benefits—arguably contrary to EU law. For example, movers became required to provide their tax numbers in order to receive support for childcare expenses and to present more detailed documentation to prove self-employment. Re-entry bans were imposed on those deemed to have committed benefit fraud. Moreover, newly arriving jobseekers, those economically inactive, and former workers with an arguable link to the German labour market became excluded from SNCBs such as basic income support. After the German Federal Social Court ruled in 2015 that movers who do not qualify for basic income support are nevertheless constitutionally entitled to general social assistance (even if they lack employment and 'sufficient resources'), German legislators adopted the 2016 Act to Regulate the Claims of Foreign Persons, which limits such assistance to four weeks only. Finally, as part of the 2020 amendments to the Freedom of Movement Act/EU, proposals were made to automatically deny social benefits to movers whose right to reside does not derive from the Directive.[275]

Notably, EU-15 states have even been trying to limit access to benefits by mobile workers. For example, in 2017, Denmark changed eligibility requirements for access to full child benefits from two to six years of continuous employment. In Germany, 2016 proposals were made to prevent workers' access to benefits during the first five years of residence and to restrict eligibility to only those who had worked full-time for at least one year. Moreover, the UK's 'New Settlement' fuelled EU-15 debates about indexation of child benefits even for workers. By its very nature, indexation of benefits negatively affects CEE movers as, among movers, they tend to both have lower incomes in host states and come from countries of origin with lower costs of living. Given that indexation of family benefits has been shown not to result in financial savings to host states,[276] such western efforts have served as a symbolic outlet for contestation around the free movement right and as a tactic to appease voters opposed to CEE mobility. In 2017, ministers from Austria, Denmark, Ireland,

---

275 These proposals were ultimately scrapped due to the *Krefeld* judgment.
276 Due to small numbers of potential claimants, upwards adjustments for movers from states with higher cost of living, and increased administrative costs entailed in calculating the indexed amounts and in enforcement efforts. See generally Blauberger et al. (2020).

and Germany asked the Commission that EU regulations be amended to explicitly permit indexation of child benefits.[277] Joined also by the Netherlands, they reiterated this stance in 2018.[278] In such examples of welfare chauvinism, despite explicitly affirming their commitment to free movement, western governments have argued that indexation is based on (a questionable understanding of) 'fairness', and have asked that rights stemming from mobility be 'adjusted' in light of 'changing circumstances'.[279] Indexation's decoupling of the right of free movement from the right to non-discrimination prompted CEE governments[280] to condemn it as unfair and incompatible with the right of free movement. Poignantly, only one EU-15 state joined CEE politicians' opposition—namely Italy, which is a significant sending country and has a lower cost of living than in north-western EU host states.

Despite its own recent judgments reducing movers' entitlements and its frequent acquiescence to western limits on (CEE) movers' rights, the EU stepped in to denounce indexation due to the risk of creating 'second-class' children.[281] Arguably, limitations on benefits intended to support children are particularly difficult to condone. Furthermore, in 2020, the Commission initiated infringement proceedings against Austria, arguing that its indexation of family-related benefits constitutes indirect discrimination. Czechia, Poland, Slovenia, and Slovakia, as well as Croatia and Romania, intervened in support of the Commission. Austria argued that its indexation policy was lawful because the UK had been allowed to pursue indexation under the 'New Settlement'. Although neither of them hosts significant numbers of movers, Denmark and Norway intervened on behalf of Austria, presumably driven by populist anti-CEE politics. The ECJ pronounced that indexation constitutes an unlawful violation of free movement and equality principles contrary to Regulation 883/2004, and Austria was forced to stop indexation in 2022.[282] As has been its practice, however, the Court was silent about the broader context across EU-15 states of consistently targeting CEE movers and limiting their rights.

In the last decade, many EU-15 states have also been adopting further obstacles to movers' access to permanent residence which, under the Directive, is available once a mover has resided lawfully for a continuous period of five years in a host state. For example, Belgium, France, and Italy require that the relevant five-year period immediately precede the date of application. Across EU-15 states, additional requirements were imposed through administrative practices, such as asking movers to prove their resources or healthcare coverage at the time of applying for permanent residence, to demonstrate continuous history of employment or social security contributions during the five-year

277 Nahles et al. (2017).
278 Poulsen et al. (2018).
279 Nahles et al. (2017).
280 Czechia, Slovakia, Estonia, Slovenia, Poland, Latvia, Hungary, as well as Romania.
281 Stupp (2017).
282 *Commission v Austria*, Case C-328/20, ECLI:EU:C:2022:468.

period, to prove knowledge of local language and customs, or to produce notarised corroborations from neighbours to confirm continuous residence. Such requirements are contrary to EU law and especially disadvantage CEE movers given how they have tended to engage in precarious, low-paid employment (often disproportionately staffed with other CEE workers), participate in circular mobility, rely on temporary accommodations, and face social exclusion from local communities.

Furthermore, EU-15 states have been interpreting the notion of 'public policy' grounds overly broadly to restrict rights of entry and residence, targeting movers who sleep rough or reside in temporary encampments. CEE movers, as well as those from Bulgaria and Romania, have been more likely to lack secure housing than movers from other parts of the EU. Thus, any such measures indirectly target them. Under the Directive, host states may restrict entry and residence rights on grounds of public policy as long as they are not 'invoked to serve economic ends' and as long as any resultant expulsion decisions are not automatic but instead take into account individual factors such as age, health, family circumstances, and level of integration. In 2017, German police distributed letters to movers who were rough sleeping, requiring them to attend immigration interviews to prove their right to reside, which is not permitted under EU law. Those who failed to attend were served with notices that any residence rights they might have had were revoked.

Finally, qualitative studies indicate CEE movers' experiences of institutional discrimination when trying to access social rights. For example, CEE movers were documented to encounter unwarranted rejections by UK government officials when applying for social benefits or trying to access support services (e.g., healthcare, homeless support, soup kitchens, housing assistance).[283] In Germany, internal guidance for job centre staff on how to combat organised welfare abuse by movers has led to turning away eligible applicants or requiring them to supply additional types of evidence not mandated by law to prove eligibility for benefits.[284] Those from the CEE region, as well as from Bulgaria and Romania, have been targeted by such practices. Furthermore, processing delays have been hindering movers' access to social rights. For example, waiting times for residency registration certificates have exceeded one year in Austria, Sweden, France, Ireland, and the UK, making it more difficult for movers to access social rights and dissuading some altogether from seeking them. Although this impacts all movers, it especially disadvantages movers from poorer regions of the EU and those overrepresented in low-paid positions such as CEE movers.

Post-2011 EU citizen complaints to EU institutions and EU advice centres reflect how CEE nationals' ability to benefit from free movement and social

---

283 E.g., Morgan (2021). Institutional discrimination against CEE nationals in the UK has continued since Brexit, with those with settled status sometimes (incorrectly) refused access to services.
284 See e.g., Lewicki (2023).

rights continues to be constrained in practice due to restrictive EU-15 regulations that do not always comply with Treaty principles or with secondary EU laws. The Commission set up SOLVIT in 2002, as a free network of centres across all Member States, to assist movers with ascertaining their EU rights and with reporting any incidents of unfair treatment by national public administrators. Of the complaints within its remit, issues most often reported (during 2016–17) were experienced by movers in the UK, Germany, and France—especially by Polish nationals—and included those regarding residence rights, access to social security, and recognition of qualifications.[285] The precise details and scale of such problems remain unknown at the EU level, however. SOLVIT is not well utilised, and the EU does not have a centralised method of monitoring domestic infringements of mobility rights. Moreover, complaints of discrimination in the experience of mobility raised at national levels are not routinely reported to the EU. Recent grievances reported to other EU bodies have come disproportionately from movers working on atypical contracts and with irregular hours, especially common among CEE movers, and indicate how inactive movers' access to residency and social rights has become further imperilled by narrow and arbitrary national interpretations of 'sufficient resources' and of 'comprehensive sickness insurance' requirements as well as through the imposition of additional requirements not mandated under EU law.[286]

The Commission has not expressed much concern about such continuing EU-15 state impediments to mobility. Experts carrying out the 2009 Parliament-commissioned study on the application of Directive 2004/38[287] had critiqued the Commission for its inadequate oversight of Member States' transposition of the Directive and for its handling of EU citizens' complaints pertaining to mobility and associated rights. Notably, in that report, specialists contrasted the Commission's inadequate support for movers' rights with its much wider support for the transposition of another directive adopted within the same time frame, which seeks to facilitate a single market for service providers.[288] This might reflect the Commission's acquiescence to western states' efforts to limit CEE nationals' mobility and access to rights and its lack of concern for how fundamental rights have been limited in practice when it comes to these 'second-class' EU citizens. Notably, despite the ongoing contestations in EU-15 states over CEE nationals' access to rights, the Commission has initiated relatively few infringement proceedings against Member States for violating movers' rights. For example, during 2010–18, only 33 infringement proceedings related to free movement and only 21 related to movers' social security rights.[289]

---

285 European Court of Auditors (2018).
286 Civic Observatory on the Rights of EU Citizens (2020).
287 European Parliament (2009).
288 Directive 2006/123 on services in the internal market.
289 Ibid.

What I also find disconcerting is that many of the impediments to mobility being reported by movers more than a decade since the transposition of Directive 2004/38 are reminiscent of the challenges identified by the High Level Panel on free movement in 1997 (mentioned earlier). Given that EU-15 nationals and politicians have highly valued the right of free movement when applied to westerners, and that post-2004 mobility has been predominantly from east to west, at least some of the apparent inefficacy of the Directive can be attributed to western opposition towards CEE nationals and to EU institutions' tolerance of this. In practice, EU-15 limitations on rights conferred by the Directive, especially social rights, have helped to institutionalise western reliance on more affordable and more exploitable CEE workers, while externalising their social costs by enabling removal of those movers who become too costly to the west.[290] Of course, this is in line with the long-standing approach towards 'Eastern Europeans' as inferior and towards the CEE region as suitable for western exploitation.

Conclusions

'[F]ormal right to move is not sufficient to establish a real freedom to move'.[291] The 1956 Spaak Report,[292] which led to the creation of the European Economic Community, predicted that prejudices would likely impede workers' mobility. Similarly, Robert Schuman, one of the EU's 'founding fathers', acknowledged that 'ethnic and political borders' within the EU are 'a historical given' but expressed hope that policy initiatives might be able to 'take away from borders their rigidity and … intransigent hostility'.[293] Such borders clearly still exist within the EU and are exemplified through the EU's conceptualisation of CEE nationals' mobility and through CEE nationals' experience thereof. CEE movers perceive that 'an East-West divide along the line of the Iron Curtain still exists' to differentiate them from western Europeans and to negatively affect their experiences.[294] Although many migrant groups and minorities tend to experience social and institutional prejudices and inequalities in the EU labour market, the Eastern Enlargement and its resultant mobility have been uniquely framed as an egalitarian undertaking and as part of the benevolent EU integration project that champions fundamental rights. Moreover, CEE movers are arguably the only Christian, white group to have faced such difficulties despite having had access to the EU citizenship right even before arriving in host Member States.

Inequalities built into the accession process, discussed in the preceding chapter, had reinforced the CEE region's economic and political struggles at the time of the Enlargement and left many CEE nationals with little choice but to seek

---

290 See generally Lewicki (2023).
291 Carens (2013).
292 Spaak (1956).
293 Cited in Maas (2013).
294 Siklodi (2014).

employment in EU-15 states. Although they have benefited in many ways from their post-accession rights their mobility has exemplified the historical divisions between east and west that continue to exist within the EU—as illustrated through the imposition of transitional mobility derogations, CEE movers' frequent experiences of de-skilling and exploitation, and the western public's ongoing opposition to CEE movers. EU institutions have, for the most part, tolerated or facilitated such chipping away of the right to free movement. Through both mobility policies and discourse, they have continued prioritising economic interests and public preferences of EU-15 states, while reinforcing and naturalising CEE nationals' second-class status.

Furthermore, the right to racial equality—which is necessary to facilitate equal access to, and equal experience of, mobility—has done little to advance CEE movers' interests in EU-15 host states. Whereas movers' nationality-based discrimination has been forbidden since the 1951 Treaty of Rome, and has always been intimately linked to the freedom of movement right, protections from inequality on grounds of race (under the Race Equality Directive) are newer and less developed. Although to some extent this stems from an issue of EU competence, there is a general policy tendency to see free movement as an isolated issue detached from the broader equality agenda. Notably, the Race Equality Directive reflects EU-15 states' economic and political concerns and is especially unfit for protecting the rights of CEE movers. Meanwhile, EU discourse has taken no account of CEE movers' racialisation and experiences of discrimination. CEE movers' interests have been overlooked or silenced—in the Directive's legislative history, in broader EU equality discourse, and in soft law measures. In the process, CEE movers' peripheral status has been naturalised, entrenching inequalities and fractures within whiteness. Overall, the right to racial equality—like the right to free movement to which it has been intimately linked—has been limited in practice and indicates a deep schism between EU ideals and actual policies. The EU's abstract rhetoric about fundamental rights to mobility and equality, discussed in the preceding chapter, has only helped to obfuscate EU policy shortcomings and inequalities in the actual experience of CEE nationals' mobility.

The new intra-EU precarious class of CEE movers epitomises the neoliberal economic framework and embodies a reconfiguration of Marx's concept of a 'reserve army of labour'. Despite the EU project's lofty promises, the Eastern Enlargement resulted in the creation of a mobile, flexible labour force willing to perform jobs that native western workers do not tolerate. More generally, the EU project has facilitated the growth of this precarious class by prioritising the three freedoms (of establishment, services, and mobility) over workers' rights and by consistently supporting an American-style, flexible, mobile labour market composed of human capital which is 'infinitely "malleable"' and adaptable to changing production systems across the EU.[295] Even during the Covid

---

295 Commission of the European Communities (1993).

pandemic, the EU continued to encourage temporary mobility of precarious CEE workers, to support western supply networks and to help western nationals vulnerable to Covid, while largely overlooking how the pandemic had exacerbated such workers' exploitation.

The creation of fungible, disposable CEE workers has been reinforced by initiatives in several EU-15 states—including Germany, France, and the UK—to weaken trade unions, deregulate businesses, and rely more on precarious labour. Relative to sourcing non-EU migrants, using movers to address labour shortages has significantly reduced western administrative and employer costs. When precarious CEE workers are unable to access welfare in EU-15 states, they often return to their countries of origin to access support therein, displacing some costs of their labour—which benefits the west—onto the east. Through policies and discourse, this transnational landscape of inequality gets overlooked when ever acknowledging it would benefit CEE movers, and it becomes reinforced whenever doing so benefits the west. Furthermore, the long-standing western rhetoric positioning the east on the periphery of 'Europe', when contextualised within the long line of pre- and post-accession policies skewed towards prioritising interests of EU-15 economies, has naturalised the peripheralisation of the CEE region and the racialisation of its nationals as less white and less 'European' than westerners. The overall dynamics of these processes exhibit features of structural racism.

Bibliography

Andriescu, Monica (2020) Under lockdown amid COVID-19 pandemic, Europe feels the pinch from slowed intra-EU labor mobility, 1 May (Migration Policy Institute), www.migrationpolicy.org/article/covid19-europe-feels-pinch-slowed-intra-eu-labor-mobility

Anthony, Andrew (2020) Fear and loathing in Dover, where Brexit and Covid meet, *The Observer*, 29 November

Barslund, Mikkel and Matthias Busse (2014) Labour mobility in the EU: Dynamics, patterns and policies, *Intereconomics* 49(3): 116–158

Baumbast and R v Secretary of State for the Home Department, C-413/99, ECLI:EU:C:2002:493

BBC News (2006) Italy police free Polish 'slaves', 19 July, http://news.bbc.co.uk/1/hi/world/europe/5193948.stm

Bell, Derrick A (1980) Brown v. Board of Education and the interest-convergence dilemma, *Harvard Law Review* 93: 518–533

Blauberger, Michael and Susanne K Schmidt (2017) Free movement, the welfare state, and the European Union's over-constitutionalization: Administrating contradictions, *Public Administration* 95(2): 437–449

Blauberger, Michael et al. (2018) ECJ judges read the morning papers: Explaining the turnaround of European citizenship jurisprudence, *Journal of European Public Policy* 25(10): 1422–1441

Blauberger, Michael et al. (2020) Free movement of workers under challenge: the indexation of family benefits, *Comparative European Politics* 18: 925–943

Boeri, Tito and Herbert Brücker (2005) Why are Europeans so tough on migrants?, *Economic Policy* 20(44): 629–703

Böröcz, József and Melinda Kovacs (eds) (2001) *Empire's New Clothes: Unveiling EU Enlargement* (Shropshire: Central Europe Review)

Bulicke v Deutsche Büro Service GmbH, Case C-246/09, ECLI:EU:C:2010:418

Cameron, Davis (2013) Free movement within Europe needs to be less free, *Financial Times*, 26 November

Carens, Joseph H (2013) Foreword, in Willem Mass (ed) *Democratic Citizenship and the Free Movement of People* 5–8 (Leiden: Martinus Nijhoff)

Carrera, Sergio and Anaïs Faure Atger (2009) Implementation of Directive 2004/38 in the context of EU Enlargement: A proliferation of different forms of citizenship? Special Report/April 2009 (Centre for European Policy Studies), http://aei.pitt.edu/10758/1/1827.pdf

Centros Ltd v Erhvervs- og Selskabsstyrelsen, Case C-212/97, ECLI:EU:C:1999:126

Centrum voor gelijkheid van kansen en voor racismebestrijding v Firma Feryn NV, Case C-54/07, ECLI:EU:C:2008:397

CHEZ Razpredelenie Bulgaria AD v Komisia za zashtita ot diskriminatsia, Case C-83/14, ECLI:EU:C:2015:480

CHEZ Razpredelenie Bulgaria AD v Komisia za zashtita ot diskriminatsia, Case C-83/14, Opinion of AG Kokott, ECLI:EU:C:2015:170

Civic Observatory on the Rights of EU Citizens (2020) Policy Paper: Analysis of the obstacles to freedom of movement and political participation—Policy Recommendations, https://ecas.org/wp-content/uploads/2020/09/CORE-Policy-paper-final.pdf

Collins v Secretary of State for Work and Pensions, Case C-138/02, ECLI:EU:C:2004:172

Commission v Austria, Case C-328/20, ECLI:EU:C:2022:468

Commission v United Kingdom, Case C-308/14, ECLI:EU:C:2016:436

Commission of the European Communities (1993) Green Paper: European Social Policy—Options for the Union, COM/93/551 final, 17.11.93

Commission of the European Communities (1996) Legal Instruments to combat Racism and Xenophobia, V/6188/97 (Brussels)

Commission of the European Communities (1997) Agenda 2000: For a stronger and wider Union, COM (97) 2000, 15.07.1997

Commission of the European Communities (2004) Green Paper—Equality and non-discrimination for all in an enlarged EU, COM (2004) 379 final, 28.05.2004

Commission of the European Communities (2005) Communication from the Commission to the Council, the European Parliament, the European Economic and Social Committee and the Committee of the Regions: Non-Discrimination and Equal Opportunities for All—A Framework Strategy, COM (2005) 224, 1.6.2005

Commission of the European Communities (2006) Green Paper: Modernising Labour Law to Meet the Challenges of the 21st Century, COM (2006) 708 final, 22.11.2006

Commission of the European Communities (2006a) Report on the Functioning of the Transitional Arrangements Set Out in the 2003 Accession Treaty (period 1 May 2004–30 April 2006), COM (2006) 48 final, 8.2.2006

Commission of the European Communities (2006b) Enlargement, Two Years After—An Economic Success, COM (2006) 200 final, 3.5.2006

Commission of the European Communities (2008) Report on the First Phase (1 January 2007–31 December 2008) of the Transitional Arrangements set out in the 2005

Accession Treaty and as Requested According to the Transitional Arrangement set out in the 2003 Accession Treaty, COM (2008) 765 final, 18.11.2008

Commission of the European Communities (2008a) Report from the Commission to the European Parliament and the Council on the application of Directive 2004/38/EC on the right of citizens of the Union and their family members to move and reside freely within the territory of the Member States, COM(2008) 840 final, 10.12.2008

Commission of the European Communities (2009) Communication from the Commission to the European Parliament and the Council on guidance for better transposition and application of Directive 2004/38/EC on the right of citizens of the Union and their family members to move and reside freely within the territory of the Member States, COM(2009) 313 final, 02.07.2009

Committee of the Regions (2000) Opinion of the Committee of the Regions on 'EU Citizenship', OJ C156/03, 06.06.2000

Committee of the Regions (2020) Brain drain in the EU: addressing the challenge at all levels, 2020/C 141/08, 29.4.2020

Consolidated version of the Treaty on the Functioning of the European Union, OJ 115, 09.05.2008

Council of Europe, European Convention for the Protection of Human Rights and Fundamental Freedoms, as amended by Protocols Nos 11 and 14 (entered into force 3 September 1953)

Council of the EU (2020) A strong Europe in a world of challenges, Programme of the Croatian Presidency of the Council of the European Union, 1 January–30 June 2020, https://vlada.gov.hr/UserDocsImages/Vijesti/2019/12%20prosinac/31%20prosinca/web_FINAL_PROGRAMME_EN_FINAL.pdf

Council of the EU (2022) Presidency Conclusions on combating racism and antisemitism, 6406/1/22 REV 1, 02.03.22

Council Recommendation of 8 November 2019 on access to social protection for workers and the self-employed 2019/C 387/01, OJ C 387, 15.11.2019

Council Recommendation 2020/1475 of 13 October 2020 on a coordinated approach to the restriction of free movement in response to the COVID-19 pandemic, OJ L 337, 14.10.2020

Council Regulation 15/61 of 16 August 1961 on initial measures to bring about free movement of workers within the Community, OJ 57/1073

Crenshaw, Kimberlé et al. (eds) (1995) *Critical Race Theory: The Key Writings that Formed the Movement* (New York: The New Press)

Crowley, Niall (2020) A perspective from the work of equality bodies on: European equality policy strategies, equal treatment directives, and standards for equality bodies (Equinet), https://equineteurope.org/wpcontent/uploads/2020/04/taking_stock_web.pdf

Currie, Samantha (2008) *Migration, Work and Citizenship in the Enlarged European Union* (Farnham: Ashgate)

Dano v Jobcenter Leipzig, Case C-333/13, ECLI:EU:C:2014:2358

Davies, Gareth (2018) Has the court changed, or have the cases? The deservingness of litigants as an element in Court of Justice citizenship adjudication, *Journal of European Public Policy* 25(10): 1442–1460

De Witte, Floris (2019) Freedom of movement needs to be defended as the core of EU citizenship, in Rainer Bauböck (ed) *Debating European Citizenship* (Springer Open)

Delgado, Richard and Jean Stefancic (2017) *Critical Race Theory* (New York: NYU Press)

Directive of 16 August 1961 on administrative procedures and practices governing the entry into and employment and residence in a Member State of workers and their families from other Member States of the Community, OJ 80/1513

Directive 2004/38/EC of 29 April 2004 on the right of citizens of the Union and their family members to move and reside freely within the territory of the Member States, OJ 2004, L 158/77

Directive 2006/123 on services in the internal market, OJ L 376, 27.12.2006

Directive 2014/54/EU of 16 April 2014 on measures facilitating the exercise of rights conferred on workers in the context of freedom of movement for workers, OJ L 128, 30.4.2014

Dougan, Michael (2004) A spectre is haunting Europe… Freedom of movement of persons and the Eastern enlargement, in Christophe Hillion (ed) *EU Enlargement: A Legal Approach* 111–141 (Oxford: Hart)

Drinkwater, Stephen et al. (2006) Poles apart? EU Enlargement and the labour market outcomes of immigrants in the UK, IZA Discussion Paper No 2410 (Bonn: Institute for the Study of Labor), http://ftp.iza.org/dp2410.pdf

Drzewiecka, Jolanta et al. (2014) Rescaling the state and disciplining workers in discourses on EU Polish migration in UK newspapers, *Critical Studies in Media Communication* 31(5): 410–425

Dustmann, Christian and Tommaso Frattini (2014) The fiscal effects of immigration to the UK, *The Economic Journal*, 124 (November), F593–F643

Elsen v Bundesversicherungsandstalt fur Angestellte, Case C-135/99, ECLI:EU:C:2000:647

Engbersen, Godfried et al. (2017) The intra-EU mobility regime: Differentiation, stratification and contradictions, *Migration Studies* 5(3): 337–355

Equality and Diversity Forum (2011) Refugees, migrants and the Equality Act 2010: A briefing for public authorities (London), www.equallyours.org.uk/wp-content/uploads/2011/06/EDF-Briefing_Public-Authorities_Web_draft-32.pdf

Erel, Umut (2007) Racism and anti-racism in Europe: A critical analysis of concepts and frameworks, *Transfer* 13(3): 359–375

Eurobarometer (1986) Public Opinion in the European Community, December

Eurobarometer (1991) Standard Eurobarometer 35: Public Opinion in the European Union, Spring, https://europa.eu/eurobarometer/surveys/detail/1425

Eurobarometer (1997) Opinion Poll no 47.1, First Results Presented at the Closing Conference of the European Year Against Racism, https://access.gesis.org/dbk/17393?download_purpose=-99

Eurobarometer (2002) Standard Eurobarometer 57: Public Opinion in the EU, Spring, https://data.europa.eu/data/datasets/s1401_57_1_st57?locale=en

Eurobarometer (2007) Special Eurobarometer 263: Discrimination in the European Union, https://data.europa.eu/data/datasets/s525_65_4_ebs263?locale=en

Eurobarometer (2011) Special Eurobarometer 363: Internal market: Awareness, perceptions, and impacts, https://data.europa.eu/data/datasets/s986_75_1_ebs363?locale=en

Eurobarometer (2013) Standard Eurobarometer 79: Public Opinion in the European Union, Spring, www.eapn.eu/wp-content/uploads/2013/09/eb79_first_en.pdf

Eurobarometer (2015) Special Eurobarometer 437: Discrimination in the EU in 2015, https://tgeu.org/wpcontent/uploads/2016/10/EU_eurobarometer_2015_437.pdf

European Anti-Racism Summit (2021), www.2021portugal.eu/en/events/european-anti-racism-summit/ (last accessed 19 June 2023)

European Anti-Racism Summit (2022), https://antiracism-eusummit2022.eu/ (last accessed 19 June 2023)
European Commission (undated) The European Pillar of Social Rights Action Plan, https://commission.europa.eu/strategy-and-policy/priorities-2019-2024/economy-works-people/jobs-growth-and-investment/european-pillar-social-rights/european-pillar-social-rights-action-plan_en (last accessed 15 June 2023)
European Commission (2001) Proposal for a European Parliament and Council Directive on the right of citizens of the Union and their family members to move and reside freely within the territory of the Member States, OJ C 270 E, COM (2001) 257 final, 25.9.2001
European Commission (2004) Green Paper: Equality and Non-Discrimination in an Enlarged European Union, COM (2004) 379 final, 28.05.2004
European Commission (2008) Employment in Europe 2008 (Brussels), https://ec.europa.eu/social/BlobServlet?docId=681&langId=en
European Commission (2008a) Report on the First Phase (1 January 2007–31 December 2008) of the Transitional Arrangements set out in the 2005 Accession Treaty and as Requested According to the Transitional Arrangement set out in the 2003 Accession Treaty, COM (2008) 765 final, 18.11.2008
European Commission (2009) EU action against discrimination: Activity report 2007–08 (Brussels), https://op.europa.eu/en/publication-detail/-/publication/9d1bc5f0-9bb1-4a30-860d-946d066fa353
European Commission (2011) Report to the Council on the Functioning of the Transitional Arrangements on Free Movement of Workers from Bulgaria and Romania, COM/2011/0729 final, 11.11.2011
European Commission (2012) Staff Working Document: Towards a Job-Rich Recovery, SWD(2012) 90 final, 18.4.2012
European Commission (2013) Impact Assessment Accompanying the Document Directive of the European Parliament and of the Council on Measures Facilitating the Exercise of Rights Conferred on Workers in the Context of Freedom of Movement for Workers, COM (2013) 236 final, 26.4.2013
European Commission (2013a) Free Movement of EU Citizens and their Families: Five Actions to Make a Difference, COM (2013) 837 final, 25.11.2013
European Commission (2014) Joint Report on the application of Council Directive 2000/43/EC of 29 June 2000 implementing the principle of equal treatment between persons irrespective of racial or ethnic origin and of Council Directive 2000/78/EC of 27 November 2000 establishing a general framework for equal treatment in employment and occupation, COM (2014) 02 final, 17.1.2014
European Commission (2016) Declaration of the European Commission on the Safeguard Mechanism referred to in paragraph 2(b) of Section D of the Decision of the Heads of State or Government, meeting within the European Council, concerning a New Settlement for the United Kingdom within the European Union, Annex VI to the European Council conclusions of 18–19 February, EUCO 1/16, CO EUR 1, CONCL 1
European Commission (2018) 2017 Annual Report on the Application of the EU Charter of Fundamental Rights, COM (2018) 396 final, 4.6.2018
European Commission (2019) Staff Working Document—Countering racism and xenophobia in the EU: fostering a society where pluralism, tolerance and non-discrimination prevail, SWD(2019) 110 final, 15.3.2019

European Commission (2020) Covid-19: Guidelines for border management measures to protect health and ensure the availability of goods and essential services, C(2020) 1753 final, 16.3.2020

European Commission (2020a) Communication: Guidelines concerning the exercise of the free movement of workers during COVID-19 outbreak, 2020/C 102 I/03, OJ C 102I, 30.3.2020

European Commission (2020b) Letter to Member State Ministers (urging EU member states to ensure that vulnerable groups, including racialised communities, receive needed support during Covid-19), 8 April, https://inar.ie/wp-content/uploads/2020/05/Letter-signed-by-Commissioners-Kyriakides-Dalli-and-Schmit-002-1.pdf

European Commission (2020c) Guidelines on Seasonal Workers in the EU in the Context of the Covid-19 Outbreak, C(2020) 4813 final, 16.7.2020

European Commission (2020d) Report on the impact of demographic change, available at https://commission.europa.eu/system/files/2020-06/demography_report_2020_n.pdf

European Commission (2020e) 2019 Annual Report on Intra-EU Labour Mobility, https://ec.europa.eu/social/main.jsp?catId=738&furtherPubs=yes&langId=en&publd=8242#:~:text=The%202019%20annual%20report%20on,active%20(employed%20and%20unemployed)

European Commission (2020f) A Union of equality: EU anti-racism action plan 2020–2025, COM (2020)565 final, 18.9.2020

European Commission (2020g) The EC reveals its new EU Action Plan on Integration and Inclusion (2021–2027), 24 November, https://ec.europa.eu/migrant-integration/news/ec-reveals-its-new-eu-action-plan-integration-and-inclusion-2021-2027_en

European Commission (2021) A long-term Vision for the EU's Rural Areas—Towards stronger, connected, resilient and prosperous rural areas by 2040, COM (2021) 345 final, 30.6.2021

European Commission (2021a) Long-term vision for the EU's rural areas: launch of the Rural Pact, 20 December, https://agriculture.ec.europa.eu/news/long-term-vision-eus-rural-areas-launch-rural-pact-2021-12-20_en

European Commission (2021b) Staff Working Document—Equality bodies and the implementation of the Commission Recommendation on standards for equality bodies, SWD(2021) 63 final, 19.3.2021

European Commission (2022) Annual Report on Intra-EU Labour Mobility 2021, https://ec.europa.eu/social/main.jsp?catId=738&langId=en&pubId=8458&furtherPubs=yes

European Commission (2022a) Possible Gaps in the Legal Protection Against Discrimination on Grounds of Ethnic or Racial Origin—Factual Summary Report Open Public Consultation, https://ec.europa.eu/info/law/better-regulation/have-your-say/initiatives/13178-Addressing-possible-gaps-in-the-Racial-Equality-Directive/public-consultation_en

European Commission (2022b) Common guiding principles for national action plans against racism and racial discrimination, https://commission.europa.eu/system/files/2022-05/common_guiding_principles_for_national_action_plans_against_racism_and_racial_discrimination.pdf

European Commission (2022c) European Equality Law Review 2022/1, www.equalitylaw.eu/downloads/5725-european-equality-law-review-1-2022-pdf-1-343-kb

European Commission (2022d) To name and address the underlying problem: Structural discrimination on the ground of racial or ethnic origin, www.equalitylaw.eu/downloads/5777-to-name-and-address-the-underlying-problem-structural-discrimination-on-the-ground-of-racial-or-ethnic-origin

European Commission (2023) The Impact of Demographic Change—in a Changing Environment, SWD(2023) 21 final, 17.01.2023
European Council (2016) Presidency Conclusions, 18–19 February, EUCO 1/16, CO EUR 1, CONCL 1, www.consilium.europa.eu/media/21787/0216-euco-conclusions.pdf
European Council (2021) The Porto Declaration, 8 May, www.consilium.europa.eu/en/press/press-releases/2021/05/08/the-porto-declaration/
European Council (2021a) European Council meeting (24 and 25 June 2021)
European Council Conclusions, EUCO 7/21, CO EUR 4, CONCL 4, www.consilium.europa.eu/media/50763/2425-06-21-euco-conclusions-en.pdf
European Court of Auditors (2018) Free Movement of Workers—the fundamental freedom ensured but better targeting of EU funds would aid worker mobility, Special Report No 06, https://op.europa.eu/webpub/eca/special-reports/eu-labour-mobility-6-2018/en/
European Economic and Social Committee (2001) Opinion on Freedom of Movement for Workers in the Single Market, 2001/C 155/10, 29.5.2001
European Monitoring Centre on Racism and Xenophobia (2006) The Annual Report on the Situation regarding Racism and Xenophobia in the Member States of the EU, https://op.europa.eu/en/publication-detail/-/publication/85974a7d-a096-4146-8824-6832db92528f
European Network Against Racism (2009) The social and employment dimensions of the EU's Lisbon Strategy for growth and jobs: what are the opportunities for monitoring and improving the situation of migrants and ethnic minorities?, www.enar-eu.org/wp-content/uploads/publicationsocialinclusion-final-lowres.pdf
European Network Against Racism (2021) The Sharp Edge of Violence: Police Brutality and Community Resistance of Racialised Groups, www.enar-eu.org/the-sharp-edge-of-violence-police-brutality-and-community-resistance-of-racialised-groups/
European Network Against Racism (2022) EU Anti-Racism Action Plan Explained: Unlocking the Potential of EU Legislation to Address Structural Racism, 4 February, www.enar-eu.org/eu-anti-racism-action-plan-explained-unlocking-the-potential-of-eu-legislation-to-address-structural-racism/
European Parliament (2005) Resolution on the Protection of Minorities and Anti-Discrimination Policies in an Enlarged Europe, OJ 2005 C 124 E/405, 25.5.2006
European Parliament (2006) Resolution on the Transitional Arrangements Restricting the Free Movement of Workers on EU Labour Markets, 2006/2036 INI, C 293 E/230, 2.12.2006
European Parliament (2009) Comparative Study on the Application of Directive 2004/38/EC on the Right of Citizens of the Union and their Family Members to Move and Reside Freely within the Territory of the Member States, PE 410.650, www.europarl.europa.eu/RegData/etudes/etudes/join/2009/410650/IPOL-JURI_ET(2009)410650_EN.pdf
European Parliament (2014) Discrimination of Migrant Workers at the Workplace: Note for the EMPL Committee, www.europarl.europa.eu/RegData/etudes/note/join/2014/518768/IPOL-EMPL_NT%282014%29518768_EN.pdf
European Parliament (2014a) Written Questions with Answers, 2014/C 179/01, 12.6.2014
European Parliament (2014b) Written Questions with Answers, 2014/C 65 E/01, 5.3.2014
European Parliament (2014c) Written Questions with Answers, 2014/C 279/01, 22.8.2014
European Parliament (2014d) Resolution on respect for the fundamental right of free movement in the EU, 2013/2960(RSP), OJ C 482, 23.12.2016
European Parliament (2016) Resolution of 14 September 2016 on social dumping in the European Union (2015/2255(INI)), OJ C 204, 13.6.2018

European Parliament (2017) European Parliament resolution of 12 December 2017 on the EU Citizenship Report 2017: Strengthening Citizens' Rights in a Union of Democratic Change (2017/2069(INI)), OJ C 369, 11.10.2018

European Parliament (2017a) Resolution of 4 July 2017 on working conditions and precarious employment (2016/2221(INI)), OJ C 334, 19.9.2018

European Parliament (2020) Resolution of 19 June 2020 on European protection of cross-border and seasonal workers in the context of the COVID-19 crisis, OJ L C 362/82, 8.9.2021

European Parliament (2020a) Press Release: Bold Measures Needed to Protect Cross-border and Seasonal Workers in EU, MEPs Say, 19 June, www.europarl.europa.eu/news/en/press-room/20200615IPR81233/bold-measures-needed-to-protect-cross-border-and-seasonal-workers-meps-say

European Parliament (2021) Resolution of 20 May 2021 on impacts of EU rules on the free movements of workers and services: intra-EU labour mobility as a tool to match labour market needs and skills (2020/2007(INI)), OJ C 15, 12.1.2022

European Parliament (2022) Resolution of 10 November 2022 on racial justice, non-discrimination and anti-racism in the EU (2022/2005(INI)), OJ C 161, 5.5.2023

European Pillar of Social Rights (2017) https://commission.europa.eu/system/files/2017-11/social-summit-european-pillar-social-rights-booklet_en.pdf (last accessed 7 June 2023)

European Union Agency for Fundamental Rights (2009) EU-MIDIS: European Union Minorities and Discrimination Survey: Main Results Report (Vienna), https://fra.europa.eu/en/publication/2012/european-union-minorities-and-discrimination-survey-main-results-report

European Union Agency for Fundamental Rights (2012) The Racial Equality Directive: Applications and Challenges, https://fra.europa.eu/en/publication/2012/racial-equality-directive-application-and-challenges

European Union Agency for Fundamental Rights (2013) Opinion on the situation of equality in the European Union 10 years on from initial implementation of the equality directives (Luxembourg), https://fra.europa.eu/en/opinion/2013/fra-opinion-situation-equality-european-union-10-years-initial-implementation-equality

European Union Agency for Fundamental Rights (2018) Making EU citizens' rights a reality: national courts enforcing freedom of movement and related rights, https://fra.europa.eu/en/publication/2018/free-movement

Eurostat (2004) News release: GDP per capita in new Member States ranges from 42% of EU25 average in Latvia to 83% in Cyprus, 3 June, www.europa.eu/rapid/press-release_STAT-04-73_en.pdf

Everson, Michelle (1995) The legacy of the market citizen, in Jo Shaw and Gillian More (eds) *New Legal Dynamics of European Union* 73–90 (Oxford: Clarendon Press)

Financial Times (2011) Poles at sharp end of Dutch politics, 24 April

Finnsdottir, Maria Sigridur (2019) The costs of austerity: Labor emigration and the rise of radical right politics in Central and Eastern Europe, *Frontiers in Sociology* 4(69), doi:10.3389/fsoc.2019.00069

Fitzpatrick, Peter (1987) Racism and the innocence of law, *Journal of Law and Society* 14(1): 119–132

Frankenberg, Ruth (ed) (1997) *Displacing Whiteness: Essays in Social and Cultural Criticism* (Durham: Duke University Press)

French, Steve (2012) Beyond ESOL? Assessing the propensity of East European migrant workers to undertake further and higher education, *Research in Post-Compulsory Education* 17(1): 125–142

Gilmartin, Mary and Bettina Migge (2015) European migrants in Ireland: Pathways to integration, *European Urban Regional Studies* 22(3): 285–299

Groenendijk, Kees et al. (2013) European Report on the Free Movement of Workers in Europe in 2011–2012 (European Commission), http://ec.europa.eu/social/BlobServlet?docId=10443&langId=en

Grzelczyk v Centre public d'aide sociale d'Ottignies-Louvain-la-Neuve, Case C-184/99, ECLI:EU:C:2001:458

Guild, Elspeth et al. (2007) European Report on the Free Movement of Workers in Europe in 2006, Part I (European Commission)

Gusa v Minister for Social Protection, Case C-442/16, ECLI:EU:C:2017:1004

Her Majesty's Revenue and Customs v Dakneviciute, Case C-544/18, ECLI:EU:C:2019:761

Holland, Dawn et al. (2011) Labour mobility within the EU—The impact of enlargement and the functioning of the transitional arrangements, Study commissioned by the Directorate-General for Employment, Social Affairs, and Equal Opportunities (London: National Institute of Economic and Social Research), https://ec.europa.eu/social/BlobServlet?docId=7191&langId=en

Horridge, Mark and Bartlomiej Rokicki (2018) The impact of European Union accession on regional income convergence within the Visegrad countries, *Regional Studies* 52(4): 503–515

Howard, Erica (2009) *The EU Race Directive: Developing the Protection against Racial Discrimination within the EU* (London: Routledge)

ICF GHK (2013) A fact finding analysis on the impact on the Member States' social security systems of the entitlements of non-active intra-EU movers to special non-contributory cash benefits and healthcare granted on the basis of residence, Final report, 14 October, https://publications.europa.eu/en/publication-detail/-/publication/c6de1d0a-2a5b-4e03-9efb-ed522e6a27f5

Ipsos MORI (2007) Immigration Poll, 2 November, www.ipsos.com/ipsos-mori/en-uk/immigration-poll

Jefferys, Steve (2015) The context to challenging discrimination against ethnic minorities and migrant workers at work, *Transfer* 21(1): 9–22

Jobcenter Berlin Neukölln v Alimanovic, Case C-67/14, ECLI:EU:C:2015:597

Jobcenter Krefeld Widerspruchsstelle v JD, Case C-181/19, ECLI:EU:C:2020:794

Johnstone, Chris (2007) Nine more countries tear down their walls, *Edmonton Journal*, 21 December, E7

Joint Declaration Against Racism and Xenophobia, OJ 1986C 158, 25.6.1986

Jyske Finans A/S v Ligebehandlingsnævnet, Case C-668/15, ECLI:EU:C:2017:278

Kahanec, Martin and Mariola Pytliková (2017) The economic impact of east–west migration on the European Union, *Empirica* 44(3): 407–434

Kahanec, Martin et al. (2016) The free movement of workers in an enlarged European Union: Institutional underpinnings of economic adjustment, in Martin Kahanec and Klaus F Zimmermann (eds) *Labor Migration, EU Enlargement, and the Great Recession* 1–34 (Berlin Heidelberg: Springer)

Kahn, Jean (1995) Final Report from: Consultative Commission on Racism and Xenophobia, 23 May (European Council), http://aei.pitt.edu/1588/

Kelner, Simon (2016) There's no such thing as racism against white people, *I Newspaper*, 31 May, https://inews.co.uk/opinion/columnists/theres-no-thing-racism-white-people/

Kofman, Eleonore et al. (2009) The equality implications of being a migrant in Britain, Project Report 19 (Equality and Human Rights Commission), https://eprints.mdx.ac.uk/5541/1/19_the-equality-implications-of-being-a-migrant-in-britain.pdf

Koning, Thomas and Brooke Luetger (2008) Troubles with transposition? explaining trends in member-state notification and the delayed transposition of EU directives, *British Journal of Political Science* 39: 163–194

Kosyakova, Yuliya and Herbert Brücker (2021) Does free movement of workers boost immigrant employment? New evidence from Germany, *Migration Studies* 9(4): 1734–1762

Krishnan, Manisha (2016) Dear white people, please stop pretending reverse racism is real, *Vice Media*, 2 October, www.vice.com/en_uk/article/dear-white-people-please-stop-pretending-reverse-racism-is-real

Land Nordrhein-Westfalen v Pokrzeptowicz-Meyer, Case C-162/00, ECLI:EU:C:2002:57

Levine-Rasky, Cynthia (2013) *Whiteness Fractured* (Farnham: Ashgate)

Lewicki, Aleksandra (2023) East–west inequalities and the ambiguous racialisation of 'Eastern Europeans', *Journal of Ethnic and Migration Studies* 49(6): 1481–1499

Maas, Willem (ed) (2013) *Democratic Citizenship and the Free Movement of People* (Boston: Martinus Nijhoff)

MacKenzie, Robert and Chris Forde (2009) The rhetoric of the 'good worker' versus the realities of employers' use and the experiences of migrant workers, *Work, Employment and Society* 23(1): 142–159

Mantu, Sandra and Paul Minderhoud (2019) Exploring the links between residence and social rights for economically inactive EU citizens, *European Journal of Migration and Law* 21(3): 313–337

Martínez Sala v Freistaat Bayern, Case C-85/96, ECLI:EU:C:1998:217

Meister v Speech Design Carrier Systems GmbH, Case C-415/10, ECLI:EU:C:2012:217

Mikl-Leitner, Johanna et al. (2013) Letter to Alan Shatter, President of the European Council for Justice and Home Affairs, www.statewatch.org/news/2013/apr/eu-4-ms-welfare-letter-to-irish-presidency.pdf

Morgan, Benjamin (2021) *Still Here: Defending the Rights of Homeless EU Citizens After Brexit and Covid-19* (London: Public Interest Law Centre), www.pilc.org.uk/wp-content/uploads/2021/06/PILC_EEA_A4_ONLINE-1.pdf

Myslinska, Dagmar (2019) Retracing the right to free movement: mapping a path forward, *Michigan State International Law Review* 27(3): 383–439

Myslinska, Dagmar (2020) Not quite right: Representations of Eastern Europeans in ECJ discourse, *International Journal of Politics, Culture and Society* 34: 271–307

Nahles, Andrea et al. (2017) Letter to European Commissioner for Employment, Social Affairs, Skills and Labour Mobility, Indexation of child benefits for children living in other EU Member States, 27 July, www.ft.dk/samling/20161/almdel/BEU/bilag/299/1781050/index.htm

Ninni-Orasche v Bundesminister für Wissenschaft, Verkehr und Kunst, Case C-413/01, ECLI:EU:C:2003:600

Nyman, Pär and Rafael Ahlskog (2018) Fiscal effects of intra-EEA migration (Uppsala University: Reminder Project), www.reminder-project.eu/wp-content/uploads/2018/03/March-2018-FINAL-Deliverable-4.1_with-cover.pdf

O'Brien, Charlotte (2015) The pillory, the precipice and the slippery slope: The profound effect of the UK's legal reform programme targeting EU migrants, *Journal of Social Welfare and Family Law* 37(1): 111–136

Office national de l'emploi v Ioannidis, Case C-258/04, ECLI:EU:C:2005:559

Organisation for Economic Co-operation and Development (2012) Free Movement of Workers and Labour Market Adjustment: Recent Experiences from OECD Countries and the European Union, www.keepeek.com/Digital-Asset-Management/oecd/social-issues-migration-health/free-movement-of-workers-and-labour-market-adjustment_9789264177185-en#page1

Organisation for Economic Co-operation and Development (2020) How COVID-19 could accelerate local labour market transitions, in *Job Creation and Local Economic Development 2020: Rebuilding Better*, https://doi.org/10.1787/a0361fec-en

Patuzzi, Liam and Meghan Benton (2020) Emigration from East to West Europe: The real test for EU free movement? (Oxford: Centre on Migration, Policy and Society), www.reminder-project.eu/publications/policy-briefings/emigration-from-east-to-west-europe-the-real-test-for-eu-free-movement/

Pensionsversicherungsanstalt v Brey, Case C-140/12, ECLI:EU:C:2013:565

Poulsen, Troels Lund et al. (2018) Letter to European Commissioner for Employment, Social Affairs, Skills and Labour Mobility Indexation of child benefits for children living in other EU Member States, 19 June, www.ft.dk/samling/20171/almdel/BEU/bilag/386/1914108.pdf

President of the European Commission et al. (2021) Porto Social Commitment, 7 May, www.2021portugal.eu/media/icfksbgy/porto-social-commitment.pdf

Prete v Office national de l'emploi, Case C-367/11, ECLI:EU:C:2012:668

Pruitt, Lisa (2015) The false choice between race and class and other affirmative action myths, *Buffalo Law Review* 63: 981–1027

Regulation 1612/68 of the Council of 15 October 1968 on freedom of movement for workers within the Community, OJ L 257, 19.10.1968

Regulation 883/2004 of the European Parliament and Council of 29 April 2004 on the coordination of social security systems (replacing Regulation 1408/71 of the Council of 14 June 1971 on the application of social security schemes to employed persons and their families moving within the Community)

Regulation 492/2011 of 5 April 2011 on freedom of movement for workers within the Union (replacing Regulation 1612/68 of the Council of 15 October 1968 on freedom of movement for workers within the Community)

Report of the High Level Panel on the Free Movement of Persons, chaired by Mrs Simone Veil, presented to the Commission on 18 March 1997, COM 7035/97

Resolution on the Protection of Minorities and Anti-Discrimination Policies in an Enlarged Europe', OJ 2005 C 124 E/405, 25.5.2006

Rzepnikowska, Alina (2019) Racism and xenophobia experienced by Polish migrants in the UK before and after Brexit vote, *Journal of Ethnic and Migration Studies* 45(1): 61–77

Saint Prix v Secretary of State for Work and Pensions, Case C-507/12, ECLI:EU:C:2014:2007

Schiek, Dagmar et al. (2015) *EU Social and Labour Rights and EU Internal Market Law* (Brussels: European Parliamentary Research Service), https://policycommons.net/artifacts/1335930/eu-social-and-labour-rights-and-eu-internal-market-law/1942742/

Siklodi, Nora (2014) Multi-level citizenship: Labour migration and the transformation of identity in the EU, in Chris Rumford and Didem Buhari-Gulmez (eds) *European Multiplicity* 129–146 (Newcastle upon Tyne: Cambridge Scholars)

Sime, Daniela et al. (2022) Performing whiteness: Central and Eastern European young people's experiences of xenophobia and racialisation in the UK post-Brexit, *Journal of Ethnic and Migration Studies* 48(19): 4527–4546

Sirkeci, Ibrahim et al. (2018) Barriers for highly qualified A8 immigrants in the UK labour market, *Work, Employment and Society* 32(5): 906–924

Sobis, Iwona (2016) Polish plumbers and Romanian strawberry pickers: How the populist framing of EU migration impacts national policies, *Migration and Development* 5(3): 431–454

Solanke, Iyiola (2009) *Making Anti-Racial Discrimination Law: A Comparative History of Social Action and Anti-Racial Discrimination Law* (London: Routledge)

Somek, Alexander (2011) *Engineering Equality: An Essay on European Anti-Discrimination Law* (Oxford: Oxford University Press)

Spaak, Paul-Henri (1956) The Brussels Report on the General Common Market (Brussels: Intergovernmental Committee on European Integration), http://aei.pitt.edu/995/1/Spaak_report.pdf

Spanish Delegation, Intergovernmental Conference on Political Union (1990) *Note on European Citizenship*, SN 2940/90, 24.09.1990

Stalford, Helen (2003) *The Impact of Enlargement on Free Movement: A Critique of Transitional Periods*, Paper Presented at Meeting of UACES Study Group on the Evolving EU Migration Law and Policy, 5 December (University of Liverpool), www.liverpool.ac.uk/media/livacuk/ewc/docs/Stalford-paper11.2003.pdf

Stupp, Catherine (2017) Thyssen slams Schäuble's proposal to cut childcare benefits for EU foreigners, *EURACTIV*, 10 February, www.euractiv.com/section/social-europe-jobs/news/thyssen-slams-schaubles-proposal-to-cut-childcare-benefits-for-eu-foreigners/

Swaddling v Adjudication Officer, Case C-90/97, ECLI:EU:C:1999:96

Tarola v Minister for Social Protection, Case C-483/17, ECLI:EU:C:2019:309

The Queen v Immigration Appeal Tribunal, ex parte Antonissen, Case C-292/89, ECLI:EU:C:1991:80

Treaty between the Kingdom of Belgium, the Kingdom of Denmark, the Federal Republic of Germany, the Hellenic Republic, the Kingdom of Spain, the French Republic, Ireland, the Italian Republic, the Grand Duchy of Luxembourg, the Kingdom of the Netherlands, the Republic of Austria, the Portuguese Republic, the Republic of Finland, the Kingdom of Sweden, the United Kingdom of Great Britain and Northern Ireland (Member States of the European Union) and the Czech Republic, the Republic of Estonia, the Republic of Cyprus, the Republic of Latvia, the Republic of Lithuania, the Republic of Hungary, the Republic of Malta, the Republic of Poland, the Republic of Slovenia, the Slovak Republic, concerning the accession of the Czech Republic, the Republic of Estonia, the Republic of Cyprus, the Republic of Latvia, the Republic of Lithuania, the Republic of Hungary, the Republic of Malta, the Republic of Poland, the Republic of Slovenia and the Slovak Republic to the European Union, OJ L 236, 23.9.2003 ('2003 Accession Treaty')

Treaty Establishing the European Coal and Steel Community, 18 April 1951 (Paris), http://aei.pitt.edu/37145/1/ECSC_Treaty_1951.pdf

Treaty Establishing the European Community (Nice Consolidated Version), OJ C 325, 24.12.2002

Treaty Establishing the European Economic Community, 25 March 1957 (Rome), www.cvce.eu/en/obj/treaty_establishing_the_european_economic_community_rome_25_march_1957-en-cca6ba28-0bf3-4ce6-8a76-6b0b3252696e.html

Treaty of Amsterdam amending the Treaty on European Union, the Treaties establishing the European Communities and certain related acts, OJ C 340, 10.11.1997

Treaty on European Union (Maastricht), OJ C 191, 29.07.1992

Trojani v Centre public d'aide sociale de Bruxelles, Case C-456/02, ECLI:EU:C:2004:488

UN General Assembly, International Convention on the Protection of the Rights of All Migrant Workers and Members of Their Families (entered into force 18 December 1990) A/RES/45/158

UN General Assembly, International Covenant on Civil and Political Rights (entered into force 23 March 1976) 999 UNTS 171

Vatsouras and Koupatantze v Arbeitsgemeinschaft Nürnberg, Case C-22/08, ECLI:EU:C:2009:344

Verwiebe, Roland et al. (2014) New forms of intra-European migration, labour market dynamics and social inequality in Europe, *Migration Letters* 11(2): 125–136

Vestische Arbeit Jobcenter Kreis Recklinghausen v García-Nieto, Case C-299/14, ECLI:EU:C:2016:114

Weisskircher, Manès et al. (2020) The only frequent flyers left: Migrant workers in the EU in times of Covid-19, *Open Democracy*, 20 April, www.opendemocracy.net/en/can-europe-make-it/only-frequent-flyers-left-migrant-workers-eu-times-covid-19/

Williams, Patricia J (1992) *The Alchemy of Race and Rights* (Cambridge: Harvard University Press)

Ziolkowski and Szeja v Land Berlin, Joined Cases C-424/10 and 425/10, ECLI:EU:C:2011:866

Chapter 4

Case Study
CEE Movers in pre-Brexit Britain

Omissions and inequalities in EU policies and discourse, discussed in the preceding chapters, have helped to support the creation of a social reality filled with ethnic stratifications which has enabled CEE movers' racialisation as second-class Europeans. Since it is at the Member State level that the lived experience of the EU's free movement and equality rights frameworks occurs, I now turn my attention to a domestic case study of CEE movers' mobility and access to social rights. To do so, I look at the example of the UK while it was still a Member State. The UK can serve as a poignant illustration of the deep schism between EU rights and the domestic experience thereof and as a warning of how rights can be disregarded even in a country with a long history of immigration and which has been considered a leader in anti-discrimination law development in Europe.

Despite higher rates of Euroscepticism than in EU-14 states, the UK was not a special case. Tensions and fractures in the experience of CEE nationals' mobility to the UK are in many ways comparable to ongoing concerns in other western Member States. Brexit itself brought to the foreground anti-CEE antipathy and domestic contestations over free movement which had been bubbling under the surface since the Eastern Enlargement. Driven by economic concerns, including increasing austerity measures, and by not feeling heard by the political elite, such consternations were capitalised on by populist politicians who provided an outlet to domestic voters who had felt left behind. Similar opposition to CEE movers and pushback against the free movement right have been observed in EU-14 states, as discussed in the preceding chapter, fuelling anti-CEE policies and rhetoric and energising populist movements.[1] EU-14 economies—especially Germany, France, and Austria, as well as Spain and Italy—have continued to rely heavily on CEE[2] workers whose mobility has persisted unabated and who are overrepresented in precarious and de-skilled positions. Whereas anti-immigrant attitudes appear to have diminished in the

---

1 Notably, in France, the Netherlands, Denmark, Finland, Germany, Sweden, Spain, and Greece.
2 Moreover, Bulgarian and Romanian net mobility has continued to increase over the recent years.

DOI: 10.4324/9781003175377-4

UK since the Brexit referendum, they have remained high across EU-14 states. Dire social consequences of economic challenges have only increased across western Member States since the Covid pandemic and Russia's invasion of Ukraine—which is only likely to further ignite anti-mover sentiment. Since the right to free movement—a fundamental EU value and raison d'être—cannot be contested at the EU level, the only option is to channel such domestic anxieties into anti-mover sentiment and policies, especially initiatives targeting the most vulnerable groups among movers such as racialised CEE nationals. Leaving the EU is simply an extreme example of this stance.

Notably, looking at the UK as a case study helps to demonstrate deep-seeded complications within the EU integration project. I suggest that contestations in the UK over CEE mobility should be seen as a product of intra-EU inequalities between eastern and western parts of the EU that have been driving CEE nationals' mobility[3] and which have been normalised and reinforced by longstanding western racialising rhetoric. Even if exiting the EU might not be in the cards for other western states—particularly given that Eurosceptic parties are highly unlikely to be able to form governments on their own without entering into coalitions with pro-EU parties—the British approach towards CEE nationals' mobility and racialisation serve as an unsettling illustration of the inequalities and failings within the right to free movement in practice.

This chapter explores how CEE movers were situated within the UK's mobility and equality frameworks and discourses which had been facilitated through, and which had been reinforcing, unequal EU policies and discourses. In line with critical race theory scholars, I question the definitions and foundations of relevant legal frameworks and legal reasoning, relating them to underlying social relations and the broader political climate, and I look closely at how policies are interpreted and enforced. My arguments are supported through a close analysis of post-04 racial discrimination claims brought by CEE nationals in the employment context. I focus on the employment field because work has been the primary driver of CEE mobility, a process further reinforced by the continuing connection of the EU freedom of movement right to movers' economic activity. Notably, discrimination often manifests itself in the labour market, and labour market outcomes are closely connected to (in) equalities in other fields. My exploration unveils some challenges that appear unique to CEE workers when relying on anti-discrimination legislation and questions whether the UK's equality regime has been capable of taking into account CEE movers' position as racialised whites. Domestic strategies targeting CEE movers' access to rights and anti-CEE rhetoric have further reinforced CEE movers' second-class Europeanness in the UK.

---

3 See also Antonucci and Varriale (2020).

CEE Nationals in the UK

Although immigrants from the CEE region had been settling in the UK for centuries, they had done so only in small numbers before the Eastern Enlargement and were largely comprised of groups fleeing political or religious persecution. According to the 1901 Census, there were fewer than 100,000 CEE nationals in the UK. CEE immigration intensified shortly after WWII and included the arrival of about 200,000 Polish soldiers and their family members under the 1947 Polish Resettlement Act and of approximately 80,000 refugees and displaced persons—largely from Poland, Latvia, and Ukraine—under the UK's European Voluntary Workers scheme which was created to cover labour shortages in low-paid, 'unskilled' work. Emigration from the CEE region was severely curtailed under communism, albeit small numbers managed to defect, especially in the aftermath of crises in the region, such as the Hungarian Revolution in 1956, Russia's invasion of Czechoslovakia in 1968, and the imposition of martial law in Poland in 1981. These asylum seekers were mostly well-educated, political dissidents. The fall of communism in 1989 ended restrictions on CEE nationals' ability to leave the region. However, entry into the UK (and the rest of the EU) was restricted and controlled through a visa regime. Some CEE nationals also arrived pursuant to their respective countries' Europe Agreements, which permitted them to establish businesses in the EU, and under Seasonal Agricultural Workers Schemes. On the eve of the Eastern Enlargement in 2004, fewer than 200,000 documented CEE nationals lived in the UK, in addition to an unknown number of undocumented[4] CEE migrants, including visa over-stayers.

CEE nationals' pre-04 presence garnered little public or media attention, although they were perceived as inferior to western Europeans. Whereas throughout the UK's history even white migrants have faced hostility—notably, the Irish, Travellers, Roma, and Jews—pre-04 CEE migrants largely escaped overt violence. This is likely because they arrived in insignificant numbers, made efforts to blend in, celebrated Christian holidays, did not concentrate as heavily in lower-skilled positions or at specific employer sites, and tended to settle predominantly in multicultural urban areas. That being said, their whiteness did not protect them from racialisation. For example, in the 1910s, Undersecretary of State Edward Troup asserted that 'aliens from Eastern Europe' were lowering British workers' wages and that 'their habits had a demoralising effect'.[5] In 1924, his successor John Pedder opposed naturalisation applications filed by 'Slavs ... and other races from Central and Eastern parts of Europe'.[6] Perceived as fundamentally 'different from the British people', those from the CEE region were portrayed as lesser than 'the Latin, Teuton and Scandinavian races', who were deemed to share 'a certain kinship with British races ... with the life and habits of this country and [to be] easily assimilated'. Thus, historically, CEE nationals came to represent a 'degenerate'

---

4 For most, status became automatically regularised at the moment of accession.
5 Cohen (2006) (citation omitted).
6 Minute by Sir John Pedder, 28 May 1924, HO 45/24765/432156/17.

whiteness which was 'contingent and had a mere degraded'[7] and 'borderline status'[8] in the hierarchies of whiteness in the UK. This racialisation intensified after large numbers of CEE nationals entered the UK after the Eastern Enlargement—reinforced through policies aiming to restrict their mobility and social rights. Meanwhile, they became positioned in the labour market as cheap, fungible, and exploitable labourers—overlooked by race-relations and equality discourses.

CEE Movers' Racialisation in the UK

After the Eastern Enlargement, CEE nationals began to move to the UK in larger numbers. Within the first two years after accession, 600,000 CEE workers arrived in the UK, although about half returned to their home countries, resulting in net figures of approximately 150,000 per year. By 2010, approximately 1.5 million CEE nationals—mostly Poles—had moved to the UK, albeit more than half had returned home. By 2016, Polish became the most common language in the UK after English. Between the Brexit referendum in 2016 and the UK's withdrawal from the EU in 2020, net EU mobility declined sharply. In 2018, approximately 3 million EU nationals resided in the UK, including 1.3 million CEE nationals and almost 500,000 Bulgarian and Romanian nationals. In 2019, Poles (646,000) and Romanians (338,000) constituted the biggest mover groups in the UK.

CEE movers were publicly unwelcome in the UK. They dispersed widely throughout the UK—including across rural areas that had not experienced large-scale immigration before. Compared to pre-04 CEE migrants, they were less likely to integrate—arguably in part due to their large numbers, propensity to settle in ethnic enclaves, over-representation in precarious and often temporary employment, concentration at low-paid employer sites staffed predominantly with other CEE workers, and frequent engagement in circular migration. They found themselves oftentimes excluded by the post-war CEE migrants already integrated in the UK. Due to increasing austerity measures further exacerbated by the 2008 financial crisis, CEE movers' arrivals were not supported by British fiscal policy measures such as expansions of housing construction or public services, and this fuelled public resentment against them.

Widespread animosity against CEE movers had built upon anti-CEE antagonism that predated both Brexit and the Eastern Enlargement. The British public has consistently highly disfavoured CEE nationals. For example, British Social Attitudes Surveys between 1983 and 1996 revealed that white Britons were prejudiced against Eastern Europeans more than any other white group measured—including EU-14 nationals, Americans, Canadians, Latin Americans, South Africans, Australians, and New Zealanders. Although Britons' attitudes towards some non-white immigrant groups appear to have improved over the

---

7 Anderson (2013).
8 Blachnicka-Ciacek and Budginaite-Mackine (2022).

years, a hierarchy among white foreigners has continued. For example, according to a 2007 immigration survey, 34% of Britons felt that EU-14 nationals should be given priority to immigrate to the UK whereas 27% supported that approach for Australians, New Zealanders, and Canadians; 9% for Americans; 1% for those from African Commonwealth countries; and 0% for CEE nationals.[9] Public concerns over migration reached a peak in 2007 and 2008 when CEE mobility was at its highest. For example, more than 40% of those polled during each month between September 2007 and April 2008 considered race and immigration among the most important issues facing Britain—ahead of worries about the economy or crime.

As a group, CEE movers were subjected to racialisation in the UK. That is, British media, public, and political discourses had ascribed negative ethnicity-based identities to CEE movers—often as welfare scroungers, criminals, and job stealers[10]—reminiscent of how non-white post-war migration had been characterised. CEE movers were typically referred to as 'migrants', akin to persons arriving from outside the EU, rather than as mobile EU citizens. For many white Britons, the word 'immigrant' connoted inherent foreignness and conjured up images of unwelcomed spongers who dilute British stock. The dominant white group in the UK actively constructed and reproduced its white privilege, while excluding CEE nationals, through everyday discourse, politics, economy, and culture. This of course repeats the many historical examples of how, as a time- and place-specific malleable construct, white privilege has not been available to all phenotypical whites, such as the Irish and Southern and Eastern European immigrants to the UK and US.

CEE movers' racialisation was accompanied by overt expressions of racism and discrimination against them. Although much media attention was devoted to racial hatred directed against CEE nationals immediately in the aftermath of the June 2016 Brexit referendum, everyday racism preceded the referendum, including incidents of hateful graffiti, threats, bullying, assaults, refusals to provide services, and property destruction.[11] Moreover, various qualitative studies indicate that CEE movers experienced discrimination in everyday interactions, in the labour market and in the housing market long before the referendum.[12] This poor treatment intensified competition between CEE groups and among CEE co-ethnics. Notably, some CEE groups felt disadvantaged compared to Polish movers (and were hence antagonistic towards them) due to Poles' larger and more long-standing presence in the UK and the consequent availability of service providers catering to them.

---

9 Ipsos MORI (2007). Bulgarians and Romanians fared particularly poorly in this survey – with 8% of those polled stating that they should not be allowed to enter the UK at all, which was higher than for any other white group measured.
10 See generally Fox et al. (2012); Lewicki (2023).
11 E.g., Burnett (2011).
12 E.g., Sumption and Somerville (2010); Rzepnikowska (2019).

Perhaps most poignantly, public opposition to CEE nationals' mobility featured prominently in Brexit debates and in the referendum outcome. While renegotiating the UK's EU membership, the then-Prime Minister David Cameron condemned Labour for having afforded CEE nationals access to the UK's labour market in 2004 and referred to Poles to illustrate immigrants' alleged exploitation of the UK's welfare system. Right-wing groups were less measured in their contempt for CEE movers whom they explicitly associated with 'violent convicted criminals', 'dangerous terror suspects',[13] and 'convicted murderers'.[14] Bulgarians and Romanians became similarly demonised. According to UKIP leader Nigel Farage, they had been 'living like animals' in their home countries, so it would have been expected of them to desire to live in a 'civilised country' like the UK.[15] Such statements are in line with historical western discourses and with institutional othering addressed in the preceding chapters. Moreover, UKIP campaigns conflated EU movers with undocumented migrants and asylum seekers (especially those of Muslim origin[16]), categorising all as unwanted 'immigrants'. Unfortunately, whereas the British political Left normally counters racism which targets groups encompassed under the 'BAME' label (Black, Asian, and Minority Ethnic), they were largely silent regarding the racialisation of CEE nationals. At the time of the Eastern Enlargement and in the context of Brexit debates, Left and Centre politicians focused on economic arguments only, reiterating EU discourses that emphasised what CEE workers could do for the UK, rather than acknowledging their EU citizenship and equality rights. In addition to being inherently degrading, this argument lost salience after the economy began to falter in 2008.

Brexit supporters cited immigration as their most important worry and were guided by identity and ethnicity anxieties more than by economic concerns. Notably, post-referendum studies showed that voter support for Brexit was inversely related to EU movers' presence in their communities[17] and was hence likely motivated by negative attitudes rather than by practical concerns or negative experiences. Both Brexit supporters and opponents showed strong preference for non-CEE white immigrants such as those from Australia.[18]

After the referendum, expressions of racism against CEE nationals continued and escalated to include increased incidents of hate crime[19] encompassing several fatal assaults.[20] Although all EU nationals as well as non-whites and

13 Vote Leave (undated).
14 Vote Leave (2016).
15 Bienkov (2013).
16 Its infamous 'Breaking Point' poster presented an image of a throng of apparently Middle Eastern asylum seekers, mostly men, presumably in continental Europe.
17 E.g., Sampson (2017).
18 Blinder and Richards (2018).
19 E.g., Younge (2016).
20 For example, Arkadiusz Jozwik, a Polish national, was beaten to death by five teenagers in Harlow, on the outskirts of London, two months after the referendum.

Muslim individuals were targeted as outsiders, CEE movers appear to have been the primary victims. For example, in 2017, an Oxfordshire fishery put up a sign warning 'NO Polish or Eastern Bloc Fishermen Allowed. No Children or Dogs'[21]—reminiscent of the post-war 'No Irish. No Blacks. No Dogs' signs. Although it is not possible to compare CEE movers' experiences to the historical (and contemporary) positioning of Blacks, the warning nevertheless attests to the fact that CEE movers' experiences were far removed from the EU's promises of equality. Disappointingly, any government statements condemning incendiary media reports and post-referendum racist incidents consistently placed blame on individual perpetrators—diverting attention from the political elite's role in propagating a climate of inequality and antagonism against CEE movers.

Anti-CEE racism has persisted since the UK formally left the EU, and this indicates how deeply engrained, and often divorced from practical concerns, anti-CEE sentiment has been. For example, almost 20% of white respondents with CEE backgrounds participating in the 2021 Evidence for Equality National Survey[22] reported that they had experienced some type of racist assault (e.g., insults, property damage, or physical attacks). CEE participants also reported encountering institutional racism, particularly in the employment setting. Post-Brexit qualitative studies have also revealed ongoing racialisation, verbal and physical abuse, vandalism, discrimination, and acts of microaggression directed against CEE nationals—including online, in school settings and public places, on public transport systems, and at places of employment.[23] When perpetrators did not know a victim's specific nationality, 'Polish' and 'Gypsy' became slur words connoting undesirability and otherness.

CEE movers' whiteness has both complicated their racialisation and bestowed some advantages on them. In pre-Brexit polls, CEE nationals were preferred by both Leavers and Remainers to many non-white groups—especially Pakistanis and Nigerians. They could go unnoticed in public spaces due to being phenotypically similar to white Britons. Their invisibility, however, would dissipate once they spoke or exhibited markers of their CEE nationalities, such as shopping at ethnic shops, using ethnic satellite dishes or CEE car registration plates, or dressing in a manner not comporting with the UK norm. In response to their racialisation, CEE movers have been known to emphasise their whiteness (and Europeanness) and to express racism against non-Caucasians and non-Christians, to try to improve their positioning within the UK's racial hierarchy. This behaviour is reminiscent of how certain Caucasian immigrants to the United States a century ago asserted their whiteness and expressed antipathy towards non-whites in order to move up on the scale of racial hierarchies.

21 Kentish (2017).
22 Evidence for Equality National Survey (Centre on the Dynamics of Ethnicity), www.ethnicity.ac.uk/research/projects/evens/.
23 E.g., Sime et al. (2022); the3million (2020).

On the other hand, CEE nationals' whiteness was a double-edged sword, as it contributed to racism, violence, and discrimination against them going unacknowledged. While directing anxieties against non-white groups is generally perceived as socially unacceptable, it is less condemnable when targeting white ethnic groups such as CEE movers, the Roma, and Travellers. As whiteness scholars have noted, whiteness is most contested at its edges. At least some white Britons appeared more comfortable directing explicit criticism against racialised whites than against non-whites[24]—similar to how the Irish and Jews were openly degraded historically and how 'chavs', the Roma, and Travellers are openly targeted today. As a participant in a study of CEE movers' experiences in a northern English city remarked, 'English people are scared of black people. Black people can take you to court and say that you are racist. You don't have this problem with Poles, so Polish people are now on the end'.[25] In another study, a CEE national declared that 'it would have been better if I was black, I mean, if I was from Africa, because people would stop treating me as an intruder..., and they feel guilty about those from Africa because of the history, because they have to make it up to them'.[26] Moreover, some members of the public assume that the concepts of racism and discrimination only apply to non-white victims.[27] For example, a jury found that an assault on a Polish mover that caused him severe head injuries did not constitute a hate crime despite the fact that the perpetrator had used phrases such as 'Polish bastard'.[28] Some police officers have even questioned whether CEE nationals deserve the same protections as visible minorities.[29]

At the same time, despite their degenerate whiteness and experiences of racialisation, CEE movers were largely absent from public debates, political discourse, and conceptual approaches towards equality and discrimination, as discussed below. Racism against them was also often attributed to 'cultural' antagonism or 'xenophobia' (fear or dislike of anything foreign), implying that it is somehow less condemnable than phenotype-based racism. Pretending that antagonism towards CEE nationals is not proper racism makes it particularly dangerous, especially as law and legal discourse tend to subscribe to the traditional black/white paradigm of privilege and lack the vocabulary to tackle wrongs that appear culturally-based or xenophobic.

The Government's Hostile Approach Towards CEE Movers

The 2004 accession was effectuated in the UK through the European Union (Accessions) Act 2003. It was accompanied by Immigration (European Economic Area) Regulation 2006, which transposed the EU Citizens' Rights

---

24 E.g., Lewis (2005).
25 Cook et al. (2010).
26 Rzepnikowska (2019).
27 E.g., Tan (2014).
28 The Scotsman (2007).
29 Johns (2014).

Directive 2004/38, and by additional regulations that limited CEE movers' access to rights during the post-accession transitional period. The government's decision to allow (regulated) labour market access to CEE nationals was largely predicated on labour shortages at the time and on forecasts of low inflows of CEE movers (of approximately between 5,000 and 13,000 per year). It was also driven by geopolitical reasons—with Margaret Thatcher having set the tone years earlier for supporting CEE accession—and by a desire to reduce potential numbers of undocumented CEE migrants.

The Worker Registration Scheme (2004–11)

The Accession (Immigration and Worker Registration) Regulations 2004 established the Worker Registration Scheme ('WRS'), which obliged newly arriving CEE nationals to register before undertaking employment[30] in the UK. Despite pre-accession labour shortages in the UK and predictions of low CEE mobility, the UK imposed these indirect transitional restrictions during the entire seven-year period allowed under the Accession Treaty.[31] Under the WRS, CEE workers were required to pay a £60 fee (later increased to £90)—which was arguably contrary to EU law[32]—and to provide confirmation of employment within 30 days of undertaking work. They also had to re-register within 30 days whenever changing employment during their first 12 months in the UK. Failure to comply resulted in losing the right to reside under the WRS. This is notwithstanding the fact that under EU Directive 2004/38, workers are entitled to retain their residence right for at least six months if they become involuntarily unemployed. Under the WRS, it was only after engaging in registered employment for 12 consecutive months that CEE workers acquired the right to reside. Until that point, they had no full access to non-contributory welfare benefits (such as jobseeker's allowance) or to contributory social benefits (such as unemployment assistance) even though during that time they might have qualified for 'worker' status under EU law. Moreover, non-compliance with the WRS scheme could have been used to deny a subsequent application for permanent residence until the Supreme Court ruled this approach unlawful.[33]

The WRS programme benefited the British purse while disadvantaging CEE workers. By the end of the transitional period in 2011, more than 1.1 million CEE workers had registered under the WRS, largely filling undesirable job vacancies. While the scheme limited their access to benefits, it enriched the

30 It did not apply to self-employed workers.
31 Even greater restrictions were imposed against Bulgarians and Romanians during 2007–14.
32 According to the European Commission, any work permits required under domestic legislation had to be issued automatically. No EU institution, however, addressed whether the UK's imposition of the WRS fee was permissible.
33 *Secretary of State for Work and Pensions v Gubeladze*, [2019] UKSC 31.

public purse through their national insurance and tax contributions. Moreover, British employers were not prosecuted for hiring workers who did not comply with the WRS. Some employers and employment agencies even encouraged CEE workers not to register (to reduce bureaucratic and financial costs of lawfully employing them) thus further limiting CEE workers' access to residence and social rights. This effect was exacerbated due to the fact that registering for the scheme was not simple. The WRS system was complicated, and the application form and explanatory notes were provided in English and online only. More generally, given CEE movers' propensity to be employed in precarious, temporary, and part-time arrangements,[34] it would have been difficult for them to satisfy the 12-month consecutive employment test and the 30-day re-registration deadlines to be eligible for benefits.

As if anticipating the ECJ's post-2010 restrictive turn (discussed in the preceding chapter), in *Zalewska v Department of Social Development*[35] the House of Lords applied the 12-month WRS registration requirement rigidly to deny income support to a Polish mover who had worked in the UK for more than 12 months but for only six months while registered under the scheme. The House of Lords ruled that limits on access to 'social advantages' under the WRS were permissible under EU law because EU Regulation 1612/68 (mandating equality in the provision of social advantages) depended on workers' compliance with all the national measures determining their eligibility for accessing the labour market (such as satisfying the WRS). Without referring to any relevant statistical data, the House of Lords also found WRS limitations on access to social advantages to be a necessary and proportionate[36] method for attaining the legitimate goals of monitoring movers and of protecting the public purse. In reaching this conclusion, the House of Lords ignored the fact that the 2003 Accession Treaty had provided for transitional derogations from only Articles 1–6 of Regulation 1612/68 (regarding entering host labour markets).[37] In a later case dealing with similar facts, the Supreme Court reiterated its rigid approach towards the WRS and did not even invoke the proportionality test.[38]

At the time of enlargement, some experts had speculated that WRS restrictions might produce negative long-term consequences for CEE workers by encouraging them to undertake and hold on to any jobs (including low-paid and precarious positions) to satisfy the registration requirement and by prompting employers to perceive them as not entirely lawful and as easily exploitable.

---

34 For example, 52% of CEE workers registered under the WRS between September 2006 and September 2007 were in temporary employment. See Border and Immigration Agency (2007).
35 [2008] UKHL 67.
36 According to EU Treaty rights, movers' right to free movement must be provided without nationality discrimination, and may only be limited through host state regulations that satisfy the proportionality test.
37 For a critique of *Zalewska*, see, e,g, Currie (2009).
38 *Mirga v Secretary of State for Work and Pensions*, [2016] UKSC 1.

Indeed, post-accession studies consistently indicated CEE workers' poor labour market outcomes and frequent experience of exploitation.[39] Notably, in 2019, the Supreme Court concluded that the WRS had imposed a substantial detriment on CEE nationals and ruled that its extension during the final transitional phase (2009–11) was contrary to EU law.[40] Employment agencies and the broader migration industry that procured CEE workers during the transitional period helped to naturalise the view that they are suitable for low-status, precarious employment, and British employers came to expect them to tolerate deskilled jobs and poor working conditions. The precarity induced by transitional post-accession measures, by increasingly restrictive ECJ case law, and by policies restricting CEE movers' access to support in the UK has been linked to CEE nationals' disadvantaged position in the post-Brexit labour market.[41] Furthermore, precarious workers found it more difficult to prove their eligibility for the post-Brexit EU Settlement Scheme. Those who were granted only pre-settled (as opposed to settled) status were excluded from welfare support.[42] More generally, the WRS propagated the widespread perception of CEE movers as temporary labour migrants only—not deserving of belonging to the British polity.

The Right-to-Reside Test

As a response to (unfounded) concerns about CEE movers' impact on the public purse, the UK also adopted Social Security (Habitual Residence) Amendment Regulation 2004 on the day of the Enlargement to help ensure that movers settling in the UK were either self-sufficient or economically active. This regulation governed newly arriving EU movers' access to most social benefits, including income support, jobseeker's allowance, pension credit, housing benefit, housing assistance, council tax benefit, child benefit, and child tax credit. To be eligible for these benefits, movers were now required to be not only 'habitually resident'[43] under EU law but also 'lawfully resident' under UK law. Unlike EU-14 nationals (who were deemed lawfully resident in the UK since the WRS did not

---

39 E.g., Kofman et al. (2009); Fernández-Reino and Rienzo (2022).
40 *Secretary of State for Work and Pensions v Gubeladze*, [2019] UKSC 31. The Court found it to be disproportionate, as it only had a small speculative mitigating effect in relation to any anticipated 'serious disturbances' in the UK's labour market.
41 See generally Currie (2022).
42 Denial of income-related benefits to those with pre-settled status was deemed lawful in *Fratila v Secretary of State for Work and Pensions*, [2021] UKSC 53, in line with the ECJ judgment in *CG v Department for Communities in Northern Ireland*, Case C-709/20, ECLI:EU:C:2021:602 (concluding that those with pre-settled status may not rely on prohibitions against nationality discrimination).
43 The habitual residence test was introduced in the UK in 1994, based on criteria established by the ECJ (e.g., length of residence, employment prospects, links to and intention to settle in the UK). It was amended during transposition of EU Directive 2004/38, to require applicants to provide more detailed evidence. In 2013,

apply to them), CEE nationals who were unemployed, jobseekers, or within the first 12 months of registered employment under the WRS did not satisfy the 'lawfully resident' test. Contrary to EU law, the UK test did not differentiate between first-time jobseekers and former workers who had subsequently become unemployed. Thus, CEE nationals could not retain 'worker' status under UK law if they involuntarily stopped working unless they had already completed 12 months of continuous registered employment.

Echoing its stance in *Zalewska*, the Supreme Court ruled in *Patmalniece v Secretary of State for Work and Pensions*[44] that these restrictions were not indirectly discriminatory against CEE movers and that, even if they were, they were proportionate by being justified due to the need to combat benefit tourism. The European Commission disagreed and instituted infringement proceedings against the UK in 2011, arguing that only the EU 'habitual residence' test should have been applied to determine movers' eligibility for social security benefits. The Commission found the additional UK right-to-reside test particularly objectionable when applied to deny jobseeker's allowance to those who had worked in the UK and had become unemployed (and hence still retained 'worker' status under EU law). The UK, however, insisted that the right-to-reside test was necessary to protect its welfare system. The eventual ECJ proceedings[45] were confined to child benefit and child tax credits only, because the ECJ's 2013 *Brey* decision (discussed in the preceding chapter) had limited the access of economically inactive movers to means-tested special non-contributory benefits. Ultimately, the ECJ sided with the UK's concerns and dismissed the infringement proceedings after finding that the right-to-reside test was a proportionate measure (as long as it was based on an individual review of each claimant's situation) that served a legitimate need (of protecting UK finances). The ECJ's acquiescence to the UK government's concerns should be contextualised within Brexit debates, as the ruling was issued four months after the UK had re-negotiated its EU membership through the 'New Settlement' and only nine days before the Brexit referendum was to be held. Nevertheless, it sent a signal to other EU-15 states that domestic measures targeting CEE movers' access to benefits could easily be justified.

Subsequent Anti-CEE Policies

Further regulatory limitations on EU movers' access to welfare benefits were imposed in 2013 and 2014 when transitional restrictions against Bulgarians and Romanians were coming to an end. For example, under the amended habitual-residence test, movers became eligible for jobseeker's allowance, child benefit,

---

the UK made the test even more demanding, with additional individualised questions and more data checks, especially pertaining to labour participation.
44 [2011] UKSC 11.
45 *Commission v United Kingdom of Great Britain and Northern Ireland*, Case 3008/14, ECLI:EU:C:2016:436.

and child tax credit only after three months of residence in the UK. To receive jobseeker's allowance and retain the right to reside after residing in the UK for six months or more, jobseekers were required to show 'compelling evidence of genuine prospects of work', which was a stricter test than under EU law (which required a showing of 'genuine chances of being engaged'). Moreover, those eligible for jobseeker's allowance, child benefit, and child tax credit could access such benefits for three months only as opposed to six months under prior regulations. Finally, jobseekers (including workers who had subsequently become unemployed) became ineligible for housing allowance, and a new minimum earnings threshold requirement (initially set at £153 per week) was imposed in order to be classified as a 'worker'. The UK's approach became even stricter in 2019, so that only EU nationals who had lived in the UK for five years and had obtained settled status would automatically meet the 'habitual residence' test and thus be eligible for benefits. Although the above restrictions applied to movers from all EU states, they were adopted to target CEE movers. Moreover, they had the most detrimental effect on CEE workers given their propensity to be engaged in precarious and low-paid employment. In turn, constraining movers' access to support served as a further barrier to any attempts to leave precarious work arrangements.

In addition to these specific, far-reaching policies that targeted CEE nationals' rights, CEE movers were impacted by how various, more general anti-migrant procedures were applied in practice. For example, the police, immigration authorities, and other governmental agencies were documented to unlawfully detain and attempt to remove homeless CEE movers—even those employed or with permanent residency rights.[46] Moreover, CEE nationals faced structural racism when trying to access benefits. For example, there is evidence that they were treated in a degrading manner by Job Centre staff during appointments to determine their welfare entitlements, and that they experienced frequent benefit payment cancellations and ID documentation confiscation by the authorities with no explanation.[47]

But the UK government's role in facilitating antagonism towards and exploitation of CEE nationals went beyond its official policies. Its political rhetoric had situated EU movers—and CEE nationals especially—as unwanted outsiders. Although prior immigration waves had faced public and right-wing opposition in the UK, hostility against CEE movers was widespread even within mainstream political culture. Both the far right and the liberal left targeted CEE movers as threatening to British identity and as responsible for the UK's social and economic problems. For example, in 2009, Phil Woolas (Labour), the then-Minister of State for Borders and Immigration, bemoaned the 'disruptive

---

46 This practice was ruled to constitute an unlawful impediment to the free movement right. See *R (On the Application of Gureckis and others) v Secretary of State for the Home Department*, Case CO/1440/2017, [2017] EWHC 3298.
47 Guma (2020).

effects' of the Eastern Enlargement on British public services.[48] In 2010, Ed Balls (Labour), the then-Secretary of State for Children, Schools and Families, stated that post-04 CEE workers had negatively impacted Britons' wages and employment conditions[49]—an assertion contradicted by empirical studies. Reiterating Tony Blair's (Labour) 2014 comments,[50] David Cameron (Conservative) specifically pointed to Poles as the reason for his 2013 proposals to curb EU movers' access to welfare benefits.[51] Contemporaneous Parliamentary debates warned against the strain on healthcare, schools, and housing posed by CEE nationals as well as by Bulgarians, Romanians, and those from farther east such as Moldovans.[52] In 2015, Members of Parliament engaged in discussions about 'the plague of aggressive begging, littering, antisocial ... and rough sleeping' migrants 'from eastern Europe' and about their organised criminal gangs.[53] To this day, the east represents an inferior region in the British political imagination. For example, in 2023, Labour's leader Keir Starmer warned that Britain's economy was doing so badly that '[i]f those trends continued, by 2030 people in the UK would each be £500 ... poorer than Poland's population ... and by 2040 would have fallen behind Hungary and Romania'.[54] His party's ambition, on the other hand, was to make living standards in the UK comparable to those in France and Germany.

Such disparaging and racist policies and statements targeting CEE nationals should also be set within the broader context of the government's proliferation of anti-immigrant ideology and hostile environment policies during the last decade which had created a climate where all those with traces of foreignness can be demonised and positioned as outsiders and parasites. Notably, the British public rarely differentiates between refugees, migrants, and movers, so policies targeting one group normalise hostility against all of these groups. The 2013 Home Office 'Go Home' campaign, officially meant to target undocumented immigrants, contributed to the creation of a racist political culture within which all immigrants became scapegoats for public discontent. Various specific strategies were implemented to effectuate internal bordering. For example, the National Health Service began to routinely profile suspected foreigners' immigration status, and all potential employees' and tenants' immigration status had to be verified. In the case of EU movers, this became further complicated as they lacked paper proof of their official immigration status (unless they already possessed permanent residency). Similarly, the EU

48 The Telegraph (2009).
49 Balls (2010).
50 Blair (2004).
51 'It's wrong that someone from Poland, who comes here, who works hard and I am absolutely all in favour of that — but I don't think we should be paying child benefit'. BBC News (2014).
52 Hansard, Immigration (Bulgaria and Romania), vol 561, debated on 22 April 2013.
53 Hansard, Immigration, vol 598, debated on 9 July 2015.
54 Islam and Hooker (2023).

Settlement Scheme provided only a digital record of status, resulting in some EU nationals' being disbelieved or indeed turned away by service providers due to lacking physical proof of their status.

CEE Movers' Disadvantaged Positioning in the Labour Market

The employment context offers an especially rich setting to explore CEE movers' disadvantage and discrimination. Ethnic discrimination happens most commonly in access to and treatment at work. Labour market outcomes serve as a key measure of exclusion. An unequal ability to benefit from the labour market has automatic consequences for social, educational, and health inequalities. Employment served as the main pull factor for CEE movers to the UK, and CEE movers' employment rates tended to be higher than those of native Britons or non-EU migrants. Of course, high rates of employment are not synonymous with equality or integration. Rather, it is the quality of employment and the ability to equally benefit from work that serve as better indicators of inclusion. CEE movers were exploited, de-skilled, and overrepresented in precarious, 3D, and low-paid positions in the UK. Notably, all the post-04 cases of CEE nationals' race discrimination that my research uncovered (discussed below) pertained to the employment context.

Empirical evidence indicates that the UK—like other EU-15 states—had benefited economically from EU mobility,[55] and especially from movers arriving after 2000.[56] EU movers were generally less likely than British or other foreign workers to receive public benefits or tax credits and less likely to live in social housing. Their income tax payments and national insurance contributions significantly enriched the public purse and outstripped what they received in tax credits and child benefits.[57] Moreover, they endowed the UK labour market with human capital with no cost to the British education system. Unlike non-EU migrants, EU movers had no significant negative effects on employment rates or wages of British workers. Instead, their taking of low-paid jobs pushed British workers into more managerial and supervisory positions.[58] There is no evidence that movers had negative effects on crime, education, health, or social housing. Among EU movers, CEE nationals were especially responsible for economic benefits to the UK. For example, post-04 CEE mobility was directly linked to an increase in the British economic output of nearly 1.5% by 2010.[59] By 2011, CEE movers' net fiscal contributions amounted to almost £5 billion.[60] Much of this benefit derived from CEE movers' high employment rates and widespread exploitation—especially in low-paid sectors.

55 E.g., Wadsworth (2016); Barnard and Ludlow (2019).
56 Dustmann and Frattini (2014).
57 E.g., HM Revenue & Customs (2016).
58 Vargas-Silva et al. (2016).
59 Fic et al. (2011).
60 Dustmann and Frattini (2014).

There is some indication that CEE nationals already working in the UK on the eve of the Eastern Enlargement were frequently de-skilled,[61] in part because many had been undocumented visa overstayers. Their labour outcomes worsened further soon after the Enlargement, especially in terms of earnings and returns from education. For example, during 2004–09, CEE movers earned 12.5% less than Britons while the average non-EU immigrants and EU-14 workers earned more than British workers. Whereas non-EU migrants and EU-14 movers had employment patterns resembling those of British workers, post-04 CEE workers tended to take up 'low-skill' positions (especially in manufacturing, distribution, construction, hospitality, and cleaning)[62] and 3D jobs (dirty, dangerous, and dull). This positioning became amplified after the UK's 2006 managed-migration strategy began phasing out non-EU low-skilled workers.

CEE movers became overrepresented in precarious and exploitative arrangements exacerbated in many cases by the involvement of employment agencies, living in tied accommodations (including in caravans, sheds, and greenhouses), and working predominantly with other CEE nationals at employment sites in remote locations devoid of support services and lacking other employment options. CEE movers tended to concentrate in the secondary labour market and to receive lower pay for comparable positions than British and EU-14 workers.[63] Being underpaid and forced to work longer hours than is lawful, sometimes in unsafe or unsanitary conditions, became the norm for many. Some employers would confiscate CEE movers' identity documents and abuse them verbally or physically. CEE movers were shown to experience significantly higher and longer-term de-skilling and lower returns on their education than other migrants groups—even in studies controlling for human capital differences such as education, experience, or language skills.[64]

Qualitative research similarly indicated CEE movers' disadvantaged position in the labour market[65]—further worsened after the 2008 economic crisis—replete with not only widespread de-skilling and being under-paid but also unlawful treatment by employers. For example, labour studies and my review of Employment Tribunal claims revealed frequent incidents of non-receipt of holiday and sick pay, unwarranted withholding of salaries and illegal wage deductions, (unlawful) advance fees to secure jobs, lack of contracts or payslips, denial of statutory breaks, denial of access to toilets, lack of health and safety protections, bullying, and harassment. Supervisors routinely ignored CEE movers' complaints of such treatment. Some CEE nationals were even trafficked into the UK and put into debt bondage and forced labour in circumstances

61 E.g., Anderson et al. (2006)
62 E.g., Drinkwater et al. (2009); Sumption and Somerville (2010).
63 Johnston et al. (2015).
64 E.g., Barslund and Busse (2014); Sirkeci et al. (2018).
65 E.g., Cook et al. (2010); Kofman et al. (2009); Anderson et al. (2008); Ciupijus (2012); East European Advice Centre (2013).

considered modern-day slavery.[66] Such treatment prompted a predominantly Polish workforce at a repackaging plant in northern England to liken their place of employment to a 'labour camp'.[67] Although analogies to Nazi atrocities are an exaggeration, labour exploitation of CEE movers was common, especially in low-skill jobs. CEE nationals' de-skilling, over-representation in low-paid jobs, exploitation, precarity, and financial woes continued after the Brexit referendum[68] and even worsened due to uncertainties over the EU Settlement Scheme[69] and during the Covid pandemic.[70]

Situating CEE Movers Among Other Non-UK Workers

It is true that many foreign-born groups tend to experience racism, inequalities, exploitation, and discrimination in the UK—especially those who are low-skilled or employed via employment agencies or gangmasters. CEE movers, however, experienced some unique challenges when compared to other disadvantaged groups and were especially prone to unfair treatment, harassment, and discrimination.[71] Employers were particularly reluctant to train CEE movers, making it harder for them to improve their human capital. Although migrants' de-skilling is typically transitory and tends to dissipate once they improve their language skills and gain local experience, CEE workers would continue to be de-skilled and to suffer wage penalties when compared to BAME, EU-14, and white British workers, even after working in the UK for a decade or longer.[72] On the other hand, their whiteness bestowed some advantages on CEE workers and made them more employable in certain settings. Similarly to how post-war displaced CEE nationals benefited from UK immigration policy preferences to fill domestic and 'low-skill' posts with affordable Caucasians, contemporary British employers sometimes preferred CEE nationals due to their whiteness especially as care workers or where they had to interact with British customers.[73]

What can explain indicators of CEE movers' widespread labour exploitation? Post-accession mobility restrictions have been linked to negative long-term effects on CEE movers,[74] by making them more accepting of semi-lawful, de-

---

66 E.g., Lawrence (2012); Harris (2013).
67 Ciupijus (2012a).
68 E.g., Barnard et al. (2022); East European Resource Centre (2018).
69 See generally Barnard et al. (2022a). Notably, Many CEE movers who had engaged in temporary, semi-lawful employment or had access to only temporary, precarious living arrangements, lacked the required documentation to prove their eligibility for the EUSS.
70 Of course, CEE workers also benefited economically and socially from their mobility to the UK, which also enhanced their labour market potential when they returned to their countries of origin.
71 See generally Kofman et al. (2009).
72 Sirkeci et al. (2018).
73 See generally Parutis (2011).
74 Kubal (2012); Currie (2009).

skilled, low-paid, and exploitative arrangements and more reliant on employment agencies. The WRS helped to naturalise employers' views of CEE workers as especially suitable for low-wage, exploitative arrangements. It also prompted their greater reliance on employment intermediaries. Post-accession CEE movers were overrepresented in agency workforces compared to other non-UK workers and were heavily concentrated at specific employment sites. For example, during 2004–09, almost half of CEE workers obtained employment through agencies.[75] Agency employment has been associated with greater rates of exploitation. At least some employment agencies were documented to treat CEE workers more poorly than other workers and to encourage employers to do the same.[76] Many UK employers did indeed specifically recruit CEE movers to fill shortages in 'low-skill' and 3D jobs due to their allegedly good work 'attitude'[77]—reminiscent of British employers' historical preferences for New Commonwealth (especially Asian) workers and those from Albania and the former Yugoslavia. Not surprisingly, CEE workers became concentrated at specific employer sites. This appears particularly prevalent among Poles in part due to their significant numerical presence. Caselaw which I reviewed (discussed below) includes examples of low-paid employment sites often in remote geographical areas where CEE workers, and sometimes Poles alone, constituted 90% or more of staff.

As Wu[78] observed in the context of the 'model minority' stereotype of far-east Asians in the United States, superficially positive stereotypes can mask disadvantage and justify inequalities. Indeed, when British employers sought out CEE movers specifically for their 'good work ethic', it was due to a hiring strategy which targeted exploitable and vulnerable workers with low labour market power who were compliant; more tolerant of poor employment conditions, lower wages, and longer working hours; and more amenable to working in isolated rural areas.[79] This view of CEE workers was facilitated and reinforced by their media, political, and public racialisation as cheap, temporary, menial labourers. This labour market positioning, aided by contemporary supranational EU economic forces and embedded within long-standing western peripheralisation of the east, was largely overlooked in British equality discourse and by UK adjudicators, as discussed below.

CEE Movers' Absence From the UK's Equality Framework

Despite their documented disadvantage, populist opposition and racism against them, and curbs imposed on their entry and other rights, CEE movers were

---

75 Jones (2014).
76 Pemberton and Stevens (2010).
77 MacKenzie and Forde (2009).
78 Wu (2002).
79 MacKenzie and Forde (2009); McKay (2009).

absent from official equality and 'race relations' discourse. For example, the Equality and Human Rights Commission's[80] 2011 Employment Statutory Code of Practice spanned 300 pages but mentioned white non-British workers only once—in an illustrative example of an employer's indirect discrimination of seasonal workers.[81] Its most comprehensive review to date of England's performance in equality and human rights measures[82] mentioned non-Britons only generally in the context of their poor health outcomes. Notably, throughout the report, 'ethnic minorities' were discussed collectively and were contrasted with 'white British' or 'white' groups (composed of 'white British', 'white Irish', and 'other white' categories). The only exception was a single mention that 'ethnic minorities (including white minorities)' are more likely to live in poverty than white Britons. In that statement, the term 'white minorities' subsumed 'white Irish', 'Gypsy, Roma and Irish Traveller', and 'other white' categories, with no mention of non-Roma CEE nationals. In its most recent report on discrimination in the employment context,[83] the Equality and Human Rights Commission acknowledged that 'migrants' often experience discrimination or marginalisation, especially in low-skill sectors, but focused on the experiences of non-white and non-Christian workers. When mentioning—in passing—EU workers, its only concern was about the challenges that employers who heavily relied on them would face after Brexit.

Publications produced by the UK government, including those posted on websites specifically devoted to equality and inclusion,[84] similarly overlooked disadvantages experienced by CEE movers and by 'other white' ethnic groups more generally. In government reports, the terms 'ethnic minority' and 'ethnic groups' are typically reserved for non-whites. CEE movers tended to be subsumed under the label 'migrant', marking them as foreigners and outsiders instead of acknowledging their right to free movement. In specific discussions of migrants' disadvantage or inequalities,[85] however, CEE (and other EU) movers tended to be excluded from the term 'migrant'. This reiterates the misconception that white privilege is equally accessible to all Caucasians. Of course, this is in line with how imprecisely the UK census categorises Caucasians: as 'White English, Welsh, Scottish, Northern Irish or British'; 'Irish Gypsy or Irish Traveller'; 'Roma' (added in 2021); or 'Any other White background'.

---

80 Non-departmental public body responsible for the promotion and enforcement of equality laws in the UK.
81 Equality and Human Rights Commission (2011).
82 Equality and Human Rights Commission (2018).
83 Equality and Human Rights Commission (2020).
84 E.g., HM Government, Equality Hub, www.gov.uk/government/organisations/the-equality-hub; HM Government, Equalities Office, www.gov.uk/government/organisations/government-equalities-office; HM Government, Race Disparity Unit, www.gov.uk/government/organisations/race-disparity-unit; HM Government, Ethnicity Facts and Figures, www.ethnicity-facts-figures.service.gov.uk/.
85 E.g., HM Government (2019).

That being said, in 2017, the government did announce that public funding is needed to encourage some groups– including Sikhs, Hindus, and 'recent arrivals from Eastern Europe'[86]–to report hate crimes being committed against them. That same year, the Equality and Human Rights Commission noted that 'there is some evidence that there is less prejudice towards Black and Asian people than towards Eastern European people'.[87] Those rare acknowledgements might be attributed to the context of the post-referendum spike in hate crimes. Since then, however, both equality discourse and policies have tended to revert to the conventional approach of overlooking CEE movers. Government-sponsored advice groups—such as the Equality Advisory and Support Service and the Advisory, Conciliation and Arbitration Service—have similarly overlooked CEE nationals' experiences of disadvantage and discrimination.

Moreover, (white) EU movers were ignored by integration and equal opportunities discourse and measures. No national integration measures have addressed white ethnic minority groups' needs.[88] What national and local integration measures do exist have been focused on the treatment of refugees and long-standing non-white minorities. Notably, three years after the Eastern Enlargement, the final report of the Commission on Integration and Cohesion—a fixed-term governmental advisory body—focused on UK-born Britons' integration issues and pointed to how CEE movers see the UK 'as an attractive place to visit and work but perhaps not always [as] a new "home"'.[89] Thus, CEE movers were portrayed as short-term workers rather than part of the British polity. Moreover, the report othered CEE movers by suggesting that they be provided welcome packs 'that cover behaviours, norms etc'. Similarly, CEE movers did not feature in the UK's equal opportunities framework. Governmental data collection also overlooked them. The UK's approach to ethnic monitoring, developed in the 1970s and 1980s, has tended to overlook non-BAME groups, at best separating non-British whites into Irish, Gypsy/Traveller, and 'other whites' groupings.[90] CEE movers' exclusion from such discourses and policies—whatever their level of effectiveness—normalised their experience of inequality.

It is true that CEE nationals' absence from equality discourse and policies can be attributed, at least in part, to their not fitting the UK's historical migration/race-relations paradigm, which has focused on addressing racisms against New Commonwealth immigrants settling in the UK and against their second-generation (non-white) progeny,[91] while at the same time greatly

---

86 HM Government (2017).
87 Equality and Human Rights Commission (2017).
88 Although there have been some discussions about integrating (typically UK-born) Gypsies and Travellers.
89 Commission on Integration and Cohesion (2007).
90 Blacks and Asians, on the other hand, are split into more precise ethnic categories, such as 'Pakistani' and 'Black Caribbean'.
91 See generally Solanke (2009). Similarly, the focus of anti-discrimination frameworks in many EU-14 states has been on protecting their former colonial subjects and newly arriving non-Caucasian migrants.

supporting the UK's economic development and business interests.[92] CEE movers had a much shorter history of disadvantage and overt discrimination in the UK than BAME individuals and were not well organised. Moreover, CEE movers were privileged due to their right of free movement and due to their (partial) whiteness. Unlike New Commonwealth migrants, a significant proportion of CEE workers engaged in only temporary migration which fluctuated with UK labour market demands. Unlike the Irish and New Commonwealth migrants, they did not engage in violent conflict as a response to racism against them. Due to their high rates of employment and low reliance on the public purse (reinforced through policies curbing their access to benefits), CEE movers made significant contributions to the UK's economy—more than native workers and more than other foreign-born groups. The government did not need to ensure their equality rights to reap these economic benefits. If anything, their exploitation at work and insufficient protections by the anti-discrimination framework (as addressed below) further reduced business costs while facilitating the UK's increasingly unregulated labour market—replete with precarious temporary and agency work, unpaid internships, zero-hour contracts, part-time work, and subcontracting arrangements.

Unfortunately, race-based wrongs cannot be effectively addressed if they are absent from legal discourse.[93] Groups overlooked by discourse tend to be more easily disregarded when adjudicators apply anti-discrimination provisions to them even though they should be included under a simple, doctrinal reading of equality laws—as indeed revealed through my analysis of Employment Tribunal claims (discussed below). More recently, there have been some glimpses of an official recognition of racism and discrimination faced by CEE nationals in the UK, but this has not made equality discourse more inclusive. Such recent steps in the right direction might be attributed to the increasing permanence of CEE movers who elected to settle in the UK after Brexit. Despite its many failings, the 2021 Sewell Report[94] did acknowledge fractures within whiteness—pointing specifically to disadvantages experienced by white Irish, Roma and Travellers, and 'Eastern Europeans'. Furthermore, when discussing the census category of 'white other', the report recommended dividing it into west and east Europeans thereby implicitly recognising differences in their experiences. It also mentioned that migrant groups, including white migrants, are more likely to experience mental health difficulties. However, the government appears to have retrenched

---

92 Akin to how EU efforts to facilitate mobility and combat discrimination have focused on supporting the internal market, the British 'race relations' approach has been privileging business interests. Immigration controls have been tied to labour needs, and anti-discrimination law has afforded workers only limited protections from exploitation, while facilitating free-market competition. Notably, the Race Relations Act 1968 was praised for decreasing the 'economic waste' of BAME workers' potential economic contributions. See Home Office (1975).
93 See generally Crenshaw (2011).
94 Commission on Race and Ethnic Disparities (2021).

on this acknowledgement of fractures within whiteness in its 2022 response[95] to the Sewell Report and in its 2023 update report[96]—returning to its pre-existing pattern of overlooking CEE nationals' racialisation and discrimination.

Post-2004 Equality Laws

Transposition of the Race Equality Directive

Although the UK was the strongest opponent of EU racial equality legislation early on—largely due to its perception as superfluous and an encroachment on UK sovereignty—the change of British leadership in 1997 resulted in the new centre-left government's support for the Race Equality Directive. This turn was also consistent with contemporaneous domestic debates about integrating Muslims and asylees and with the post-Stephen Lawrence political commitment to addressing institutional inequalities. The prospect of the Eastern Enlargement and the potential arrival of CEE movers in the UK does not appear to have been taken into account despite the UK's historical experience of recognising another form of anti-white racism—namely that against the Irish.

The EU Race Equality Directive's transposition—mandated by the EU to be finalised by 2003—was met with little opposition within British political and legal spheres. By then, the UK already had a well-developed anti-discrimination framework. To assuage any concerns about constraining UK businesses, the government emphasised that the transposed anti-discrimination protections would not impose 'unnecessary burdens' and would in fact increase productivity[97]—in line with the traditional EU approach to equality measures. The Race Relations Act 1976 (Amendment) Regulations 2003 implemented the Directive by amending pre-existing legislation. In line with the Directive, the UK included new definitions of indirect discrimination and harassment and shifted the burden of proof to make it easier for victims to prove discrimination. The Directive also prompted more resource-consuming comprehensive reforms in the UK through the adoption of a new single, consolidated anti-discrimination legislation. The Equality Act 2006 was implemented to prohibit discrimination due to age, disability, gender, gender reassignment, race, sexual orientation, and religion or belief.[98]

---

95 HM Government (2022).
96 HM Government (2023).
97 Cabinet Office (2001).
98 Concurrently, greater immigration controls were being imposed (on non-EU migrants), including through the 2008 points-based system. This is in line with the UK's traditional approach towards race relations – implementing more stringent immigration controls, while at the same time, expanding anti-discrimination laws.

Case Study

The Equality Act 2010

Background and Legislative History

In response to a decade of lobbying by human rights and equality groups, in 2005, Tony Blair commissioned the most extensive review of inequalities, social policies, and anti-discrimination legislation since the 1970s. After review reports were issued in 2007,[99] a year-long consultation process followed before the Equality Bill was presented in 2009. The Bill garnered cross-party support. Implemented in stages, the Equality Act 2010 consolidated and clarified nine pre-existing anti-discrimination legislations, close to 100 statutory instruments, and more than 2,500 pages of guidance and codes of practice developed over more than four decades. Composed of 218 sections, the 2010 Act is far more detailed than previous equality legislations. Notably, it increased protections by allowing (limited) positive action and (narrow) collective remedies in employment claims, permitting reliance on hypothetical comparators, and prohibiting associative and perceived discriminations. The Act's most innovative provisions, however, were not brought into force as they were considered too burdensome for the business sector.

During more than a decade of lobbying efforts preceding the adoption of the Equality Act 2010, migrant and mover voices were not heard. There were no lobbying initiatives by migrant or white ethnic minority groups during the adoption of the Act or during the promulgation of earlier UK anti-discrimination laws. My review of all Commons and Lords debates about proposals for the 2010 Act revealed that migrants and movers were never considered. Moreover, they were not mentioned in any Parliamentary discussions between the time of the Eastern Enlargement and the adoption of the Equality Act in 2010 that referred to the concepts of 'discrimination' or 'inequality'. Instead, legislative deliberations focused on BAME groups and tended to lump whites into one (allegedly privileged) group.[100]

Key publications during the Act's consultation process also tended to ignore fractures within whiteness—coinciding with how British empirical studies of economic outcomes and of markers of social inclusion tend to lump all whites together. For example, the lengthy publication presented by the Equalities Office[101] during the parliamentary consultation period made no mention of immigrants despite being drafted after conferring with two migrant rights organisations. Moreover, by noting that 'if you are from an ethnic minority you are a fifth less likely to find work than if you are white', the report approached 'ethnic minority' and white groups as mutually exclusive—thus overlooking whites' heterogeneity. The final report of the Equalities Review[102] did

---

99 Discrimination Law Review (2007); Equalities Review (2007).
100 E.g., Hansard, Black and Minority Ethnic People: Workplace Issues, vol 771, debated on 3 May 2016.
101 Equalities Office (2008).
102 Equalities Review (2007).

acknowledge that equality policies should target groups not traditionally emphasised by anti-discrimination measures, but it referred only to British working-class whites. The report spanned more than 170 pages but did not devote any attention to CEE movers despite the fact that their significant numbers were already being met with media and public hostility. After the Equality Act 2010 was passed, its lengthy explanatory notes[103] did not mention migrants, movers, or non-UK nationals.

Notably, during the Equality Act's legislative process, the government recognised a fracture within whiteness (that has also been implicated in CEE movers' experiences)—the relationship between low socio-economic class and inequality. But a provision addressing class was ultimately scrapped, and discourse surrounding this proposal focused on poor white Britons only. Section 1 of the Equality Bill sought to 'reduce the gap between rich and poor' and to ensure 'that public bodies systematically and strategically take account of people who are poor and clearly disadvantaged'.[104] Thus, in all their decision-making, public bodies were to reflect on how to decrease inequalities in education, health, and housing stemming from socio-economic disadvantage.[105] This duty applied to all groups regardless of race. By that time, intersections between poverty and inequalities in housing, education, employment, and healthcare were well documented,[106] and it was well known that ethnicity- and class-based economic inequalities[107] had been increasing over time in the UK. In supporting this provision, the Labour Party emphasised that socio-economic legislation is crucial to promoting fairness[108]—moving beyond the traditional economic justifications for equality measures.

My research indicates that political debates in the context of the socio-economic duty ignored migrants and movers. The 1999 White Paper 'Opportunity for All: Tackling Poverty and Social Exclusion',[109] which had prompted the drafting of Section 1, referred to immigrants only once—in the context of providing second-generation students with extra language support. In advocating for the socio-economic duty, Labour politicians drew attention to inequalities experienced by poor white Britons and by well-established minority groups including Muslims, Travellers, Jews, Afro-Caribbeans, and disadvantaged Indian castes.[110] New migrants and Christian white ethnic groups were ignored. This oversight occurred despite the fact that the National Equality Panel,

---

103 Explanatory Notes (2010).
104 House of Lords Debates, 15 December 2009, col 1407.
105 Explanatory Notes (2010).
106 E.g., Hills et al. (2009).
107 National Equality Panel (2010).
108 E.g., Hansard Report, 18 November 2010, vol 518, Fiona Mactaggart.
109 Department of Social Security (1999).
110 E.g., Hansard Report, House of Lords, 18 November 2010, vol 722, Baroness Thornton.

established by the Labour Government in 2008, had noted that migration status plays a role in disadvantage—even for EU movers.[111]

Driven by a desire to cut down public expenditures, lessen administrative burdens on businesses, and facilitate the free market by reducing worker protections, the Coalition government ultimately scrapped socio-economic duty in 2013. The socio-economic duty proposal did provide, however, a rare official recognition that (lower) class is linked to the experience of disadvantage and that some whites have incomplete access to white privilege. Intersections between white-skin privilege and socio-economic disadvantage demand close scrutiny.[112] Ambalavaner Sivanandan, the then-director of the Institute of Race Relations, had drawn attention to racism against 'impoverished strangers even if they are white' such as CEE asylum seekers before the fall of communism.[113] This racism became naturalised in post-Cold War Europe and was facilitated by the CEE region's relative poverty when compared to western Europe.[114]

I argue that this state of affairs is still ongoing—having been facilitated through the western-centric approach towards the CEE region during its accession process and through the continuing economic and political inequalities between east and west which are both embedded within the long-standing western gaze that inferiorises the east. Relatively lower wages in the CEE region, which continue to this day, have situated CEE nationals within lower strata of intra-EU class hierarchies. Moreover, once in the UK, CEE movers were pushed into low-paid employment by the Worker Registration Scheme. Many CEE movers came from regions in their home countries with high unemployment rates and believed that being exploited in de-skilled jobs was the price they had to pay in order to retain employment—especially if they had poor English skills.

Notably, they became subjected by Britons to class-inspired inferiorisation about physical appearance, lifestyle, type of work, poverty, and cultural practices and were positioned as not good enough to be accepted into the (middle-class) British way of life.[115] Some white Britons also perceived CEE movers as innately inferior, possessing 'alien values', and exhibiting primitive and criminal traits, while being 'not quite white' enough to integrate into English life. For example, some questioned whether CEE movers were phenotypically white and described them instead as 'pale' or 'not black'.[116] White British people conflate belonging with whiteness—but only of the sufficiently British kind which depends on unaccented speech, British cultural practices, and visible markers of stereotypical white middle-class British appearance and behaviour.[117] CEE movers did not fit that image.

111 National Equality Panel (2010).
112 See generally Pruitt (2015).
113 Fekete (2009).
114 See generally Fekete (2001).
115 See generally Moore (2013).
116 Halej (2014).
117 Samaluk (2014).

That being said, one should not get distracted by debates regarding whether class or race is more implicated in social injustices. Oppression Olympics do a disservice to all disadvantaged or marginalised groups. Instead, it is the various intersecting fractures within race and within class that affect the experience of equality and determine whether groups have a voice in the promulgation of laws and in shaping legal discourse. All CEE movers were affected by anti-CEE sentiment in the UK, and some middle-class CEE movers have been victims of discrimination—as my review of Employment Tribunal claims revealed (discussed below). Unfortunately, the scrapping of the socio-economic duty provision overlooked such nuances in the experience of inequality and legitimated existing social and class structures.

Key Provisions of the Equality Act 2010

The Equality Act 2010 protects against discrimination, harassment, and victimisation based on nine protected characteristics—including race—in employment and when using private or public services. The Act continues to define 'race' as initially formulated under the Race Relations Act 1976, to encompass 'colour, nationality, and ethnic or national origin'. CEE national groups clearly fall under these protected grounds. 'Colour' includes, for example, 'being black or white'.[118] Movers retain their 'nationalities' through citizenship of their countries of origin. This also typically determines their 'national origins' (that is, connection to a nation through birth or ancestry). White groups' protection due to their specific national origins has been recognised since the Irish became widely acknowledged in the UK as having a vulnerable national origin.

In the context of employment, discrimination is prohibited in hiring, employment terms, promotions, transfers, training opportunities, and dismissal. Hence, in theory at least, persons of all races are to be integrated into the labour market and provided equal opportunities once hired. Workers engaged via temporary contracts as well as those hired through employment agencies are also protected. The Act additionally safeguards some self-employed workers.

In line with the Race Equality Directive's burden of proof provisions, the Equality Act 2010 extended reversal of the burden of proof to all discrimination claims. Thus, if the claimant presents facts from which a court could conclude that the respondent had contravened a provision of the Act, and if the respondent fails to offer a non-discriminatory explanation, the court must conclude that the alleged contravention had occurred. First, the claimant must prove, on the balance of probabilities, facts from which a reasonable court *could* properly conclude, based on all the evidence (including the respondent's explanation), that the respondent had committed a proscribed act. If the claimant satisfies this stage, the burden shifts to the respondent to prove, on the balance of probabilities, that the treatment 'was in no sense whatsoever' due to race.

118 Explanatory Notes (2010).

Courts expect 'cogent evidence' that race was 'not any part' of the reason for the unequal treatment.[119] This two-stage test need not be applied in a mechanical way (especially when dealing with hypothetical comparators) as long as the court focuses on determining why the respondent treated the claimant as she did. This provides adjudicators some flexibility and discretion to make the burden more or less challenging.

I. DIRECT DISCRIMINATION

'A person (A) discriminates against another (B) if, because of a protected characteristic, A treats B less favourably than A treats or would treat others'.[120] This definition is closely in line with the EU Race Equality Directive. Race need not have been the main cause as long as it was 'an effective cause' of the allegedly discriminatory conduct.[121] Direct discrimination can be based on the respondent's perception, however incorrect, that the victim had a protected trait.[122] This might protect workers if their employers discriminate against them yet do not accurately differentiate between their specific ethnicities—as illustrated by some of the cases discussed below. The respondent's motive for discriminating is not relevant.[123] Thus, even discrimination due to an unconscious prejudice is unlawful. The fact that the respondent might share the same race as the victim is also not relevant. To function as a comparator, an employee must be employed by the same employer (at the same or different location) and under the same terms as the claimant.

Although an inference of discrimination cannot be drawn from the mere fact that an employer treated an employee who has a protected characteristic unfairly or unreasonably,[124] courts must scrutinise particularly carefully situations in which only the claimant was affected by poor treatment.[125] To infer discrimination, adjudicators must consider each allegation individually and must also adopt a holistic approach. There is no defence to direct discrimination based on race. As worded, protections against direct discrimination aim to attain formal equality only—by focusing on equal treatment. Moreover, as my review of Employment Tribunal cases uncovered, adjudicative discretion in inferring a link between poor treatment and race led to dismissals of some CEE movers' arguably strong claims. Furthermore, tribunals often did not engage in

---

119 *Prasil v Orchard House Foods*, Case 3400534/2014, Employment Tribunal Cambridge, 12 April 2018.
120 Equality Act 2010, Section 13(1).
121 *Wreczycka v Care In Style Limited*, Case 3200984/2017, Employment Tribunal East London, 7 March 2018.
122 *Law Society v Bahl*, [2004] EWCA Civ 1070.
123 *R (E) v Governing Body of JFS*, [2009] UKSC 15.
124 *Glasgow City Council v Zafar*, [1998] ICR 120.
125 *Kowalewska-Zietek v Lancashire Teaching Hospitals NHS Foundation Trust*, UKEAT/0269/15/JOJ, 21 January 2016.

rigorous or accurate comparator analysis—further complicated by low-paid CEE workers' tendency to work alongside their co-ethnics or other CEE nationals.

II. INDIRECT DISCRIMINATION

'A person (A) discriminates against another (B) if A applies to B a provision, criterion or practice which is discriminatory in relation to a relevant protected characteristic of B's'.[126] A provision, criterion or practice ('PCP') is discriminatory if A applies (or would apply) it to persons with whom B does not share the characteristic; the PCP puts (or would put) persons with whom B shares the characteristic 'at a particular disadvantage' when compared with persons with whom B does not share it; and the PCP puts (or would put) B at such disadvantage. However, A can present a defence if A shows that the PCP satisfies the proportionality test (i.e., it is a proportionate means of achieving a legitimate aim). To do so, A must prove that A had considered other, less discriminatory means when formulating the PCP at issue. Unlike direct discrimination, indirect discrimination does not require a causal link between the victim's race and the disadvantageous treatment, but it does require a causal link between the PCP and the disadvantage suffered. In determining a 'particular disadvantage', a pool of hypothetical comparators may be used, including through national, regional, or employer-specific statistics—although such comparators do not constitute conclusive proof by themselves.

Although this definition of indirect discrimination allows adjudicators to scrutinise facially neutral actions which in practice disadvantage people with protected characteristics, it has lesser potential to achieve substantive equality than the EU Race Equality Directive's definition of indirect discrimination. Whereas, under EU law, indirect discrimination may be found when only one person was put at a disadvantage, the Equality Act 2010 requires evidence that the PCP disadvantages the group sharing the claimant's protected characteristic. Moreover, an indirectly discriminatory PCP may be justified under UK law if it constitutes 'proportionate means' of achieving a 'legitimate aim'. This strives to attain formal equality only. Finding a justification for indirect discrimination under the Directive is more difficult as the means must be both 'appropriate' and 'necessary'.

Notably, both the Directive and the Equality Act rely on comparator groups, which supports a formal approach to equality. That is, merely requiring that likes should be treated alike allows for levelling down while ignoring social inequalities. Moreover, appropriate use of hypothetical comparators necessitates taking account of societal inequalities, and a long line of case law, to develop rigorous methodology. This appears problematic for CEE movers, whose widespread racialisation was normalised in the UK and who had not been addressed by a long line of jurisprudence. Although the requirement that

126 Equality Act 2010, Section 19(1).

the group to which the claimant belongs suffer a 'disadvantage' appears to create space for adjudicators to consider broader power relations and specific groups' racialisation, the lack of relevant national and regional statistics makes such analysis challenging in the context of non-BAME groups. Additionally, in line with popular and political discourses, adjudicators appeared to lack sensitivity to acknowledge CEE nationals' widespread racialisation, exclusion, and lack of access to equal opportunities—factors which could have potentially supported CEE claimants' arguments about their groups' disadvantages. My review of CEE applicants' cases revealed that they asserted indirect racial discrimination claims very infrequently, and such claims were rarely successful.

III. HARASSMENT

'A person (A) harasses another (B) if (a) A engages in unwanted conduct related to a relevant protected characteristic, and (b) the conduct has the purpose or effect of (i) violating B's dignity, or (ii) creating an intimidating, hostile, degrading, humiliating or offensive environment for B'.[127] 'Conduct' has been interpreted broadly by courts to include written, oral, and physical actions (such as gestures or images). A single act may be significant enough to create a hostile environment if its effects are of longer duration. No comparator is needed, and the unwanted conduct does not have to be directed at the claimant. In determining whether the conduct at issue had the purpose or effect of violating the claimant's dignity or creating an intimidating or hostile environment, each of the following must be taken into account: (a) the claimant's perceptions, (b) all the facts of the case, and (c) whether it is reasonable for the conduct to have had the alleged effect.

This test would have been easier for CEE claimants to satisfy if adjudicators were willing to take into account the broader context of CEE movers' racialisation in the UK and how it had impacted individual claimants' experiences. Given how normalised such racialisation became in public and political discourse, however, courts tended not to do so, as my discussion below indicates. Notably, the Employment Appeal Tribunal warned against encouraging 'a culture of hypersensitivity', noting that 'not every racially slanted adverse comment or conduct may constitute the violation of a person's dignity', especially if it is unintended[128] or causes only 'minor upsets'.[129] This left much discretion to adjudicators and reinforced their ability to ignore the wider context of anti-CEE sentiment and peripheralisation. Moreover, employers are not liable for acts that might constitute harassment if they are committed by claimants' co-workers or by third parties. This is problematic in the context of groups that are widely racialised. Employers could ignore even widespread harassment of CEE workers by their colleagues with impunity.

127 Equality Act 2010, Section 26(1).
128 *Richmond Pharmacology v Dhaliwal*, [2009] IRLR 336, EAT/0458/08.
129 *Grant v HM Land Registry & EHRC*, [2011] EWCA Civ 769.

IV. VICTIMISATION

'A person (A) victimises another person (B) if A subjects B to a detriment because (a) B does a protected act, or (b) A believes that B has done, or may do, a protected act'.[130] Treatment amounts to a 'detriment' if a reasonable worker would or might take the view that, given all the factual circumstances, it was to her detriment. There is no need to show a less favourable treatment. Doing the protected act need not be the only cause, but must be a significant cause, of the detrimental treatment. As with the test for harassment, the 'reasonable person' standard was unlikely to account for the wider climate of CEE nationals' disadvantage and racialisation.

V. LANGUAGE RULES

The Equality Act makes no mention of language or accent discrimination. Case law, however, has been developed to determine when English-only rules in the workplace might be discriminatory. English-only rules that are found unlawful typically constitute indirect discrimination. Such rules are more likely impermissible if applied to casual conversations between employees, in social areas, or during break times. Blanket English-only rules applied during the performance of work duties, however, are likely lawful if they constitute a proportionate method for achieving a legitimate aim—such as to ensure better work performance or good work relations (by not making others feel excluded) or to fulfil health and safety obligations. Moreover, targeting specific foreign-language speakers or only specific languages might constitute direct discrimination or harassment. A co-worker's complaint about feeling excluded by others' private conversations in a different language might constitute a sufficient reason to forbid such conversations, especially if they are frequent or appear to have been intended to exclude or to create a hostile environment.[131] Given the widespread antipathy towards CEE movers in the UK, as well as competition and strife among CEE groups of different nationalities, some workers might have been overly sensitive to feeling excluded by CEE speakers, especially if a specific CEE group constituted the majority of a workforce, as indeed was suggested by my review of Employment Tribunal claims.

General Critique of the Equality Act 2010

Although the Equality Act 2010 expanded pre-existing anti-discrimination protections, it fails to step beyond some of the key weaknesses of the EU Race Equality Directive and, in some provisions, merely follows its minimum

---

130 Bringing proceedings, providing information related to proceedings, or alleging (in good faith) a violation under the Act.
131 *Griffin v Hyder Brothers Ltd*, Case 2406224/2011, Employment Tribunal, 25 April 2012.

requirements. Notably, the Act did not implement proposals made by many experts that employers with more than ten employees should be required to conduct periodic employment and pay-equity reviews to determine whether members of disadvantaged groups have access to fair participation and equal pay. Overall, many of the Act's provisions only offer formal protections—divorced from equal opportunities or integration goals—that do not accurately address the reality of discrimination, especially when it comes to groups traditionally ignored by equality discourse such as migrants (or movers) and poorer claimants. Discrimination claims continue to be very challenging for victims to prove even when claimants have legal representation. Among all discrimination claims, complaints of race discrimination appear to be the least likely to succeed. For example, of the race discrimination claims brought in 2015–16, 5% were successful at full hearing, 23% were dismissed at preliminary hearing, 18% were unsuccessful at full hearing, 21% were withdrawn, and 33% were settled.[132]

A fundamental reason for the Equality Act's lack of efficacy is because the British equalities framework contains an overarching economic core—consistent with market capitalism and with protecting the elite's economic privilege. Statements made by Members of Parliament at the time of the Equality Act's adoption mentioned its anticipated economic benefits.[133] Even concepts that sound far removed from economic goals are nevertheless intertwined with economic concerns. For example, the notion of equal opportunities has been premised on eliminating barriers to free competition between individuals,[134] and the initial proposal for the imposition of socio-economic duty emphasised that injustice and poverty are 'economically foolish'.[135] At the same time, the widespread rhetoric of equal opportunity, further reinforced by praises of how advanced the UK anti-discrimination framework is,[136] has served to conceal such economic priorities—obscuring the law's politics in service of the privileged class. This disingenuous approach is congruous with the economic core of the EU's anti-discrimination framework[137] which has been embedded within lofty narratives of fundamental rights and benevolence. In addition, the Equality Act contains numerous discrete limitations, some of which seemed particularly challenging in the context of CEE claimants—as discussed below.

132 McColgan (2017).
133 E.g., Hansard Report, House of Lords, 26 April 2011, col WA39, Baroness Garden of Frognal.
134 See generally Solomos (1989).
135 Department of Social Security (1999).
136 For example, the 2021 Sewell Report applauded the UK for being a progressive, multi-ethnic and multi-cultural community, and for being on its way towards becoming a 'beacon to the rest of Europe and the world'.
137 Arguably, the origins of all equality measures in western Europe fall at the intersection of post-war human rights concerns and free market agendas. See generally Hepple (2014).

I. INSUFFICIENT DEFINITION OF 'RACE'

The legal system is not equipped to redress many race-based wrongs because it does not have the vocabulary to do so. Fundamentally, anti-discrimination law implies that only racism covered by legislation is unacceptable enough to warrant political intervention.[138] This, of course, is problematic in societies where racism is prevalent. It also presents a challenge for CEE movers given how widespread and normalised their exploitation and racialisation were. For starters, the material scope of the Equality Act 2010 tolerates racism in most of the private sphere. Moreover, its definition of 'race' does not always capture racialised whites' peripheralisation.

Although 'race' under the Equality Act encompasses ethnic origin, national origin, and nationality—and thus begins to recognise the fact that colour-based groups are not homogeneous—this does not always suffice to reflect migrants' complicated experiences of racism and disadvantage. Although all immigrants fall under one or more of these protected race characteristics, the discrimination they suffer is not always tied specifically to such categories. Notably, the Equality Act does not protect having migrant (or mover) status, or being a foreigner, and does not include explicit statutory prohibitions of language or accent discrimination. Poor treatment due to birth abroad (without a specific national origin being mentioned) does not constitute discrimination. The Act also overlooks 'cultural racism'. Thus, poor treatment of CEE claimants due to their general foreignness or mover background, where perpetrators did not specify their national origin or nationality, was not covered by anti-discrimination legislation, especially when adjudicators applied the concept of 'race' in an inflexible way. These gaps left CEE workers vulnerable to non-actionable acts of discrimination.

Indeed, *Nikolova v M & P Enterprises London Ltd*[139] illustrates how characteristics protected under the Equality Act are not sufficient to address exploited movers' (or migrants') discrimination. In *Nikolova*, the Employment Appeal Tribunal attributed a Bulgarian budget-hotel cleaner's exploitation to her economic vulnerability rather than to her race. Like the claimant, all full-time cleaners at the hotel were Bulgarian, and all were similarly exploited. The Employment Tribunal ignored the claimant's suggestion of a hypothetical (white) British comparator and instead looked to exploited part-time receptionists of BAME backgrounds. Notably, the Employment Tribunal expounded that:

> many other nationalities seeking work in the UK have poor English, and many from Eastern Europe ... will ... accept low waged work which is still better than can be found at home. The fact that the respondent mainly

---

138 See generally Fitzpatrick (1987).
139 UKEAT/0293/15/DM, 4 February 2016.

employed Bulgarians is likely to result from word of mouth recruitment, rather than selecting Bulgarians because of their economic vulnerability.... Economically rational employers ... tak[e] advantage of whomever they can find who will accept less than the minimum wage rate, or poor safety standards.... This may include people with race as a protected characteristic, but also many without. Further, there may be many non-English nationals, or those for whom English is not a first language, who are not in the group prepared to take low paid work in poor conditions.

On appeal, the claimant argued that the lower tribunal had focused on irrelevant facts (the respondent's recruitment practices and presumed lack of intention) and had relied on materially different actual comparators. The Appeal Tribunal dismissed her arguments.[140] After acknowledging that the lower tribunal had made only limited comparator observations (and only implicitly and in passing), and that its reasoning (in the above quoted paragraph) was 'somewhat discursive' and 'elliptical', the Appeal Tribunal nevertheless found it sufficiently detailed. The Appeal Tribunal sought to bolster these conclusions by itself relying on irrelevant facts. Notably, it pointed out that this employer was willing to exploit any vulnerable employees including two British receptionists (neither of whom was an appropriate comparator[141]) and a Greek cleaner later hired to replace the claimant.

The outcome in *Nikolova* indicates that (direct) discrimination might be more difficult for claimants to prove if an exploitative employer predominantly recruits workers of only one national origin or similarly exploits workers of various national backgrounds—both of which might be (erroneously) treated as evidence of the employer's lack of ill will toward a specific claimant. This ignores the fact that, as discussed earlier, some employers adopted recruitment strategies to target East European movers or workers of particular CEE ethnicities specifically because they were deemed easier to exploit. Moreover, *Nikolova* points to the fact that intersectionality and/or socio-economic duty provisions would have been helpful in making anti-discrimination law more relevant to reality of discrimination. The court's spurious analysis—based on irrelevant facts and on a poor application of the comparator standard—illustrates significant liberties that adjudicators may take with legal reasoning under the Equality Act, and this is particularly problematic in the context of groups whose racialisation and poor treatment have become naturalised.

The *Nikolova* ruling demonstrates how equality law would be strengthened by the addition of more protected grounds to the definition of 'race' such as

---

140 Her appeal was allowed, however, because the lower tribunal had failed to address whether a hypothetical comparator would have been subjected to the same treatment, and had failed to apply the burden of proof correctly.

141 They worked part-time, mainly as receptionists, and there was no indication that they were exploited.

being born abroad, being an immigrant (or mover), or being foreign—all of which are covered by international human rights instruments. Two recent Supreme Court cases heard together, *Taiwo v Olaigbe and Onu v Akwiwu*,[142] also illustrate this point. Both claimants were Nigerian and in the UK pursuant to domestic-worker visas which tied their residence rights to their (abusive) employers. The Employment Tribunal dismissed their race discrimination claims after attributing their mistreatment to their 'vulnerable migrant worker' status rather than their nationality. The Court of Appeal explicitly noted that 'immigration status' should *not* be equated with 'nationality' for the purposes of the Equality Act. The Supreme Court agreed, ruling that their abuse was not due to their nationality but rather due to their 'vulnerability as a particular kind of migrant worker'. Resembling the reasoning in *Nikolova*, the Supreme Court mentioned that many other non-British workers are not vulnerable and would not have been abused the same way. Of course, such persons are not accurate comparators, so it is difficult to understand the value of this observation. As both *Nikolova* and *Taiwo and Onu* indicate, exploitation sometimes stems from migration status (or from associated economic vulnerability), which is not covered under the definition of 'race'. More generally, other characteristics that are related to 'race' and impact the experience of inequality—such as social origin, lack of social or cultural capital, and inability to access political power—get overlooked entirely by the law.

II. OVERLOOKING INTERSECTIONALITY

A significant weakness of the UK's anti-discrimination framework stems from its single-axis model of discrimination which overlooks intersectionality. Initially borne out of the inability of race or gender dimensions alone to capture black women's experiences of structural subjugation,[143] the intersectional framework exposes how various axes of marginalisation intersect through interlocking systems of power.[144] Although intersectionality has most frequently been applied to characteristics such as gender, (non-white) race, religion, and class, recent scholarship has expanded it to additional axes of subjugation. Notably, Levine-Rasky[145] points out the importance of fractures within whiteness due to being foreign, a migrant, or of non-majoritarian ethnic origin.

Some British adjudicators appear aware of the importance of intersectionality. In *Hewage v Grampian Health Board*, the Supreme Court accepted Employment Tribunal findings of direct discrimination on the grounds of sex and race, without requiring the claimant to identify separate facts to support each claim.[146]

---

142 [2016] UKSC 31, 22 June 2016.
143 E.g., hooks (1982).
144 See generally Brah and Phoenix (2004).
145 Levine-Rasky (2011).
146 [2012] UKSC 37, 25 July 2012.

Instead, the two grounds were approached as combined. Moreover, the Employment Appeal Tribunal has upheld a finding of indirect discrimination based on combined sex and national origin discrimination when a foreign-born, single mother was disciplined for work absences due to childcare difficulties.[147] The Tribunal aptly noted that 'the nature of discrimination is such that it cannot always be sensibly compartmentalised into discrete categories'.

The Equality Act 2010, however, does not account for intersectionality of various protected characteristics in the experience of discrimination. For example, direct discrimination claims are based on unfavourable treatment due to '*a* protected characteristic'.[148] Although early bill proposals included combining multiple grounds,[149] and academics had supported an intersectional approach, the business lobby opposed it due to being perceived as too burdensome for businesses. Thus, only the limited 'combined discrimination' provision was included in the final bill—allowing direct discrimination claims to be brought on the ground of two protected characteristics, each of which had to be proven separately. This failed to account for 'the synergy inherent in intersectionality'.[150] Ultimately, even that narrow proposal was not implemented by the Coalition government which deemed it too costly for businesses.[151]

Not recognising intersectionality forces complainants to choose only one form of discrimination to pursue and thus risks creating a hierarchy of discrimination grounds. Critically, without an intersectional approach, equality law makes it easier for perpetrators to act with impunity. For example, an employer might avoid liability when being sued by an unsuccessful black female job applicant by presenting evidence that he hires both black people and women. Critically, the single-axis approach does not reflect lived experience. For many CEE workers, their exploitation and discrimination stemmed from an intersection of ethnicity, low socio-economic status, and migration status. Moreover, even if discrimination of CEE movers due to race could be recognised in specific cases, discrimination experienced by those who possessed additional protected traits (such as being disabled or female) was unlikely to be captured.

III. INDIVIDUAL ENFORCEMENT

For anti-discrimination law to even approach attaining substantive equality, it needs to provide collective rights and collective remedies.[152] That is not possible under the Equality Act 2010. For one, no class actions are permitted. Although during the Act's legislative history class actions were considered by the

---

147 *Ministry of Defence v DeBique*, [2010] IRLR 471, Employment Appeal Tribunal, 12 October 2009.
148 Equality Act 2010, Section 13(1) (emphasis added).
149 Equalities Office (2008).
150 Solanke (2011).
151 Osborne (2011).
152 See generally Lacey (1998).

Equalities Office and were recommended by the European Commission, they were ultimately not included in the Act due to allegedly increasing legal costs for the business sector. Moreover, although the agency enforcement model—which was initiated with the creation of the Commission for Racial Equality under the Race Relations Act 1976—had acknowledged the need to address structural or institutional discrimination where no individual victim might be in a position to sue, the current legislation contains no provision for organisations to engage in proceedings on behalf of complainants. The Work and Pensions Committee[153] had recommended allowing representative actions by bodies such as trade unions or the Equality and Human Rights Commission, but the proposal never came to fruition due to business lobby pressure. In addition, current legislation removed the Equality and Human Rights Commission's ability, under the Equality Act 2006, to apply for injunctions even if no particular victims had been identified.[154]

Redress based on individual claims has many drawbacks. It is difficult for low-paid employees to have access to sufficient resources to pursue claims—especially with legal representation. CEE movers were particularly disadvantaged in this regard due to frequently engaging in precarious employment, working long hours and irregular shifts with little advance notice, and having limited access to advocacy groups or legal aid.[155] Moreover, the amount of damages awarded through individual claims—with no penalties for employers found to repeatedly discriminate—was unlikely to have a deterrent effect on larger employers even if they routinely exploited and discriminated against CEE movers.

Even conceptually, an individual-based approach does not fit the reality of inequality, because it fails to acknowledge that racism has been a normalised part of some groups' conditions of employment. Incidents of discrimination are divorced from their social contexts and become framed as rare, individual aberrations only—a view which is far from reality. The law overlooks pre-existing disadvantages faced by some groups and ignores the underlying social conditions that contribute to disadvantage. As my review of Employment Tribunal cases revealed, evidence that goes beyond individual claims—such as of CEE movers' widespread disadvantage and racialisation—was infrequently used and given little weight by adjudicators. Fundamentally, the Equality Act only takes account of what specific respondents have done to individual claimants—and only if the allegations happen to fall within the small number of closely delineated causes of action. Approaching inequality from the perpetrator's perspective makes anti-discrimination law inherently ineffective.[156] Furthermore, focusing on the facts of

153 Work and Pensions Committee (2009).
154 Although the EHRC may investigate potential violations and issue non-binding compliance notices (specifying respondent actions that would be required to ensure conformity with the legislation).
155 See generally Barnard et al. (2018).
156 See generally Freeman (1990).

individual disputes encourages adjudicators to rely more on their own—typically majoritarian—values and forms of conceptualising social relations,[157] thus making it unlikely that CEE claimants' perspectives would be taken into account. Instead, such an approach is more likely to preserve the status quo.

IV. LIMITED REMEDIES

Remedies under the Equality Act appear driven by economic concerns rather than by integration or equal opportunities goals. Enforcement mechanisms remain focused on aggrieved individuals, with the main remedy being monetary damages. This includes compensation for financial loss (typically loss of earnings), damages for injury to feelings[158] (which may be awarded even if no other damages are granted), and aggravated or exemplary (punitive) damages.[159] In indirect discrimination claims, if the respondent proves that discrimination was unintentional, damages may only be awarded if the court considers it just and equitable to do so. Since it is easier for respondents to prove lack of their intent rather than for claimants to prove the existence of such intent, this approach benefits respondents. There is no upper limit on the amount of damages that can be awarded in discrimination cases, but, in practice, median awards in race discrimination cases under the Act have typically ranged between £5,000 and £14,000, which is unlikely to be sufficient to deter large employers from discriminating against other similarly situated workers. This has been particularly problematic in the context of CEE movers who tended to congregate at specific exploitative employment sites.

Courts can also order limited non-financial remedies including recommendations that respondents implement certain actions to reduce adverse effects of discrimination, but this power has been rarely used.[160] Moreover, to lessen the burden on businesses, the Deregulation Act 2015 repealed the Employment Tribunal's initial ability to make wider recommendations aimed at reducing the effects of discrimination not only on the claimant but also on the respondents' other employees. Wider recommendations would have greatly benefited exploited and racialised workers, such as low-paid CEE movers, who tended to work alongside many other exploited CEE workers. Finally, unlike in unfair dismissal cases, courts lack the power to order victims' hiring or reinstatement in discrimination cases under the Act. This further disincentivises potential claimants from pursuing legal action—especially those who had already resigned themselves to taking on precarious positions and engaging in circular mobility, such as CEE movers.

157 See generally Fitzpatrick (1987).
158 Typically awarded below £10,000.
159 Rarely awarded, and only when respondent had behaved in a malicious or oppressive manner.
160 For example, in 2013, Tribunals made recommendations in 30 cases (eight of which related to individual claimants only).

V. PROCEDURAL HURDLES

Claims under the Equality Act must be brought before courts within six months and before Employment Tribunals within three months of occurrence of the relevant act.[161] Such short time limits have a significant impact on anyone who is not familiar with the legal system or has poor language skills. But they presented a particular hurdle for CEE movers, who often engaged in circular, temporary migration. My analysis of cases brought by CEE nationals indicates that many indeed failed to timely prosecute their claims due to traveling back home or due to changing their temporary employment or temporary housing locations. Furthermore, CEE movers tended to work long hours, often in remote locations with little access to legal advice, and some relied on employer-provided tied accommodations which necessitated long commutes to their employment sites. All of these factors further complicated their ability to meet short deadlines.

Moreover, between 2013 and 2017,[162] claimants had to pay a £1,200 fee for filing an employment discrimination claim and a £1,600 fee for filing an appeal. This reduced filings by approximately 75% without producing a change in claimants' success rates—indicating that many of the claims which were not filed had merit.[163] The imposition of filing fees more heavily impacted low-paid workers and particularly those who had little incentive to assert their rights such as transient CEE movers taking on temporary jobs or engaging in circular migration.

CEE Movers' Race Discrimination Claims in the Employment Context

Although there are no ethnicity-specific statistics, the limited research that exists indicates that CEE movers filed fewer employment[164] cases, but more race discrimination claims, than would have been expected based on their population size in the UK. Barnard's review of Employment Appeal Tribunal judgments between 2005 and 2012[165] identified only 13 appeals brought by CEE claimants. Barnard's and Ludlow's study of Employment Tribunal judgments between 2010 and 2013[166] also indicated low levels of enforcement by CEE claimants. During that time, CEE nationals filed approximately 200 cases (0.06% of all cases) which is 85% less than would be expected based on their

---

161 In their discretion, courts may allow late claims if to do so would be 'just and equitable'.
162 The Supreme Court determined these fees to have been unlawful. See *R (UNISON) v Lord Chancellor*, [2017] UKSC 51.
163 McColgan (2017).
164 E.g., unfair dismissal, unpaid wages, breach of contract.
165 Barnard (2014).
166 Barnard and Ludlow (2016).

population size. These low levels of enforcement might be attributed to a variety of factors, such as temporary migration motivations, mistrust of authorities (stemming from experiences of governmental corruption under communism and during the post-1989 period), their home countries' legal cultures (with a weak sense of workers' rights), and practical obstacles (e.g., precarious employment, language difficulties, employer-tied accommodations, inability to afford representation, working in sectors with no trade unions).[167] Notably, the most overrepresented claims brought by CEE claimants in Barnard's and Ludlow's study were for race discrimination (11% of CEE workers' claims compared to an average of 2% for all workers). Due to lack of ethnicity-based statistics, and the fact that not all Tribunal cases get reported, it is difficult to determine how well CEE claimants fared compared to other groups of claimants. The aforementioned 2016 study by Barnard and Ludlow and my review of case law suggest that their race discrimination claims have had low success rates which is in line with the low success rates of race discrimination claims generally.

Unlike the above quantitative studies, I set out to engage in a close qualitative analysis of only race discrimination cases brought by CEE claimants in order to better understand how the Equality Act was applied to them. I reviewed all reported Supreme Court, Court of Appeal, Employment Appeal Tribunal, and Employment Tribunal decisions pertaining to race discrimination claims (within the employment context), filed under the Equality Act 2010. Among those, I identified more than 800 cases filed by claimants of CEE nationalities.[168] All the cases I reviewed concerned allegations of racial discrimination before the EU's withdrawal from the EU, and based on factual details, it appears that most if not all of the claimants were EU movers (as opposed to pre-2004 immigrants or arrivals under the new Points-Based System). To better identify patterns in judicial reasoning and discourses when it comes to 'Eastern Europeans', I also looked at claims filed by Bulgarian and Romanian movers.

Most of my discussion below focuses on Employment Tribunal judgments. Although they, unlike Employment Appeal Tribunal decisions, are not binding, they are important to legal research because they apply anti-discrimination law in a highly predictable way—due to the Tribunal's specialised training and its large number of decisions. Moreover, the rulings of courts of first instance tend to engage in much more detailed factual analysis than do appellate judgments where jurisdiction is confined to errors of law. My review of cases is not exhaustive, of course, as most claims get disposed without a hearing (by being withdrawn, settled, or dismissed), and because public access to Employment Tribunal cases is not comprehensive. Furthermore, some claimants'

---

167 See also Barnard et al. (2018).
168 Given that Poles constituted by far the largest mover group in the UK, especially before transitional mobility derogations imposed against Romanians and Bulgarians ended in 2014, Polish claimants were overrepresented in the cases I located.

nationalities might not be evident from their surnames or mentioned in court discussions. However, my close qualitative discourse analysis[169] helps to highlight the types of claims frequently brought by CEE movers and their factual circumstances and indicates how adjudicators tended to approach specific legal or factual issues prevalent in the context of CEE claimants. In the process, I was able to identify some unique challenges that CEE movers had faced when asserting their rights under the Equality Act and to recognise particular shortcomings of anti-discrimination protections when applied to them.

Direct Discrimination Claims

Most of the cases I found involved direct discrimination claims. This might be because direct discrimination constitutes an intuitive claim and is defined in a more straightforward manner than other claims under the Equality Act. Hence, it is likely especially appealing to litigants who are not familiar with the litigation process, are not fluent in English, or lack representation. The cases I reviewed suggest that the Employment Appeal Tribunal did tend to fulfil its role by stepping in when the Employment Tribunal had failed to apply the correct legal test or failed to accurately interpret applicable rules or if it had failed to address all potentially relevant allegations. In many such instances, the Employment Appeal Tribunal appeared to enforce scrupulous application of relevant legal tests and recommended that the case be remitted before a different first-instance adjudicator to ensure fairness in the proceedings. Based on the small number of reported appeals, however, it is difficult to decipher how the Employment Appeal Tribunal would have addressed underlying factual allegations in direct discrimination claims brought by CEE movers. Judgments of the Employment Tribunal, however, offered insights into some unique challenges CEE movers faced when asserting direct discrimination claims and into how adjudicators approached claimants' factual allegations.

Successful Direct Discrimination Claims

My review of CEE nationals' direct discrimination claims before the Employment Tribunal indicates that they were more likely to succeed if, in addition to being represented by counsel, claimants (1) were employed in skilled or managerial positions, (2) did not have CEE co-workers in comparable roles, or (3) successfully asserted additional claims or presented evidence of a pattern of mistreatment. Given these observations, asserting successful claims would have been especially challenging for CEE movers because they concentrated in 'low-skill' (low-paid) positions, often worked predominantly alongside co-ethnics or other CEE workers, and frequently found it too costly or difficult to retain counsel. I also noticed that successful claims were most often predicated on the

---

169 See generally Van Dijk (2001); Wodak and Reisigl (2001).

tribunal's holistic evaluation of claimants' facts, especially where an ongoing pattern of poor treatment could be demonstrated, as well as on a correct application of the two-step burden of proof test and on the use of correct comparators (often hypothetical). In practice, judges were inconsistent in how holistically they approached allegations.

Moreover, the burden-of-proof and the comparator tests were often clumsily or even incorrectly applied. It is difficult to determine whether this was due to adjudicators' general imprecision or incompetence, carelessness in regard to CEE claimants, or backwards reasoning (that is, relying on spurious reasons to substantiate their pre-determined decisions to dismiss claims). Regardless of the precise reasons, since adjudicators appeared to apply burden-of-proof and comparator provisions inconsistently, outcomes of CEE claimants' cases might have been easily affected by subjective factors—for example, whether individual adjudicators subscribed to the anti-CEE political climate, were aware of CEE nationals' racialisation, or felt sympathy towards claimants. Adjudicators' broad understanding of 'race' and appreciation of CEE movers' widespread racialisation also supported findings of direct discrimination, although I observed this rarely in the caselaw I reviewed. Cases discussed below illustrate such patterns in addition to providing glimpses into CEE movers' work experiences.

For example, in *Krupa v B&M Retail Ltd*,[170] witnesses confirmed that a Polish warehouse cleaner's British line manager urinated on the toilet floor right after he had asked her to clean it (which was not part of her duties). The manager did not offer an explanation, but instead blankly denied claimant's allegations. He also argued that he could not be liable because he knew that the claimant was somewhere from the CEE region but had allegedly not realised that she was Polish. The first-tier tribunal sided with the claimant's assertion of direct discrimination in addition to finding harassment and victimisation. To support its finding of direct discrimination, the tribunal reasoned that the manager would not have treated non-Polish employees, especially British ones, this way. The tribunal inferred a causal link between his actions and the claimant's race, based on a holistic factual analysis—pointing specifically to facts that it was not the claimant's duty to clean toilets, they had been cleaned an hour earlier, and the manager dirtied the floor immediately after she had finished cleaning it.

Similarly, in finding for the claimant in *Besz v Multi Packaging Solutions Limited*,[171] the tribunal relied on an appropriate hypothetical comparator and found the respondent liable for another infraction (harassment). Moreover, the Polish warehouse worker's arguments were strengthened by the fact that he could demonstrate a pattern of racially-based mistreatment by his British line manager who had made three derogatory statements directly to the claimant[172]

---

170 Case No 2400660/2016, Employment Tribunal Liverpool, 28 March 2017.
171 Case No 2602118/2016, Employment Tribunal Nottingham, 26 September 2017.
172 Including 'after Brexit I will vote to send you back to Poland'.

and one derogatory remark about the claimant to his co-worker.[173] The tribunal concluded that although personal animus might have motivated this treatment, it had an underlying racial element because the respondent provided no explanation to show that the treatment had nothing to do with the claimant's race and because he would not have treated a British worker this way. The tribunal also correctly rejected, as irrelevant, the respondent's argument that he did not treat all Polish or all CEE workers in an equally hostile manner.[174] Similarly, a pattern of derogatory remarks supported a finding of direct discrimination in *A v B & C*,[175] where a Polish shop assistant had been repeatedly told by her supervisor that the national minimum-wage and holiday-pay regulations did not apply to Poles but only to British nationals.

Nazarczyk v T J Morris Limited[176] illustrates that, when the tribunal applied the hypothetical comparator test correctly, even a single comment could suffice to support direct discrimination claims. In response to a Polish warehouse worker's request that his daughter's shift be made to coincide with his so that he could walk her home at night, his English supervisor responded along the lines of 'if you do not like it, pack yourself and your family up and go back to Poland'. The respondent argued that he would have treated a hypothetical British worker the same—for example, suggesting that his daughter go back to Bath if she were from there and did not feel safe in Liverpool. The tribunal correctly disregarded that proposed comparator scenario because it did not have the same racial connotation. The tribunal noted that a comparable situation would have been to say 'if you do not like it here, go back to Poland' to a hypothetical British worker. That, of course, would have been non sensical. This illustrates how challenging it sometimes is to find a correct and useful comparator in racial claims based on national origin or nationality. Of course, adjudicators have the option not to use comparators and instead to focus on the question of why a specific claimant was subjected to the treatment at issue. That approach, however, opens the door to more subjective decision-making.

A finding of direct discrimination could also be based on a long-standing pattern of less-overtly negative treatment, especially when combined with an inference of discriminatory attitudes among those in managerial and disciplinary positions. In *Michalak v The Mid Yorkshire Hospitals NHS Trust*,[177] a Polish medical consultant presented evidence of a secret campaign by the management team, which spanned six years and included 22 instances of harassment and false allegations, that culminated in her unwarranted dismissal. In secret meetings, her managers had referred to her Polish origin and had questioned her competence due to her Polish medical training. The respondents did

173 'I hope it's a one way ticket', while the claimant was in Poland.
174 Some adjudicators, however, did consider such arguments in finding against claimants, as discussed below.
175 Case No 2403142/2017, Employment Tribunal Manchester, 4 February 2019.
176 Case No 2401275/2017, Employment Tribunal Liverpool, 10 August 2017.
177 Case No 1808465/2007, Employment Tribunal Leeds, 14 June 2010.

not offer any satisfactory explanations and failed to show that their behaviour was in no way tainted by race. Without relying on a comparator, the tribunal found the respondents liable for direct discrimination (as well as for sex discrimination and unfair dismissal). The tribunal inferred that senior managers held discriminatory attitudes because they were all white Britons, despite the fact that half of the consultants had BAME backgrounds. Drawing a (debatable) connection between those two facts illustrates the tribunal's flexibility in inferring discriminatory attitudes. Although a similar inference could have been drawn in many of the cases I reviewed, this is the only decision in which I observed it. Perhaps this is attributable to the fact that, as a result of this treatment, the claimant was diagnosed with a chronic personality change, making it unlikely that she would work again as a doctor. It might also have been due to the fact that she was highly skilled which would suggest the importance of a claimants' class to case outcomes.

Other tribunal cases I reviewed also indicate that it might have been easier for CEE nationals to support their direct discrimination claims if they were employed in semi- or highly-skilled positions not populated by co-ethnics or other CEE workers. For example, in *Procek v Oakford Farms Ltd*,[178] a Polish farm manager claimant was not paid at the same rate as the other farm managers (all of whom were British), was not given the correct job title or recognition, and had his qualifications questioned. The tribunal used those other managers as actual comparators. The tribunal then inferred a causal link between the unequal treatment and the claimant's race by pointing to items of evidence that are not particularly convincing (that he was not allowed time off to attend English classes, and he was forced to cancel holidays on short notice). The respondent could not provide an adequate explanation that this treatment was in no sense due to his race.

Similarly, in *Ruda v TEi Ltd*,[179] the tribunal ruled in favour of the claimant, a Polish quality assurance engineer, who had been repeatedly called 'Borat' by a colleague over a period of four weeks. Other employees (none of whom were from the CEE region) had been given nicknames associated with their personal characteristics rather than with their national origins. *Ruda* also offers yet another illustration of complications that arise when using comparators in cases of verbal discrimination. The tribunal in *Ruda* reasoned that somebody who shared all of the claimant's other characteristics but who was not from Poland or the CEE region would not have been called 'Borat'. Of course, since the satirical character of Borat is based on an amalgamation of CEE and Balkan traits and languages, it would have been nonsensical to call a Dane that, for example.

---

178 Employment Tribunal Liverpool, 2009. Although this case was decided under the Equality Act 2006, I included it in my analysis because direct discrimination law has not changed significantly since then.
179 Case No 1807582/10, Employment Tribunal Leeds, 23 August 2011.

Among reported cases, it was common for CEE claimants to have numerous co-workers from the same ethnicity or from other CEE states, especially when employed in 'low-skill' positions. In such circumstances, it appeared even more critical for claimants to be able to prove a pattern of very poor treatment and to be represented by counsel. For example, in *Kowal and Obieglo v Peter Leslie & Sons t/a David Leslie Fruits*,[180] two Polish seasonal strawberry pickers won their direct discrimination claims after the tribunal found that the respondent would not have treated (hypothetical) Scottish workers the same way. The respondent's approximately 200 farm workers (mostly Poles, Czechs, and Slovakians) were all underpaid and housed on site in converted metal containers with no running water and with access to only 12 showers.[181] After the claimants complained to their manager about poor working conditions they were escorted off the premises by the police. Unlike the later precedent set by the Employment Appeal Tribunal in *Nikolova* (discussed earlier), the first-tier tribunal in *Obieglo* found for the claimants, even though they made no allegations about race-based treatment and they could have easily been found to be simply 'economically vulnerable'. Adjudicators clearly have a great deal of flexibility when inferring causal links between adverse treatment and race, and the decisions I located have not been consistent. Of course, since tribunal decisions are not binding, any leniency or goodwill they might have exhibited towards exploited CEE workers had little impact beyond the individual claimants concerned.

Some adjudicators who ruled for claimants in direct discrimination cases did so by instead interpreting statutory provisions with substantial flexibility. Notably, in some cases, judges applied an understanding of 'race' broader than under the Equality Act's definition. For example, in *Wilk v Wackers*,[182] the tribunal concluded that calling a Hungarian live-in-carer an 'idiot' alluded to his speaking English as a second language and thus was linked to his race. Such flexibility implicitly indicates that 'race' is defined too narrowly under the Equality Act to reflect the lived experience of discrimination.

At least some adjudicators who ruled in favour of specific CEE claimants approached CEE workers collectively as a similarly poorly treated group. For example, in *Besz*, the tribunal noted in passing that the respondent may not have treated all workers 'of either Polish or eastern European origin in an equally hostile manner', and, in *Ruda*, the tribunal reasoned that a hypothetical comparator 'who was neither from Poland nor perceived of Eastern European origin' would not have been treated the same way as the claimant. Although looking at CEE workers collectively in direct discrimination claims does not strictly follow the statutory definition of direct discrimination, it indicates some

---

180 Case Nos 113343/09 and 113344/09, Employment Tribunal Dundee, 6 April 2010.
181 Following a newspaper investigation, David Leslie Fruits Ltd became the first company in Scotland prosecuted under the Gangmasters (Licensing) Act, and was fined £500 for using an unlicensed gangmaster. It is doubtful that a fine in that amount can serve as a regulatory deterrent for large companies.
182 Case No 3313268/2019, Employment Tribunal Watford, 11 March 2020.

adjudicators' awareness that post-04 CEE movers were prone to exploitation and racialisation in the UK. This was a double-edged sword. Approaching all CEE workers as inherently vulnerable extended them protections in individual cases but also arguably propagated their stigmatisation and undermined their agency.

Failed Direct Discrimination Claims

On the other hand, CEE movers tended to lose their direct discrimination claims when tribunals did not strictly follow applicable legal tests especially when their reasoning hinged on careless or spurious analyses of comparators or on the (irrelevant) fact that other workers sharing the claimant's ethnicity (or more generally, workers of any CEE national origin) did not appear to complain of comparably poor treatment. Both of these hurdles to legal reasoning were facilitated by CEE movers' tendency to work at employment sites heavily populated by their co-ethnics or other CEE workers—especially in low-paid occupations. Having many co-ethnic or CEE co-workers was a double-edged sword for many CEE claimants. Some tribunals incorrectly relied on this as evidence of a lack of discrimination (especially when others did not complain of mistreatment), while other tribunals applied levelling-down and incorrectly relied on other exploited workers as comparators. In line with *Nikolova*, some respondents also escaped liability by arguing that their treatment of CEE claimants was motivated not by race but by their 'economic vulnerability'—a common condition given how many CEE movers were de-skilled and employed in low-paid, temporary positions.

The cases discussed below also illustrate how difficult it was for some CEE workers to support their direct discrimination claims due to tribunal inconsistencies and discretion when inferring causation between poor treatment and race, due to approaching 'race' in an overly narrow way, and due to overlooking CEE movers' racialisation. The inherent flexibility in judicial engagement with relevant facts also served to disadvantage some CEE claimants, potentially reflecting judicial biases against them. Moreover, in many of the above cases, facts were disputed. Like any claimants who do not belong to the privileged group (from which adjudicators tend to come) CEE claimants appeared disadvantaged in cases with disputed facts, where judges had to take account of witness credibility. This is inherently a subjective determination which hinges on being sensitive to claimants' culture, race, and class and which further complicated due to claimants' imperfect British language skills or the use of interpreters.

In many cases where claimants lost, the tribunal hesitated to use comparators who were either British or from other CEE states. For example, in *Prasil v Orchard House Foods*,[183] Polish and Slovakian food production operatives, each with excellent work records, were dismissed for taking unauthorised breaks. Most of their co-workers were Polish, one-third were British, and the rest were from other

---

[183] Case No 3400534/2014, Employment Tribunal Cambridge, 12 April 2018.

CEE states. Claimants proposed several actual comparators, both Britons and non-UK nationals, who had not been dismissed following incidents of gross misconduct. The tribunal deemed them all too factually dissimilar. Notably, although the tribunal attempted to justify why the two proposed British comparators were materially different, it did not even try to explain why all of the proposed non-UK operatives were not suitable. The tribunal did not fashion a hypothetical comparator. Instead, it sought to infer the reason why the claimants were dismissed and concluded that it was due to their misconduct rather than to race. Similarly, in *Nemec v Concept Recruitment Group Ltd*,[184] the tribunal did not use a comparator but instead inferred that the claimant was dismissed due to alleged poor attendance rather than to his race. The claimant, a Czech worker at a card factory, had asserted that Poles—who constituted a majority of the workforce—were better treated. The tribunal referred to the respondents' argument that they had dismissed a Polish worker after only two weeks due to poor attendance. The court did not, however, analyse a specific comparator in detail but instead inferred that the claimant's treatment was not due to his race. In both *Prasil* and *Nemec*, Poles constituted the majority of the workforce. Such challenges in adjudicators' use of comparators might be explained by the fact that there was not a long line of cases pertaining to CEE movers' claims.

Furthermore, in cases where claimants' direct discrimination claims were found unsubstantiated, adjudicators often displayed great flexibility in creating arguably erroneous hypothetical comparators, occasionally adding subjective descriptors that led to more discretionary decision-making. For example, in *BDW Trading Ltd v Kopec*,[185] the tribunal defined a hypothetical comparator for the Polish claimant as 'male … with the same work history and characteristics as the Claimant, including his weak performance in the softer skills, save that he is of a non-Eastern European ethnicity'. Defining the comparator in this way revealed the adjudicator's inherent prejudice against the claimant and foreshadowed the actual outcome of the case.

To justify dismissing CEE workers' direct discrimination claims, some judges would point to other co-ethnic workers who appeared to be treated decently—or, who at least did not voice any complaints against respondents. For example, in *Skrzydlo v CRC Recruitment Ltd*,[186] when a Polish warehouse worker informed her employment agency that she was pregnant, she stopped being offered work consistently. After finding the actual British comparator proposed by the claimant too dissimilar, the tribunal relied on an incorrect actual comparator—another Polish worker who continued to work for the same agency while pregnant albeit under materially different circumstances (for another client and under different conditions). The tribunal improperly reasoned that this indicated that nationality played no part in the claimant's treatment.

---

184 Case No 1800244/2022, Employment Tribunal Leeds, 14 November 2022.
185 UKEAT/0197/19/OO, 13 December 2019.
186 Case No 3400728/2016, Employment Tribunal Cambridge, 3 April 2018.

Similarly, in *Grzyb v Lidl*,[187] where a Polish cashier was suspended for failing to scan one of his co-worker's purchases, the tribunal noted that there had been no complaints against the manager (who had dismissed him) from the many other Polish employees he had supervised. Likewise, in dismissing a direct discrimination claim by a Latvian food production operative who had been declined employment in *Bouzir v Country Style Foods Ltd*,[188] the adjudicator pointed to the respondent's having hired several other Latvians. Furthermore, in *Skarbek-Cielecka v Holy Rise Consultants Ltd*,[189] the adjudicator disregarded a British comparator proposed by the Polish claimants (care workers employed via an agency) and instead looked at one specific co-worker who was also Polish and who had testified for the respondent about having been treated decently.

More generally, working for respondents who employed mostly non-British staff complicated some CEE claimants' ability to assert direct discrimination. Some adjudicators would misinterpret respondents' reliance on multi-ethnic workforces as indicative of their lack of ill will towards foreign workers, overlooking the fact that exploitative employers often tend to hire mostly non-UK workers because they are morevulnerable. Such line of reasoning also allowed for levelling down—so that employers who treated all of their employees poorly could more easily escape liability if their workforce was comprised largely of non-British workers. For example, in *Matuzewicz v 2 Sisters Food Group Ltd*,[190] a Polish food production worker complained of being subjected to poor treatment and verbal abuse. The tribunal dismissed her concerns with little factual or legal analysis. It mentioned the element of detriment only once and did not address the less favourable treatment. The tribunal also pointed out the irrelevant fact that the respondent was employing 'a multi racial workforce which get along well, have a joke with each other and swear in each other's languages', overlooking the fact that similar swear words carry different connotations in different languages (and depending on gender). Finally, it noted that, had the claimant's allegations been even partly accurate, her co-workers would have contacted the employer's third-party whistle blower hot line. This is not only legally irrelevant but also insensitive towards the reality of exploited workers' circumstances. Many are hesitant to complain even by using what appear to be anonymous methods. Similarly, in *Kozakiewicz v Futon Ltd*,[191] in ruling for the respondent, the tribunal noted its 'nationally and racially diverse workforce' which was comprised of many Poles (including some in managerial positions at other locations). Hence, the tribunal found it unproblematic that a British manager had refused to recruit additional Poles because she did not want to turn the establishment into an 'all-Polish' store. Likewise, in dismissing

---

187 Case No 2600945/2016, Employment Tribunal Leicester, 25 November 2017.
188 [2011] EWCA Civ 1519, 8 December 2011.
189 Case No 2303648/2017, Employment Tribunal London South, 9 August 2019.
190 Case No 2500043/17, Employment Tribunal North Shields, 10 August 2017.
191 Case No 2600264/2017, Employment Tribunal Nottingham, 12 December 2017.

direct-discrimination claims in *Juszczyk v Kettle Produce Ltd*[192] and *Dzierzanowski v Cranswick Country Foods Plc*,[193] the adjudicators noted that the respondents' workforces included, respectively, 45% CEE nationals and 55% Polish nationals, although this is not legally relevant.

In line with such tribunal patterns of reasoning, respondents tended to emphasise, as part of their defence, the fact that they employed many non-British workers. For example, in *Januszewski v Ultima Furniture Systems Limited*,[194] the respondent pointed out that half of its workforce was Polish and that its supervisors were even learning Polish due to this fact, therefore his treatment of the Polish claimant could not have been discriminatory. Similarly, in *Winczewski v MAM Transport Services Ltd*,[195] the employer testified that it had employed many Polish drivers over the years. Notably, when the Polish claimant pointed out that many of them had been dismissed, the tribunal uncritically reiterated the respondent's testimony that some of such employees had been dismissed only to be re-engaged as contractors instead, because 'it suited them to operate that way'. The tribunal took this comment at face value, overlooking the fact that this practice likely benefited the employer financially while making such workers' labour positions more precarious.

In finding against claimants, adjudicators often failed to engage in a holistic analysis of potentially discriminatory incidents and also tended to minimise the significance of patterns of potential discrimination, especially where facts were disputed. For example, in aforementioned *Winczewski*, various Polish drivers were mistreated by British co-workers over the years and had complained about this to their managers. The adjudicator did not deem this relevant. Furthermore, employers were able to avoid liability in cases where they did nothing in response to potentially discriminatory acts, even repeated ones, which were committed by third parties or by co-workers who were not in managerial positions vis-à-vis claimants. In aforementioned *BDW Trading Ltd v Kopec*, a Polish concierge at a residential building was repeatedly called a 'f***ing Eastern European' and a 'f***ing Russian' by customers and by third parties, was physically attacked during the course of some of such incidents, and was ultimately disciplined and suspended after reporting one such incident to the police. The tribunal acknowledged that his line manager had no diversity training and did nothing to help pre-empt or to address such incidents, yet it concluded that she was not at fault for the claimant's poor treatment. The tribunal reasoned that she was not racist because she had tried to assist the claimant to overcome his 'lack of softer skills'. Through this observation, the tribunal also placed some blame on the claimant himself.

---

192 Case No S/4103971/2016, Employment Tribunal Dundee, 2 March 2017.
193 Case No 1808685/2018, Employment Tribunal Hull, 22 March 2019.
194 Case No 1805191/2019, Employment Tribunal Sheffield, 17 February 2021.
195 Case No 3311620/2021, Employment Tribunal Cambridge, 19 January 2023.

Moreover, some adjudicators would mis-attribute ongoing racist bullying by co-workers to 'jovial' comments and office 'banter'. For example, in *Kabzinski v Vistajet International Ltd*,[196] a Polish customer-experience analyst was subjected to repeated private and public comments from a co-worker regarding being a 'Gypsy' or a 'cheap Gypsy' not suited for working in a skilled position. The tribunal attributed this to their 'friendly' relationship, having socialised after work a few times, and to their 'common interest' in the Borat character.

Furthermore, cases I reviewed indicate that claimants and adjudicators defined 'race' in the context of CEE movers inconsistently, even within cases, further complicating legal analysis. For example, a Latvian national was described by the tribunal as having an 'Eastern European background' and a 'Latvian national origin'.[197] In another case, the judge referred to a claimant's race as 'Polish nationality', 'Polish national origin', and 'Eastern European ethnic origin'.[198] The tribunal described another claimant's race as 'from the Czech Republic or ... not Polish'.[199] In yet another case, the Employment Appeal Tribunal approached all whites as homogeneous and found that a claimant's poor treatment should not be attributed to his being 'white' or of 'Polish origin'.[200] Similarly, CEE claimants themselves defined their origins broadly and inconsistently, often using the pan-ethnic 'Eastern European' label—for example, as 'Lithuanian/Eastern European',[201] 'eastern European',[202] or 'Polish, Eastern European ethnicity'.[203]

It is difficult to imagine a German or French claimant being referred to or describing herself as of 'western European' race, indicating how the eastern parts of Europe are indeed homogenised in the western imagination and how this fact has had palpable implications for CEE claimants. CEE claimants, as well as Bulgarian and Romanian movers, were indeed aware of their racialisation. For example, a Bulgarian investment banker alleged that he was treated more poorly than 'Western European' employees would have been.[204] Although subsuming CEE claimants within the pan-ethnic 'Eastern European' label is in line with the widespread anti-CEE sentiment and racialisation—and indeed supports my collective approach and arguments throughout this book—it complicated legal analysis, especially when trying to identify suitable comparators.

---

196 Case No 2200745/2021, Employment Tribunal London Central, 31 October 2022.
197 *Borodinova v Stateside Food Limited*, Case No 2407202/2021, Employment Tribunal Manchester, 9 December 2022.
198 *Kabzinski*, Case No 2200745/2021, 31 October 2022.
199 *Nemec*, Case No 1800244/2022, 14 November 2022.
200 *Medrysa v The London Borough of Tower Hamlets*, UKEAT/0208/20, 29 April 2021.
201 *Kolaitis v DX Network Services Ltd*, Case No 1300522/2019, Employment Tribunal Birmingham, 1 February 2021.
202 *Angelov v Marston Group Ltd*, Case No 3330861/2018, Employment Tribunal Reading, 15 April 2020.
203 *BDW Trading Ltd v Kopec*, UKEAT/0197/19/OO, 13 December 2019.
204 *Mechkarov v Citibank N.A.*, UKEAT/0006/19, 31 July 2019.

On the other hand, some judges failed to recognise the role of race and racialisation in CEE nationals' discrimination claims, making respondents' behaviours not actionable. This supports my argument that the definition of 'race' is indeed too narrow under the Equality Act. For example, in *Glogowska v F A Gill Ltd*,[205] the claimant was bullied by her supervisor for having poor English skills. Concluding that her mistreatment was not connected to her nationality, the tribunal noted that an 'inability to speak good English is not a protected characteristic'. Similarly, bullying statements about a Bulgarian arrest officer's 'unprofessional' body language (attributed to his being 'from another country')—which eventually contributed to complaints being made against him and to his dismissal—were also deemed not related to race.[206] Notably, in *Jutrenzka v Chinnocks Wharf Management Co Ltd*,[207] the tribunal concluded that any alleged bullying and derogatory comments made against all 'Eastern Europeans' cannot support a claim under the Equality Act because they encompass multiple ethnicities. The tribunal emphasised that allegations must be based on one specific nationality, such as Polish national origin. Thus, racist behaviour directed against all CEE workers at a place of employment, especially if the respondent was not aware of the claimant's specific national origin or did not refer to it, would not be actionable.

Moreover, in line with *Nikolova* (discussed earlier), I found multiple instances of judges attributing claims of race discrimination to CEE nationals' economic vulnerabilities or mover statuses—categories not actionable under the Equality Act. For example, in aforementioned *Winczewski*, the tribunal pointed out that a company which recruited drivers specifically from Poland and paid them less than British drivers could not be accused of discrimination. Instead, the employer's actions were excused and attributed to his rational behaviour as 'a man that would save costs where he could'. The tribunal went on to observe that 'if one group of drivers (quite irrespective of race) insisted on a higher rate than another, ... [the employer] was content to pay them differently to save money where he could, rather than treat his workforce fairly'. Similarly, in *Petrica v Central London Community Healthcare NHS Trust*,[208] a Romanian statistics administrator argued that his immigration status (as a CEE mover) had made him especially vulnerable in the aftermath of the Brexit referendum. The tribunal agreed with the respondent's reliance on *Taiwo* and *Onu* (discussed earlier) and concluded that 'immigration status per se' is not a protected characteristic under the Equality Act.

Indirect Discrimination Claims

Indirect discrimination claims are generally more rarely asserted and more difficult to prove than direct discrimination claims. The few reported Employment

---

205 Case No 1303719/2019, Employment Tribunal Birmingham, 26 October 2020.
206 *Angelov*, Case No 3330861/2018, 15 April 2020.
207 Case No 3201751/2019, Employment Tribunal East London, 31 March 2022.
208 UKEAT/0059/20/AT, 12 May 2021.

Tribunal indirect discrimination cases involving CEE claimants reinforced some observations made in my discussion of direct discrimination claims, suggesting how intrinsically difficult it would have been for CEE workers to pursue them successfully. Notably, indirect discrimination claims appeared more likely to succeed if adjudicators defined the concept of 'race' more broadly than under the Equality Act and where they took a holistic look at not only specific claimants' but also their co-ethnics' patterns of discrimination (especially if actual British comparators were available). Unfortunately, in practice, adjudicators could have easily not adopted such approaches—especially if they were swayed by their own prejudices against CEE movers or by their lack of understanding of their widespread racialisation. Moreover, as with any claims, obtaining legal advice seems to have increased chances of success. In practice, this was not common as CEE movers experienced challenges in accessing legal counsel and tended to work in sectors that were less likely to be unionised.

Firstly, in cases where CEE claimants were successful, adjudicators tended to define 'race' broadly, which implicitly indicates that its definition under the Equality Act might be too narrow to offer meaningful anti-discrimination protections. For example, in *Zaluski v NSL Ltd*,[209] a Polish claimant (a civil enforcement officer) argued that a policy or practice in place that limited bereavement leave disadvantaged him (and his two other foreign-born colleagues—another Pole and an Indian). The Employment Tribunal agreed and defined 'race' as 'being from an overseas home country (i.e., a foreign national working in the UK)', with a person whose home country is the UK serving as comparator. Similarly, in *Skwarczynska v Sturts Community Trust*,[210] the tribunal concluded that an employer's disciplinary hearing conducted in English only was indirectly discriminatory against the Polish claimant (a carer). The tribunal acknowledged that language skills do not constitute 'race' under the Equality Act, yet it nevertheless concluded that most British people speak English as their first language, and thus Poles would be put at a particular disadvantage in comparison with them. In both these cases, a narrow application of 'race' by adjudicators would have likely led to dismissals of CEE workers' claims.

Secondly, indirect discrimination claims appeared more successful where a PCP could be shown to have placed all workers of the same nationality at a disadvantage and where the claimant was supported by a trade union. In *Kosik v Montgomery Transport Ltd*,[211] the Polish claimant, whose lorry had tipped over during a delivery, argued that all Polish workers at the haulage company (which employed mostly British and Polish drivers) were treated more poorly than their British co-workers by being given older, more accident-prone vehicles. The Employment Tribunal agreed. The claimant was represented by counsel and had the support of his trade union. Many low-paid CEE movers

---

209 Case No 2305243/2021, Employment Tribunal, 24 February 2023.
210 Case No 1400540/2019, Employment Tribunal Southampton, 12 October 2021.
211 Employment Tribunal Manchester, 2015. See also Unite Legal Services (2015).

would have been in a weaker position than Mr Kosik since they tended to be employed in non-unionised industries, alongside predominantly other co-ethnics or CEE workers (with no British workers to serve as comparators), by employers who similarly exploited all workers. Moreover, it would have been difficult for many CEE movers to provide evidence of their group's disadvantage at the hands of specific employers since many CEE workers were temporary, and my review of cases indicates that they rarely provided statements or shared information to support claimants—presumably due to fear of employer reprisals or due to co-ethnic economic competition. The lack of relevant data collection also would have complicated their ability to support indirect discrimination claims.

Harassment Claims

Harassment cases brought by CEE workers suggest that lower-tier adjudicators displayed a great deal of flexibility when applying statutory test elements, especially in determining a causal connection to race and when applying the 'reasonable person' standard. This opened the door for inconsistent decisions and enabled findings to be made against claimants, especially if adjudicators were unsympathetic towards them. The few harassment claims that were appealed suggest that the Employment Appeal Tribunal might not have been consistent in applying rigorous legal analysis in such claims.

For example, in *Kowalewska-Zietek v Lancashire Teaching Hospitals NHS Foundation Trust*,[212] the Employment Appeal Tribunal agreed with the Employment Tribunal's dismissal of a harassment claim by a Polish neurologist. After the respondent had received some complaints from patients and registrars about the claimant, her responsibilities were reduced. In a personnel report, her supervisor then questioned her training in Poland. In dismissing her claim, the lower-tier tribunal emphasised that 'any stereotypical assumption in the report was about the quality of Polish training, not about Poles themselves'. The tribunal's reasoning focused on the fact that these comments would not have been made had the claimant been trained in Britain but would have been made had a British doctor been trained in Poland. Although this reasoning is not entirely convincing, and is irrelevant to the legal test for harassment (which does not look to comparators), the Appeal Tribunal concluded that the lower-tier tribunal had engaged in sufficient factual analysis and dismissed her appeal.

The appellate ruling in *Quality Solicitors v Tunstall*[213] offers another illustration of poor judicial analysis of a harassment claim. The Employment Tribunal ruled in favour of the claimant—a Polish paralegal who had overheard her boss telling a potential client that 'she is Polish but very nice'. The respondent claimed that he had stated 'she is Polish *and* very nice'. The lower-tier tribunal concluded that, regardless of the exact phrase used, her race should have been irrelevant to

212 UKEAT/0269/15/JOJ, 21 January 2016.
213 UKEAT/0105/14/RN, 28 July 2014.

her introduction to a client, and thus its mention was patronising. The Employment Appeal Tribunal, however, ruled that the lower-tier tribunal had failed to perform statutory harassment analysis. Notably, instead of remitting the case to the first-instance tribunal, as is the usual practice, the Appeal Tribunal set aside the finding of harassment, reasoning that it was based on only a single remark which had been made in the context of 'encouraging' a client to be assisted by this claimant. The Appeal Tribunal overlooked the fact that this 'encouragement' is precisely the reason why the remark was patronising, as it was based on an assumption that the client would not want the claimant working on his case due to an inherent prejudice against Poles.

In the above two cases, the Employment Appeal Tribunal's approach to potential lower-tier tribunal errors in statutory analysis was inconsistent. In *Quality Solicitors*, the lower-tier tribunal did not explicitly address the reasonableness of the claimant's reaction and had combined two separate elements of the statutory test to conclude that the comment had made the claimant feel humiliated and degraded (rather than stating whether the effect of the respondent's conduct had (1) violated her dignity or (2) created a degrading or humiliating environment). This error was sufficient for the Appeal Tribunal to set aside the lower-tier tribunal's findings. On the other hand, in *Kowalewska-Zietek*, where the lower-tier tribunal did not apply facts to the statutory test at all, the Employment Appeal Tribunal did not find its analysis inadequate. In both cases, the result was the same and claimants were unsuccessful.

Employment Tribunal analyses of harassment claims also appeared unpredictable, with adjudicators dismissing harassment more readily if they incorrectly or carelessly applied relevant statutory provisions, or if they failed to engage in a holistic analysis of facts presented to them or failed to adopt a victim's perspective. On the other hand, successful harassment claims tended to include additional successful claims, such as in aforementioned *Besz* and *Krupa*. One wonders whether the rigour of judicial analysis and case outcomes depended on how sympathetically predisposed specific adjudicators were towards claimants or on the underlying claims' strengths.

For example, when dismissing a harassment claim in aforementioned *Matuzewicz*, the Employment Tribunal did not apply statutory elements of harassment. Instead, it attributed the claimant's poor treatment to her being too sensitive, 'obstinate and opinionated'. It is difficult to imagine such unnecessary descriptors being applied to claimants (especially males) of other races. Repeated derogatory comments or bullying incidents that targeted a specific employee were mis-attributed by some tribunals to friendly 'banter'—for example, in aforementioned *Kabzinski*.[214] Moreover, employers appeared to be able to avoid liability where degrading comments or behaviours were prevalent but where each specific employee was targeted only on a few occasions. For example, in aforementioned *Januszewski*, the respondent eluded responsibility for harassment where British supervisors shouted

---

214 For a general discussion of bullying disguised as 'banter', see Soutar (2023).

and reprimanded the Polish claimant in front of others, grabbed him, and escorted him off the premises. In concluding that there was no link between such incidents and the claimant's nationality, the tribunal disregarded the cumulative effect of other degrading incidents at that workplace—replete with British supervisors' calling other Polish workers 'Polish bast**d'. It is difficult to imagine adjudicators tolerating such employer behaviour had the claimant been non-white.

Victimisation Claims

Despite its straightforward statutory definition, I was able to locate only a few reported victimisation claims asserted by CEE nationals. It is likely that CEE movers, especially those without legal representation, were not familiar with the concept of victimisation since it was not traditionally recognised by equality laws across the CEE region before the transposition of the Race Equality Directive. Moreover, my review of cases indicates that many CEE workers tended not to complain about their poor, and arguably discriminatory, treatment until after resigning or after being dismissed.[215] Furthermore, once they severed all ties with their employers, it would have been unlikely that they would have been subsequently placed at an actionable detriment. CEE movers' being accustomed to frequently working in temporary positions and in precarious labour arrangements also likely made many more accepting of such treatment, and dissuaded some from pursuing potential victimisation claims.

In the one notable case where a CEE worker successfully asserted a victimisation claim, it was backed by plentiful evidence, and the respondent could not present convincing support for a non-discriminatory reason for her dismissal. In aforementioned *Krupa*, the respondent had dismissed the claimant, a warehouse cleaner, after she had sent three emails to the company's CEO to complain about the management's breaches of their legal obligations and unlawful behaviours—including poor treatment of Polish workers. The respondent argued that the claimant had been dismissed due to her poor skill set, being costly (as an agency employee), and being 'obstructive' and 'annoying'. The tribunal noted that there was no evidence of her poor skill set and no explanation as to why she, as opposed to other agency employees, was too costly. After applying all elements of the statutory test, the tribunal inferred that her protected disclosures had a material effect on her dismissal because the respondent had found her 'annoying' and a 'nuisance' at least in part due to her grievances.

Language Rule Claims

Language rules that prohibit speaking languages other than English at work might support harassment, indirect discrimination, or direct discrimination claims, depending on the specific circumstances of each case. The few reported

---

215 E.g., aforementioned *Jutrenzka v Chinnocks Wharf Management Co Ltd*.

claims asserted by CEE workers in this context indicate somewhat inconsistent judicial analysis which often hinged on nuanced factual details and which was susceptible to judicial discretion and subjective interpretation. For example, some respondents who had targeted specific employees for not using English were found not to have breached the Equality Act if claimants were judged to speak English sufficiently well. Respondents could also avoid liability by phrasing a warning to speak English only in a way that did not explicitly refer to a claimant's native language. Such judicial approaches would have likely disadvantaged CEE claimants, especially if adjudicators were guided by majoritarian values and perspectives. Furthermore, it was oftentimes complaints (of feeling excluded), made by co-workers who did not share the claimants' CEE ethnicity, that had led to arguably discriminatory language rules. Given how widespread anti-CEE sentiment was in the UK, one can only assume that CEE workers were subjected to such complaints and resultant potentially discriminatory treatment more often than reported caselaw indicates.

English-only rules appeared more likely to constitute indirect discrimination when they were not rationally justified by health and safety concerns—and thus failed the proportionality test. Notable examples include aforementioned *Skwarczynska*, in which the employer rejected (with no justification) the claimant's request for an interpreter to be used during disciplinary hearings. Similarly, in *Sokolova v Humdinger Ltd*,[216] a Latvian production operative at a food supplier company successfully asserted indirect discrimination based on not being offered, and not being allowed to bring, an interpreter to any of her grievance and disciplinary meetings. The tribunal concluded that this placed 'those of Latvian nationality and/or those who did not speak English as a native language' at a particular disadvantage which the employer could not show to be justified. Arguably, the outcome of these two cases might have hinged on how particularly reprehensible the tribunal had found the denial of the right to an interpreter during disciplinary meetings.

However, even if English-only rules were not justified by health and safety concerns but instead were linked to an employer's animus towards claimant's national group, they were sometimes deemed not to constitute indirect discrimination, especially if claimants were judged to have sufficient English skills. For example, in *Konieczna v Whitelink Seafoods Ltd*,[217] the claim of indirect discrimination was dismissed where a Polish HR assistant at a food-processing factory was not allowed to speak Polish during HR meetings with Polish staff who did not speak English. The blanket English-only rule was adopted after the claimant had been working for the respondent for a while and it could not be justified by health and safety concerns as it was applied away from the factory floor. Her supervisors forced her to use interpreters when meeting with Polish employees who did not speak English. The rule appeared to have been

---

216 Case No 1805866/2020, Employment Tribunal Hull, 23 July 2021.
217 Case No 4113137/2014, Employment Tribunal Aberdeen, 14 December 2015.

implemented as part of the management's attempts to dismiss the claimant, and was applied in an increasingly hostile environment filled with derogatory anti-foreigner and anti-Polish remarks by supervisors (which were found to support the claimant's harassment claim). The tribunal admitted that the claimant's speaking Polish in HR meetings was sensible and that this rule disadvantaged Polish workers who were not fluent in English. Despite this, the tribunal dismissed her indirect discrimination claim because she was able to speak English, and therefore she was found not to have been personally disadvantaged by the rule. This decision is not easy to reconcile with labour market realities faced by CEE movers. Specific CEE co-ethnics—often with only minimal English skills—tended to congregate at employment sites, particularly in low-paid sectors, and some specific employers' recruitment strategies even targeted specific CEE countries—hiring translators and line managers who spoke specific CEE languages to facilitate this process. At the same time, such employers could have been allowed to apply English-only rules, even if driven by apparent animus and with no legitimate justification, and could avoid liability for indirect discrimination if specific claimants were judged to possess 'sufficient' English skills.

Konieczna also illustrates the difficulty in asserting direct discrimination claims even in cases of English-only rules shown to have been applied in a way as to target specific claimants. The tribunal admitted that Ms Konieczna's speaking in Polish during HR meetings with non-English speaking Polish workers was 'practical'. Her direct discrimination claim was dismissed, however. The tribunal concluded that she was not treated less favourably than a hypothetical comparator (someone who did not speak Polish as her first language) would have been, because she spoke fluent English. The tribunal appears to have misinterpreted the test of direct discrimination. The claimant, after all, was targeted and ultimately dismissed and had been exposed to a generally hostile anti-Polish environment. This could have been sufficient to infer direct discrimination due to her being Polish. There was no objective basis for the tribunal to conclude that an HR assistant of another nationality would have been treated as poorly.

Outcomes of direct discrimination decisions appear somewhat inconsistent, however, as some CEE claimants singled out for speaking their native language were successful, especially where such prohibitions extended to casual conversations not part of work duties or if they were applied to target a specific employee only. For example, in *Rowinski v Kuehne and Nagel Ltd*,[218] a Polish team leader at a logistics company successfully asserted a direct discrimination claim against his employer who had a policy that only English was to be used 'during working activities'. Half of the company staff—including many Poles—did not speak English as a first language. When training two new Polish staff members who had difficulty understanding instructions in English, the claimant spoke Polish to them when he felt that this was necessary to ensure that they

218 Case No 3327184/2019, Employment Tribunal Reading, 10 December 2021.

learn correct work procedures. He also spoke Polish to a Polish colleague during a break. On both occasions, he was rudely and aggressively reprimanded by a supervisor not to use Polish, and his subsequent grievance about this treatment was rejected. The tribunal looked to the wording and the stated purpose of the employer's English-only rule—to ensure an inclusive working environment by using English only during all 'working activities'—and concluded that, on both occasions, the claimant did not infringe it.

Even when a specific employee was targeted, however, direct discrimination claims were not always easy to support, as illustrated by *Dziedziak v Future Electronics Ltd*,[219] the first case in which a language bar was found to support a claim of direct discrimination. After a non-Polish colleague had complained that she felt distracted by a Polish asset manager's work-related conversation in Polish, a supervisor instructed the latter not to speak 'in own language'. The employer had no general English-only policy. Other foreign-language speakers who had not been reprimanded for using their native language served as actual comparators. The respondent offered no explanation for this discrepancy in treatment. In finding for the claimant, the Employment Tribunal ruled that being forbidden to speak one's own language was intrinsically linked to one's nationality. Notably, the tribunal pointed out that the claim would have failed had the claimant been told not to speak Polish specifically. This is presumably because such an instruction could apply to non-Poles who speak Polish. I am not convinced by this reasoning. When a Pole is instructed not to speak Polish, such an admonition is intrinsically tied to her nationality, and a Pole is likely to feel an emotional attachment to using the Polish language. The same cannot be said of someone for whom Polish is a second language. Moreover, the tribunal observed that the claim would have failed had the claimant been told to speak only English, since that rule would be applicable to workers of any race. According to the tribunal, either of such instructions would have lacked the necessary causal link to her race. Thus, *Dziedziak* illustrates how a simple rephrasing by an employer of their instruction could offer an easy method of avoiding liability for direct discrimination.

Some CEE claimants were able to successfully assert harassment claims based on language rules, especially if they were not only singled out but also presented evidence of additional discriminatory treatment. For example, in *Exec Catering Ltd v Kaczynska*,[220] the tribunal found a harassment claim to be well-founded when a Polish café worker was told by her manager not to speak Polish to her Polish co-workers even though the employer did not have a general language rule. In aforementioned *Konieczna v Whitelink Seafoods Ltd*, the claim of harassment also succeeded due to cumulative evidence of not only being singled out and aggressively reprimanded for using Polish but also being exposed to several derogatory comments by British supervisors about 'f***ing Poles'. Similarly, in

219 UKEAT/0270/11/ZT, 28 February 2012.
220 UKEAT/0182/13/JOJ, 31 January 2014.

Jurga v Lavendale Montessori Ltd,[221] a Polish teacher and other Polish staff were repeatedly told by their supervisor not to speak Polish, even outside work duties, after another teacher had complained about feeling excluded. Given the widespread public antipathy towards CEE movers (by both Britons and workers of other CEE ethnicities), it is not unfathomable that co-workers might have been especially prone to feeling excluded by conversations in CEE languages. Notably, in *Jurga*, Italian workers were not given comparable warnings. The tribunal considered this harassment because, although the respondent had a blanket rule that only English should be spoken in a formal work setting, the claimant and other Poles were singled out, reprimanded individually, and instructed not to speak Polish even during break times.

Practical and Procedural Hurdles

Practical hurdles[222] in asserting and proving discrimination claims were often exacerbated in CEE movers' cases that I examined. Claimants were often employed in temporary and precarious arrangements which generally tend to be associated with exploitation and discrimination. Although tribunal discussions do not always mention details of specific employment arrangements, in many of the cases discussed at length above, CEE claimants engaged in precarious employment. For example, Obieglo and his co-claimant worked as seasonal fruit pickers; Skrzydlo, Matuzewicz, and Skarbek-Cielecka were employed through agencies; Grzyb had a ten-hour contract; and Kaczynska worked variable hours. Generally, those employed in 'low-skill', low-paid jobs tend to be overworked and focused on their day-to-day survival only.

Moreover, CEE movers often engaged in circular and temporary migration. A sense of being transient makes the burden of racist subjugation easier to bear. It also prompts workers to feel less invested in asserting their rights—an attitude likely exacerbated because employment discrimination claims take months, or often years, to resolve. Post-communist tendencies to mistrust authorities and to be submissive as employees likely also prompted some CEE movers not to pursue potential claims. Of course, those who work semi-lawfully or without proper documentation—which was also not uncommon among CEE movers— avoid making any complaints. Some CEE movers also subscribed to the view that their mistreatment could not be considered racism or discrimination because they are white.

---

221 Case No 3302379/2012, Employment Tribunal Watford, 30 September 2013.
222 Discrimination claims are generally challenging to assert and prove. Equality law has become more complex over time. Respondents possess most of the evidence, and typically have better access to legal representation. All claimants who are poor, not familiar with the British legal system, or not proficient at English are especially disadvantaged. Moreover, many victims of race discrimination hesitate to seek legal redress – due to fearing retaliation or doubting that they will be believed.

CEE claimants also tended to be especially impacted by procedural obstacles. Many of the claims that I reviewed were dismissed because they were out of time. Some were untimely due to claimants' having received incorrect guidance from the migration industry or friends. Poles and Hungarians, as well as Bulgarians and Romanians, have been documented to rely for advice on the unscrupulous migration industry that developed to cater to large CEE mover groups. Comprised of largely unregulated immigration, financial, travel, and recruitment agencies, communication businesses, ethnic media, and ethnic food shops, the migration industry is profit-driven, sometimes operated by organised crime groups, and not well informed about the legal regime. Furthermore, CEE movers' tendency to work surrounded by co-ethnics or other CEE nationals, whom they tended to mistrust and compete against, likely did little to facilitate their knowledge of worker rights or Employment Tribunal procedures. Notably, in *Ruda v TEi Ltd* (discussed earlier), the tribunal acknowledged that, in general, foreign workers—even those fluent in English and employed in skilled jobs—tend to suffer from unfamiliarity and a 'degree of vulnerability' with respect to British working practices. In most of the cases I reviewed, however, adjudicators were not sympathetic to CEE workers' out-of-time claims.

Overall, the cases I examined suggest that CEE claimants did not appear to fare well when trying to substantiate their discrimination claims. It is difficult to imagine that adjudicators would so easily dismiss or tolerate, without reprimand, some of the treatment experienced by unsuccessful CEE claimants—such as in *Kozakiewicz*,[223] *Quality Solicitors*,[224] *Kabzinski*,[225] *Januszewski*,[226] *Konieczna*,[227] or *Winczewski*[228]—had it been directed against non-white workers.

Conclusions

Labour needs two decades ago prompted the UK to support CEE states' accession and their nationals' (regulated) access to the UK labour market. As CEE movers became more and more visible, they provoked overt public opposition which led to incidents of racism and eventually contributed to the outcome of the Brexit referendum. Moreover, CEE movers became embedded within anti-CEE public, media, and political rhetoric and subsumed within the government's general anti-immigrant discourse. Their experiences of discrimination, disadvantage, and racialisation, and their unique positioning within the British hierarchies of privilege and disadvantage, were overlooked by the British equality discourse and inadequately addressed by statutory anti-discrimination provisions—in line with how they have been overlooked by the EU equality frameworkas discussed in the preceding chapter.

223 Refusing to recruit additional Poles to avoid becoming an 'all-Polish' store.
224 'She is Polish but very nice'.
225 Repeated bullying by being called a 'gypsy', 'cheap gypsy, and 'b*tch'.
226 Workers being called 'Polish bast*rd'.
227 Repeated comments about 'f*cking Poles'.
228 All Poles being paid less than British workers in identical roles.

The statutory definition of 'racial or ethnic origin' under the Equality Act 2010 is not sufficient in practice when it comes to protecting the rights of migrants or movers. Oftentimes, the reason for discrimination is due to a victim's being a migrant, being foreign, or—in the case of my study group—having generic 'Eastern European' origin. If courts define 'race' in an inflexible way, such cases fall beyond the grasp of equality law. Shortcomings of anti-discrimination measures also appeared compounded when applied in the context of CEE claimants—in part due to adjudicators' unpredictable and inconsistent analyses facilitated by imprecise wording of some statutory elements. Although, in general, interpretive leeway also permits adjudicators to apply statutory provisions as to benefit claimants, employment adjudicators did not appear to have frequently taken advantage of this in the context of CEE movers.

While I have not found consistent evidence of adjudicators' explicitly favouring employers over CEE workers, unfavourable decisions often relied on careless or erroneous application of statutory provisions or on references to irrelevant facts. It is not clear whether this reflects a poor grasp of relevant doctrine, majoritarian values and experiences, or adjudicators' personal prejudices. Moreover, CEE 'low-skill' movers' tendency to work for exploitative employers alongside many (if not predominantly) co-ethnics or with workers from other CEE states presented unique challenges in asserting their equality rights—which are not shared by all migrants or all socio-economically disadvantaged groups. Specifically, this made it more difficult to find comparators who were treated more favourably, and some adjudicators erroneously considered the employment of many CEE nationals as evidence of employers' lack of discrimination.

The inadequate attention of British equality law and discourse to the experiences of my study group might be attributable to the fact that CEE movers did not fit the UK's traditional approach towards 'race relations' and migration. Historically, mounting racism against immigrants and their increasingly permanent settlement would prompt both immigration restrictions and, eventually, greater equality protections. CEE movers complicated this dynamic. As a EU Member State, the UK could not impose direct mobility restrictions except for post-accession transitional derogations. Although the Brexit referendum promised to curb CEE nationals' numbers,[229] no attention has been devoted to the equality framework's responsiveness to their experiences. Of course, protecting white movers from discrimination would not have had much to contribute to the dominant group's interests, especially since CEE movers did not engage in overt conflict with other groups, many were in the UK temporarily, and they made significant contributions to the British purse despite (or due to) having inadequate equality protections. Moreover, the government might have felt a lesser sense of guilt when ignoring their rights. No post-colonial

---

229 And in fact, all EU nationals' access to the UK labour market has been significantly diminished under the current Points-Based System, especially among 'low-skilled' workers.

nostalgia applied in the movers' contexts, and their whiteness did bestow upon them (partial) access to privilege while also making prejudices and racism against them more challenging to conceptualise as actionable discrimination.

The position of CEE movers within the UK's equality framework also has implications for the EU project. Freedom of movement is intrinsically not free without better national responses to movers' racialisation and discrimination. Having enabled CEE workers' mobility and enacted the Race Equality Directive, the EU has stepped back from paying attention to what happens in host states to EU citizens who actually engage in mobility. Although its competence in affecting equality of outcomes is very limited, the EU does have the power to shape discourse, monitor inequalities, implement initiatives to support movers' integration, and point out shortcomings in how national equality regimes approach movers. It has largely remained silent,[230] however, even refraining from condemning post-referendum hate crimes against CEE movers which were brought to its attention. The EU should play a greater role in this area, particularly since CEE mobility to EU-14 states shows no signs of abating.

Bibliography

A v B & C, Case No 2403142/2017, Employment Tribunal Manchester, 4 February 2019

Anderson, Bridget (2013) *Us and Them?: The Dangerous Politics of Immigration Control* (Oxford: Oxford University Press)

Anderson, Bridget et al. (2006) *Fair Enough? Central and East European Migrants in Low-Wage Employment in the UK* (Oxford University: COMPAS)

Anderson, Bridget et al. (2008) *New EU Members? Migrant Workers' Challenges and Opportunities to UK Trades Unions: A Polish and Lithuanian Case Study* (Oxford University: COMPAS)

Angelov v Marston Group Ltd, Case No 3330861/2018, Employment Tribunal Reading, 15 April 2020

Antonucci, Lorenza and Simone Varriale (2020) Unequal Europe, unequal Brexit: How intra-European inequalities shape the unfolding and framing of Brexit, *Current Sociology* 68(1): 41–49

Balls, Ed (2010) We were wrong to let so many eastern Europeans in Britain, *The Guardian*, 5 June

Barnard, Catherine (2014) Enforcement of employment rights by migrant workers in the UK: The case of EU-8 nationals, in Cathryn Costello and Mark Freedland (eds) *Migrants at Work: Immigration and Vulnerability in Labour Law* 193–215 (Oxford: Oxford University Press)

Barnard, Catherine and Amy Ludlow (2016) Enforcement of employment rights by EU-8 workers in Employment Tribunals, *Industrial Law Journal* 45(1): 1–28

---

230 Unlike EU bodies, the independent European Commission against Racism and Intolerance has bemoaned Eastern Europeans' low labour market outcomes, condemned scaremongering by UKIP and Conservative MPs for contributing to public xenophobia, and recommended that integration measures target CEE movers. See European Commission against Racism and Intolerance (2016).

Barnard, Catherine and Amy Ludlow (2019) "Undeserving" EU Migrants "Milking Britain's Benefits"? EU citizens before social security tribunals, *Public Law* 2: 260–280
Barnard, Catherine et al. (2018) Beyond employment tribunals: Enforcement of employment rights by EU-8 migrant workers, *Industrial Law Journal* 47(2): 226–262
Barnard, Catherine et al. (2022) (Legal) Assistance in employment matters to low-paid EU migrant workers in the east of England, *Legal Studies* 42(3): 491–507
Barnard, Catherine et al. (2022a) The changing status of European Union nationals in the United Kingdom following Brexit: The lived experience of the European Union Settlement Scheme, *Social and Legal Studies* 31(3): 365–438
Barslund, Mikkel and Matthias Busse (2014) Labour mobility in the EU: Dynamics, patterns and policies, *Intereconomics* 49(3): 116–158
BBC News (2014) Andrew Marr's interview with David Cameron, 5 January, www.bbc.co.uk/news/av/uk-politics-25611459
BDW Trading Ltd v Kopec, UKEAT/0197/19/OO, 13 December 2019
Besz v Multi Packaging Solutions Limited, Case No 2602118/2016, Employment Tribunal Nottingham, 26 September 2017
Bienkov, Adam (2013) Nigel Farage: Romanians want to move to a 'civilised country', *Politics*, 6 September
Blachnicka-Ciacek, Dominika and Irma Budginaite-Mackine (2022) The ambiguous lives of 'the other whites': Class and racialisation of Eastern European migrants in the UK, *The Sociological Review* 70(6): 1081–1099
Blair, Tony (2004) Speech to the Confederation of British Industry on Migration, 27 April, www.guardian.co.uk/politics/2004/apr/27/immigrationpolicy.speeches
Blinder, Scott and Lindsay Richards (2018) *UK Public Opinion toward Immigration: Overall Attitudes and Level of Concern* (Oxford University: Migration Observatory)
Border and Immigration Agency (2007) *Accession Monitoring Report*, May 2004—September 2007
Borodinova v Stateside Food Limited, Case No 2407202/2021, Employment Tribunal Manchester, 9 December 2022
Bouzir v Country Style Foods Ltd, [2011] EWCA Civ 1519, 8 December 2011
Brah, Avtar and Ann Phoenix (2004) Ain't I a woman? Revisiting intersectionality, *Journal of International Women's Studies* 5(3): 75–86
Burnett, Jon (2011) Eastern European workers under attack, 26 May (Institute of Race Relations), www.irr.org.uk/news/eastern-european-workers-under-attack/
Cabinet Office (2001) *Consultation Paper: Towards Equality and Diversity—Implementing the Employment and Race Directives* (London: HM Government)
CG v Department for Communities in Northern Ireland, Case C-709/20, ECLI:EU:C:2021:602
Ciupijus, Zinovijus (2012) EU Citizens or Eastern European labour migrants? The peculiar case of Central Eastern Europeans in Britain, *Politeja* 2/3: 29–46
Ciupijus, Zinovijus (2012a) Talking about 'Labour Camps' in post-2004 Europe: Lived experiences of work, transnational mobility and exploitation among Central Eastern European migrants, *EMECON* 1: 1–12
Cohen, Robin (2006) *Migration and its Enemies: Global Capital, Migrant Labour and the Nation-State* (Farnham: Ashgate)
Commission v United Kingdom of Great Britain and Northern Ireland, Case 3008/14, ECLI:EU:C:2016:436

Commission on Integration and Cohesion (2007) Our Shared Future, www.equallyours.org.uk/commission-on-integration-and-cohesion-final-report/
Commission on Race and Ethnic Disparities (2021) The Report, https://assets.publishing.service.gov.uk/government/uploads/system/uploads/attachment_data/file/974507/20210331_-_CRED_Report_-_FINAL_-_Web_Accessible.pdf
Cook, Joanne et al. (2010) The experiences of accession 8 migrants in England: Motivations, work and agency, *International Migration* 49(2): 54–79
Crenshaw, Kimberlé (2011) Race, reform, and retrenchment, *German Law Journal* 12(1): 247–284
Currie, Samantha (2009) Challenging the UK rules on the rights of EU8 workers, *Journal of Social Welfare and Family Law* 31(1): 47–58
Currie, Samantha (2022) Scapegoats and guinea pigs: Free movement as a pathway to confined labour market citizenship for European Union accession migrants in the UK, *Industrial Law Journal* 51(2): 277–317
Department of Social Security (1999) *Opportunity for All: Tackling Poverty and Social Exclusion, First Annual Report*, Cm 4445 (London)
Discrimination Law Review (2007) *A Framework for Fairness: Proposals for a Single Equality Bill for Great Britain—A Consultation Paper* (London: Department for Communities and Local Government)
Drinkwater, Stephen et al. (2009) Poles apart? Enlargement and the labour market outcomes of immigrants in the United Kingdom, *International Migration* 47(1): 161–190
Dustmann, Christian and Tommaso Frattini (2014) The Fiscal Effects of Immigration to the UK, *The Economic Journal* 124: F593–F643
Dziedziak v Future Electronics Ltd, UKEAT/0270/11/ZT, 28 February 2012
Dzierzanowski v Cranswick Country Foods Plc, Case No 1808685/2018, Employment Tribunal Hull, 22 March 2019
East European Advice Centre (2013) *East Europeans in London: A Peer Led Study of the Issues Faced by East Europeans in London Relating Housing, Employment, Household Income and Support Needs* (London)
East European Resource Centre (2018) *Eastern Europeans at Work: Lessons from Outreach 2017*, www.eerc.org.uk/wordpress/wpcontent/uploads/2018/02/Report-Eastern-Europeans-at-work-Lessons-from-outreach.pdf
Equalities Office (2008) *Framework for a Fairer Future—The Equality Bill*, Cm 7431 (London)
Equalities Review (2007) *Fairness and Freedom: The Final Report of the Equalities Review* (London)
Equality Act 2010 (London: HMSO)
Equality and Human Rights Commission (2011) Employment Statutory Code of Practice, www.equalityhumanrights.com/sites/default/files/employercode.pdf
Equality and Human Rights Commission (2017) When prejudice turns into discrimination and unlawful behaviour, 29 July, www.equalityhumanrights.com/en/our-work/blogs/when-prejudice-turns-discrimination-and-unlawful-behaviour
Equality and Human Rights Commission (2018) Is England fairer? The state of equality and human rights 2018, www.equalityhumanrights.com/sites/default/files/is-england-fairer-2018.pdf
Equality and Human Rights Commission (2020) Recruitment of workers into lowpaid occupations and industries: An evidence review, www.equalityhumanrights.com/sites/default/files/recruitment-of-workers-into-low-paid-occupations-and-industries.pdf

European Commission against Racism and Intolerance (2016) ECRI Report on the United Kingdom, 4 October (Council of Europe), www.refworld.org/docid/5836d07c7.html
Evidence for Equality National Survey (Centre on the Dynamics of Ethnicity), www.ethnicity.ac.uk/research/projects/evens/ (last accessed 23 June 2023)
Exec Catering Ltd v Kaczynska, UKEAT/0182/13/JOJ, 31 January 2014
Explanatory Notes (2010) Equality Act 2010, Revised Edition (London), www.legislation.gov.uk/ukpga/2010/15/pdfs/ukpgaen_20100015_en.pdf
Fekete, Liz (2001) The emergence of xeno-racism, *Race and Class* 43(2): 23–40
Fekete, Liz (2009) *A Suitable Enemy: Racism, Migration and Islamophobia in Europe* (London: Pluto)
Fernández-Reino, Mariña and Cinzia Rienzo (2022) *Migrants in the UK Labour Market: An Overview* (Oxford: The Migration Observatory)
Fic, Tatiana et al. (2011) *Labour Mobility within the EU—The Impact of Enlargement and the Functioning of the Transitional Arrangements*, Study Commissioned by the Directorate-General for Employment, Social Affairs, and Equal Opportunities (London: National Institute of Economic and Social Research)
Fitzpatrick, Peter (1987) Racism and the innocence of law, *Journal of Law and Society* 14(1): 119–132
Fox, Jon et al. (2012) The racialization of the new European migration to the UK, *Sociology* 46(4): 680–695
Fratila v Secretary of State for Work and Pensions, [2021] UKSC 53
Freeman, Alan David (1990) Antidiscrimination law: The view from 1989, *Tulane Law Review* 64(6): 1407–1442
Glasgow City Council v Zafar, [1998] ICR 120
Glogowska v F A Gill Ltd, Case No 1303719/2019, Employment Tribunal Birmingham, 26 October 2020
Grant v HM Land Registry & EHRC, [2011] EWCA Civ 769
Griffin v Hyder Brothers Ltd, Case 2406224/2011, Employment Tribunal, 25 April 2012
Grzyb v Lidl, Case No 2600945/2016, Employment Tribunal Leicester, 25 November 2017
Guma, Taulant (2020) Turning citizens into immigrants: state practices of welfare 'cancellations' and document retention among EU nationals living in Glasgow, *Journal of Ethnic and Migration Studies* 46(13): 2647–2663
Halej, Julia Oktawia (2014) *Other Whites, White Others: East European Migrants and the Boundaries of Whiteness*, PhD Dissertation (UCL, School of Slavonic and East European Studies)
Hansard, Black and Minority Ethnic People: Workplace Issues, vol 771, debated on 3 May 2016 (House of Lords)
Hansard, Immigration, vol 598, debated on 9 July 2015 (House of Commons)
Hansard, Immigration (Bulgaria and Romania), vol 561, debated on 22 April 2013 (House of Commons)
Hansard Report, 18 November 2010, vol 518, Fiona Mactaggart
Hansard Report, House of Lords, 18 November 2010, vol 722, Baroness Thornton
Hansard Report, House of Lords, 26 April 2011, col WA39, Baroness Garden of Frognal
Harris, Katie (2013) Forced labour in the UK: 'There was no escape. I lived every day in fear', *The Guardian*, 20 November
Hepple, Bob (2014) *Equality: The Legal Framework* (Oxford: Hart)
Hewage v Grampian Health Board, [2012] UKSC 37, 25 July 2012

Hills, John et al. (eds) (2009) *Towards a More Equal Society? Poverty, Inequality and Policy Since 1997* (Bristol: Policy Press)

HM Government, Equalities Office, www.gov.uk/government/organisations/government-equalities-office (last accessed 24 June 2023)

HM Government, Equality Hub, www.gov.uk/government/organisations/the-equality-hub (last accessed 24 June 2023)

HM Government, Ethnicity Facts and Figures, www.ethnicity-facts-figures.service.gov.uk/ (last accessed 24 June 2023)

HM Government, Race Disparity Unit, www.gov.uk/government/organisations/race-disparity-unit (last accessed 24 June 2023)

HM Government (2017) Press release—New hate crime package to target groups at need, 26 January, www.gov.uk/government/news/new-hate-crime-package-to-target-groups-at-need

HM Government (2019) Interventions supporting ethnic minority labour market participation: part one, www.gov.uk/government/publications/ethnic-minority-labour-market-participation-interventions-part-1/interventions-supporting-ethnic-minority-labour-market-participation-part-one

HM Government (2022) Inclusive Britain: Government response to the Commission on Race and Ethnic Disparities, CP 625, www.gov.uk/government/publications/inclusive-britain-action-plan-government-response-to-the-commission-on-race-and-ethnic-disparities/inclusive-britain-government-response-to-the-commission-on-race-and-ethnic-disparities

HM Government (2023) Inclusive Britain update report, www.gov.uk/government/publications/inclusive-britain-update-report/inclusive-britain-update-report

HM Revenue & Customs (2016) Statistics on recently arrived non-UK EEA nationals subject to income tax and National Insurance contributions or receiving HMRC administered benefits, https://assets.publishing.service.gov.uk/government/uploads/system/uploads/attachment_data/file/522811/HMRC-Ad_Hoc_Stats_Release-EEA_Nationals_net_contribution_2013-2014.pdf

Home Office (1975) Command Paper 6234: On Racial Discrimination (London)

hooks, bell (1982) *Ain't I A Woman? Black Women and Feminism* (London: Pluto Press)

House of Lords Debates, 15 December 2009, col 1407

Ipsos MORI (2007) *Immigration Poll*, 2 November, www.ipsos.com/ipsos-mori/en-uk/immigration-poll

Islam, Faisal and Lucy Hooker (2023) Sir Keir Starmer says he's not talking down UK economy, *BBC News*, 27 February, www.bbc.co.uk/news/business-64780112

Januszewski v Ultima Furniture Systems Limited, Case No 1805191/2019, Employment Tribunal Sheffield, 17 February 2021

Johns, Michael (2014) *The New Minorities of Europe: Social Cohesion in the European Union* (Lanham: Lexington Books)

Johnston, Ron et al. (2015) East versus West? Over-qualification and earnings among the UK's european migrants, *Journal of Ethnic and Migration Studies* 41(2): 196–218

Jones, Katharine (2014) It was a whirlwind. A lot of people made a lot of money: The role of agencies in facilitating migration from Poland into the UK between 2004 and 2008, *Central and Eastern European Migration Review* 3(2): 105–125

Jurga v Lavendale Montessori Ltd, Case No 3302379/2012, Employment Tribunal Watford, 30 September 2013

Juszczyk v Kettle Produce Ltd, Case No S/4103971/2016, Employment Tribunal Dundee, 2 March 2017

Jutrenzka v Chinnocks Wharf Management Co Ltd, Case No 3201751/2019, Employment Tribunal East London, 31 March 2022

Kabzinski v Vistajet International Ltd, Case No 2200745/2021, Employment Tribunal London Central, 31 October 2022

Kentish, Benjamin (2017) Oxfordshire fishery facing legal action over 'NO Eastern Europeans' sign, *The Independent*, 19 December

Kofman, Eleonore et al. (2009) *The Equality Implications of Being a Migrant in Britain*, Research Report 19 (London: Equality and Human Rights Commission)

Kolaitis v DX Network Services Ltd, Case No 1300522/2019, Employment Tribunal Birmingham, 1 February 2021

Konieczna v Whitelink Seafoods Ltd, Case No 4113137/2014, Employment Tribunal Aberdeen, 14 December 2015

Kosik v Montgomery Transport Ltd, Employment Tribunal Manchester, 2015

Kowal and Obieglo v Peter Leslie & Sons t/a David Leslie Fruits, Case Nos 113343/09 and 113344/09, Employment Tribunal Dundee, 6 April 2010

Kowalewska-Zietek v Lancashire Teaching Hospitals NHS Foundation Trust, UKEAT/0269/15/JOJ, 21 January 2016

Kozakiewicz v Futon Ltd, Case No 2600264/2017, Employment Tribunal Nottingham, 12 December 2017

Krupa v B& MRetail Ltd, Case No 2400660/2016, Employment Tribunal Liverpool, 28 March 2017

Kubal, Agnieszka (2012) *Socio-Legal Integration: Polish Post-2004 EU Enlargement Migrants in the United Kingdom* (Farnham: Ashgate)

Lacey, Nicola (1998) *Unspeakable Subjects: Feminist Essays in Legal and Social Theory* (Oxford: Hart)

Law Society v Bahl, [2004] EWCA Civ 1070

Lawrence, Felicity (2012) Workers who collected Freedom Food chickens 'were trafficked and beaten', *The Guardian*, 29 October

Levine-Rasky, Cynthia (2011) Intersectionality theory applied to whiteness and middle-classness, *Social Identities* 17(2): 239–253

Lewicki, Aleksandra (2023) East–west inequalities and the ambiguous racialisation of 'Eastern Europeans', *Journal of Ethnic and Migration Studies* 49(6): 1481–1499

Lewis, Miranda (2005) Asylum: Understanding public attitudes (Institute for Public Policy Research), www.ippr.org/publications/asylum-understanding-public-attitudes

MacKenzie, Robert and Chris Forde (2009) The rhetoric of the 'good worker' versus the realities of employers' use and the experiences of migrant workers, *Work, Employment and Society* 23(1): 142–159

Matuzewicz v 2 Sisters Food Group Ltd, Case No 2500043/17, Employment Tribunal North Shields, 10 August 2017

McColgan, Aileen (2017) Country Report—Non-discrimination: United Kingdom (European Network of Legal Experts in the Non-discrimination Field), https://publications.europa.eu/en/publication-detail/-/publication/188dafa2-8168-11e7-b5c6-01aa75ed71a1

McKay, Sonia (2009) Employer use of migrant labour—motivations, experiences and HR responses, Research Paper 03/09 (Advisory, Conciliation and Arbitration Service), https://ec.europa.eu/migrant-integration/sites/default/files/2009-12/docl_11355_460027890.pdf

Mechkarov v Citibank N.A., UKEAT/0006/19, 31 July 2019

Medrysa v The London Borough of Tower Hamlets, UKEAT/0208/20, 29 April 2021

Michalak v The Mid Yorkshire Hospitals NHS Trust, Case No 1808465/2007, Employment Tribunal Leeds, 14 June 2010

Ministry of Defence v DeBique [2010] IRLR 471, Employment Appeal Tribunal, 12 October 2009

Minute by Sir John Pedder, 28 May 1924, HO 45/24765/432156/17

Mirga v Secretary of State for Work and Pensions, [2016] UKSC 1

Moore, Helen (2013) Shades of whiteness? English villagers, Eastern European migrants and the intersection of race and class in rural England, *Critical Race and Whiteness Studies* 9(1): 1–19

National Equality Panel (2010) *An Anatomy of Economic Inequality in the UK: Report of the National Equality Panel* (London: Equalities Office), https://eprints.lse.ac.uk/28344/1/CASEreport60.pdf

Nazarczyk v TJ Morris Limited, Case No 2401275/2017, Employment Tribunal Liverpool, 10 August 2017

Nemec v Concept Recruitment Group Ltd, Case No 1800244/2022, Employment Tribunal Leeds, 14 November 2022

Nikolova v M & P Enterprises London Ltd, UKEAT/0293/15/DM, 4 February 2016

Osborne, George (2011) Chancellor of the Exchequer, George Osborne MP Budget Statement, 23 March

Parutis, Violetta (2011) White, European, and hardworking: East European migrants' relationships with other communities in London, *Journal of Baltic Studies* 42(2): 263–288

Patmalniece v Secretary of State for Work and Pensions, [2011] UKSC 11

Pemberton, Simon and Claire Stevens (2010) The recruitment and retention of Central and Eastern European migrant workers in the United Kingdom: A panacea or a problem under the new policies of 'managed migration'?, *Regional Studies* 44(9): 1289–1300

Petrica v Central London Community Healthcare NHS Trust, UKEAT/0059/20/AT, 12 May 2021

Prasil v Orchard House Foods, Case 3400534/2014, Employment Tribunal Cambridge, 12 April 2018

Procek v Oakford Farms Ltd, Employment Tribunal Liverpool, 2009

Pruitt, Lisa R (2015) Who's afraid of white class migrants? On denial, discrediting, and disdain (and toward a richer conception of diversity), *Columbia Journal of Gender and Law* 31: 196–254

Quality Solicitors v Tunstall, UKEAT/0105/14/RN, 28 July 2014

R (E) v Governing Body of JFS, [2009] UKSC 15

R (On the Application of Gureckis and others) v Secretary of State for the Home Department, Case CO/1440/2017, [2017] EWHC 3298

R (UNISON) v Lord Chancellor, [2017] UKSC 51

Richmond Pharmacology v Dhaliwal, EAT/0458/08, [2009] IRLR 336

Rowinski v Kuehne and Nagel Ltd, Case No 3327184/2019, Employment Tribunal Reading, 10 December 2021

Ruda v TEi Ltd, Case No 1807582/10, Employment Tribunal Leeds, 23 August 2011

Rzepnikowska, Alina (2019) Racism and xenophobia experienced by Polish migrants in the UK before and after Brexit vote, *Journal of Ethnic and Migration Studies* 45(1): 61–77

Samaluk, Barbara (2014) Whiteness, ethnic privilege and migration: A Bourdieuian Framework, *Journal of Managerial Psychology* 29(4): 370–388

Sampson, Thomas (2017) Brexit: The economics of international disintegration, *Journal of Economic Perspectives* 31(4): 163–184

Secretary of State for Work and Pensions v Gubeladze, [2019] UKSC 31

Sime, Daniela et al. (2022) Performing whiteness: Central and Eastern European young people's experiences of xenophobia and racialisation in the UK post-Brexit, *Journal of Ethnic and Migration Studies* 48(19): 4527–4546

Sirkeci, Ibrahim et al. (2018) Barriers for highly qualified A8 immigrants in the UK labour market, *Work, Employment and Society* 32(5): 906–924

Skarbek-Cielecka v Holy Rise Consultants Ltd, Case No 2303648/2017, Employment Tribunal London South, 9 August 2019

Skrzydlo v CRC Recruitment Ltd, Case No 3400728/2016, Employment Tribunal Cambridge, 3 April 2018

Skwarczynska v Sturts Community Trust, Case No 1400540/2019, Employment Tribunal Southampton, 12 October 2021

Sokolova v Humdinger Ltd, Case No 1805866/2020, Employment Tribunal Hull, 23 July 2021

Solanke, Iyiola (2009) *Making Anti-Racial Discrimination Law: A Comparative History of Social Action and Anti-Racial Discrimination Law* (London: Routledge)

Solanke, Iyiola (2011) Infusing the silos in the Equality Act 2010 with synergy, *Industrial Law Journal* 40(4): 336–358

Solomos, John (1989) From Equal Opportunity to Anti-Racism: Racial inequality and the limits of reform, Policy Paper in Ethnic Relations No 17 (University of Warwick, Centre for Research in Ethnic Relations)

Soutar, Liam (2023) The 'banter' excuse just keeps popping up in employment tribunals, 28 April, www.hrgrapevine.com/content/article/2023-04-27-the-banter-excuse-just-keeps-popping-up-in-employment-tribunals

Sumption, Madeleine and Will Somerville (2010) *The UK's New Europeans: Progress and Challenges Five Years After Accession* (London: Equality and Human Rights Commission)

Taiwo v Olaigbe and *Onu v Akwiwu*, [2016] UKSC 31, 22 June 2016

Tan, Clarissa (2014) Britain has many major problems—Racism isn't one of them, *The Spectator*, 15 February

The Scotsman (2007) Ex-goalie guilty of attempted murder, 7 August

The Telegraph (2009) Phil Woolas admits government got it wrong over eastern European immigration, 13 May

the3million (2020) The written evidence submitted to the UK Parliament (FRE0048), https://committees.parliament.uk/writtenevidence/7861/pdf/

Unite Legal Services (2015) Polish worker receives £14,850 settlement in discrimination case thanks to Unite Legal Services, 30 April, www.unitelegalservices.org/news-stories/polish-worker-receives-14-850-settlement-in-discrimination-case-thanks-to-unite-legal-services

Van Dijk, Teun (2001) Critical discourse analysis, in Deborah Schiffrin et al. (eds) *The Handbook of Discourse Analysis* 352–371 (Oxford: Blackwell)

Vargas-Silva, Carlos et al. (2016) The impacts of international migration on poverty in the UK (Joseph Rowntree Foundation), www.jrf.org.uk/report/impacts-international-migration-poverty-uk

Vote Leave (undated) www.voteleavetakecontrol.org/why_vote_leave.html (last accessed 12 May 2023)

Vote Leave (2016) Economist interviews Vote Leave Campaign Director Dominic Cummings, 22 January, www.voteleavetakecontrol.org/economist_interviews_vote_leave_campaign_director_dominic_cummings.html

Wadsworth, Jonathan et al. (2016) Brexit and the Impact of Immigration on the UK, Brexit Analysis Paper No 5 (LSE: Centre for Economic Performance), https://cep.lse.ac.uk/pubs/download/brexit05.pdf

Wilk v Wackers, Case No 3313268/2019, Employment Tribunal Watford, 11 March 2020

Winczewski v MAM Transport Services Ltd, Case No 3311620/2021, Employment Tribunal Cambridge, 19 January 2023

Wodak, Ruth and Martin Reisigl (2001) Discourse and racism, in Deborah Schiffrin et al. (eds) *The Handbook of Discourse Analysis* 372–397 (Oxford: Blackwell)

Work and Pensions Committee (2009) The Equality Bill: how disability equality fits within a single Equality Act, 3rd Report of Session 2008–2009, vol I, 29 April, www.publications.parliament.uk/pa/cm200809/cmselect/cmworpen/158/158i.pdf

Wreczycka v Care In Style Limited, Case 3200984/2017, Employment Tribunal East London, 7 March 2018

Wu, Frank H (2002) *Yellow: Race in America Beyond Black and White* (New York: Basic Books)

Younge, Gary (2016) 'Eggs thrown, windows smashed, a family attacked in a park': How Brexit impacted east Europeans, *The Guardian*, 31 August

Zalewska v Department of Social Development, [2008] UKHL 67

Zaluski v NSL Ltd, Case No 2305243/2021, Employment Tribunal, 24 February 2023

Chapter 5

Conclusions

Fractures and Peripheries, Past and Future

On 23 February 2018, Jozef Chovanec, a 38-year-old Slovak entrepreneur whose business included hiring Slovak workers for Belgian construction projects, was trying to board a flight at Charleroi Airport in Brussels. An altercation with airport staff ensued after he apparently failed to produce his boarding pass. As a result, he was detained and taken to a police cell. He died several days later at a hospital after suffering from cardiac arrest and coma. Security camera footage of the incident leaked in 2020 revealed what had happened before he was transported to the hospital. After being put in a cell, he banged his head against the wall until it was covered in blood. In response, six police officers entered his cell to restrain him. He was placed face-down on the floor, his face covered with a blanket, and an officer knelt on his chest for about 16 minutes. Meanwhile, another officer made a mock Nazi salute, and the remaining officers smiled in amusement. Next, medical personnel were called, and, approximately 40 minutes later, Mr Chovanec was given a sedative injection.

The release of this footage led to public outrage in both Belgium and Slovakia. Slovak Members of the European Parliament asked the Parliament to bring to justice perpetrators of these acts, and the Slovak government called for the EU Justice Commissioner's involvement in the Belgian investigation. However, EU representatives declined these pleas on the grounds that the EU does not have competence to interfere in Member States' domestic affairs. As Black Lives Matter protests broke out in the United States, prompting a global movement against police brutality, Slovakia's President labelled the incident a matter of police brutality. In early 2023, the Belgian Public Prosecutor's Office announced that none of the six police officers would be prosecuted. The decision did not produce a mass outcry, and it was barely noticed by media and political commentators. My hope is that this book helps to explain both how such an incident could have occurred and how it failed to result in a mass protest movement. Specifically, I submit that Mr Chovanec's death and its aftermath must be situated within the western-centric construction of the EU project, the ongoing peripheralisation of CEE states and nationals through discourse and policies, and the shortcomings of approaching whiteness as a homogeneous construct.

DOI: 10.4324/9781003175377-5

Whereas generally, cleavage between the EU's lofty fundamental-rights ideals and the reality of its policies has been attributed to the EU's limited competence and its inability to enforce its values or to ensure Member State compliance, I propose that the EU project has been founded on and propagates a reality that differentiates between the west and the east, benefiting the former. This has had repercussions on inequalities built into the Eastern Enlargement process and on CEE nationals' unequal experiences of mobility. Anti-CEE racism forms an integral part of the western-centric EU project as reflected in EU discourses and policies that have marginalised the CEE region and its nationals—placing them at the periphery of proper 'Europe'. Brexit was simply one manifestation of this sentiment—a misguided outlet for contestations about east-to-west mobility.

As my discussion in the preceding chapters illustrates, the EU equality regime, the enlargement project, and CEE nationals' mobility have been embedded within values and ideologies that prioritise neo-liberal economic expansionism and interests of the western Member States. Despite abstract myths of a progressive, benevolent, and inevitable integration project based on respect for fundamental rights, in identity discourses, EU-15 states have served as a synecdoche for the entire 'Europe' and the entire EU, and the CEE region has been pushed to the periphery. In the process, CEE nationals have been othered—reinforcing historical east-west power differentials. Power inequalities between the two parts of Europe were prominently displayed, and reinforced, during the Eastern Enlargement process. The one-sided political, legal, and economic course was accompanied by EU rhetoric which othered the CEE region as being in need of 'civilising' through westernisation. Inequalities built into the Enlargement process became reinforced through EU institutions' and EU-15 states' initiatives to limit CEE workers' access to mobility and to social rights, thereby creating hierarchies of EU citizenship and of whiteness within the EU.

CEE nationals' unequal access to the freedom of movement right has been accompanied by their exploitation and discrimination in receiving EU-15 states, which have greatly benefited economically from their labour. It is true that all migrants face challenges, especially at first, but CEE movers have been unique: the overall EU project has been framed as egalitarian, and, unlike most historical migrant groups, movers have been endowed with residence and employment rights on arrival. —Moreover, racial equality discourse has not recognised the need to protect them. Instead, in equality discussions, white race typically appears homogeneous and invisible, normalised as privileged. This reproduces white privilege accruing to those who fit the western norm while silencing marginalised and racialised whites and legitimising existing social structures and class relations. This impact has been amplified by anti-discrimination policies which have been especially unfit for protecting CEE movers' rights. More generally, the right to equality, which has been intimately linked to the right of free movement, reflects western economic and political concerns and is far removed from the EU's fundamental rights narratives. The case study of how CEE movers were approached in the UK while it was still a Member State has helped to reinforce these findings while providing an illustration of the lived experience of CEE nationals' mobility.

My approach throughout the book illustrates how a more nuanced application of critical whiteness studies can be greatly beneficial to analyses of EU and Member State policies and discourses in the context of contemporary mobilities. Whiteness and white privilege of the (western) dominant group have been actively reproduced by excluding and racialising white CEE movers through discourse; laws; and economic, political, and cultural structures. By contextualising CEE nationals' mobility within both historical and contemporary transnational power dynamics, my analysis arrived at a more nuanced picture of today's micro-level ethnic power relations which are shaping the boundaries of whiteness and its time- and place-specific fractures.

Racism and the concept of race cannot be fully addressed without also paying attention to the role of capitalism and economic exploitation, class, and other forms of oppression[1] not only within countries but also transnationally. In 2017, the then-President of France warned the then-Polish Prime Minister: 'You have principles, we [EU] have structural funds'. As my findings indicate, CEE nationals' mobility experiences might be best understood through the intersection of (1) the CEE states' and their nationals' positioning within EU-wide economic hierarchies, and (2) the western conceptualisation of the CEE region as ethnically inferior—not belonging to proper 'Europe' and not fully 'white'. EU and western state policies limiting access to welfare benefits, imposing financial tests to access the right of free movement, and encouraging precarious employment have disproportionately disadvantaged CEE nationals—especially those who are poorer or lower-paid. It is not their class alone, however, that can explain their experience of inequalities and racialisation. Notably, non-CEE Member States that have struggled economically—such as Portugal or Greece—and their nationals have not elicited as much opposition or exclusionary discourse as CEE nationals have. Moreover, as my review of employment discrimination claims filed by CEE nationals in the UK indicated, even highly-skilled, well-paid, middle-class CEE workers have been targets of racial discrimination due to being perceived as inherently lesser because of their eastern ethnicities. Thus, it is the various intersecting fractures within whiteness and within class that have been affecting CEE movers' experiences of inequality and discrimination. Future research, as well as policymakers and adjudicators, must take account of this.

By problematising the construction of white privilege and disrupting public and private inclinations to essentialise whiteness, the book serves the central goal of critical whiteness studies—of disrupting white privilege,[2] helping to subvert it, and taking a step towards undermining racism. White privilege is dangerous and whiteness is a double-edged sword.[3] Unmarked skin colour has

1 See generally Valdes (2002).
2 See generally Lopez (2005).
3 See, e.g., Bridges (2019).

been facilitating CEE nationals' post-war migration and post-2004 mobility to western states and has made them preferred for customer-facing jobs. However, it has also alleviated any unease about victimising them through unequal policies and about oppressing them with racist language and discriminatory behaviours which would not as easily escape condemnation if directed against non-whites. Of course, critical reflections on fractures within whiteness should not lose sight of a detailed examination of white supremacy, which must be dismantled. Both methodologies must be set within collaborative praxis among all those who engage in anti-capitalist, anti-colonial, and intersectional scholarship and equality advocacy.

As Fitzpatrick expounded, it is through the otherness of the primitive and non-western that the occident's legal structures get bestowed modern and praiseworthy attributes.[4] Colonialism has been the extreme example of this project, characterised by western exploitation of colonised states and its peoples accompanied by the application of allegedly modern western structures to redeem those perceived as 'savage'. I argue that the west's ongoing relationship with the CEE region, with many markers of coloniality, reflects and reinforces this construction of western law. The Eastern Enlargement was framed as the west's rescuing of the east and benevolently returning it to 'Europe'. Meanwhile, colonial-like EU processes of economic extraction, unequal policies, and the silencing of CEE voices—embedded within the long-standing western approach of othering the east—have shaped, at least in part, post-accession dynamics of east/west inequality and of racialising mobile CEE citizens in EU-15 states. Although applying postcolonial theory to a context far divorced from its original milieu might not seem intuitive at first, the usefulness of its core concepts to my project has proven its malleability and persisting utility in helping to expose and disrupt contemporary incarnations of colonial-like relations. Theories and ideas can only become re-invigorated by new contexts in which they are applied.[5]

A Path Forward

My findings have broader implications for exploring how legal rules and institutional discourse conceptualise equality and race when it comes to marginalised whites. Whiteness continues to play a role in how 'Europe' is defined and how Europeans encounter the lived experience of mobility. The myth of a 'post-racial' Europe—driven by crushing Nazism and by narratives about egalitarianism and the benevolence of the EU project—must be challenged, and critical race frameworks should be applied more to the exploration of power dynamics within the EU and within continental Europe.[6] 'Given the compulsive human need to categorize others, "color-blindness" is an absurd concept'.[7] Race—with

---

4 Fitzpatrick (1992).
5 See generally Said (1983).
6 See generally Möschel (2014); Blaagaard (2008).
7 Morrison (1992).

nuanced fractures and intersections within it—continues to determine hierarchies of privilege which become embedded within specific political, economic, and social contestations at discrete geographical and historical locations. At the same time, 'race' and 'whiteness' are constructs, and there is therefore potential to de-construct and re-define them. Whiteness itself must be marked and explored as a racialised position within the EU, which is transnational and relational, with privilege and disadvantage shaped by markers such as migration status, ethnicity, and class.

CEE nationals' right to free movement continues to be contested across EU-14 states—with anti-immigrant, welfare chauvinistic parties in positions of influence in countries as diverse as Austria, Sweden,[8] Finland, France, and Italy—and with Macron's 2017 calls for protectionist measures against posted CEE workers. Although this book approaches CEE states and nationals collectively, in line with western antipathy towards 'Eastern Europeans', it should serve as a provocation for closely scrutinising how each CEE state and its nationals have been approached by EU discourse and policies and how each CEE state's nationals experience EU citizenship and mobility rights. Additionally, there is great need for critical studies devoted to Bulgarians and to Romanians who have been understudied despite being especially racialised and disadvantaged among intra-EU movers. Little attention has also been devoted to Croatians. Similar explorations should be conducted of Roma people, and Romany studies have much to gain from adopting critical whiteness and postcolonial frameworks.[9] Finally, akin to my analysis of the experience of mobility and inequality by CEE nationals in the pre-Brexit Britain, case studies of each EU-14 receiving state would shed light on interactions between EU rights and the domestic experience thereof. Of course, white CEE movers have also been perpetrators of racism, exploitation, and discriminations against their own co-ethnics, other CEE groups, the Roma, and non-white[10] host state nationals. Such inter- and intra-group tensions are also in need of greater scholarly attention.

More generally, not only intra-EU mobilities but the evolving EU project itself—the world's second-largest democracy and third-largest economy—needs to be subjected to greater ongoing critical scrutiny. The EU's western-centric approach raises fundamental questions about the meaning of EU citizenship, the legitimacy of the EU project, and the construction of 'Europeans'. The top-down process of the EU citizenship right, further complicated by association of the EU with (privileged) whiteness only, has made the meaning and experience of citizenship hollow for many. Protections against nationality discrimination

8 Far-right Sweden Democrats even assumed presidency of the European Council during 2023.
9 E.g., Vajda (2015).
10 Reminiscent of how Slavic workers in the United States a century ago sided with the capitalist local class to oppose black workers, in order to partake more fully of white privilege. See Roediger (1991).

within the right to free movement and protections against race discrimination should be seen as inherently interconnected and as linked to the broader EU equality agenda. Key arguments advanced in this book should also provoke more profound concerns about how 'Europeanness' is constructed and about the lack of a cohesive socio-political 'European' identity that becomes evident whenever EU citizens are faced with internal or external crises.[11] The process that culminated in Brexit also prompts broader questions about EU integration—arguably further de-stabilised due to frictions exposed when responding to the 2008 economic crisis, the 2015 refugee 'crisis', the 2020 Covid pandemic, and Russia's invasion of Ukraine in 2022. Notably, after the 2019 European Parliament elections, 29% of its members represented Eurosceptic parties—the highest percentage in its history.

In addition to academic implications, my work has policy ramifications. For starters, an acknowledgement of and measures to reduce internal fractures within the EU are needed to safeguard the continuation and the legitimacy of the integration endeavour. The east continues to be on the periphery of the EU project—facing French-German hegemony. To expand their own economies, western EU states have been penetrating eastern markets and financial infrastructures while exploiting more affordable supply chains and labour sources. This has only reinforced the continuing gap in wealth and living standards between east and west. Poignantly, western companies have been approaching the CEE region and its nationals as unequal. For example, identical brands of western food products were sold at higher prices, while made with cheaper ingredients, in eastern Member States, leading the then-Bulgarian Prime Minister to denounce the practice as 'food apartheid'.[12] This has been complemented by attempts to impose western social and political values onto CEE states, with the EU often withholding funding if such values are not deemed to be followed. At the same time, the west has continued to ignore the CEE regions' prerogatives—including in the contexts of economic and migration 'crises' and warnings about Russia long before its invasion of Ukraine. Analyses of Member States' influence on EU policy-making have shown that CEE states tend to wield less power than their western counterparts.[13] Moreover, although individual ECJ judges' impact on jurisprudence is difficult to determine, EU-15 judges have been overrepresented in the Court's leadership positions.[14] It remains to be seen whether the CEE region's increasing geopolitical importance—driven by Lukashenko's totalitarian repression in Belarus and Russia's attack on Ukraine—might affect east/west power dynamics.[15]

11 See also Ammaturo (2019).
12 EURACTIV (2017).
13 E.g., Busse et al. (2020); Janning (2018); Lehne (2019).
14 See generally Dumbrovsky (2013). As of 2023, there have been no Presidents or Vice Presidents of the ECJ from CEE states, Bulgaria, or Romania.
15 Moreover, EU candidacy for Ukraine (and potentially, Moldova, and additional Balkan states) might push the EU's eastern racialised peripheries farther east and make the CEE region become more 'central' in decision-making and discourse.

Furthermore, EU and western policies must better tackle CEE movers' inequalities. If the EU project's legitimacy is to be restored—or, arguably, ever attained—it must be accompanied by more inclusive discourses and more meaningful rights in line with its professed ideals of equality and unity in diversity. The promise of the EU project dictates that its policies are inclusive and more responsive to contemporary varieties of otherings. Only then might it become possible to imagine—and ultimately, effectuate—a continent that comes closer to its lofty goals. Having endowed movers with EU citizenship and having enabled their mobility, the EU must play a role in addressing CEE movers' exploitation. Although EU governance is limited and more akin to administrative than constitutional rule, and its equality laws are mere frameworks, the EU should create more inclusive equality discourse, take into account CEE movers' racialisation when creating and applying policies, and better monitor movers' experiences of inequality in host states. Token anti-racist initiatives should be replaced with nuanced approaches that take into account various axes of oppression.

Importantly, to better reflect the nature of today's discrimination and racisms, domestic equality laws and related policies must take account of contemporary demographic changes, transnational contexts, and intersectionality. Legislators have a role to play in setting a more responsive framework for courts to follow and in contributing to a more inclusive equality discourse. The fact that CEE movers are white and have access to formal EU rights does not mean that they 'cannot be in need of special measures of social inclusion and social protection'.[16] Adjudicators should approach specific claimants' experiences more holistically—situating them within broader patterns of exploitation and widespread racialisation.[17] More nuanced data collection, with attention to victims' and claimants' national origins, is needed to help support such efforts. Moreover, the media, advocacy groups, and educators should engage in more responsible and inclusive debates about race, mobility, and equality to help shift awareness and discourses about CEE movers. Ultimately, of course, laws alone cannot bring about change in this area. Instead, equality policies need to be accompanied by a western cultural shift and self-transformation in westerners' attitudes so that the CEE region and its nationals are no longer imagined and treated as inferior.

Finally, since laws, legal myths, and legal discourse contain resistant elements on which excluded groups can draw in order to contest existing power structures, CEE nationals themselves should mobilise their agency to facilitate their greater inclusion and equality protections. Openly acknowledging all CEE nationals' victimisation through racialisation and racism is necessary to form

---

16 Henrard (2011).
17 I am not discounting politically-driven problems of social inequality or economic exploitation, which affect the experience of all non-privileged groups, and which need to be addressed through broader policy initiatives.

collaborative cross-ethnic grass-roots policy efforts based on common conscience and ideology. Emotional empowerment should be accompanied by economic empowerment—for example, by consistently speaking up against economic exploitation in host states, soliciting relevant trade unions' support, and forming workers' associations where no trade unions exist. All such initiatives can be further advanced by seeking out allyships, learning from other disadvantaged groups, and collaborating with them. CEE national leaders should be involved in similar conversations and efforts at domestic and supranational governmental levels, taking heed of the recent Polish Prime Minister's aspirational call for 'a union of strong, equal and free nations'.[18] As the second decade after the Eastern Enlargement draws to a close, that vision woefully remains an embodiment of a lofty dream rather than a lived reality.

Bibliography

Ammaturo, Francesca Romana (2019) Challenges to European identity and European citizenship in light of Brexit and the 'refugees/migrants crisis', *European Journal of Social Theory* 22(4): 548–566

Blaagaard, Bolette (2008) European Whiteness? A Critical Approach, *Kvinder, Køn & Forskning* 4, https://doi.org/10.7146/kkf.v0i4.27942

Bridges, Kharia (2019) White privilege and white disadvantage, *Virginia Law Review* 105: 449–482

Busse, Claire et al. (2020) EU Coalition Explorer, 8 July (European Council on Foreign Relations), https://ecfr.eu/special/eucoalitionexplorer/

Dumbrovsky, Tomas (2013) *The European Court of Justice After the Eastern Enlargement: an emerging inner circle of judges*, Paper Presented at EUSA Conference (Boston), https://dx.doi.org/10.2139/ssrn.2551211

EURACTIV (2017) Eastern Europeans bite back over 'food apartheid', 3 July, www.euractiv.com/section/agriculture-food/news/eastern-europeans-bite-back-over-food-apartheid/

Fitzpatrick, Peter (1992) *The Mythology of Modern Law* (New York: Routledge)

Henrard, Kristin (2011) An EU perspective on new versus traditional minorities: On semi-inclusive socio-economic integration and expanding visions of 'European' culture and identity, *Columbia Journal of European Law* 17: 57–99

Janning, Josef (2018) The "more Europe" core four, 26 July (European Council on Foreign Relations), https://ecfr.eu/article/commentary_the_more_europe_core_four/

Lehne, Stefan (2019) Europe's east-west divide: Myth or reality?, 11 April (Carnegie Europe) https://carnegieeurope.eu/2019/04/11/europe-s-east-west-divide-myth-or-reality-pub-78847

Lopez, Alfred J (ed) (2005) *Postcolonial Whiteness: Critical Reader on Race and Empire* (New York: State University of New York Press)

Morawiecki, Mateusz (2019) Poland's vision for Europe, *Politico*, 30 April, www.politico.eu/article/poland-vision-for-europe-mateusz-morawiecki/

Morrison, Toni (1992) *Playing in the Dark: Whiteness and the Literary Imagination* (Cambridge: Harvard University Press)

---

18 See Morawiecki (2019).

Möschel, Mathias (2014) *Law, Lawyers and Race: Critical Race Theory from the US to Europe* (London: Routledge)
Roediger, David (1991) *The Wages of Whiteness: Race and the Making of the American Working Class* (New York: Verso)
Said, Edward (1983) *The World, the Text, and the Critic* (Cambridge: Harvard University Press)
Vajda, Violeta (2015) Towards 'critical whiteness' in Romani studies, *Roma Participation in Policy Making and Knowledge Production* 2(1): 47–56, www.errc.org/uploads/upload_en/file/roma-rights-2-2015-nothing-about-us-without-us.pdf
Valdes, Frank et al. (eds) (2002) *Crossroads, Directions, and a New CRT* (Philadelphia: Temple University Press)

Index

Note: Page numbers followed by 'n' refer to notes.

Accession Country Regular Reports 23
accession process 46; accession referenda in CEE states 50–52; accession treaty safeguard clauses 49–50
Accession (Immigration and Worker Registration) Regulations 2004 (UK) 168
Accession Treaty 70, 117, 120–123, 125, 168, 169
accession treaty safeguard clauses 49–50
Act of Accession 2003 25
'Agenda 2000' plan 22
Agreements on Trade and Commercial and Economic Cooperation (T&C Agreements) 34, 35, 116
agricultural policies 54, 55
Alimanovic 132–134
Amsterdam Treaty 1999 123
anti-CEE animus 124
anti-CEE antipathy 160
anti-CEE policies 171–174
anti-CEE policy climate 2
anti-CEE political climate 200
anti-CEE racism 166, 230
anti-CEE sentiment 2, 91, 112, 166, 185, 208
anti-discrimination: acquis 130; framework 181, 193; law 2, 104, 106, 113, 135, 160, 180n92, 191, 192, 194, 195, 198; legislation 161, 182, 191; measures 103, 118–119, 219; policies 119, 230; protections 4, 85, 99, 101, 119, 181, 189, 199; provisions 104
anti-immigrant ideology 173
anti-immigrant populism 120
anti-mover sentiment and policies 161

anti-Polish environment 215
Anti-Racism Action Plan 116
antiracist initiatives 235
anti-Slavic sentiment 6, 15
anti-Soviet sentiments 24
Aristotle 21
Articles 1–6 of Regulation 1612/68 169
Article 4 of Regulation 883/2004 133
Article 7(3)(c) of Directive 2004/38 132
Article 7(3) of Directive 2004/38 95, 129
Article 10 of Regulation 492/2011 134
Article 14(3) of the Directive 92
Article 14(4)(b) of Directive 2004/38 139
Article 18 of the EC Treaty 122
Article 24(2) of Directive 2004/38 134
Articles of Agreement of the International Monetary Fund 40

Balls, Ed 173
Baltic states 26, 28, 30–32, 35, 39, 56, 80
Barnard, Catherine 197, 198
BDW Trading Ltd v Kopec 205, 207
Bell, Derrick 25, 85, 100
'benefit tourism' 70
Besz v Multi Packaging Solutions Limited 200
Black, Asian, and Minority Ethnic (BAME) 165
Black Lives Matter (BLM): movement 109, 114; protests 229
Blair, Tony 173, 182
Bouzir v Country Style Foods Ltd 206
Brexit referendum 2, 70, 131, 163, 164, 171, 176, 219
British education system 174
British equality discourse 11, 218

British equality law 219
British Euroscepticism 2
British 'race relations' approach 180n92
British Social Attitudes Surveys 163
budgetary policies 44
Bush, George 28

Cameron, David 130, 165, 173
carbon-dioxide emission 53
case law 187, 189, 198; ECJ 69, 110, 170
Caucasian 4, 21, 100, 113, 119, 176, 178; immigrants 166; intra-EU movers 101; migrants 7
Central and Eastern European (CEE) states 1, 4, 10, 11, 23, 34–38, 41, 47, 49, 55–57, 60, 74, 84, 92, 123, 145–147; accession, economic and political dynamics of 25–26; accession referenda in 50–52; economically inactive movers' rights 126–127; immigration 119; mobility 2, 6, 11, 120; mobility to EU-15 states, economic benefits of 82–83; movers: disadvantaged positioning in labour market 174–177; exploitation and discrimination in EU-15 states 71–79; in pre-Brexit Britain (see pre-Brexit Britain, CEE movers in); region, explicit othering of 22–24; region before the fall of communism 26–27; rights 98–99, 127–138; self-employed movers' rights 125 126; nationals' mobility, experience and impact of 71; nationals' rights during transitional period 124–125; negative long-term impact of mobility on 79–82
child benefit indexation proposal 131
Chovanec, Jozef 229
Cicero 21
citizenship laws 98
Citizens' Rights Directive 2004/38 10, 69, 83, 87–99, 125, 126, 167–168
Citizens Signpost Service 92, 92n126
Claims (UK): direct discrimination 199–209; discrimination 190, 217n221; Employment Tribunals 175, 180, 185, 189; harassment 211–213; indirect discrimination 209–211, 215; language rule 213–217; victimisation 213
CMEA 33
collective citizenship 85
colonialism 232

COMECON 26, 28–30, 32
Commission for Racial Equality 195
Commission v United Kingdom 133
Common Agricultural Policy (CAP) 48, 56, 79n53
communism 7, 9, 16, 22, 24, 25, 28n91, 32, 33, 117, 162, 198
communist leaderships 27
communist one-party political system 32
communist rule 116
'comprehensive sickness insurance' 93, 94
Copenhagen Summit Conclusions 1993 41
critical race methodologies 9
critical race theory 8
critical whiteness studies 11
Currie, Samantha 120
Czechoslovakia 28–30, 33, 37n125, 162

Declaration on European Identity 20–21
Delors, Jacques 22
Deregulation Act 2015 (UK) 196
direct discrimination (UK) 186–187; claims 199–209
direct transitional post-accession mobility derogations 86
discrimination 4, 5, 10, 11, 164, 167; claims 190, 217n221
documentary qualitative analysis 9
domestic equality rights organisations 107
domestic ethnic majorities 108
domestic immigration laws 116
domestic immigration rules 116
domestic labour law enforcement 78
domestic policies 127; reforms 46; regimes 108
domestic transitional arrangements 121
dominant white group 164
Du Bois, W.E.B. 8
Durkheim 21
Dziedziak v Future Electronics Ltd 216
Dzierzanowski v Cranswick Country Foods Plc 207

Eastern Enlargement 1, 2, 4, 5, 8–10, 16–20, 23–26, 45, 46, 56, 58–60, 70, 74, 75, 84, 87, 92, 93, 96, 99, 100, 116, 117, 123, 160, 163, 165, 173, 175, 182, 230, 232
east-to-west mobility 2, 69–71; CEE: economically inactive movers' rights 126–127; movers' exploitation and discrimination in EU-15 states 71–79;

movers' rights 127–138; nationals' rights during transitional period 124–125; self-employed movers' rights 125–126; Citizens' Rights Directive 2004/38 87–99; economic benefits of CEE mobility to EU-15 states 82–83; ethnicity-based discrimination 99–116; EU-15 states: approach towards CEE nationals' mobility 119–120; limits on access to free movement and social rights 138–145; EU institutions' approach towards CEE nationals' mobility 117–119; experience and impact of CEE nationals' mobility 71; negative long-term impact of mobility on CEE region 79–82; right to free movement 83–84; transitional mobility derogations 116–117, 120–124
economic crisis 24, 28, 81, 130, 175, 234
economic freedoms 32, 108
economic inequalities 16, 26, 57, 76, 82
economic initiatives 19, 27
economic integration 19, 102
'economic migrants' 1
economic reforms 32, 40
economic restructurings 26, 31, 40
economic safeguard clause 49
economic 'shock therapy' 29
EC Treaty Article 12 84n88, 125
EC Treaty Article 39(2) 120
Emissions Trading System policies 53
employment, race discrimination claims in (UK) 197–198; direct discrimination claims 199–209; harassment claims 211–213; indirect discrimination claims 209–211; language rule claims 213–217; practical and procedural hurdles 217–218; victimisation claims 213
Employment Appeal Tribunal (UK) 188, 191, 194, 197, 199, 203, 208, 211, 212
Employment Equality Directive 2000/78 108
Employment Statutory Code of Practice (UK)178
Employment Tribunals (UK) 185, 186, 189, 193, 197, 210; claims 175, 180, 185, 189
Enlightenment 3, 15, 19
Equality Act (UK) 11, 181–199, 203, 209, 210, 214, 219; background and legislative history 182–185; general critique of 189–197; key provisions of 185–189
Equality and Human Rights Commission (UK) 178, 179, 195

Equality Bill (UK) 182
equality law 192, 194
equality policies 235
equal treatment and access to social assistance 97
Erasmus 21
ethnic discrimination 174
ethnicity-based discrimination 99–116
ethnic stratifications 160
EU-15 60, 70, 73, 92, 93, 95, 103, 108, 110, 121, 124, 124n221, 132; economies 117, 118; labour markets 76; policies 4, 92; state limits on access to free movement and social rights 138–145; states' approach towards CEE nationals' mobility 119–120; state welfare systems 83
EU Anti-Racism Action Plan 2020–25 114
EU Anti-Racism Summit 115
EU (Citizens' Rights) Directive 2004/38 10, 69, 83, 87–99, 125, 126, 167–168
EU equality discourse 114–116
EU (Race Equality) Directive 181, 186, 187, 189
EU Regulation 1612/68 169
EU Rhetoric 10, 20, 58, 59, 71, 128, 135, 137, 230; Western Gaze in 16
Europe Agreements 25n81, 38, 38n126, 39, 39n132, 44
European Coal and Steel Community 16n7
European Commission 1, 79n54, 168n32
'European' community 3, 23
European Council 17, 24, 47, 130, 138
European Court of Justice (ECJ) 18, 24, 88–90, 96, 104, 105, 108, 122, 125, 125n222, 126–131, 133, 133n251, 134, 140, 142; case law 69, 110, 170; jurisprudence 109
European cultural heritage 20
European cultural identity 21, 22
European culture 21
European Economic and Social Committee 118
European Economic Community (EEC) 33, 145
European Equality Law Review 116
European heritage 3, 21, 23
European integration project 69
European Monetary Union 81
Europeanness 21, 22, 52, 71, 234
European Network Against Racism (ENAR) 115, 116

European Parliament 23, 75, 92, 112
European Pillar of Social Rights Action Plan 2020 137
European polity 23
European Trade Union Confederation 118
European Union (EU): accession partnership agreements 41; discourse on free movement and social rights 135–1338; equality framework 112, 218; equality principles 125; Europe Agreements 37–41; fiscal policies 81; freedom of movement right 161; funding 56; gender equality legislation 111; gradual geographical expansion of 1; institutions 69, 76; institutions' approach towards CEE nationals' mobility 117–119; integration project 8; law 5, 128, 140, 143, 144, 168, 170, 187; mobility framework 128–135; one-sided approach towards negotiations 47–49; policies 2; policy statements 17; post-war relationship 16; pre-04 policies on CEE and EU-15 states 42–46; racial equality legislation 181; trade and cooperation agreements 34–37
European Union (Accessions) Act 2003 167
European Voluntary Workers scheme 162
Europe: Giving Shape to an Idea 17
Eurosceptic factions 52
Euroscepticism 160
Eurosceptic parties 57, 161
EU Settlement Scheme (UK) 173–174
EU soft laws 16
EU Treaty rights 169n36
EU VAT regulations 57
Evidence for Equality National Survey 2021 166
Exec Catering Ltd v Kaczynska 216

Farage, Nigel 165
fascism 101
final transitional phase 124
Firma Feryn 105, 109n167
Fitzpatrick, Peter 8, 106, 232
forced labour 15
foreign bank ownership 44
foreign debt 44
foreign direct investment (FDI) 31
foreign investment 42–43
Fortress Europe 3
freedom of capital 46

freedom of movement 97, 99, 220; laws 10; right 77, 83, 86, 87, 108, 146, 230
Freedom of Movement Act 141
Freedom Party 104
free-market capitalist models 30
free market competition 2
free-market economies 31, 57
free-market model 30
Free Movement of Persons 87
free movement rights 2, 10, 70, 71, 76, 77, 83–87, 118, 121, 123, 127–130, 141, 142, 145, 160, 161, 178, 233, 234
free-movement rules 123
Fundamental Rights Agency 113, 115
fundamental-rights narratives 19

Garner, Steve 7
GATT 33, 34
gender equality 111
geo-political stability 56
German labour market 141
'Go Home' campaign 173
Gorbachev, Mikhail 28, 33
Green Paper: Equality and Non-Discrimination in an Enlarged European Union 2004 119
gross foreign debt 44
Grzyb v Lidl 206

habitual residence test 99, 170n43, 171, 172
Hague Congress 1948 17
harassment 111–112, 188; claims 211–213
hard-laws 9, 19
Health and Consumer Protection 50
Hegel, Georg Wilhelm Friedrich 21
Hewage v Grampian Health Board 193
Hobsbawm, Eric 21
Hofbauer, Hannes 44
hostile approach towards CEE movers: right-to-reside test 170–171; subsequent anti-CEE policies 171–174; Worker Registration Scheme 167–170
'hostile environment' element 111
hostile environment policies (UK) 173
Hungarian law 37
Hungarian Revolution 162
Hungary 28, 29, 33, 36, 37, 43, 44, 56
hypothetical comparator test 201

'imagined community' 21
Immigration (European Economic Area) Regulation 2006 (UK) 167

242 Index

income tax payments 174
indirect discrimination 111, 187–188; claims 209–211, 215
indirect transitional restrictions 168
individual enforcement 106–107, 194–196
inequalities 2, 10, 16, 20, 55, 57; in east-to-west mobility (*see* east-to-west mobility); role of 5
inferiorised groups 7
Institute of Race Relations (UK) 184
institutional discrimination 111
institutional heritage 21
institutional racism 166
internal-market safeguard clause 49
international anti-discrimination instruments 109
international financial institutions 36
international food aid 27
international human rights instruments 103, 193
International Monetary Fund (IMF) 27, 29, 31, 32, 36, 37, 40, 44, 45, 81
intersectionality 193–194
intra-EU east-to-west mobility 59
intra-EU inequalities 78, 161
intra-EU labour mobility 70
intra-EU mobilities 10, 11, 69, 82, 90, 233
Irish and New Commonwealth migrants 180
Iron Curtain 34; Baltic states 30–31; Slovenia 32; Visegrád Group 28–30

Januszewski 212
Januszewski v Ultima Furniture Systems Limited 207
Jobcenter Krefeld judgment 134, 135
Joint Declaration 'One Europe' 25
Joint EEC-CMEA Declaration 1988 33
Jozwik, Arkadiusz 165n20
Jurga v Lavendale Montessori Ltd 217
Juszczyk v Kettle Produce Ltd 207
Jutrenzka v Chinnocks Wharf Management Co Ltd 209
Jyske Finans 105, 109n167

Kabzinski v Vistajet International Ltd 208
Kahn Report 1995 102
Kalmar, Ivan 26
Kant, Immanuel 21
Konieczna v Whitelink Seafoods Ltd 214, 216
Kosik v Montgomery Transport Ltd 210
Kowal and Obieglo v Peter Leslie & Sons t/a David Leslie Fruits 203

Kowalewska-Zietek v Lancashire Teaching Hospitals NHS Foundation Trust 211
Kozakiewicz v Futon Ltd 206
Krupa v B&M Retail Ltd 200

labour camp 176
labour exploitation 120
labour flexibilisation 72
labour-intensive farming 56
labour market 10, 45, 107, 118, 124, 136, 161, 163, 164, 175, 177, 180; CEE movers' disadvantaged positioning in 174–177; disturbances 121; flexibilisation 83, 130; integration 82; outcomes 174; segregation 110
labour mobility 79, 80, 90
Labour Party (UK) 183
labour regulation enforcement 72
language rule 189; claims 213–217
Levine-Rasky, Cynthia 193
Lisbon Strategy 2000 46
Ludlow, Amy 197, 198
Lukashenko, Aleksandr 234
Luxembourg Summit 1997 46

Maastricht Treaty 85, 87, 102, 123
market-oriented economies 29
Marshall Plan 26
martial law 27, 162
Marx, Karl 21, 146
Matuzewicz v 2 Sisters Food Group Ltd 206
Michalak v The Mid Yorkshire Hospitals NHS Trust 201
Middle Ages 15
migrant-advocacy groups 102
migrant rights organisations 102
Mitteleuropa 3
mobilities: contemporary 6; derogations 122, 123, 126; east-to-west (*see* east-to-west mobility); intra-EU 10, 11, 69, 82, 90, 233; labour 79, 80, 90; post-accession (*see* post-accession mobility); restrictions during earlier enlargements 123–124; right of 99; transitional (*see* transitional mobility)
'model minority' stereotype 177
Molotov Plan 26
Monnet, Jean 85
Monnet Lecture 24

national discrimination sanctions 104
national equality laws 112
national equality regimes approach 220

National Health Service (UK) 173
national insurance contributions 174
nationality-based discrimination 117
national social assistance system 133
Nazarczyk v T J Morris Limited 201
Nazism 232
Nemec v Concept Recruitment Group Ltd 205
neo-liberal economics 8; approach 83; climate 75; expansionism 230; market 100
New Commonwealth migrants 179, 180
Nikolova v M & P Enterprises London Ltd 191
non-contributory welfare benefits 168
non-discrimination frameworks 110
non-majoritarian groups 5
non-UK workers in UK 176–177
non-white ethnic groups 76
non-white ethnic minority groups 3, 76
non-white groups 167
non-white immigrant groups 163
non-white post-war migration 164

oil crisis 1973 27
Oppression Olympics 185

Patmalniece v Secretary of State for Work and Pensions 171
Pedder, John 162
peripheralisation 2
Petrica v Central London Community Healthcare NHS Trust 209
PHARE 36, 40, 42
Polish-Lithuanian Commonwealth 15
Polish Resettlement Act 1947 162
political instabilities 58
population drain 80
populist anti-CEE politics 142
Porto Declaration 138
post-04 CEE mobility 174
post-2004 Equality Laws: Equality Act 2010 182–197; transposition of Race Equality Directive 181
post-accession derogations 118
post-accession mobility 101; derogations 10, 75, 86, 127, 128; restrictions 176
post-accession public opinion 57
post-accession transitional mobility derogations 82
post-Brexit labour market 170
post-Brexit qualitative studies 166

postcolonial theory 8, 11, 232
post-communist CEE states 30
post-communist economic transformations 54
post-communist economic transition 32
post-communist political environment 32
post-Maastricht EU citizenship rights 123
post-Maastricht Treaty 117
post-racial Europe 232
post-referendum studies 165
post-transitional mobility derogations 117
post-war collectivisation 32
'poverty immigration' 70
Prasil v Orchard House Foods 204
pre-04 CEE migrants in UK 163
pre-accession agreements 9, 116
pre-accession initiatives 37
pre-accession labour shortages in UK 168
pre-accession policies 5, 45
pre-Brexit Britain, CEE movers in 160–161; CEE nationals in the UK 162–181; post-2004 Equality Laws 181–197; race discrimination claims in employment 197–218
pre-Brexit polls 166
private litigation 106
Procek v Oakford Farms Ltd 202
pro-EU market economic reforms 40
pro-EU parties 161
proportionality test 187
protective clauses 50
provision, criterion or practice (PCP) 187, 210
public health insurance 94
public international law 33
public national health service 94

Quality Solicitors v Tunstall 211

race 3, 232–233; discrimination cases 11; discrimination claims in employment (*see* employment, race discrimination claims in); insufficient definition of 191–193
race-based inequalities 100
Race Equality Directive 2000/43 10, 83, 86–87, 99, 103, 104, 108, 114, 119, 181, 185, 213, 220
Race Relations Act 1968 (UK) 180n92
Race Relations Act 1976 (Amendment) Regulations 2003 (UK) 181, 185, 195
racial and ethnic discrimination 101

racial anti-discrimination laws 113
racial capitalism 4, 26
racial discrimination 112, 113
racial equality discourse 230
racial equality protections 102
racialisation 2, 3, 5, 7, 10, 11, 58, 75, 83, 101, 106, 107, 110, 147, 161–164, 188, 191, 195, 200, 204, 208–210, 235; CEE movers' 115, 123, 146, 160; and discrimination. 10, 11; and inequalities 2, 114; inferiorised groups 7; in the UK, CEE movers' 163–167
racialised minorities 78
racialised whites 114
racism 2–5, 10, 11, 73, 100, 101, 111, 113, 136, 164, 167, 177, 191, 195, 219, 231; institutional 166; structural 109, 114, 115, 172
racist political culture 173
radical-right parties 80
refugee crisis 6
Resolution on the Protection of Minorities and Anti-Discrimination Policies in an Enlarged Europe 2005 119
right of equality 87, 99, 230
right of mobility 99
right of permanent residence 95–96
right-to-reside test 170–171
right-wing groups 165
Rome Summit 59
Rousseau, Jean-Jacques 21
Rowinski v Kuehne and Nagel Ltd 215
Ruda v TEi Ltd 202, 218

safeguard clause 50n201
Schimmelfennig 24
Schröeder, Gerhard 120
Schuman, Robert 145
Seasonal Agricultural Workers Schemes (UK) 162
seasonal labour 15
secondary domestic legislations 92
Section 1 of the Equality Bill (UK) 183
Sivanandan, Ambalavaner 184
Skarbek-Cielecka v Holy Rise Consultants Ltd 206
Skrzydlo v CRC Recruitment Ltd 205
Skwarczynska v Sturts Community Trust 210
social assistance 95, 133; benefits 93; element 133; systems 86
social disparities 25

social dumping 136
social inequalities 45, 82
social justice issues 100
'social market economy' 84
social policies 86
social rights 137, 138
Social Rights Pillar Action Plan 138
social rights policies 6
Social Security Act 2006 (Germany) 97
Social Security (Habitual Residence) Amendment Regulation 2004 (UK) 170
social security benefits systems 86
social security rights 144
social security systems 131
socio-economic duty proposal 184
socio-economic equality 100
socio-economic legislation 183
soft-laws 9, 19
Sokolova v Humdinger Ltd 214
SOLVIT 144
Somek, Alexander 100
Southern Enlargement 123, 124
Soviet-era social security systems 45
Soviet trade subsidies 27
special non-contributory cash benefits (SNCB) 86, 89, 99, 132, 133, 140
Stalin, Joseph 26
Starmer, Keir 173
Starting Line Group (SLG) 102
statutory anti-discrimination provisions 218
structural racial discrimination 116
structural racism 109, 114, 115, 172

Taiwo v Olaigbe and Onu v Akwiwu 193
tax-reduction packages 43
Thatcher, Margaret 168
Tocqueville 21
trade 42
trade liberalisation policies 31
traditional mobility hierarchy 128
transitional derogations 10, 121n215, 122, 128
transitional mobility: derogations 116–117, 120–125, 139; limitations 70; restrictions 75, 82, 123
transitional post-accession mobility derogations 1
treaty equality rights 84
Treaty of Amsterdam 103, 103n149
Treaty of Nice 2001 46

Treaty of Paris 1951 84
Treaty of Rome 84, 85, 146

UK: anti-discrimination framework 190; CEE movers' racialisation in 163–167; CEE nationals in the 162–181; equality framework 177–181; immigration policy 176; labour market 174, 180, 218
UKIP campaign 165
Union of Industrial and Employers' Confederations of Europe 118

victimisation 189; claims 213
Visegrád Group 28–30
Voltaire 21
volunteer worker schemes 4

wage penalties 72
'welfare migration' 140
'welfare tourism' 87

western financial institutions 46, 60
western labour markets 74, 130
western labour organisations 118
White Paper 'Opportunity for All: Tackling Poverty and Social Exclusion' 1999 183
Wilk v Wackers 203
Winczewski v MAM Transport Services Ltd 207
Work and Pensions Committee (UK) 195
Worker Registration Scheme (WRS) (UK) 11, 167–170, 177, 184
worker status, retention of 95
World Bank 29, 31, 36, 40
Wu, Frank H 177

Zalewska v Department of Social Development 169
Zaluski v NSL Ltd 210
zero-hour contracts 139
zero-tolerance policy 50